Barabbas: A Dream Of The World's Tragedy

Marie Corelli

BARABBAS

A DREAM OF THE WORLD'S TRAGEDY

'And they consulted how they might take Him, *by subtilty.*'
—*Matthew xxvi. v. 4.*

BARABBAS

DREAM OF THE WORLD'S TRAGEDY

BY

MARIE CORELLI

AUTHOR OF

'THELMA' 'A ROMANCE OF TWO WORLDS' 'ARDATH'
'VENDETTA!' 'WORMWOOD: A DRAMA OF PARIS'
'THE SOUL OF LILITH'

FIFTH EDITION

𝕸𝖊𝖙𝖍𝖚𝖊𝖓 & 𝕮𝖔.
18 BURY STREET, LONDON, W.C.
1894

'And they had then a notable prisoner called Barabbas.'—*Matthew xxvii. v.* 16.

'One named Barabbas which lay bound with them that had made insurrection with him.'—*Mark xv. v.* 7.

'Barabbas, who for a certain sedition made in the city and for murder was cast into prison.'—*Luke xxiii. v.* 19.

'Now Barabbas was a robber.'—*John xviii. v.* 40.

BARABBAS

A DREAM OF THE WORLD'S TRAGEDY

———+———

I

A LONG sultry Syrian day was drawing near its close.
The heavy heat was almost insupportable, and a poisonous stench oozed up from the damp earth-floors of the Jewish prison, charging what little air there was with a deadly sense of suffocation. Down in the lowest dungeons complete darkness reigned, save in one of the cells allotted to the worst criminals ; there, all through the slow hours a thin white line of light had persistently pierced the thick obscurity. It was the merest taper-flame reflection of the outside glowing Eastern sky, yet narrow as it was, it had vexed the eyes of the solitary prisoner on whom it fell, and he had turned from its hot flash with a savage curse and groan. Writhing back as far as his chains would allow, he covered his face with his manacled hands, pressing his eyelids down, and gnawing his lips in restless fury till his mouth was bitter with the taste of his own blood. He was seized with such impotent rages often. He mentally fought against that poignant light-beam cutting like a sword through deep darkness,—he regarded it as a positive foe and daily source of nervous irritation. It marked for him

the dismal time,—when it shone he knew it was day,
—when it vanished, it was night. Otherwise, whether
minutes or hours passed, he could not tell. His
existence had merged into one protracted phase of
dull suffering, varied with occasional fits of maniac
ferocity which only relieved him for the moment and
left him more stupefied and brutish than before. He
had no particular consciousness of anything except
of that needle-pointed ray, which falling obliquely
upon him, dazzled and hurt his eyes. He could have
endured the glare of the Syrian sun in the free and
open country,—no one better than he could have
turned a bold gaze to its amber flame radiating
through the vast blue dome of ether,—but here and
now, that thin shaft of brightness pouring slantwise
through the narrow slit in the wall which alone
served as an air-passage to the foul den in which he
was caged, seemed an aggression and a mockery.
He made querulous complaint of it, and, huddling
on his bed of dirty straw in the furthest darkness
refreshed himself anew with curses. Against God
and Fate and man, he railed in thick‑throated
blasphemies, twisting and turning from side to side
and clutching now and again in sheer ferocity at the
straw on which he lay. He was alone, yet not
altogether lonely, for close beside him where he
crouched like a sullen beast in the corner there was
a crossed grating of thick iron bars, the only air-
aperture to the neighbouring cell, and through this
there presently came a squat grimy hand. After
feeling about for a while, this hand at last found and
cautiously pulled the edge of his garment, and a faint
hoarse voice called him by name:

'Barabbas!'

He turned with a swift savage movement that set
his chains clanking dismally.

'What now?'

'They have forgotten us,' whined the voice. 'Since early morning they have brought no food. I am perishing with hunger and thirst! Ah, I would I had never seen thy face, Barabbas, or had aught to do with thine evil plotting!'

Barabbas made no answer.

'Knowest thou not,' went on his invisible fellow-felon, 'what season this is in the land?'

'How should I know!' retorted Barabbas disdainfully. 'What are seasons to me? Is it a year or years since we were brought hither? If thou canst tell, I cannot.'

''Tis eighteen months since thou didst slay the Pharisee,' replied his neighbour with marked malignity of accent,—'And had it not been for that wicked deed of thine, we might have missed this present wretchedness. Verily it is a marvel we have lived so long, for look you, now it is Passover.'

Barabbas uttered no word, either of surprise or interest.

'Rememberest thou the custom of the Feast?' pursued the speaker, 'How that one captive chosen by the people shall be set at liberty? Would that it might be one of us, Barabbas! There were ten of our company,—ten as goodly men as ever were born in Judæa, always excepting thee. For thou wert mad for love, and a frenzied lover is the worst of fools!'

Barabbas still kept silence.

'If innocence hath any merit,' continued the voice behind the grating anxiously, 'then perchance the choice will fall on me! For am I not an innocent man? The God of my fathers knoweth that my hands are not stained with the blood of the virtuous; I slew no Pharisee! A little gold was all I sought' ——

'And didst thou not take it?' rejoined Barabbas suddenly and with scorn,—'Thou hypocrite! Didst thou not rob the Pharisee of all he had upon him even to his last jewel? Did not the guard capture thee in the very act of breaking with thy teeth the gold band from his arm ere the breath left his body? Cease thy prating! Thou art the worst thief in Jerusalem and thou knowest it!'

There was a sound behind the bars as of something between a grunt and a snarl, and the squat hand thrust itself through with vicious suddenness, to be as suddenly withdrawn. A pause ensued.

'No food all day!' moaned the voice again presently,—'And not a drop of water! Surely if they come not I shall die! I shall die in this darkness,— this dense pitch blackness'— and the faint accents grew feebly shrill with fear,—'Dost thou hear me, thou accursed Barabbas? I shall die!'

'And so there will be an end of thee,' returned Barabbas indifferently,—'And those who hoard gold in the city can sleep safely henceforth with open doors!'

Out came the ugly hand again, this time clenched, giving in its repulsive shape and expression a perfect idea of the villainous character of its unseen owner.

'Thou art a devil, Barabbas!' and the shadowy outline of a livid face and wild hair appeared for an instant against the grating,—'And I swear to thee I will live on, if only in the hope of seeing thee crucified!'

Barabbas held his peace, and dragged himself and his clanking chains away from his spiteful fellow-prisoner's vicinity. Lifting his eyes distrustfully he peered upwards with a smarting sense of pain,—then heaved a deep sigh of relief as he saw that the burning arrowy line of white radiance no longer lit the cell. It had changed to a beam of soft and dusky crimson.

'Sunset!' he muttered. 'How many times hath the sun gone down and risen since I beheld her last!

This is the hour she loves,—she will go with her maidens to the well behind her father's house, and underneath the palm-trees she will rest and rejoice, while I,—I,—O God of vengeance!—I may never look upon her face again. Eighteen months of torture! Eighteen months in this tomb and no hope of respite!'

With a savage gesture he rose and stood upright; his head almost touched the dungeon ceiling, and he stepped warily, the heavy fetters on his bare legs jangling harshly as he moved. Placing one foot on a notch in the wall he was able to bring his eyes easily on a level with the narrow aperture through which the warm fire-glow of the sunset fell, but there was little to be seen from such a point of observation. Only a square strip of dry uncultivated land belonging to the prison, and one solitary palm-tree lifting its crown of feathery leaves against the sky. He stared out for a moment, fancying he could discern the far-off hazy outline of the hills surrounding the city,— then, too faint with long fasting to retain his footing, he slipped back and returned to his former corner. There he sat, glowering darkly at the rose-light reflected on the floor. It partially illumined his own features, bringing into strong prominence his scowling brows and black resentful eyes,—it flashed a bright life-hue on his naked chest that heaved with the irregular and difficult breath of one who fights against long exhaustion and hunger-pain,—and it glittered with a sinister coppery tint on the massive iron gyves that bound his wrists together. He looked much more like a caged wild beast than a human being, with his matted hair and rough beard,—he was barely clothed, his only garment being a piece of sackcloth which was kept about his loins by means of a coarse black rope, twisted twice and loosely knotted. The heat in the cell was intense, yet he shivered now and then as he crouched in the stifling gloom, his knees drawn nearly up to his chin, and his shackled hands resting on his knees, while he stared with an owl-like pertinacity at the crimson sunbeam which with every second grew paler and dimmer. At first it had been an ardent red,—as red as the blood of a slain Pharisee, thought Barabbas with a dark smile,—but now it had waned to a delicate wavering pink like the fleeting blush of a fair woman,—and a great shudder seized him as this latter fancy crossed his sick and sullen mind. With a smothered cry he clenched his hands hard as though assailed by some unendurable physical pang.

'Judith!—Judith!' he whispered, and yet again— 'Judith!'

And, trembling violently, he turned and hid his face, pressing his forehead close against the damp and slimy wall. And thus he remained, motionless,— his massive figure looking like a weird Titanesque shape carved in stone.

The last red flicker from the sunken sun soon faded, and dense darkness fell. Not a sound or movement betrayed the existence of any human creature in that noxious gloom. Now and again the pattering feet of mice scurrying swiftly about the floor made a feeble yet mysterious clamour,—otherwise, all was intensely still. Outside, the heavens were putting on all their majesty; the planets swam into the purple ether, appearing to open and shine like water-lilies on a lake,—in the east a bar of silvery cloud showed where the moon would shortly rise, and through the window slit of the dungeon one small star could be just discerned, faintly glittering. But not even an argent ray flung slantwise from the moon when at last she ascended the skies could illumine the dense thicket of shadows that gathered in that dreary cell, or touch with a compassionate brightness the huddled form of the wretched captive within. Invisible and solitary, he wrestled with his own physical and mental misery, unconscious that the wall against which he leaned was warm and wet with tears,—the painful tears, worse than the shedding of blood, of a strong man's bitter agony.

II

HOURS passed, — and presently the heavy silence was broken by a distant uproar,—a hollow sound like the sudden inrush of a sea, which began afar off, and gathered strength as it came. Rolling onward and steadily increasing in volume, it appeared to split itself into a thousand angry echoes close by the dungeon walls, and a confused tumult of noisy tongues arose, mingling with the hurried and disorderly tramping of many feet and the clash of weapons. Voices argued hoarsely,—there were shrill whistlings,—and now and then the flare of tossing torches cast a fitful fire-gleam into the den where Barabbas lay. Once a loud laugh rang out above the more indistinct hubbub followed by a shout—

'Prophesy! Prophesy! Who is he that smote thee?'

And the laughter became general, merging itself swiftly into a frantic chorus of yells and groans and hisses. Then came a brief pause, in which some of the wilder noises ceased, and an angry disputation seemed to be going on between two or three individuals in authority, till presently the ocean-like roar and swell of sound re-commenced, passed slowly on, and began to die away like gradually diminishing peals of thunder. But while it remained yet within distinct hearing, there was a slow dragging of chains inside the dungeon and a feeble beating of manacled

hands at the interior grating, and the voice that had
called before now called again :

'Barabbas!'

No answer was returned.

'Barabbas! Hearest thou the passing multitude?'
Still silence.

'Barabbas! Dog! Assassin!' and the speaker
dealt an angry blow with his two fists at the dividing
bars,—'Art thou deaf to good news? I tell thee
there is some strife in the city,—some new sedition,—
it may be that our friends have conquered where we
have failed! Down with the law! Down with the
tyrant and oppressor! Down with the Pharisees!
Down with everything!' And he laughed, his
laughter being little more than a hoarse whisper,—
'Barabbas! We shall be free! Free!—think of it,
thou villain! A thousand curses on thee! Art
thou dead or sleeping that thou wilt not answer me?'

But he exhausted his voice in vain, and vainly beat
his fists against the grating. Barabbas was mute.
The moonlight, grown stronger, pierced the gloom of
his cell with a silvery radiance which blurred objects
rather than illumined them, so that the outline of his
figure could scarcely be discerned by his fellow-
captive who strove to see him through the bars of
the lower dungeon. Meanwhile the noise of the
crowd in the streets outside, had retreated into the
distance, and only a faint murmur arose from time to
time like the far-off surge of waves on a rocky shore.

'Barabbas! Barabbas!' and the vexed weak voice
grew suddenly loud with an access of spite and fury
—'An' thou wilt not respond to good tidings thou
shalt listen to evil! Hear me!—hear thy friend
Hanan who knows the wicked ways of women better
than thou! Why didst thou kill the Pharisee, thou
fool? 'Twas wasted pains,—for his boast was a true
one and thy Judith is a '——

The opprobrious term he meant to use was never uttered, for with a sudden spring, fierce and swift as that of an enraged lion leaping from its lair, the hitherto inert Barabbas was upon him, clutching at the two hands he had thrust through the grating to support himself, and squeezing and bending them against the bars with a terrific ferocity that threatened to snap the wrists asunder.

'Accursed Hanan! Dog! Breathe but her name again and I will saw thy robber hands off on this blunt iron and leave thee but the bleeding stumps wherewith to steal!'

Face to face in the faintly moonlit gloom, and all but invisible to one another, they writhed and wrestled a little space with strange impotence and equally strange fury, the chains on their fettered arms clashing against the bars between, till with a savage scream of pain, Hanan tore his maimed fingers and lacerated wrists from the pitiless grasp that crushed them, and fell helplessly downward into the darkness of his own den, while Barabbas flung himself away and back on his bed of straw, breathing hard and heavily, and shuddering through every fibre of his frame.

'If it were true,' he whispered between his set teeth,—'if it were true,—if she were false,—if the fair flesh and blood were but a mask for vileness,—God! —she would be worse than I,—a greater sinner than I have ever been!'

He buried his head in the hollow of his arm and lay quite still, striving to think out the problem of his own wild nature, his own blind and unbridled passions. It was a riddle too dark and difficult to solve easily, and gradually his mind wandered, and his thoughts began to lose themselves in a dizzy unconsciousness that was almost pleasure after so much pain. His clenched hands relaxed, his breathing became easier, and presently, heaving a deep sigh of exhaustion, he stretched himself out on the straw like a tired hound and slept.

The night marched on majestically. The moon and her sister planets paced through their glorious circles of harmonious light and law ; and from all parts of the earth, prayers in every form and every creed went up to heaven for pity, pardon and blessing on sinful humanity that had neither pity, pardon nor blessing for itself,—till, with a magic suddenness the dense purple skies changed to a pearly grey,— the moon sank pallidly out of sight,—the stars were extinguished one by one like lamps when a feast is ended, and morning began to suggest its approach in the freshening air. But Barabbas still slept. In his sleep he had unconsciously turned his face upward to what glimmering light there was, and a placid smile smoothed the fierce ruggedness of his features. Slumbering thus, it was possible to imagine what this unkempt and savage-looking creature might have been in boyhood ; there was something of grace in his attitude despite his fettered limbs,—there were lines of tenderness about his mouth, the curve of which could be just seen through his rough beard ; and there was a certain grave beauty about the broad brow and closed eyelids. Awake, he fully appeared to be what he was, a rebellious and impenitent criminal,—but in that perfect tranquillity of deep repose, he might have passed for a brave man wronged.

With the first faint light of the dawn, a sudden unwonted stir and noise began in the outer courts of the prison. Barabbas, overpowered by slumber as he was, heard it in a semi-conscious way, without realising what it might mean. But presently, as it grew louder, he opened his eyes reluctantly and raising himself on one arm, listened. Soon, he caught, in the

distance the sound of clashing weapons and the steady
tramp of men, and while he yet wondered, vaguely
and sleepily, at the unusual commotion, the clashing
and jangling and marching drew nearer and nearer,
till it came to an abrupt halt outside his very cell.
The key turned in the lock,—the huge bolts were thrust
back,—the door flew open, and such a blaze of light
flared in that he put up his hands to shield his eyes
as if from a blow. Blinking like a scared owl, he
roused himself and struggled into a sitting posture,
staring stupidly at what he saw,—a group of glittering soldiery headed by an officer who, holding a
smoking torch aloft, peered into the drear blackness
of the dungeon with a searching air of command.

'Come forth, Barabbas!'

Barabbas gazed and gazed, dreamily and without
apparent comprehension.

Just then a shrill voice yelled,

'I, also! I, Hanan, am innocent! Bring me also
before the Tribunal! Give me justice! Barabbas slew
the Pharisee, not I! The mercy of the Feast for
Hanan! Surely ye will not take Barabbas hence and
leave me here?'

No heed was paid to these clamourings, and the
officer merely repeated his command:

'Come forth, Barabbas!'

Growing more broadly awake, Barabbas stumbled
up on his feet and made an effort to obey, but his
heavy chains prevented his advance. Perceiving this,
the officer gave order to his men, and in a few minutes
the impeding fetters were struck off, and the prisoner
was immediately surrounded by the guard.

'Barabbas! Barabbas!' shrieked Hanan within.

Barabbas paused, looking vaguely at the soldiers
who pressed him in their midst. Then he turned his
eyes upon their commander.

'If I go to my death,' he said faintly,—'I pray thee

give yonder man food. He hath starved and thirsted all day and night,—and he was once my friend.'

The officer surveyed him somewhat curiously.

'Is that thy last request, Barabbas?' he inquired. 'It is Passover, and we will grant thee anything in reason!'

He laughed, and his men joined in the laughter. But Barabbas only stared straight ahead, his eyes looking like those of a hunted animal brought to bay.

'Do thus much for charity,' he muttered feebly; 'I have also starved and thirsted, but Hanan is weaker than I.'

Again the officer glanced at him, but this time deigned no answer. Wheeling abruptly round, he uttered the word of command, placed himself at the head of his men, and the whole troop, with Barabbas in their centre closely guarded, strode onward and upward out of the dark dungeon precincts to the higher floors of the building. And as they tramped through the stone passages, they extinguished the torches they carried, for the night was past and the morning had come.

III

MARCHING into the courtyard of the prison, the party halted there, while the heavy gates were being unfastened to allow an exit. Outside was the street,—the city,—freedom!—and Barabbas, still staring ahead, uttered a hoarse cry and put his manacled hands to his throat as though he were choking.

'What ails thee?' demanded one of the men nearest him, giving him a dig in the ribs with the hilt of his weapon,—'Stand up, fool! Never tell me that a breath of air can knock thee down like a felled bullock!'

For Barabbas reeled, and would have fallen prone on the ground insensible, had not the soldiers caught at his swaying figure and dragged him up, roughly enough, and with much coarse swearing. But his face had the pallor of death, and through his ragged beard his lips could be seen, livid and drawn apart over his clenched teeth like the lips of a corpse,—his breathing was scarcely perceptible.

The commander of the troop advanced and examined him.

'The man is starved'—he said briefly,—'Give him wine.'

This order was promptly obeyed, and wine was held to the mouth of the swooning captive, but his teeth were fast set and he remained unconscious.

Drop by drop however, the liquid was ungently forced down his throat, and after a couple of minutes, his chest heaved with the long laboured sighs of returning vitality, and his eyes flashed widely open.

'Air,—air!' he gasped, 'The free air,—the light'——

He thrust out his chained hands gropingly, and then, with a sudden rush of strength induced by the warmth of the wine, he began to laugh wildly.

'Freedom!' he exclaimed, 'Freedom! To live or die, what matter! Free! Free!'

'Hold thy peace, thou dog!' said the commanding officer sharply,—'Who told thee thou wert free? Look at thy fettered wrists and be wise! Watch him closely, men! March!'

The prison-gates fell back on their groaning hinges and the measured tramp, tramp of the little troop awakened echoes of metallic music as they defiled across the stony street and passed down a steep flight of steps leading to a subterranean passage which directly communicated with the Tribunal of Justice, or Hall of Judgment. This passage was a long vaulted way, winding in and out through devious twists and turnings, and was faintly lit up by oil lamps placed in sconces at regular distances, the flickering luminance thus given only making the native darkness of the place more palpable. Gloom and imprisonment were as strongly suggested here as in the dungeons left behind,—and Barabbas, his heart sickening anew with vague dread, shrank and shivered, stumbling giddily once or twice as he strove to keep pace with the steady march of his escort. Hope died within him; the flashing idea of liberty that had stirred him to such a sudden rapture of anticipation, now fled like a dream. He was being taken to his death; of that he felt sure. What mercy could he expect at the hands of the judge by whom he knew he must be tried and condemned? For was

not Pontius Pilate governor of Judæa? and had not
he Barabbas, slain, in a moment of unthinking fury,
one of Pilate's friends?   That accursed Pharisee!
His sleek manner,—his self-righteous smile,—his
white hand with the glittering blazon of a priceless
jewel on the forefinger, and all the trifling details of
costume and deportment that went to make up the
insolent and aggressive personality of the man,—
these things Barabbas remembered with a thrill of
loathing. He could almost see him as he saw him
then, before with one fierce stab he had struck him to
the earth, dead, and bleeding horribly in the brilliant
moonlight, his wide open eyes glaring to the last in
dumb and dreadful hate upon his murderer. And
a life must always be given for a life; Barabbas
admitted the stern justice of this law. It was only
what he knew to be the ordained manner of death
for such criminals as he, that caused his nerves to
wince with fear and agony. If, like the Pharisee, he
could be struck out of existence in a moment, why,
that were naught,—but to be stretched on beams of
wood there to blister for long hours in the pitiless sun,
—to feel every sinew strained to cracking, and every
drop of blood turning first to fire and then to ice,—
this was enough to make the strongest man shudder;
and Barabbas, weakened by long fasting and want of
air, trembled so violently at times that he could
scarcely drag his limbs along. His head swam and
his eyes smarted; there were dull noises in his ears
caused partly by the surging blood in his brain, and
partly by the echo of a sound which with every
onward step grew more distinct,—a clamour of angry
voices and shouting, in the midst of which he fancied
he heard his own name,

'Barabbas! Barabbas!'

Startled, he looked inquiringly into the faces of
the soldiers that surrounded him, but their impassive

bronze-like features betrayed no intelligence. Vainly he strove to listen more attentively,—the clanking weapons of his guard and the measured thud of their feet on the stone pavement, prevented him from catching the real purport of those distant outcries. Yet surely,—surely there was another shout—

'Barabbas! Barabbas!'

A sickening horror suddenly seized him,—a swift and awful comprehension of his true position. The mob, relentless in all ages, were evidently clamouring for his death, and were even now preparing to make sport of his torments. Nothing more glorious to a brutal populace than the physical agony of a helpless fellow-creature,—nothing more laughter-moving than to watch the despair, the pain, and the writhing last struggle of a miserable human wretch condemned to perish by a needlessly slow and barbarous torture. Thinking of this, great drops of sweat bathed his brow, and as he staggered feebly on, he prayed dumbly for some sudden end,—prayed that his hot and throbbing blood might rush in merciful full force to a vital centre of his brain that so he might fall into oblivion swiftly like a stone falling into the sea. Anything—anything, rather than face the jeers and the mockery of a pitiless multitude trooping forth as to a feast to see him die!

Closer and closer came the hubbub and roar, interspersed with long pauses of comparative stillness, and it was during one of these pauses that his enforced journey came to an end. Turning sharply round the last corner of the underground passage, the soldiers tramped out into the daylight, and ascended several wide marble steps, afterwards crossing an open circular court, empty and cool in the silver-grey hues of early dawn. Finally passing under a columnar arch, they entered a vast Hall, which was apparently divided into two square spaces,—one almost clear,

2

save for a few prominent figures that stood forth in statuesque outlines against a background of dark purple hangings fringed with gold,—the other densely crowded with people who were only kept from rushing into the judicial precincts by a line of Roman soldiery headed by their centurion.

On the appearance of Barabbas with his armed escort, heads were turned round and hurried whispers were exchanged among the crowd, but not one look of actual interest or compassion was bestowed upon him. The people's mind was centred on a far weightier matter. Such a trial was pending as had never yet been heard within the walls of a human tribunal, and such a Captive was being questioned as never before gave answer to mortal man! With a sudden sense of relief, Barabbas, stupefied though he was, began dimly to realise that perhaps after all his terrors had been groundless; there was no sign here, at least, not at present, of his death being wanted to make an extra holiday for the mob, and, infected by the prevailing spirit of intense curiosity and attention, he craned his neck forward eagerly in order to obtain a view of what was going on. As he did so, the people directly in front of him shrank away in evident aversion, but he paid little heed to this mutely expressed repugnance, as their unanimous recoil made a convenient opening through which he could plainly see the judgment daïs and all its imposing surroundings. There were seated several members of the Sanhedrim, several of whom he knew by sight, among them the high-priest Caiaphas, and his colleague Annas,—a few scribes occupied lower benches and were busily engaged in writing,—and among these dignified and exalted personages, he perceived, to his astonishment, a little lean, wrinkled, crouching moneychanger, a man well known and cursed throughout all Jerusalem for his high rates of usury and cruelty to the poor. How came so mean a villain there? thought Barabbas wonderingly; but he could not stop to puzzle out the problem, for the chief person his eyes involuntarily sought for and rested upon was the Roman judge,—that very judge of whose stern sad face he had dreamed in the darkness of his dungeon, — Pilate the calm, severe, yet at times compassionate arbiter of life and death according to the codes of justice administered in Judæa. Surely to-day he suffered, or was weary!—for did ever legal 'tyrant' before look so sick at heart? In the grey morning light his features seemed to have an almost death-like rigidity and pallor—his hand played absently with the jewelled signet depending from his breast,—and beneath the falling folds of his robe of office, one sandalled foot beat impatiently upon the floor. Barabbas stared at him in dull fascination and fear,—he did not look a cruel so much as a melancholy man,—and yet there was something in his classic profile, and in the firm lines of his thin closely compressed lips that augured little softness of character. What was likely to be his verdict on an assassin who had slain one of his friends? And while Barabbas vaguely pondered this, an irrepressible cry rose up all at once from the multitude around him, like the noise of breaking waters roaring in thunderous repetitions through the vaulted Hall,—

'Crucify him! Crucify him!'

The wild shout was furious and startling, and with its thrilling clamour, the lethargic torpor that had held Barabbas more or less spell-bound was suddenly dispersed. With a swift shock he came to himself like one roughly shaken from sleep.

'Crucify him!'

Crucify—whom? Whose life was thus passionately demanded? Not his? No, not his, most surely, for the people scarcely heeded him. Their looks were all turned another way. Then if he were not the offender, who was?

Pushing himself yet more to the front, he followed the angry glances of the mob and saw, standing patiently below the judgment-seat one Figure,—saw, and seeing, held his breath for very wonderment. For that Figure seemed to absorb into itself all the stateliness, all the whiteness, all the majesty of the lofty and spacious Tribunal, together with all the light that fell glimmeringly through the shining windows,—light that now began to form itself into the promise rays of the rising sun. Such radiance, such power, such glorious union of perfect beauty and strength in one human Form, Barabbas had never seen or imagined before, and he gazed and gazed till his soul almost lost itself in the mere sense of sight. Like one in a trance he heard himself whisper,

'Who is yonder Man?'

No one answered. It may be no one heard. And he repeated the query softly over and over again in his own mind, keeping his eyes fixed on that tall and god-like Being, whose sublime aspect seemed to imply an absolute mastery over men and things, but who nevertheless waited there silently in apparent submission to the law, with a slight dreamy smile on the beautiful curved lips, and a patient expression in the down-dropt eyelids, as of one who mutely expected the public declaration of what he had himself privately decreed. Still as a statue of sunlit marble He stood, erect and calm, His white garments flowing backward from His shoulders in even picturesque folds, thus displaying His bare rounded arms, crossed now on His breast in a restful attitude of resignation, yet in their very inertness suggesting such mighty muscular force as would have befitted a Hercules. Power, grandeur, authority and invincible supremacy were all silently expressed in His marvellous and incomparable Presence,—and while Barabbas still stared fascinated, awed, and troubled in mind, though he knew not why, the shouts of the populace broke forth again with hoarser reiteration and more impatient ferocity,—

'*Away with him! Away with him! Let him be crucified!*'

And far back from the edge of the crowd, a woman's voice, sweet and shrill and piercing, soared up and rang out with a cruel music over all the deeper uproar,—

'*Crucify him! Crucify him!*'

IV

THE clear vibration of the woman's cry acted like a strange charm to stimulate afresh the already feverish excitement of the people. A frenzied hubbub ensued,—shrieks, yells, groans and hisses filled the air, till the noise became absolutely deafening, and Pilate, with an angry and imperious gesture suddenly rose and faced the mob. Advancing to the front of the daïs, he lifted up his hand authoritatively to command silence. Gradually the din decreased, dying off in little growling thuds of sound down to a few inaudible mutterings, though before actual stillness was restored, the sweet soprano voice rang forth again melodiously, broken by a bubbling ripple of laughter,—

'Crucify him!'

Barabbas started. That silvery laugh struck to his heart coldly and made him shiver,—surely he had heard an echo of such scornful mirth before? It sounded bitterly familiar. Pilate's keen eyes flashed a vain search for the unseen speaker,—then, turning towards the people with an air of pacific dignity, he demanded,—

'*Why, what evil hath he done?*'

This simple question was evidently ill-timed, and had a disastrous effect. The sole answer to it was a bellowing roar of derision,—a thunderous clamour of wild rage that seemed to shake the very walls of the

Tribunal. Men, women, and little children alike joined in the chorus of 'Crucify him! Crucify him!' and the savage refrain was even caught up by the high-priests, elders and scribes, who in their various distinctive costumes and with their several attendants, were grouped behind Pilate on the judgment daïs. Pilate heard them, and turned sharply round, a dark frown knitting his brows. Caiaphas, the chief priest, met his eyes with a bland smile, and repeated under his breath 'Crucify him!' as though it were a pleasing suggestion.

'Of a truth it were well he should die the death,' murmured Annas, his portly colleague, casting a furtive glance at Pilate from under his pale eyelashes; —'The worthy governor seemeth to hesitate, yet verily this traitor is no friend of Cæsar's.'

Pilate vouchsafed no answer save a look of supreme and utter scorn. Shrugging his shoulders, he re-seated himself and gazed long and earnestly at the Accused. 'What evil hath he done?' It might have been more justly asked what evil could He do? Was there any mark of vileness, any line of treachery on the open beauty of that fair and lustrous Countenance? No! Nobleness and truth were eloquently declared in every feature; moreover there was something in the silent Presence of the Prisoner that made Pilate tremble,— something unspoken yet felt,—a vast and vague Mystery that seemed to surround and invest Him with a power all the more terrific because so deeply hidden. And while the troubled procurator studied His calm and dignified bearing, and wondered doubtfully what course it were best to pursue, Barabbas from his coign of vantage stared eagerly in the same direction, growing more and more conscious of an unusual and altogether wonderful fascination in the aspect of this Man the people sought to slay. And presently his vivid curiosity gave him courage to address one of the soldiers near him.

'Prithee tell me,' said he, 'what captive King stands yonder?'

The soldier gave a short contemptuous laugh.

'King! Ay, ay! He calls himself King of the Jews,—a sorry jest, for which his life will pay forfeit. He is naught but a carpenter's son, known as Jesus of Nazareth. He hath stirred up rebellion, and persuadeth the mob to disobey law. Moreover he consorteth with the lowest rascals,—thieves and publicans and sinners. He hath a certain skill in conjuring; the people say he can disappear suddenly when most sought for. But he made no attempt to disappear last night, for we trapped him easily, close by Gethsemane. One of his own followers betrayed him. Some there be who deem him mad,—some say he hath a devil. Devil or no, he is caught at last and must surely die.'

Barabbas heard in incredulous amazement. That royal-looking Personage a carpenter's son?—a common working-man, and one of the despised Nazarenes? No, no!—it was not possible! Then, by degrees he began to remember that before he, Barabbas, had been cast into prison for robbery and murder, there had been strange rumours afloat in the country of Judæa, concerning one Jesus, a miracle-worker, who went about healing the sick and the infirm, giving sight to the blind, and preaching a new religion to the poor. It was even asserted that He had on one occasion raised a man named Lazarus from the dead after three days' burial in the ground, but this astounding report was promptly suppressed and contradicted by certain scribes in Jerusalem who made themselves generally responsible for the current news. The country people were known to be ignorant and superstitious, and any one possessing what was called 'the gift of healing' in provinces where all manner of loathsome physical evils abounded, could obtain undue and almost supernatural influence over the miserable and down-trodden inhabitants. Yet surely if this Man were He of whom rumour had spoken, then there seemed no reason to doubt the truth of the miraculous powers attributed to Him. He was Himself an embodied Miracle. And what were His powers actually? Much had been said concerning this same Jesus of Nazareth, of which Barabbas had no distinct recollection. His eighteen months of imprisonment had obliterated many things from his memory, and what he had chiefly brooded upon in his dreary dungeon had been his own utter misery, and the torturing recollection of one fair woman's face. Now, strange to say, he could find no room for any thought at all, save the impending fate of Him on whom his eyes were fixed. And as he looked, it seemed to him that all suddenly the judgment-hall expanded hugely and swam round in a circle of bright flame through which he saw that angelic white Figure shine forth with a thousand radiations of lightning-like glory! A faint cry of terror broke from his lips,—

'No, no!' he stammered—'No, I tell you! You cannot, you dare not crucify Him! Yonder is a Spirit! . . . no man ever looked so . . . He is a god!'——

As he uttered the word, one of the Roman soldiers hearing, turned and struck him fiercely on the mouth with his steel gauntlet.

'Fool, be silent! Wilt thou too be one of his disciples?'

Wincing with pain, Barabbas strove to wipe the trickling blood from his lips with his fettered hands, and as he did so, caught a straight full look from the so-called Jesus of Nazareth. The pity and the

tenderness of that look pierced him to the soul; no
living being had ever given him a glance so instantly
comprehensive and sympathetic. With a quick reckless movement, he thrust himself more to the front of
the crowd to gain a closer view of One who could so
gently regard him. A passionate impulse of gratitude
moved him to rush across the whole width of the Hall,
and fling himself in all his rough brute strength in
front of this new-found Friend to serve as a human
buckler of defence in case of need. But bristling
weapons guarded him, and he was too closely surrounded for escape. Just at that moment, one of the
scribes, a tall lean man in sober-coloured raiment, rose
from his place in the semi-circle of priests and elders
grouped on the judicial platform, and, unfolding a
parchment scroll began to read in a monotonous
voice the various heads of the indictment against the
Accused. These had been hastily summed up by the
Sanhedrim, during the brief trial which had taken
place in the house of Caiaphas the high-priest on the
previous evening. A great stillness now reigned in
lieu of the previous uproar; a deep hush of suspense
and attention, in which the assembled mob seemed to
wait and pant with expectation, as a crouching beast
waits and pants for its anticipated prey. Pilate
listened frowningly, one hand covering his eyes.
During the occasional pauses in the scribe's reading,
the noise of traffic in the outside stony streets made
itself distinctly audible, and once the sound of a little
child's voice singing, came floating merrily upwards
like the echo of a joy-bell. The skies were changing
rapidly from pearl-grey hues to rose and daffodil; the
sun was high above the horizon, but its light had not
yet found a way through the lofty windows of the
judgment-hall. It beamed on the crowd beyond the
barrier with iridescent flashes of colour,—now flashing
on a red kerchief tying up a woman's hair, or on the

glittering steel corselet of a Roman soldier, while the Tribunal itself was left in cold and unillumined whiteness, relieved only by the velvet hangings pertaining to it, which in their sombre purple tint suggested the falling folds of a funeral pall.

The reading of the indictment finished, Pilate still remained silent for some minutes. Then, lifting his hand from his eyes, he surveyed, somewhat satirically, his companions in authority.

'Ye have brought me this man as one that perverteth the people,' he said slowly,—'What accusation bring ye against him?'

Caiaphas, and Annas, who was then vice-president of the Sanhedrim, exchanged wondering and half indignant glances. Finally Caiaphas with an expression of offended dignity looked round appealingly upon his compeers.

'Surely ye have all heard the indictment,' he said, —'And the worthy governor's question seemeth but vain in this matter. What need we of further witnesses? If yonder man were not a malefactor would we have brought him hither? He hath blasphemed; for last night we did solemnly adjure him in the name of the living God, to declare unto us whether he were the Christ, the Son of the Blessed, and he answered boldly and said "*I am! And hereafter ye shall see the Son of Man sitting on the right hand of Power and coming in the clouds of heaven!*" What think ye? Is he not worthy of death?'

An emphatic murmur of assent went round the semi-circle of the priests and elders. But Pilate gave a gesture of contempt and flung himself restlessly back on the judgment-seat.

'Ye talk in parables, and do perplex the ends of justice. If he himself saith he is the Son of Man, how do ye make him out to be the Son of God?'

Caiaphas flushed an angry red, and was about to make some retort, but on a moment's reflection, suppressed his feelings and proceeded, smiling cynically—

'Of a truth thou art in merciful mood, Pilate, and thine Emperor will not blame thee for too much severity of rule! In our law, the sinner that blasphemeth shall surely die. Yet if blasphemy be not a crime in thy judgment, what of treason? Witnesses there are who swear that this man hath said it is not lawful to give tribute unto Cæsar; moreover he is an evil boaster, for he hath arrogantly declared that he will destroy the Holy Temple. Yea verily, even unto the Holy of Holies itself, he saith he will destroy, so that not one stone shall remain upon another, and in three days, without the help of hands, he will build up a new and greater tabernacle! Such mad ranting doth excite the minds of the populace to rebellion,—moreover he deceiveth the eyes of the vulgar and uninstructed by feigning to perform great miracles when all is but trickery and dissimulation. Finally, he hath entered Jerusalem in state as a King;'—here he turned to his colleague in office— 'Thou, Annas, canst speak of this, for thou wert present when the multitude passed by.'

Annas, thus appealed to, moved a little forward, pressing his hands together, and casting down his pale-coloured treacherous eyes with a deferential air of apologetic honesty.

'Truly it would seem that a pestilence in this man's shape doth walk abroad to desolate and disaffect the province,' said he,—'For I myself beheld the people, when this traitor entered the city by the road of Bethphage and Bethany, rush forth to meet him with acclamations, strewing palm-branches, olive-boughs and even their very garments in his path, as though he were a universal conqueror of men. And shouts of triumph rent the air, for the multitude received him both as prophet and king, crying "*Hosanna! Blessed is he that cometh in the name of the Lord! Hosanna in the highest!*" Whereat I marvelled greatly, and being troubled in mind, returned unto Caiaphas to tell him straightway those things which I had seen and heard concerning the strange frenzy of the mob, which of a surety is dangerous to the maintenance of law and order. 'Tis an unseemly passion of the vulgar to thus salute with royal honour one of the accursed Nazarenes.'

'Is he in truth a Nazarene?' inquired one of the elders suddenly, with a dubious air,—'I have heard it said that he was born in Bethlehem of Judæa, and that Herod, the late king, was told of certain marvels at his birth'——

'An idle rumour,' interrupted Annas hastily; 'We took him before the tetrarch yesternight, where, had he chosen, he could have made his own defence. For Herod asked him many questions which he could not or would not answer, till the noble tetrarch's patience failing, he sent him on to Pilate to be sentenced. He is known to be of Nazareth; for his parents have their home and calling in the village so named.'

Pilate listened, but said nothing. He was ill at ease. The statements of Caiaphas and Annas seemed to him a mere babble of words without meaning. He was entirely opposed to the members of the Sanhedrim;—he knew they were men who chiefly sought their own interest and advancement, and he also knew that the real cause of their having denounced the so-called 'prophet of Nazareth,' was fear,—fear of having their theories shaken, their laws questioned, and their authority over the people denied. He saw in the dignified Prisoner before him, one who, whatever He was, or wherever He

came from, evidently thought for Himself. Nothing
more terrorising to sacerdotal tyranny than liberty of
thought!—nothing more dangerous than freedom of
conscience, and indifference to opinion! Pilate himself was afraid, but not with the same dread as that
which affected the Jewish priests,—his misgivings
were vague and undefined, and all the more difficult
to overcome. He was strangely reluctant to even
look at the 'Nazarene,' whose tall and radiant form
appeared to shine with an inward and supernatural
light amid the cold austerity of the judicial surroundings; and he kept his eyes down, fixed on the floor,
the while he hesitatingly pondered his position. But
time pressed,—the Sanhedrim council were becoming
impatient,—he was at last compelled to act and to
speak, — and slowly turning round in his chair he
fully confronted the Accused, who at the same instant
lifted His noble head and met the anxious, scrutinising
regard of His judge with an open look of fearless
patience and infinite tenderness. Meeting that look,
Pilate trembled,—but anon, forcing himself to assume
an air of frigid composure, he spoke aloud in grave
authoritative accents:

'*Answerest thou nothing? Hearest thou not how
many things are witnessed against thee?*'

Then and only then, the hitherto immovable white-
robed Figure stirred,—and advancing with slow
and regal grace, approached Pilate more nearly, still
looking at him. One bright ray of the risen sun fell
slantingly through a side-window and glistened star-
like on the bronze-gold of the rich hair that clustered
in thick waves upon His brow, and as He kept His
shining eyes upon His judge, He smiled serenely
even as one who pardons a sin before hearing its
confession. But no word passed His lips. Pilate
recoiled,—an icy cold chilled the blood in his veins,—
involuntarily he rose, and fell back step by step,

grasping at the carved gold projections of his judicial throne to steady his faltering limbs, for there was something in the quiet onward gliding of that snowy-garmented Shape that filled his soul with dread, and suggested to his mind old myths and legends of the past, when Deity appearing suddenly to men, had consumed them in a breath with the lightning of great glory. And that one terrific moment while he stood thus face to face with the Divine Accused seemed to him an eternity. It was a never-to-be-forgotten space of time in which all his life, past and present, appeared reflected as a landscape is reflected in a drop of dew,—moreover, the premonition of a future, dark and desolate, loomed indistinctly upon his mind, like a shadow on the horizon. All unconsciously to himself his countenance paled to a ghastly haggardness, and scarcely knowing what he did, he raised his hands appealingly as though to avert some great and crushing blow. The learned Jews who were grouped around him, stared at his terror-stricken attitude in wonderment, and exchanged glances of vexation and dismay, while one of the elders, a dark-eyed crafty-visaged man, leaned forward hastily and touched him on the shoulder, saying in a low tone—

'What ails thee, Pilate? Surely thou art smitten with palsy, or some delusion numbs thy senses! Hasten, we beseech thee, to pronounce sentence, for the hours wear on apace,—and at this season of the Passover, 'twere well and seemly that thou should'st give the multitude their will. What is this malefactor unto thee? Let him be crucified, for he is guilty of treason, since he calls himself a King. Full well thou knowest we have no King but Cæsar, yet yonder fellow boldly saith he is King of the Jews. Question him, whether or no he hath not thus boasted falsely of power!'

Pilate gazed round at his adviser bewilderedly,—he

felt as though he were entangled in the mazes of an evil dream where demons whispered dark hints of unworded crimes.   Sick and cold to the very heart, he yet realised that he must make an effort to interrogate the Prisoner as he was bidden, and, moistening his parched lips, he at last succeeded in enunciating the necessary query, albeit his accents were so faint and husky as to be scarcely audible.

'*Art thou the King of the Jews?*'

An intense silence followed.   Then a full, penetrating Voice, sweeter than sweetest music, stirred the air,—

'*Sayest thou this thing of thyself or did others tell it thee of me?*'

Pilate's face flushed, and his hand grasped the back of his chair convulsively.   He gave a gesture of impatience, and answered abruptly, yet tremulously,—

'*Am I a Jew? Thine own nation and the chief priests have delivered thee unto me; what hast thou done?*'

A light as of some inward fire irradiated the deep lustrous eyes of the 'Nazarene;' a dreamy, meditative smile parted His lips.   Looking so, and smiling thus, His glorious aspect made the silence eloquent, and Pilate's authoritative demand 'What hast thou done?' seemed answered without speech.   And the voiceless response might have been rendered into words like these,—

'What have I done?   I have made Life sweet, and robbed Death of bitterness; there is honour for men and tenderness for women; there is hope for all, Heaven for all, God for all!—and the lesson of Love,—Love divine and human as personified in Me, sanctifies the Earth for ever through My Name!'

But these great facts remained unuttered, for, as yet they were beyond dull mortal comprehension, and, with the faint dreamy smile still giving a poetic languor of deep thought to every line of His countenance, the Accused answered slowly, every word He spoke vibrating melodiously through the stillness,—

'*My kingdom is not of this world. If my kingdom were of this world then would my servants fight that I should not be delivered to the Jews. But—now is my kingdom not from hence!*'

And, drawing His majestic figure up to its full height, He raised His head and looked up towards the loftiest window of the Hall, now glittering diamond-like in the saffron-tinted rays of the swiftly ascending sun. His attitude was so unspeakably grand and suggestive of power, that Pilate again recoiled, with that sickening sense of helpless terror clutching at his heart anew. He stole a furtive and anxious glance at the chief priests and elders, who were leaning forward on their benches listening attentively,—they all appeared unmoved and coldly indifferent. Caiaphas smiled satirically and exchanged a side-whisper with Annas, but otherwise no one volunteered to speak. Sorely against his will, Pilate continued his examination. Feigning an unconcern he was far from feeling, he asked his next question half carelessly, half kindly,—

'*Art thou a King, then?*'

With a sublime gesture, the Accused flashed one burning glance upon all who waited breathlessly for His reply,—then looked straightly and steadily, full into Pilate's eyes.

'*Thou sayest!*'

And, as He uttered the words, the sun, climbing to the topmost arch of the opposite window, beamed through it in a round blaze of glory, and flooded the

3

judgment - hall with ripples of gold and crimson, circling the Divine brows with a glittering rainbow radiance as though the very heavens had set their crown and signet upon the splendour of a Truth revealed!

V

THERE was a moment's pause.

Pilate sat dumb and irresolute,—but among the assembled members of the Sanhedrim there ran various broken murmurs of indignation and impatience. '*What need we of further witness?*' 'He is convicted out of his own mouth!' 'He hath spoken treason!' '*Let him die the death!*' The sunlight showering its prolific gold on the white garments of the Prisoner flashed into prismatic glimmerings now and again as though it had encountered some other light with which it joyously played and harmonised. And Pilate's sight grew misty and strained,—his temples throbbed and ached. He was tired, confused, pained and perplexed; the extraordinary beauty of the Figure confronting him was too singularly unique to be otherwise than powerfully impressive, and he knew as thoroughly as ever mortal judge knew anything, that to condemn this Man to a hideous and unmerited death would be to commit a crime the consequences of which he could not quite foresee, but which he instinctively dreaded. He was perfectly aware of the active part the high-priests Caiaphas and Annas had played in the work of hunting down the 'Nazarene' and bringing Him before the Tribunal, and he also realised the manner in which they had laid their plans. A certain wild and lawless young man named

Iscariot, the only son of his father, had banded himself with the disciples of this Jesus of Nazareth, and
the elder Iscariot, a wealthy usurer, was a close
friend and confidant of Caiaphas. It was therefore
not difficult to perceive how the father, prompted by
the high-priest, and himself displeased at his son's
sudden fanaticism for a stranger, had brought all the
weight of religious and parental authority to bear in
persuading the young man to give up his so-called
'Master' to justice. There were other far more
deeply hidden motives than these of which Pilate
was ignorant, but what little he knew, or thought
he knew, was sufficient to make him distrust the
unsupported witness of the priests and elders alone.
Pondering the matter within himself a while, he
presently turned to the council and demanded,

'Where is Iscariot?'

Anxious looks were exchanged, but no reply was
offered.

'Ye tell me it was he who brought the guard to
where this Nazarene lay hidden,' proceeded Pilate
slowly,—'An' he hath taken so chief a part in the
capture, he should be here. I would fain know what
he hath to say concerning the doings of the man
whom first he chose to follow and then forsake. Let
him be brought before me.'

Annas leaned forward with an air of apologetic
servility.

'The young man hath fled from the city out of
fear,' said he; 'He hath been seized with some fool's
panic, for lo, he came to us at late midnight, madly
bemoaning his sins and bringing back the silver
which we had given him as guerdon for his service
and obedience to the law. Some evil fever surely
worked within his blood, for while we yet gently
reasoned with him in hope to calm his frenzy, all
suddenly he dashed the money down before us in

the Temple and departed in haste, we know not whither.'

'Strange!' muttered Pilate abstractedly. The absence of Iscariot from the present scene of trial vexed him sorely. He had a strong desire to ask the man who had betrayed his Master the cause of his sudden disaffection, and now that this was impossible, he felt more jaded and worn-out than before. His head swam,—and in the confused trouble of his mind, a great darkness seemed to grow up out of the air and envelop him swiftly and resistlessly. And in that darkness he fancied he saw a ring of fire which swung round and round like a rolling wheel, becoming narrower with every rotation, and binding him in closely as with a burning zone. The horrible sensation increased, stifling his breath and blinding his eyes till he felt he must leap from his chair and cry aloud in order to save himself from suffocation, —when,—all at once, his nameless inward suffering ceased,—a cool breath seemed to be wafted across his brow, and looking up, he saw that the deep and loving gaze of the Accused was fastened upon him with an infinity of tenderness and pity that opened to him, as it were, a new and exquisite and wondrous sense of life and limitless desire. For that one moment all his perplexities were swept away, and his course seemed clear. Turning to the chief priests and elders he said in firm emphatic tones,—

'*I find no fault in this man!*'

His words were received with a general movement of indignation, and Caiaphas losing all his wonted dignity, rose up in wrath, exclaiming loudly,

'No fault! No fault? Art thou mad, Pilate? *He stirreth up the people, teaching throughout all Jewry, beginning from Galilee to this place*'——

'And look you,' interposed Annas, craning his thin neck and ill-favoured visage forward,—'He consorteth with none but outcasts, publicans and sinners, and against all the virtuous he pronounceth openly the damnation of hell. Here sitteth the Rabbi Micha who hath heard him make outcry in the public streets, and hath taken note of certain sayings wherewith he seeketh to mislead the people. For he is one that perverteth truth while feigning most boldly to proclaim it. Speak, Micha,—for it seemeth that the worthy governor needeth more witness than ours against this rogue and blasphemer.'

Micha, an elderly Jew, with a keen, dark, withered face and hard cold eyes, rose at once and drew a set of tablets from his breast.

'These words,' said he in a dry even tone, 'are veritably set down here as I received them with mine own ears while standing in the Temple itself. For this misguided and fanatical young man hesitated not to preach his unscrupulous theories in the established place of holy doctrine. Judge ye for yourselves whether such language be not violent,'— and bringing his memoranda close to his eyes, he read slowly,

' *Woe unto you, scribes and Pharisees, hypocrites ! for ye shut up the kingdom of heaven against men, and ye neither go in yourselves, nor suffer them that are entering to go in.*

' *Woe unto you, scribes and Pharisees, hypocrites ! for ye devour widows' houses, for pretence making long prayer, therefore ye shall receive the greater damnation.*

' *Woe unto you, scribes and Pharisees, hypocrites ! for ye compass sea and land to make one proselyte, and when he is made, ye make him twofold more the child of hell than yourselves !*

' *Woe unto you, scribes and Pharisees, hypocrites ! for ye are like unto whited sepulchres, which indeed appear beautiful outward, but are within full of dead men's bones and all uncleanness.*

'Ye serpents, ye generation of vipers, how can ye escape the damnation of hell!'

Here pausing, Micha looked up.

'Of a truth,' he remarked in the same monotone,— 'for one whom the country folk strive to screen by the spreading of false rumours concerning his gentle and harmless character, such words as these are mere raving devilry, and full of bitterness, spite and malice prepense, set forth as wilful onslaughts upon those who do maintain virtue, law and order. Little gentleness will ye find in them, but much misguided vanity and spleen.'

A slight dawning smile lifted the rigid corners of Pilate's stern mouth. In his heart he secretly admired the magnificent physical and moral courage of a man who could boldly enter the Temple itself and thus plainly and publicly denounce hypocrisy in the very place where it was most practised.

'I tell thee, good Micha, and thou, Caiaphas, and Annas also,' he said decisively, 'I find no fault in him at all, touching those things whereof ye accuse him. No, nor yet Herod,—for ye went to him last night, and lo, nothing worthy of death is found in him '——

'Stay, noble Pilate!—listen to *me!*' interrupted a querulous, cracked voice, and the little ape-like figure of the old usurer whom Barabbas had, to his surprise, perceived occupying a prominent place on one of the judgment-benches, rose up in tremulous excitement—'Listen I pray thee!—for art not thou set here to administer justice to the wronged and oppressed in Judæa? Look you, most excellent sir! this malefactor, this accursed devil, this vile traitor and deceiver '—here the wrinkled old wretch gasped and sputtered for breath in the sheer extremity of

rage,—'this pretended prophet came insolently into
the Temple two days agone and saw me there at my
accustomed place,—thou knowest, noble Pilate, I am
an honest poor man!—and lo, like a furious madman
he seized me,—ay, and he hath a clutch like iron!—
and taking up a whip of knotted cords scourged me,
great Pilate!—scourged me, *me!*' and his voice rose
to a shrill yell of fury—'out of the holy place!   And
his mouth was full of blasphemy and cursing, for he
said, "*My house is called the house of prayer, but ye
have made it a den of thieves!*"   Mark that, worthy
Pilate! he did claim the very Temple as his own, even
as he hath claimed to be King of the Jews, and hath
sought to reign over all Judæa.   Crucify him, noble
governor!—crucify him in the name of God!   And
scourge him!—scourge him till the proud and sinful
blood flows in torrents from his veins!—scourge him,
for he hath scourged one of the children of Levi,—
yea, he hath scourged me, even *me!*'   Here he
stopped, half choked with malice and fury, while
Pilate regarded him, coldly smiling.

'Verily, Zacharias, thou tellest me of one good
service this man hath rendered the State,' he said
deliberately—'Long hast thou merited a whipping,
and that thou hast at last received it will help to
satisfy some few of thy money clients in Jerusalem!'
An involuntary murmur of approving laughter broke
from some of the members of the council, but was
quickly suppressed as the high-priest frowned darkly
upon the offenders.   Zacharias shrank back, scowling
and muttering, while Pilate calmly continued—'More
than ever am I persuaded that there is no evil in this
youthful preacher to the poor, and no fault at all
worthy of death, wherefore as ye have a custom at
this Feast requiring the liberation of a prisoner, I will
release him unto you and let him go.'

'The multitude will rend thee, Pilate, for an act so

impolitic !' exclaimed Caiaphas hotly—' What !—shall
an innocent man like this aged Zacharias, who hath
no fault save the common fault of his trade, be publicly
scourged, and thou the governor of Judæa find no
remedy? Thou art no friend to Cæsar if thou let
this man go. Moreover they demand the release of
Barabbas, who hath been imprisoned for more than a
year, and whose sin of rebellion was one of impulse,
not of malignant intention. He hath been brought
hither by my order, and waits below the barrier,
guarded, but prepared for freedom.'

'Then he is ill prepared !' declared Pilate sharply—
'For by all the gods of Rome he shall be crucified !
Freedom for Barabbas? Have ye no memory? Did
he not raise an insurrection against Roman law, and
harangue the people in the open streets far more
wildly and arrogantly than this harmless Nazarene
hath done? And did he not slay all unprovokedly
one of your own tribe, Gabrias the Pharisee, a man of
excellent learning and renown? Go to! Envy doth
prompt ye to demand the nobler life and give liberty
to the vile,—and ye have sorely misguided the mob
in this matter. But now will I myself address them,
and release unto them him whom they call King of
the Jews.'

And, rising from his chair he prepared to descend
from the Tribunal. Caiaphas made a hasty step
forward as though to prevent his movements, but
Pilate waved him aside disdainfully, and he stood
rooted to the spot, the picture of baffled rage and
dismay, his thin white hands nervously clenched,
and the great jewel on his breast heaving up and
down with the passionate quickness of his breathing. Annas sat still in his place, utterly taken
aback by the governor's decision, and stared fixedly
in front of him as though he found it difficult to
believe the evidence of his senses. Zacharias the

money-lender alone gave violent vent to his feelings
by throwing up his hands wildly in the air and
anon beating his breast, the while he loudly bewailed
himself—

'Ai! ai! There is no justice left in Jerusalem!
Woe, woe unto the children of Abraham who are
ground down beneath the iron heel of Rome! Woe
unto us who are made the spoil of the heathen tyrant
and oppressor!'

And as he thus raved and rocked his lean body to
and fro, the Divine Prisoner suddenly turned and
regarded him steadily. A rapid change came over
his wicked features,—he ceased yelling,—and drawing
himself together in a wrinkled heap till he looked like
some distorted demon, he began to mutter curses in
a thick whisper that was more awful than any audible
speech. The 'Nazarene' watched him for a moment,
a noble wrath clouding the fairness of His brows,—
but the shadow of righteous indignation passed even
more swiftly than it had come, leaving His face serene
and smiling and patient as before. Only the bright
pure Eyes were more steadily uplifted to the sunlight,
as though they sought to drink in glory for susten-
ance. Meanwhile, an old, white-bearded man, a
prominent and much-respected member of the
Sanhedrim, interposed, and pulling the mouthing
Zacharias back to his place with a stern injunction to
be silent, he himself ventured to address Pilate in
calm conciliatory accents.

'Believe me, worthy Pilate, thou art not altogether
wise in this matter. Why, for the sake of one man
wilt thou give cause of offence to both the priests and
people? A rebellious rogue and murderer such as
Barabbas hath proved himself to be, is far less dangerous to the community than yonder young Teacher of
new doctrines, who out of very arrogance, arising
perchance from the consciousness of a certain superior

physical force and outward beauty, doth maintain himself thus boldly, striving to terrorise thee and avert true justice. Lo, there are many such as he among the wandering Egyptian aliens, who, by reason of an imposing presence, and a certain vague sublimity of speech, do persuade the less crafty to believe in their supernatural powers. Look you, even Barabbas himself hath assumed this same imperial attitude when haranguing the mob and inciting the idle and dis-affected to rioting and disorder, for he hath been a student of many books and speaketh with the tongue of eloquence. Nevertheless none of the rebellious have presumed so far as this misguided Nazarene, who, forsaking his trade, and collecting about him the veritable scum of Judæa (with the exception of Iscariot, who is well connected, and whose fanaticism for this man hath sorely grieved his father) doth pretend to open Heaven only to the poor and vile. He hath declared it easier for a camel to pass through the eye of a needle than for a rich man to enter the Kingdom of God! Wherefore, by such exaggerated parable he doth imply that even imperial Cæsar shall not escape damnation. Should such teachings prevail there will be an end of all restraint in Judæa, and thine Emperor will most surely blame thee for thy lack of discipline. Take heed, good Pilate!—mercy is nobly becoming in thee, but with mercy, forget not judgment!'

Pilate listened to this little homily with manifest reluctance and impatience, and his level brows drew together in a worried frown. After a pause he said irritably,

'*Take ye him then and judge him according to your law!*'

Caiaphas turned upon him indignantly.

'*It is not lawful for us to put any man to death*,' he answered haughtily —'Thou art the governor, and to thee we are compelled to look for justice.'

At that moment there was a slight stir and movement in the waiting crowd beyond the barrier, and people were seen to be making way for the entrance of a new-comer. This was a slim, dark-eyed youth of a graceful form and delicate beauty,—he was gorgeously attired in a silken garment of pale blue, bound about him with a scarlet girdle and richly embroidered in gold and silver. He advanced in haste, yet timidly, and as he crossed the judgment-hall, cast an anxious and awe-stricken look at the stately figure of the 'Nazarene.' Pilate watched his approach with a good deal of surprise and impatience, —he recognised his wife's favourite page, and wondered what had brought him thither at such a time and in so unaccustomed a place. Arriving at the judgment daïs the youth dropped on one knee and proffered a folded scroll. Snatching it in haste, Pilate opened it and uttered a smothered exclamation. It was from his wife, one of the most beautiful of Roman women, known in the city for her haughty and fearless disposition, and for her openly pronounced contempt for the manners and customs of the Jews. And what she had written now ran simply thus,—

'Have thou nothing to do with that just man, for I have suffered many things this day in a dream because of him.'

With an abrupt sign of dismissal to the page, who at once retired by the way he had come, Pilate crushed the missive in his hand and sat lost in thought. Round the Tribunal, the sunshine spread in a sea of gold,—a bell striking the hour, slowly chimed on the deep stillness,—the white-robed figure of the Accused stood waiting as immovably as a sculptured god in the midst of the dazzling beams

of the morning,—and through Pilate's brain the
warning words of the woman he loved more than
all the world sent jarring hammer-strokes of
repetition—

'Have thou nothing to do with that just man.'

VI

IF he could have prolonged his deliberations thus
for ever it would have seemed to him well.   He
was not actually conscious of time.   Something vast,
indefinite and eternal appeared to surround and make
of him but a poor, helpless, stupid block of perishable
humanity, unfit to judge, unfit to rule.   He felt as
though he had aged suddenly,—as though a score of
years had passed in withering haste over his head
since the ' Nazarene' had confronted him as a prisoner
waiting to be condemned.   And with this mysterious
sense of inward age and incapacity freezing his very
blood, he had the goading consciousness that all the
members of the Sanhedrim council were watching him,
wondering at his indecision and impatiently expecting
judgment on what to them was a matter of perfectly
plain common-sense and social justice, but which to
him had assumed almost gigantic proportions of
complexity and trouble.   At last, with an effort, he
arose, and gathering his robes about him, again
prepared to descend from the Tribunal.   With a
half-appealing, half-authoritative gesture he beckoned
the Accused to follow him.   He was instantly
obeyed, and the Man of Nazareth walked patiently
yet proudly after His judge, whose trailing garment
served to sweep the ground for the passing of His
footsteps.   In the rear of the twain came all the
priests and elders, whispering together and shaking

their heads over the Roman governor's incomprehensible conduct, and after them in turn the crooked-limbed and evil-visaged usurer, Zacharias, shuffled along, supporting himself on a stick of which the knob was heavily encrusted with gold and jewels, this one piece of gorgeousness being in curious contrast to the rest of his otherwise beggarly attire. And as the whole vari-coloured group moved forward, a murmur of satisfaction and interest hummed through the expectant multitude,—at last the long-deferred sentence was to be finally pronounced.

Arrived within a few feet of the barrier which divided the judicial precincts from the common Hall, Pilate paused. Lifting up his voice so that it might be heard on the very outskirts of the throng, he addressed himself to the people, at the same time pointing to the regal Figure standing a little way behind him.

'*Behold your King!*'

Yells of derisive laughter answered him, intermingled with hooting and hisses. Caiaphas smiled disdainfully, and Annas appeared to be convulsed with a paroxysm of silent mirth. Pilate's glance swept over them both with a supreme and measureless scorn. He loathed the Jewish priests, their ritual and their doctrine, and made no secret of his abhorrence. Holding up one hand to enjoin silence he again appealed to the irritated and impatient mob.

'*I have examined this man before you,*' he said, in deliberate far-reaching accents, '*and I find in him no fault worthy of death.*'

Here he paused, and a sudden hush of stupefaction and surprise fell on the listening crowd. The governor resumed,—

'*But ye have a custom that I should release unto you one at the Passover; will ye therefore that I release unto you the " King of the Jews " ?*'

A roar of furious denial interrupted and drowned his voice.

'*Not this man!*'

'*Not this man, but Barabbas!*'

'Barabbas!' 'Barabbas!'

The name was caught and taken up by the people as though it were a shout of triumph, and echoed from mouth to mouth till it died away of itself in the outer air. Pilate stepped back, disappointed and irate,—he realised the position. The populace had evidently been intimidated by the priests, and had come prepared to stand by their monstrous demand, —the life of a notorious criminal in place of that of an innocent man. And they had a certain right to enforce their wishes at the season of Passover. With a short vexed sigh, Pilate flashed a searching glance over the now closely serried ranks of the people.

'Where is Barabbas?' he demanded impatiently— 'Bring him forth!'

There was a moment's delay, and then Barabbas, wild-eyed, uncouth, half starved and almost naked, yet not without a certain defiant beauty in his fierce aspect, was thrust to the front between two armed soldiers of the Roman guard. Pilate eyed him with strong disfavour, — Barabbas returned him scornful glance for glance. Conscious that the attention of the mob was now centred upon him, the whole soul of the long-imprisoned and suffering man rose up in revolt against the 'Roman tyrant' as Pilate was not unfrequently called by the disaffected Jews, and the old pride, rebellion and lawlessness of his disposition, began to make new riot in his blood. If it had not been for the wondrous, almost luminous Figure that maintained such an attitude of regal calm close at hand, Barabbas felt that he would have willingly struck his judge on the mouth with the very gyves that bound his wrists together. As

it was, he remained motionless, his eyes blazing forth
anger,—his bare brown chest heaving quickly with
the irregular fluctuations of his passionate breath,—
and in that attitude he might have stood as a
representative type of strong, barbaric, untaught,
untamed Humanity. Facing him was the sublime
contrast, Divinity, — the grand Ideal, — the living
symbol of perfect and spiritualised Manhood, whose
nature was the nearest akin to God, and who for this
very God-likeness was deemed only worthy of a
criminal's death. Some glimmering idea of the
monstrous incongruity between himself and the silent
Accused, struck Barabbas forcibly even while he
confronted Pilate with all that strange effrontery
which is sometimes born of conscious guilt; and the
thought crossed his brain that if, in agreement to
the public voice he were indeed released, the first use
he would make of his liberty would be to persuade
the people to mercy on behalf of this kingly-looking
Man, whose noble aspect exerted on his dark and
tortured soul, a secret, yet potent spell. And while
this idea was in his mind, Pilate, steadily regarding
him, spoke out with harsh brevity—

'So! Thou didst slay Gabrias the Pharisee?'
Barabbas smiled disdainfully.

'Yea! And so would I slay another such an one
could there be found in all the city so great a liar!'

Pilate turned to the high-priests and elders.

'Hear ye him? Yet this is the man ye would set
at liberty? Impenitent and obstinate, he hath no
sense of sorrow for his crime,—how then doth he merit
pardon?'

Caiaphas, vaguely embarrassed by the question,
lowered his eyes for a second, then raised them,
conveying into his long thin face an admirably affected
expression of serious pity and forbearance.

'Good Pilate,' he replied blandly and in a low tone,

4

—'Thou knowest not the whole truth of this affair. Barabbas hath indeed been guilty of much sin, but look you, his evil passions were not roused without a cause. We, of the Holy Temple, are prepared to instruct him how best his crime may be expiated in the sight of the Most High Jehovah, and his offering shall not be rejected, but received at the altar. For the ill-fated Gabrias, though eminent in learning and of good renown, had a hasty and false tongue, and it is commonly reported that he did most vilely slander a virtuous maiden of this city whom Barabbas loved.'

Pilate lifted his eyebrows superciliously.

'These are but base pandering matters,' he said, 'wherewith thou, Caiaphas, should'st have nought to do. And Gabrias surely was not the only possessor of a false tongue! Thy words savour of a woman's tale-bearing and are of idle purport. Murder is murder,—theft is theft,—excuses cannot alter crimes. And this Barabbas is likewise a robber.'

And again confronting the multitude, he reiterated his previous demand in a more directly concise form.

' *Which will ye that I release unto you? Barabbas or Jesus which is called Christ?*'

With one accord the populace responded tumultuously,

'Barabbas!' 'Barabbas!'

Pilate gave a gesture which might have meant despair or indignation or both, and turned a wistful look over his shoulder at the 'Nazarene,' who at the moment seemed absorbed in grave and tranquil meditation, of which the tenor must have been pleasing, for He smiled.

Once more Pilate addressed the crowd:

' *What will ye then that I do unto Him whom ye call the King of the Jews?*'

'Crucify him!' 'Crucify him!'

The answer came in yells and shrieks of rage, but above all the frantic din, there rose that one silver flute-like woman's voice that had been heard before—
'*Crucify him!*'
Barabbas started at the sound as a racehorse starts at the prick of a spur. Wildly he looked about him,— with an almost ravenous glitter in his eyes he scanned the shouting throng, but could discover no glimpse of the face he·longed yet feared to see. And, yielding to a nameless attraction, he brought his wandering glances back,—back to the spot where the sunlight seemed to gather in a fiery halo round the form of Him who as Pilate had said was 'called Christ.' What was the meaning of the yearning love and vast pity that was suddenly reflected in that fair Countenance? What delicate unspoken word hovered on the sensitive lips, arched like a bow and tremulous with feeling? Barabbas knew not,—but it suddenly seemed to him that his whole life with all its secrets good and evil, lay bare to the gaze of those soft yet penetrating eyes that met his own with such solemn warning and tender pathos.

'No, no!' he cried loudly on a swift inexplicable impulse—'*She* did not speak! She could not thus have spoken! Women are pitiful, not cruel, — *she* seeks no man's torture! O people of Jerusalem!' he continued, his deep voice gathering a certain sonorous music of its own, as, turning himself about, he faced the crowd—'Why do ye clamour for this prophet's death? Surely he hath not slain a man among ye, —neither hath he stolen your goods nor broken into your dwellings. Rumour saith he hath healed ye in your sicknesses, comforted ye in your sorrows, and performed among ye many wondrous miracles, so ye yourselves report, — wherefore then for these things should he die? Are ye not just?—have ye not the gift of reason? Lo, it is I who merit punishment!

I, who slew Gabrias and rejoice in mine iniquity!—
and look you, I, blood-stained, guilty and impenitent,
deserve my death, whereas this man is innocent!'

Shouts of derisive laughter and applause and
renewed cries of 'Barabbas! Barabbas! Release unto
us Barabbas!' were the only result of his rough
eloquence.

'Stop his mouth!' exclaimed Annas angrily—'He
must be mad to prate thus!'

'Mad or no, ye have yourselves elected him for
freedom'—observed Pilate composedly—'Mayhap ye
will now retract, seeing he hath shown a certain
generosity towards yon defenceless Nazarene!'

While he spoke, there was a threatening movement
of the mob towards the barrier,—the line of Roman
soldiery swayed as though it were likely to be broken
through by superior force,—and a multitude of hands
were tossed aloft in air and pointed at the unmoved
patient figure of the Christ.

'*Crucify him! Crucify him!*'

Pilate advanced swiftly, close to the ranks of the
turbulent populace, and demanded sternly,

'*Shall I crucify your King?*'

Amid a chorus of groans and hisses, more than a
hundred voices gave reply,—

'*We have no king but Cæsar!*'

'Verily, by thy hesitancy, Pilate, thou wilt have the
whole city in tumult!' said Caiaphas reproachfully.
'Seest thou not the mob are losing patience?'

At that moment a tall man whose grizzled head
was adorned with a showy scarlet turban, detached
himself from the rest of the throng and stood boldly
forward, exclaiming in loud excited tones—

'*We have a law, and by that law he ought to die,
because he made himself the Son of God!*'

As he heard these words, Pilate retreated some few
steps away from the barrier, with the strange stunned

sense of having been struck a sharp blow from an invisible hand. The Son of God! Such an assertion was assuredly blasphemous, if indeed the Accused had asserted it! But this was just what Pilate doubted. When Caiaphas had previously spoken of it, he had received the report with contempt, because he knew the high-priest would stop at no falsehood, provided his own immediate ends were thereby attained. But now that one of the populace had come forward with the same accusation, Pilate was forced to look at it in a different light. After all, he was set in his place to administer justice to the Jews, and in the Jewish law blasphemy was regarded as a crime almost worse than murder. He, Pilate himself, as a citizen of Rome, took a different and much lighter view of the offence. For the Roman deities were all so mixed, and so much worse than human in their vengeances and illicit loves, that it was not always easy to perceive anything more lofty in the character of a god than in that of a man. Any warrior who had won renown for fierce brute courage and muscular prowess, might report himself in Rome as the son of a god without affronting popular feeling, and in time, many-mouthed Tradition would turn his lie into a seeming truth. And in that mysterious land through which the Nile made its languid way, did not travellers speak with awe and wonderment of the worship of Osiris, the incarnate god in human semblance? The idea was a popular one,—it arose from an instinctive desire to symbolise the divine in humanity, and was a fable common to all religions, wherefore there seemed to be little actual harm in the fact of this dreamy-looking poetic young philosopher of Nazareth seeking to associate himself with the favourite myths of the people, if, indeed, he did so associate himself. And Pilate, his thoughts still busy with the romances told of the gods in Egypt, beckoned the Accused

towards him. His signal was complied with, and the
'Nazarene' moved quietly up to within reach of His
judge's hand. Pilate surveyed Him with renewed
interest and curiosity, then in a low tone of friendly
and earnest appeal, asked,

'*From whence art thou?*'

No verbal answer was vouchsafed to him,—only a
look; and in the invincible authority and grandeur of
that look there was something of darkness and light
intermingled,—something of the drear solemnity of the
thunder-cloud before the lightning leaps forth, sword-
like, to destroy. A great anguish and foreboding
seized Pilate's soul,—with all the force of his being he
longed to cry out,—to give voice to his secret trouble,
and to openly express before priests and people his
abhorrence and rejection of the judicial task he was
set to do. But all words seemed strangled in his
throat,—and a desperate sense of hopelessness and
helplessness paralysed his will.

'*Speakest thou not unto me?*' he continued, in
accents that were hoarse and tremulous with excess
of feeling; '*Knowest thou not that I have power to
crucify thee, and power to release thee?*'

Still steadily the large lustrous eyes regarded him,
with something of compassion now in their glance,—
and after a moment's pause, the rich full voice once
more cast music on the air:

'*Thou couldest have no power at all against me except
it were given thee from above!*' Then, with a slight
sigh of pity and pardon; '*Therefore, he that delivered
me unto thee hath the greater sin.*'

And the penetrating look flashed upward from
Pilate to the tall rigid form of Caiaphas, who shrank
from it as though suddenly scorched by a flying
flame. Pilate, more than ever impressed by the air
of command, power, and entire fearlessness expressed
in the whole demeanour of the Prisoner, once again

began to puzzle his brain with the recollection of the
various stories that were current concerning Egypt,—
stories of exiled monarchs, who, banished from their
realms by an untoward series of events or for some
self-imposed religious intention, went wandering
about in all the countries of the world, teaching the
mystic wisdom of the East, and performing miracles
of healing. Was it not probable that this young
Preacher, so unlike the Jewish race in the fair open-
ness and dignity of His countenance, the clear yet
deep dark blue of His eyes, and the wonderfully
majestic yet aerial poise of His figure, might, notwithstanding the popular report of His plebeian origin,
after all be one of these discrowned nomads? This
idea gained on Pilate's fancy, and impelled by its
influence he asked for the second time,—

'Art thou a King?'

And by marked accentuation of the question he
sought to imply that if such were the original distinction of the Captive, release might yet be obtained.
But the 'Nazarene' only gave a slight sigh of somewhat wearied patience as He replied,—

'THOU *sayest that I am a King!'* Then, apparently moved by commiseration for the vacillating
perplexity of His judge, He continued gently,—'*To
this end was I born and for this end came I into the
world,—That I should bear witness unto the Truth!
Every one that is of the Truth knoweth my voice.'*

While He thus spoke, Pilate gazed upon Him
in solemn astonishment. Here was no traitor or
criminal, but simply one of the world's noblest madmen! More convincing than all the other accusations
brought against Him by priests and people was His
own unqualified admission of folly. For whosoever
sought to 'bear witness unto the Truth' in a world
kept up by lies, could not be otherwise than mad!
Had it not always been thus? And would it not

always be thus? Had not the Athenian Socrates met his death nearly five hundred years agone for merely uttering the Truth? Pilate, more instructed than the majority in Greek and Roman philosophy, knew that no fault was so reprehensible in all classes of society as simple plain-speaking; it was almost safer to murder a man than tell the truth of him! Thus thinking he gave a hopeless gesture of final abandonment to destiny; and with an ironical bitterness he was scarcely conscious of, uttered the never-to-be-forgotten, never-to-be-answered query—

'What is Truth?'

Then, glancing from the Accused to the accusers, from the priests to the people, from the people in turn to Barabbas, who waited before him sullenly expectant, he sighed impatiently, and with the desperately resolved air of one compelled to perform the very act his soul most abhorred, he beckoned to a clerk in attendance and gave him a whispered order. The man retired, but returned almost immediately bearing a large silver bowl filled with pure water. Flinging back his rich robe of office and allowing it to trail in voluminous folds behind him, Pilate, closely followed by the attendant carrying the silver vessel, stepped forward again to confront the populace who were becoming more contentious and noisy with every moment's delay. On perceiving the governor's advance however, they ceased their turbulent murmurings and angry disputations, and concentrated all their attention upon him, the more particularly as his movements were somewhat strange and unexpected. Rolling up his gold-embroidered sleeves well above his wrists, he raised his bare hands aloft and showed them, palms outward, to the multitude, the great jewels on his fingers flashing like stars in the morning sun. He held them so uplifted for a minute's space, while the people, wondering, looked on in silence,—then, slowly lowering them, he dipped them deep in the shining bowl, rinsing them over and over again in the clear cold element which sparkled in its polished receptacle like an opal against fire. And as he shook the bright drops away from him, he cried in a loud penetrating voice—

'I am innocent of the blood of this just person! See ye to it!'

The multitude shouted and yelled. They understood and accepted the position. Their Roman judge publicly declined all responsibility in the matter,—even so let it be!—but they, they the elect of God, the children of Judæa, eagerly embraced, and not for the first time in their annals, the righteous opportunity of slaying the innocent. And with one mighty roar they responded, men and women alike,

'His blood be upon us and on our children!'

The hideous, withering, irrevocable Curse rose shudderingly up to Heaven,—there to be inscribed by the Recording Angel in letters of flame as the self-invoked Doom of a people.

VII

AFTER this nothing more could be said. An ignorant and callous mob has neither justice, reason nor pity, yet the popular verdict had to be accepted as final. No appeal could be made against such a grimly resolved and unanimous decision. Pilate saw that had he still ventured to plead the cause of the Divine Accused, the impatience of the crowd, strained to its last limit, would probably break out in riot and bloodshed. He therefore, like a man driven along by a resistless whirlwind, sacrificed his own will to the desire of the people; and Caiaphas, seeing that he had at last yielded to the force of necessity, heaved a sigh of relief. Hesitation was at an end,—the Man of Nazareth was to die the death. And the great high-priest murmured his satisfaction in the ear of his father-in-law Annas, who listened servilely, rubbing his fat hands together and every now and then rolling up his small treacherous eyes in pious thanksgiving,—thanksgiving that the Holy City of Jerusalem was to be finally freed from the troublous and alarming presence of the 'Nazarene.'

'Once dead,' whispered Caiaphas, with a contemptuous side-glance at the fair-faced enemy of his craft, the silent 'Witness unto the Truth'—'and, moreover, slain with dishonour in the public sight, he will soon sink out of remembrance. His few disciples will be despised, — his fanatical foolish doctrine will be sneered down, and we,—*we* will take heed that no chronicle of his birth or death or teaching remains to be included in our annals. A stray street preacher to the common folk!— how should his name endure?'

'Nay, it shall not endure,' returned Annas with an unctuous air of perfect assurance—'Thou, most holy and exalted Caiaphas, hast ever dwelt too ardently upon this fellow's boasting. Many there are, such as he, who thus idly vaunt themselves, and swear that though unknown and all unhonoured by their own generation, they shall be acclaimed great and wonderful hereafter. Arrogant philosophers prate thus,—mad poets who string rhymes as children string beads, and call such fool's work valuable,— heretical thinkers too of all degrees,— yet lo, their vaunting comes to naught! Verily, if History make no mention of this man, who will believe he ever lived?'

Caiaphas smiled coldly.

'Little word will there be of him in History,' said he. 'For his crazed followers are ignorant of letters, and our scribes must write only what *we* shall bid them!'

Part of this low-toned conversation was overheard by Zacharias, the old usurer, and he nodded emphatic approval, laughing silently the while. The condemnatory sentence passed on the immortal Captive by the Jewish populace was balm to his mean and miserable soul,—he rejoiced in it as in some excellent and satisfying jest, and he struck his jewelled stick now and then on the pavement, with an ecstatic thump, by way of giving outward expression to his inwardly gratified feeling. Pilate, meantime, having, by the washing of his hands before the people, openly signified his repugnance and refusal to personally participate in the crime (for so

he truly considered it) about to be committed, proceeded with the rest of his enforced duty in feverish
haste and something of horror. Nothing could now
be done quickly enough to please him,—he grew
nervous and excited,—a shamed flush at times burned
in his cheeks, and anon he grew ghastly pale again,
every line of his features becoming drawn and livid
as the features of the dead,—and in all his hurried
movements he carefully avoided turning his eyes
towards the Man Condemned. At his abrupt signal
some twenty soldiers with drawn weapons surrounded the grand white Figure that stood, divinely
silent, in the glory of the morning sun,—coarse-
visaged, squat-bodied men who laughed and swore
among themselves as they eyed their Prisoner up
and down and made mocking comments on His
stately and unmoved bearing. He,—Himself,—
appeared to be almost unconscious of their prox-
imity,—some happy fancy seemed to hover, spirit-
like, across His mind, for judging by His radiant
aspect, He might have been a crowned Apollo
dreaming of realms wherein his smile alone created
light and sound and life. And in the same moment
that the military cohort thus fenced Him in with
their bristling spears, the two soldiers who had
guarded Barabbas until now retired to the rear,
leaving their man to receive his formal release at
the hands of the governor. Alone,—facing Pilate,—
Barabbas waited,—the iron manacles still weightily
dragging down his arms and showing where their
long and corroding pressure had bruised and cut
the flesh beneath. He was giddy with fatigue and
excitement, but his black eyes were brilliant, and
every nerve and muscle in his body thrilled to the
rapturous thought of liberty. His suspense did not
last long, for Pilate was now in no humour for delays.
Snatching from an attendant officer the implement

used for such purposes, he struck at the heavy links of the rescued criminal's chains with such irate violence that they were soon parted asunder and fell, clanging harshly on the marble pavement. The noise made by their fall was sufficient to excite the populace to a burst of triumphant shouting.

'Barabbas!'

'Freedom for Barabbas!'

'Hail, Barabbas!'

Barabbas meanwhile stared at the cast-off fetters with a stupefied air as though they had all at once become curious and unfamiliar objects. He had worn them day and night for eighteen months, yet now it seemed he knew them not. He lifted his arms and swung them to and fro with a sense of bodily ease and lightness,—but where was the buoyancy of spirit that had but a moment before elated him? It was gone; and gone quite suddenly, he knew not how. He had hoped and longed and prayed for freedom,— his hope was fulfilled,—and now, with fulfilment, hope was dead. A heavy despondency overcame him, and he stood dully inert, while he heard Caiaphas say,

'Wilt thou not fasten yon bracelets upon the Nazarene, good Pilate? Who knoweth but that in going to his death he may not prove rebellious?'

Pilate frowned.

'What now! Hath he fought with the guard? Hath he moved? Hath he murmured? Hath he spoken aught of violence? He disputeth not judgment,—he doth most mutely accept the fate ye give him. Therefore why bind that which maketh no resistance? Let Jews be what they will, ye shall not make a coward of a Roman!'

And with this he turned abruptly to Barabbas.

'Why dost thou wait there, fellow? Get thee hence!' and the suppressed irritation he felt quivered in his usually calm voice—'Impenitent murderer and thief as thou art, the laws of thy nation set thee free, to slay and steal again at thy pleasure!'

Barabbas winced, and his dark face flushed. The scathing words cut him deeply, but he found nothing to say in reply. His head drooped somewhat wearily on his chest,—he fully understood he was at liberty,—yet liberty did not now bring with it the complete sense of joy he had thought to find in its possession. Beyond the barrier the people outside waited to receive him with triumphant acclamations,—but his limbs seemed to be fastened to the spot where he stood, and for the life of him he could not help gazing wistfully and remorsefully at the One condemned in his stead.

'It would have been better,' he said within himself, 'to have died for yonder Man, than live on, free.'

As this thought crossed his mind, it seemed to him that a sudden soft light shone round the uplifted head of the 'Nazarene,'—a ring of pale and misty radiance that gradually deepened into a warm glow of golden flame. He gazed at this phenomenon affrighted,—surely others saw the glory as well as himself? Judge, priests, soldiers and people, could it be possible they were blind to what was so distinctly visible? He tried to speak and tell them,—but his tongue clove to the roof of his mouth, and he could only stare like one distraught, striving to utter words that refused to become audible. Caiaphas, impatient at his apparent stupidity and unwillingness to move, stepped up to him.

'Didst thou not hear the governor's command, thou fool? Get thee hence quickly! Take heed to thy ways, and see thou venture not near the house of Iscariot!'

This injunction pronounced in an angry whisper, roused Barabbas from his amazed contemplation of the Christ to a sudden silent access of personal fury.

The glory-light vanished from the brows of the prophet of Nazareth,—there was no more wonder, no more mystic terror;—material life and its demands rose paramount in his mind. With a look of indignant scorn and rebellion flashed full in the face of the great high-priest, he straightened himself proudly to his full height, and turning his back on the Hall of Judgment strode swiftly towards the barrier dividing him from the populace, the Roman soldiers making way for him to pass. A moment more, and he had sprung into the midst of the crowd, where he was received with frenzied yells of delight and prolonged cheering. An exultant mob gathered round him, shouting his name,—men embraced him,—women caught his grimy hands and kissed them,—little children danced about him whooping and shrieking with joy, not knowing why they did so, but simply infected by the excitement of their elders,—one man in the height of enthusiasm tore off a rich upper mantle from his own shoulders and flung it around the half-naked, half-starved form of the newly-released criminal, shedding tears of emotion the while. Not a trace was left of the previous aversion shown towards him when first he had been marched into the Tribunal, a prisoner under armed escort,—the public, more fickle than the wind, were full of rejoicing over the fact that *their* word and *their* will had obtained his release,—and, to judge by their jubilant cries, the once notorious murderer might have been a king returning to throne and country after long exile. A large section of the crowd forgot for the moment that Other, who was left to His fate and condemned to die,—they were content to press round their own rescued man with joyous greeting and laughter, praying him to partake of food and wine with them at the nearest inn, or urging him to accompany them in turn to their several homes.

Breathless and bewildered, and incongruously clad in
the silk and gold-threaded garment his philanthropic
admirer had wound about him, Barabbas looked from
right to left, wondering how best he might elude the
enthusiastic attentions which threatened to overwhelm his small stock of patience. For he himself
was not elated with his triumph; he knew, better
than most men the true value of 'friends' as this
world goes; and he felt more weariness and impatience than anything else, as his eyes roved
anxiously over the surging sea of heads in search of
one face that he fancied was sure to be there,—a face
that for him was all he realised of heaven. But he
failed to discover what he sought, and, chilled by his
disappointment, he scarcely heard the various items
of news and gossip some of his former acquaintances
were pouring into his ears. All at once a murmur
ran from lip to lip,—

'Look you, they scourge him!'

Like an ocean wave rolling inshore, the crowd
moved by one instinct turned, swaying impetuously
back towards the Hall of Judgment. Standing on
tip-toe they craned their necks over each other's
shoulders to see what was going on,—men lifted tiny
children in their arms,—some few, principally women,
uttered smothered exclamations of pity,—but on the
whole a mercilessly pleased air of expectation pervaded
the throng. Barabbas, carried along by the force of
the mob, found himself facing the Tribunal once more,
and being a tall man he was able to command a better
view than most of those immediately around him.

'Brutes!' he muttered as he saw—'Dogs! Devils!
To strike a man defenceless! O coward bravery!'

And with strained eyes and heavily beating heart
he watched the scene. The Tribunal seemed now to
be well-nigh possessed by the Roman guards, for
several extra soldiers had been summoned to aid in

the pitiless deed about to be done. In the centre of
a ring of bristling spears and drawn battle-axes stood
the 'Nazarene,' offering no resistance to the rude
buffetings of the men who violently stripped Him of
His upper garments, leaving His bare shoulders and
breast exposed to view. An officer meantime handed
the scourge to Pilate,—a deadly-looking instrument
made of several lengths of knotted whip-cord, fringed
with small nail-like points of sharpened iron. It was
part of the procurator's formal duty to personally
chastise a condemned criminal,—but the unhappy
man upon whom, in this dreadful instance, the allotted
task now fell, shuddered in every limb, and, pushing
away the barbarous thong, made a faint mute gesture
of denial. The officer waited, his dull heavy face
exhibiting as much surprise as discipline would allow.
The soldiers waited, staring inquisitively. And in
equable sweetness and silence the Man of Nazareth
also waited, the sunlight giving a polished luminance
to His bared shoulders and arms, dazzling in their
whiteness, statuesque in their symmetry,—the while
He lifted His deep pensive eyes, and regarded His
miserable judge with a profound and most tender
pity. Caiaphas and his father-in-law exchanged
vexed glances.

'Dost thou yet delay justice, Pilate?' questioned
the high-priest haughtily—'Time presses. Do what
thy duty bids thee,—strike!'

5

VIII

BUT Pilate still hesitated, gazing blankly out into nothingness. His face was pallid, — his lips were set hard,—his erect figure, clothed in rich attire, looked curiously stiff and lifeless like that of a frozen man. Would that the sick qualm at his heart might overcome him altogether, he thought, so that, falling in a senseless swoon, he might escape the shame and horror of striking that kingly Gentleness, that embodied Patience! But life and consciousness throbbed through him, albeit painfully and confusedly; the people whom he was set to govern, demanded of him the full performance of his work. Mechanically he at last stretched forth his hand and grasped the scourge, — then, with a faltering step and downcast eyes approached the Condemned. The soldiers, anticipating the scourging, had, notwithstanding Pilate's objection to bind 'that which maketh no resistance,' tied their passive Captive's hands with rope, lest He should attempt to defend Himself from the falling blows. On these needless and unmerited bonds, Pilate first of all fixed his glance, a great wrath and sorrow contending within him. But he was powerless to alter or soften the conditions of the law,—he was the wretched tool of destiny,—and with a bitter loathing of himself and the shameful thing he was compelled to do, he turned away his eyes and, . . lifted the lash It dropped heavily

with a stinging hiss on the tender flesh,—again and
again it rose, . . . again and again it fell, . . . till
the bright blood sprang from beneath its iron points
and splashed in red drops on the marble pavement.
. . . But no sound passed the lips of the Divine
Sufferer,—not so much as a sigh of pain,—and no
prophetic voice uplifted itself to proclaim the truth,—
*'He was wounded for our transgressions, and by His
stripes are we healed!'*

Meanwhile, a strange and unaccountable silence
possessed the people watching outside,—pressing
close against one another, they peered with eager
curious eyes at the progress of the punishment,—till
at last, when the scourge caught in its cruel prongs a
strand of the Captive's gold-glistening hair, and, tearing it out, cast it, wet with blood, on the ground, a
girl in the crowd broke out into hysterical sobbing.
The sound of woman's weeping scared Pilate in his
dreadful task,—he looked up, flushed and fevered,
with wild eyes and a wilder smile and paused.
Zacharias the usurer hobbled forward, excitedly
waving his jewelled staff in the air.

'To it again, and harder, most noble governor!'
he yelled in his cracked and tremulous voice, 'To it
again, with better will! Such blows as thine would
scarcely hurt a child! He scourged others,—let him
taste of the thong himself! Look you, he hath not
winced nor cried out,—he hath not yet felt the lash!
To it again in justice, excellent Pilate! in simple
justice! He hath scourged me, an aged man and
honest,—verily it is right and fitting he should
receive the sting in his own flesh, else shall he die
impenitent! Again, and yet again, most worthy
governor,—but let the stripes be heavier!'

As he spoke, gesticulating violently, his stick
suddenly slipped from his shaking hand and dropped
on the marble floor, and a great pearl, loosened from

its setting in the jewelled handle, flew out, rolled away like a bead, and disappeared. With a shriek of anguish, the miserable man fell on his knees and began to grope along the pavement with his yellow claw-like fingers, shedding maudlin tears, while he entreated the impassive soldiers standing by to aid him in looking for the precious lost gem. A grim smile went the round of the band, but not a man moved. Moaning and whimpering, the wretched usurer crept slowly on all-fours over the floor of the Tribunal, keeping his eyes close to the ground, and presenting the appearance of some loathly animal rather than a man, the while he every now and again paused and prodded with his filthy hands into every nook and corner in hope to find the missing jewel. The loss was to him irreparable, and in his grief and rage he had even forgotten his desire of vengeance on the 'Nazarene.' Pilate, watching him as he crawled about, weeping childishly, was moved by such a sense of pleasure at his discomfiture as to feel almost light-hearted for the moment, — and, breaking into a loud laugh of unnatural hilarity, he flung away the blood-stained scourge with the relieved air of one whose disagreeable task was now finished. But Caiaphas was by no means satisfied.

'Thou hast given yon condemned malefactor but the mildest scourging, Pilate,' he said—'Why hast thou cast aside the lash so soon?'

Pilate's eyes flashed fire.

'Press not my humour too far, thou vengeful priest!' he muttered breathlessly—'I have done my accursed work. See ye to the rest!'

Caiaphas retreated a step or two, somewhat startled. There was something in the expression of Pilate's face that was truly terrifying,—a dark and ghastly anguish that for the moment disturbed even the high-priest's cold and self-satisfied dignity. After a brief pause however, he recovered his wonted composure, and by a sign to the centurion in command, intimated that the scourging was over, and that the Prisoner was now abandoned to His fate. And, this culminating point having been reached, all the members of the Sanhedrim, together with the scribes and elders present, saluted the governor ceremoniously and left the Tribunal, walking slowly down two by two into the lower hall called 'Prætorium.' Thither too, the soldiers were preparing to lead or drag the doomed Nazarene. Filing away in solemn and dignified order, the sacerdotal procession gradually disappeared, and only Pilate lingered, chained to the spot by a sort of horrible fascination. Sheltering himself from the public view behind a massive marble column, he leaned against that cold support in utter weariness, broken in body and mind by the fatigue and, to him, inexplicable anguish of the morning's trial. In his dazed brain he strove hard to realise what it was, what it could be, that made him feel as if the most unutterable crime ever committed on earth was about to be perpetrated this very day in this very city of Jerusalem. He had become a torturing problem to himself, — he could not understand his own overwhelming emotion. His wife's message had greatly disturbed him ; he had thrust the scroll hurriedly in his breast, but now he drew it out and once more re-read the strange injunction,—

'*Have thou nothing to do with that just man, for I have suffered this day many things in a dream because of him.*'

Mysterious words!—what could they mean ? What could she, Justitia, the proud, fearless and beautiful woman of Rome have 'suffered'? In a dream, too, —she who scarcely ever dreamed,—who laughed at auguries and omens, and had even been known to say satirical things against the gods themselves! She was totally unimaginative; and to a certain extent her nature was hard and pitiless, or what her own people would have termed 'heroic.' She would look on, pleased and placid, at the most hideous gladiatorial contests and other barbarous spectacles then in vogue in her native city,—when she was but twelve years of age she had watched unmoved the slow torturing of a slave condemned to be flayed alive for theft and perjury. Hence, this action of hers in protesting against the condemnation of any particular criminal, was sufficiently unusual and unlike her to be remarkable. '*Have thou nothing to do with that just man!*' What would she say if she could see that same 'just man' now! Pilate, looking fearfully round from his retired coign of vantage, turned sick and cold at the horror of the scene that was being enacted,—but though he would have given his life to interfere, he knew that he dared not. The people had declared their will,—and that will must needs be done. There was no help and no hope for a Truth unanimously condemned by this world's liars. There never has been, and there never shall be!

The previous intense silence of the multitude had given way to fierce clamour; the air resounded with discordant bellowings as though a herd of wild beasts had broken loose to ravage the earth. The soldiery, no longer restrained by the presence of sacerdotal authority, and moreover incited to outrage by the yells of the mob, were violently pushing their Prisoner along with the butt-ends of their weapons in a brutal endeavour to make Him lose His footing and fall headlong down the steps that led into the Prætorium. Their savage buffetings were unprovoked assaults, dealt out of a merely gratuitous desire to insult the sublime Sufferer,—for He Himself gave them no cause of affront, but went with them peaceably. His shoulders still bare, were bleeding from the scourge,—His hands and arms were still tightly bound,—yet neither pain nor humiliation had lessened the erect majesty of His bearing or the aerial pride of his step,—and His beautiful eyes kept the lustrous, dreamy splendour of a thought and a knowledge beyond all human ken. Pressing close about Him His ruffianly guards derided Him with mocking gestures and laughter, shouting obscenities in His ears and singing scraps of ribald songs. A scarlet mantle had been left by chance on one of the benches in the Hall, and this was spied out by one of the men who snatched it up in haste and flung it across the Captive's wounded shoulders. It trailed behind Him in regal flowing folds; and the fellow who had thrown it thus in position, gave a wild shout, and pointing with his pike exclaimed derisively,

'*Hail, King of the Jews!*'

Shrieks of applause and bursts of laughter answered this ebullition of wit, and Barabbas alone out of all the callous crowd made protest.

'Shame!' he cried,—'Shame on you, Romans! Shame on you, people of Jerusalem! Why mock that which is condemned?'

But his voice was lost in the uproar around him, or if not utterly lost, it fell unheeded on the ears of those who did not choose to hear. And anon, a fresh burst of taunting merriment split the air into harsh echoings,—a new phase of bitter jesting moved the crowd,—the 'King' was being crowned! A spearman acting on the initiative given by his fellow, had leaped into the outer garden-court, and had there torn from the wall three long branches of a climbing rose, thick with thorns. Pulling off all the delicate buds, blossoms and leaves, he twisted the prickly stems into a coronal, and with this approached the silent Christ, his companions greeting him with hoarse yells of approving laughter.

Hail, King of the Jews!' he cried, as he placed it

on the Divine brows, pressing the spiky circlet fiercely down into the tender flesh till the pained blood sprang beneath its pressure—'Hail, all hail!'

And he struck the fair and tranquil Face with his steel gauntlet.

'A sceptre! A sceptre for the King!' shouted a little lad, running out from the crowd excitedly, and waving a light reed aloft as he came. The soldiers laughed again, and snatching the reed, set it upright between the bound wrists of their blameless Captive. Then with devilish howlings and wild gestures, a group of disorderly ruffians rushed forward pell-mell and dropped on their knees, turning up their grimy grinning faces in pretended worship and mocking servility, the while they yelled in frantic chorus,

'Hail! *Hail, King of the Jews!*'

They might as well have stormed the Sun, or flung insults at a Star. Mystically removed above and beyond them all was the Man of Sorrows,—His lips, close set in that wondrous curve of beauty such as sculptors give to the marble god of song, opened not for any utterance of word or cry;—scarcely indeed did He appear to breathe, so solemn and majestic a stillness encompassed Him. That tranquil silence irritated the mob,—it implied perfect courage, indifference to fate, heroic fortitude, and sublime endurance,—and thus seemed to be a dignified, dumbly declared scorn of the foolish fury of the people.

'A curse on him!' cried a man in the crowd— 'Hath he no tongue? Hath he no more doctrines to teach before he dies? Make him speak!'

'Speak, fellow!' roared a soldier, striking him heavily on the shoulder with the handle of his spear, 'Thou hast babbled oft of both sin and righteousness,—how darest thou now hold thy peace?'

But neither taunt nor blow could force an answer

from the immortal 'King.' His noble features were composed and calm,—His luminous eyes looked straight ahead as though beholding some glory afar off in shining distance,—and only the slow drops of blood starting from under the sharp points of His thorny crown, and staining the bright hair that clustered on His temples, gave any material evidence of life or feeling.

'*He hath a devil!*' shouted another man—'He is hardened in impenitence and feels nothing. *Away with him! Let him be crucified!*'

While this incessant clamour was going on, Pilate had stood apart, watching the scene with the doubtful and confused sensations of a man in delirium. As in some horrid vision, he beheld the stately Figure, draped in the scarlet robe and crowned with thorns, being hustled along the Prætorium towards the open court outside, which had to be reached by yet another descending flight of steps,—and, yielding to a sudden impulse he moved quickly forward, so that he came in the way of the advancing guard. Seeing him appear thus unexpectedly, the centurion in command paused. The soldiers too, somewhat taken aback at being caught in their brutal horse-play by no less a personage than the governor himself, ceased their noisy shouts abruptly and rested on their weapons, sullenly silent. Once more, and for the last time on earth, Pilate ventured to look straight at the Condemned. Bruised, bound and bleeding, the twisted rose-thorns setting their reluctant prongs ever more deeply into his brows, the 'Nazarene' met that questioning, appealing, anguished human gaze with a proud yet sweet serenity ; while Pilate, staring wildly in terror and wonderment, saw that above the crown of thorns there glittered a crown of Light,—light woven in three intertwisted rays of dazzling gold and azure, which cast prismatic reflections upward, like meteor-flames flashing between earth and heaven. A Crown of Light! . . . a mystic Circle, widening, ever widening into burning rings that seemed endless, . . . how came such glory there? What could it mean? Like a drowning man desperately clutching at a floating spar while sinking in the depths of the sea, so Pilate clutched vaguely and half blindly at the flowing scarlet mantle, which, as a symbol of the world's mockery robed the regal form of the world's Redeemer, and dragged at it as though he sought to pull its wearer forward. The clamorous touch was obeyed; the Man of Nazareth suffered Himself to be led by His judge to the summit of the last flight of steps leading downwards and outwards from the Prætorium. There, He fully faced the assembled multitude in all His sorrowful sublimity and tragic splendour; and for a moment deep silence ruled the throng. Then, suddenly heart - stricken and over-whelmed at the sight of such pure and piteous majesty, Pilate dropped the edge of the scarlet robe as though it had scorched his flesh.

'ECCE HOMO!' he exclaimed, tossing up his arms as he shrieked the words out in his native tongue, careless as to whether they were understood or not by the startled Jewish crowd—'ECCE HOMO!'

And breaking into a wild fit of delirious laughter and weeping, he flung his mantle desperately across his mouth to stifle the agonised convulsion, and swerving aside giddily, fell, face forward on the ground, insensible.

IX

A LOUD cry went up from the multitude, and in the consternation and confusion which ensued, the crowd swiftly divided itself into various sections. Some rushed to proffer assistance in lifting the unconscious governor and carrying him to his palace; others gathered once more around the released Barabbas with fresh adulation and words of welcome,—but by far the larger half of the mob prepared to follow the Divine Condemned and see Him die. Fearful and unnatural as it seems, it is nevertheless true that in all ages the living have found a peculiar and awful satisfaction in watching the agonies of the dying. To be alive, and to look on while a fellow-creature gasps out in torture the last reluctant breath, is a position that has always given a mysteriously horrible pleasure to the majority. And on this particular day more than the customary morbid diversion was expected, for a rumour had gone the round of the populace that two notorious thieves were to be executed at the same time as the young 'prophet' out of Galilee. Such a spectacle was assuredly worth waiting for !—and accordingly they waited, a motley-garbed, restless, expectant mass of men and women, the perpetual hum of their voices sounding like the noise made by thousands of swarming bees, the while they occasionally varied the monotony of speech by singing, stamping and whistling. The Roman soldiers, greatly disconcerted by Pilate's sudden and inexplicable illness, and in their own mind superstitiously connecting it with some spell they imagined to have been secretly wrought by the 'Nazarene, were now in no mood for trifling. Dragging off the scarlet robe from their Prisoner, they hastily flung His own raiment upon Him, and with many dark and threatening looks, led Him forth, closely guarded.

The morning was intensely hot and bright,—in the outer court a fountain was in full play, casting up a silvery column of foam-dust to the burning blue of the sky. The whole band of soldiers halted while their centurion conferred apart with the criminal executioner, whose duty it was to provide crosses suitable for the legal mode of punishment then in vogue, and who also was bound to assist in nailing those condemned in the barbarous position needful to ensure a lingering and horrible death. Three crosses were required that day, he said,—and he was in doubt as to whether any that he had were sufficiently strong to sustain the powerful and splendid figure of the Captive now pointed out to him.

'I' faith I am sorry he is condemned,' he muttered with a touch of commiseration in his rough accents,— 'He hath a noble presence, and of a surety to slay him thus shamefully is an error, Petronius. Believe me, so thou wilt find it! Rememberest thou not how one of thine own calling, dwelling in Capernaum, had his servant sick of a palsy, and yonder man did heal him without so much as visiting the house where he lay? I tell thee, mischief will come of his death. And now I look at thee, thou hast a sober air,—thou art not in tune with this deed, methinks?'

Petronius lowered his eyes, and meditatively traced out the pattern of the pavement with the point of his drawn weapon.

'Our governor hath not condemned him'—he said in a low tone,—'And therefore Rome is not responsible. Pilate would have saved him,—but the Jews have willed otherwise.'

'Ay, ay!' grumbled the executioner, himself a native of Apulia,—'The Jews, the Jews! Dark and bloody are their annals, Jove knoweth!—and they have been known to murder their own children to please the savage deity they worship. Look you, the fat priests devour the firstlings of a flock in their own houses, pretending 'tis their God who hath such greedy appetite,—and those among them who accumulate more gold than is lawful will swear that even high rates of usury are the divine blessing on the righteous! Hypocrites all, Petronius!—but yonder Prisoner is not a Jew?'

The centurion looked wistfully at the Condemned, now re-clothed in His own white garments, but still wearing the crown of thorns. A smile irradiated His fair face,—His soft eyes were watching with tenderness the dainty caperings of a butterfly that fluttered for mere joyous caprice just near enough to the fountain to catch a drop or two on its azure wings, and then danced off again high up into the sunshine. Even so absorbed and gentle might have been His aspect when He said, '*Behold the lilies of the field! They toil not, neither do they spin,—and yet I say unto you, that Solomon in all his glory was not arrayed like one of these!*'

'He is not—he cannot be a Jew?' repeated the executioner questioningly.

'Yea, verily he is a Jew,' replied Petronius at last with a slight sigh,—'Or so it is reported. He is of that vile Nazareth; the son of Joseph the carpenter there,—and Mary his mother is, or was, here a while ago with the women.'

The executioner shook his head obstinately.

'Thou wilt never make me believe it!' he said,— 'He hath the air of an alien to this land. Look you, there is no face like his in the crowd,—he is neither Greek nor Roman nor Egyptian,—but though I cannot fix his race I would swear his father was never a Jew! And as for the cross, ye will all have to wait while I go and test which is the strongest and least worn, for, on my life, it must lift up a Hercules! Seest thou not what height and muscle?—what plenitude of vigour?—By Jupiter! an' I were he I would make short work of the guard!'

Chuckling hoarsely at what he considered an excellent jest, he disappeared on his gruesome errand, taking three or four of the soldiers with him. The rest of the troop remained surrounding the 'Nazarene,' while the crowd of spectators increased every moment, extending itself far into the street beyond. All the people were growing more and more excited and impatient,—some of them were conscious of a certain vague disappointment and irritation. There was no amusement in seeing a Man condemned to death if He refused to be interested in His own fate, and stood waiting as resignedly and patiently as this 'prophet of Nazareth,' who looked more happy than pained. Several minutes elapsed, and the cross had not yet been brought. The enforced delay seemed likely to be prolonged, and several thirsty souls edged themselves out of the crush to get refreshment while they had time and opportunity. Among these was Barabbas. Some former old acquaintances of his had taken possession of him, and now insisted upon his accompanying them, somewhat against his will, into an inn close by, where they drank his health with boisterous acclamations. Barabbas ate and drank

with them,—and the natural avidity of an almost
starving man enabled him to assume the air of a boon
companionship he was far from feeling, but when his
appetite was moderately appeased, he pushed away
the remaining morsels and sat silent and abstracted
in the midst of the loud laughter and jesting around
him.

'What ails thee, man?' cried one of his entertainers
presently—'Thou art duller than a dying dog!
Where is thy once reckless merriment?'

'Gone!' answered Barabbas harshly, his black eyes
growing more sombre and serious as he spoke,—'In
the old days I was merry, and I knew not why,—
now I am sad, and know not the cause of my sadness.
I have suffered long,—I am weary!—and, . . . and,
. . . methinks it is a crime to slay yon Nazarene!'

His words were met with laughter.

'By my soul, Barabbas,' exclaimed one man,
clanking his pewter goblet on the table as a sign
that he desired it refilled—'Thou hast come out of
prison with the sentiments of a woman! Thou, the
wolf, hast crawled forth a lamb! Ha ha ha ha!
Who would have thought it? Thou that didst so
neatly slip thy knife into the mealy maw of Gabrias,
thou, of all men whimperest for another death which
concerns thee not, and is, by all the laws, deserved.'

''Tis not deserved!' muttered Barabbas—'The
Man is innocent!'

He paused, and rose from his seat involuntarily.
His companions stopped drinking and stared at
him.

'I tell ye all,' he continued firmly—'there is no sin
in that young Prophet. He hath done many good
things by your own report,—and,—looking at him
a while since I saw'——

He broke off,—there was a strange terror in his
eyes, and he shuddered.

'What?' cried his friends in chorus—'Surely thou hast a devil, thou also! What sawest thou?'

'Nothing!' and Barabbas turned upon them with a chill smile—'Nothing that ye would have seen or cared to see!'

They all regarded him in open-eyed wonderment. Was this indeed Barabbas?—this meditative, wistful, thinking man? Was this the lawless, wild associate of the roystering band of rebels who, with a little surface knowledge and bombastic prating in the open streets had actually succeeded, not so very long ago, in disturbing the peace of the city of Jerusalem? And while they remained silent, dumbfoundered and perplexed, a calm voice, melodious yet ironical, suddenly addressed them—

'Pardon me, excellent sirs, for breaking in upon cheerful converse,—but I seek to pay homage where homage is due, and I would fain give humble greeting, I also, to him who is elected of the people. Great are the children of Israel, beloved in all ages of the one true God who naturally hath no sort of interest in the fates of other nations!—great is their verdict on every question, and for ever unerring their decision! Great must he be who fortunately wins their favour,—therefore, great is Barabbas, and to him I proffer salutation!'

No language could adequately describe the various inflections of tone in which this little speech was given. Every note in the gamut of delicate satire seemed sounded,—and instinctively all present turned to look at the speaker. And as they looked, many shrank back in evident apprehension,—Barabbas however, being unacquainted with the new-comer, regarded him indifferently as he would any other stranger, though not without a certain touch of curiosity. He saw before him an olive-complexioned man of rather small stature, slight in build, yet apparently wiry and vigorous, with a somewhat long oval face, straight black brows, and eyes so glittering and strangely-coloured that they might have been iridescent jewels set in his head rather than organs of vision. They were dark eyes apparently, but there was a curious dull gold tint in the iris like clouded amber, that made them look almost light at times, and gave them a singularly unearthly lustre and expression. Their owner was clad in a foreign garb of soft yellowish material girded about him with a broad band of flexible gold,—the upper part of his loose mantle formed a kind of hood or cowl which was partially pulled over his thick black hair, and fastened at his throat with a clasp of opals. He seemed discreetly amused at the disquieting effect his appearance had on most of the men assembled at the inn, but he advanced nevertheless and bowed profoundly to Barabbas, who gave him no other response than a stare.

'Excellent Barabbas!' he continued in the same curiously cold, yet perfectly sweet accents,—'Deny me not, I pray thee, the satisfaction of thy friend-ship! I am but a wanderer and an alien in these provinces of Judæa so specially favoured by a dis-criminating Jehovah,—a veritable barbarian in my ways, knowing little, though studying much,—but in matters pertaining to thy welfare, thou shalt perchance find me useful, whether thy quest be of war or—love!'

Barabbas started,—one of his friends pulled him aside, whispering,—

''Tis Melchior. Best humour him! He hath an evil name and holdeth sovereignty over devils!'

'I know him not'—said Barabbas aloud, disdain-ing the warning nods and winks of the various members of the company present,—'And therefore his greeting profiteth me nothing.'

6

The stranger smiled.

'I love honesty!' he said suavely,—'And thou, Barabbas, art honest!' A rough ripple of subdued mirth went the round of the men, and Barabbas winced as though the point of a lash had stung his flesh. 'True it is that thou knowest me not; equally true it is that thou *shalt* know me. Melchior is my name as thy ear-whisperer hath stated, but of sovereignty over devils I am innocent, inasmuch as I rule no men!' His eyes lightened and flashed a topaz brilliancy under the heavy blackness of his brows as he continued—'What motley garb is this?' and he felt between finger and thumb the texture of the embroidered mantle which had been flung round Barabbas on his release from prison—'Thou art all but naked beneath this glistering show,—a noble emblem of humanity in very truth! Even thus did I expect to find thee,—robed as a king without, but within, the merest squalid nudity! Follow me and be cleansed of thy prison foulness,—I have my dwelling for the present here in this hostelry,—and in mine upper chamber thou canst prank thyself out in fitting attire to meet the eyes of thy beloved, for as thou art, most surely she will laugh at thee! Hath she not laughed at thee before? Come and be garmented for festival!'

But Barabbas held his ground, though his dark cheek flushed at the stranger's familiar allusions to his 'beloved.' Drawing the rich robe he wore more closely about him, he gave a gesture of haughty refusal.

'I obey no man's bidding,' he said,—'I have not been so lately set at liberty that I should now become a slave. Think me not churlish that I refuse thy proffered service,—time passes swiftly, and behold, in the space of moments I go hence with the multitude,—I fain would see the death of the condemned Nazarene.'

Melchior's face changed. A dark shadow swept across his features,—an expression of mingled sorrow and solemnity.

'Thou shalt most assuredly behold that death!' he said,—'For will not all the world be there? 'Tis Humanity's great Feast of Slaughter!—the apotheosis of the Jews! A true gala!—a thing to remember!— mark me, a thing to remember I tell thee! For in ages to come, perchance, the story of how this Man of Nazareth was slain to satisfy the blood-thirstiness of the God-elected children of Israel, may serve as a wonder and terror to time!' He paused,—his countenance cleared, and he resumed his former ironical tone, 'Yea, thou shalt see the prophet die,—but believe me when I tell thee that she whom thou lovest will also be there, and hast thou the look of a lover?—clad thus foolishly, and uncouth as an escaped bear?' He laughed lightly. 'Yet nevertheless I will not ask thee to do my bidding, most self-reliant and excellent Barabbas! I do but tell thee that in my upper chamber here, thou canst be decently garbed if so thou willest. And maybe thou shalt hear private news of import. Please thy humour! Follow, not me, but thine own inclination!'

He nodded carelessly to the staring company, and passing through the room with a soft, almost cat-like tread, he began to ascend a dark and narrow flight of stone stairs leading to the second floor of the inn. Startled and bewildered by his mysterious words and manner, Barabbas watched the yellow glimmer of his garments vanishing upwards by degrees till he had quite disappeared,—then, like a man driven by some irresistible necessity, he muttered an incoherent excuse to his amazed companions, and in a blind, unreasoning, unconquerable impulse, rushed after him.

X

'HE is mad!'
        'Melchior, or Barabbas,—which?'
'Both!'

These and other similar exclamations broke from
most of the men assembled in the common room of
the inn. Melchior's sudden entrance, his conversation
with the newly - liberated criminal, and finally, his
departure followed by the headlong exit of Barabbas
himself, had all taken place within a few minutes,
and the incident had left an impression of stupefied
wonderment on those who had witnessed it.

'Who is this Melchior?—what is his calling?' demanded one man suspiciously—'What country is he
of?—how cometh he here in Jerusalem?'

There was a silence. No one seemed ready with a
reply. The keeper of the inn, a middle-aged Jew of
servile and propitiatory manners, edged himself gradually within the circle of his customers, and coughing
softly to attract attention, said—

'Methinks, good sirs, ye mistake him greatly in
giving him an evil repute merely for the unexplained
frequency of his visits to the city. He is assuredly a
man of wealth and wisdom,—though as to what land
he journeyeth from, none can say truly, though of my
own poor opinion, I would deem his birthplace in
Egypt. Concerning his business here he hath none
save the following of his own pleasure,—he comes and

goes,—and hath ever left some poor man the richer for his sojourn.'

'Like enough thou speakest well of him, Ben Ezra!' laughed one of his auditors—'Thou knowest the trick of lining thy pouch with gold! 'Twould be but a fool's error to wag thy tongue against this alien whom thou shelterest while thou dost charge him double fees for food and lodgment! Go to! Thou canst not judge of him fairly,—good ready money doth quickly purchase good opinion!'

Ben Ezra smiled amicably and began to clear away some of the emptied pewter flagons.

'Doubtless ye are all well-skilled in such matters,' he replied indifferently—'No host maligns a paying customer. Nevertheless, the worthy Melchior comporteth himself with such excellent good discretion that I see no cause wherein ye should take fear of him,—he hath done no man harm.'

'Not that thou knowest of, belike'—said a surly fellow, rising from his seat, and preparing to depart, 'But they that are reported harmless, often by spells and incantations, inflict most deadly injuries. Witness yon crazed and sinful Prophet of Nazareth! —hath he not the face of an angel?—and yet he hath cursed the Holy Temple, and sworn that not one stone shall remain upon another to show what it hath been! Lo, for such evil boasting his death shall scarce atone! And did not his mere glance this morning send Pilate almost mad, and plunge him in a deadly swoon?'

'Ay, ay! Thou sayest truly!'

And, reminded of the impending triple execution about to take place, the whole company rose up to leave the inn, and began to pay their various reckonings with the landlord. While they were thus engaged, a great roar went up from the waiting multitude outside,—a hoarse discordant sound of savagery and menace. Glancing comprehensively at one another, the party of wine-drinkers hastily settled their accounts and made a general rush from the inn, out into the street, where, though they knew it not, the most strangely imposing and wondrous spectacle that was ever seen or would ever be seen in the world awaited them,—the spectacle of a God led forth to die!

The crowd had increased so enormously that the road was completely blocked. Tradesmen with hand-carts and pedlars leading pack-mules could not pass, and had to turn back and find their way through the dark and tortuous by-streets of the city to their various destinations. Children lost themselves in the crush and went about crying, in search of their parents,—a party of travellers newly arrived from Damascus by the caravan route, got wedged with their worn-out horses and mules in the thick of the mob and could not move an inch. As far as the eye could see, the vari-coloured throng heaved restlessly to and fro under the blaze of the brilliant sun, and moving slowly and majestically in the midst of all, came the thorn-crowned 'Nazarene.' His hands and arms had been newly and more strongly bound, and were now tied behind Him so that He could not touch anything, or attempt by so much as a gesture to awaken the sympathies of the people. Soldiers encircled Him with a ring of glittering spears,—and following Him closely came four men, of whom one was the executioner, labouring under the cumbrous weight of a huge Cross some ten feet in height, the lower end of which scraped gratingly along in the dust, the thick beam being too heavy to lift up completely. As they caught sight of the cruel instrument of death, the populace set up an ecstatic yell of ferocious applause and satisfaction, and turned their faces all with one accord

towards the place of execution, which they understood to be a small hill outside the town, sometimes
called Golgotha, and sometimes Calvary. At the
moment when the huge human mass thus began to
move in one pre-determined direction, two additional
spectators joined the swarming rabble, — they were
Barabbas and Melchior. Barabbas, clad in tunic,
vest and mantle of a dense blackish purple, bordered
with gold, his rough beard combed and trimmed, and
a loose hood of white linen pulled over the thick
mass of his wild black hair, looked a very different
personage to the half-naked, reckless ruffian who had
been set free of the criminal dungeons that very
morning. He kept close beside his mysterious new
acquaintance, watching him anxiously from time to
time as though afraid to lose sight of him. His
countenance was grave and composed and not
without a certain harsh beauty of expression,—and
he walked with an informal grace and ease that was
almost dignity. Now and then his eyes wandered
over the crowd in front of him to the white figure
of the condemned 'King of the Jews,' whose shining
head, circled with the prickly coronal, rose visibly
like a featured Star above all the rest of the surging
thousands.

''Tis a crime to slay the innocent,'—he muttered.
'Condone it as they will, it is a crime.'

Melchior gave him a keen critical glance.

'Nothing is a crime if the people swear by it'—
he said—'And to slay the innocent hath ever been
man's delight. Doth he not trap the singing-birds
and draw his knife across the throat of the fawn?
Doth he not tear up the life of a blameless tree and
choke the breath of flowers in the grasp of his hand?
What would'st thou, thou meditative black-browed
son of Judæa? Physically or morally, the innocent
are always slain in this world. No one believes in a

pure body—still less do they believe in a pure soul. Pure soul and pure body are there in yonder thorn-crowned Monarch of many lands,—and lo you how we all troop forth to see him die!'

Barabbas was silent, troublously revolving in his own mind the phrase 'Monarch of many lands.'

'What is death?' pursued Melchior,—'Why doth it seem so hard a matter? 'Tis the end of all men. Yet whosoever slays the guilty shall be punished,—witness thyself, Barabbas, who didst rid the world of a lying knave. Clad in the skin of hypocrisy was the eminent Gabrias, and thou didst send him into outer darkness with one thrust of thy blade! That was not wisely done, thou fierce-blooded rascal! for he was an evil man protected by the law, whereas a good and just Man walketh yonder to His death, condemned by the Jews, and the Jews are not punished—*yet!*'

As he finished speaking there was a loud crashing noise and a shout, and the march of the multitude suddenly stopped. The great Cross had slipped from the grasp of the men supporting it, and its huge weight falling heavily sideways had well-nigh crushed one of the crowd who had ventured too near it. It was a matter of some difficulty to get it up from the ground again, and when the bearers had at last succeeded in partially raising it, they paused to take breath and looked about them for assistance. At that moment a huge, broad-shouldered, black-haired, tawny-skinned fellow was seen to be elbowing his way along in a contrary direction to that in which the mob were pressing, and as he came, many of the people shouted noisy and derisive greetings. His great height made him conspicuous, for he towered above all the heads of the throng except that of the 'Nazarene'—and the long almond shape of his eyes, his dark skin and manner of dress bespoke him of a very different race to the elect of Judæa. As he pushed through the press like a giant thrusting aside pigmies, some of the soldiers recognised him and shouted his name:

'Simon!'

'Come hither, Simon! Lend thine aid! Hast thou Rufus and Alexander with thee?'

'What news from Cyrene?'

'Thou art here in good time, Simon! For once we shall find use for thee!'

Hearing these and sundry other vociferations, the black-browed Cyrenian paused and looked scornfully about him. .

'What is this fool's feast of howling?' he demanded in an angry tone—'Are ye emptying Jerusalem of her thieves and rascals? Then shall the city be left desolate! Whither go ye?' Then, as his fiery eyes roved over the throng and he caught sight of the fair face of the doomed Captive—'What enslaved Prince have ye there?'

Wild yells and execrations drowned his voice, and a considerable portion of the mob closed in and began to hustle him roughly.

'Art thou drunken with new wine that thou dost see a prince in a malefactor? Thieves and rascals dost thou call us, thou dog!'

'Let him bear the Cross of the Nazarene!' shouted one of the roughs,—'He hath often boasted he hath the strength of four men!'

'Ay, ay! Let him carry the Cross! 'Tis fitting toil for a Cyrenian jack-ass such as he!'

And they continued to press round him with much hooting and swearing. The huge Simon was about to strike out with his fists and fight his way free of them all, when suddenly,—right across the heads of the multitude,—he met the straight, luminous, penetrating look of the Christ. Something shot through his veins like fire,—his strong limbs trembled,—a strange surprise and fear benumbed his mental faculties,—and he mechanically allowed himself to be pushed along to the spot where the bearers of the Cross still rested, taking breath, and wiping the sweat from their brows.

'Welcome, Simon!' said one of them with a grin, 'Thy broad back shall for once do us good service! Where are thy sons?'

'What need ye of them?' growled Simon roughly—'Surely they have been in Jerusalem these many days.'

'Rufus hath been wine-bibbing,' piped a lad standing by,—'And Alexander hath been seen oft at the money-changers!'

'And thou art a prating infant,' retorted Simon—'Who gave thee leave to note the actions of grown men? In Cyrene thou would'st be whipped for opening thy mouth before thy betters.'

'Callest thou thyself my betters!' said the boy derisively,—'Thou mud-skinned rascal! Take up the Cross and see thou stumble not!'

For one second Simon looked as though he were about to strike the lad to the earth,—but he was surrounded by the Jewish mob and the Roman soldiers, and there was the magnetic impression upon him of two splendid sorrowful Eyes that had, in one lightning glance, expressed a silent wish,—a dumb yet irresistible command ;—and therefore he stood mute, displaying no resentment. Nor did he make the least attempt to resist when, with jeers and laughter, the soldiers lifted the great Cross and laid its entire unsupported weight upon his shoulders.

'How likest thou that, thou giant of the mountain and the sea!' screamed an excitable old woman in the crowd, shaking her wrinkled fist at him,—'Wilt vaunt again of thy city set on a hill, and the vigour thou inhalest from thy tufts of pine? Shall we not hear thy sinews crack, thou ruffian of Cyrene, who doth dare to mock the children of Israel!'

But Simon replied not. He had settled the Cross steadily in position, and now, clasping its lower beam with both muscular arms, appeared to carry its massive weight with extraordinary and even pleasurable ease. The soldiers gathered round him in amaze,—such herculean vigour was something of a miracle,—and awakened their reluctant admiration. Petronius, the centurion, approached him.

'Canst thou in very truth bear the Cross?' he asked,—he was a mercifully-minded man, and of himself would neither have incited a mob to cruelty nor soldiers to outrage—''Tis some distance yet to Calvary,—wilt venture thus far?'

Simon lifted his black leonine head,—his eyes had grown soft and humid, and a faint smile trembled on his bearded lips.

'I will venture with this burden to the end of the world!' he answered, and there was a deep thrill of tenderness in his voice that made its roughness musical; 'To me 'tis light as a reed newly plucked by the river! Waste no words concerning my strength or my body's ableness,—lead on with yonder crowned Man—I follow!'

Petronius stared at him in undisguised wonderment, but said no more. And once again the multitude began to move, crushing onward like the troublous waves of a dark sea, all flowing in one direction, and illumined only by the golden beacon-splendour of that Divine Glory in their midst, the god-like visage, the steadfast eyes and radiant head of the 'King of the Jews.' And the tramping feet of the hurrying thousands awakened from the stones of the road a sullen continuous echo of thunder, as with shouts and shrieks and oaths and laughter they pressed forward, athirst for blood,—forward, and on to Calvary!

XI

THE sun now rode high in the heavens, and the scorching heat became almost unendurable. The morning's trial had begun earlier and lasted longer than in ordinary cases, owing to Pilate's indecision, and after the final pronouncement of the people's verdict, there had still been delays, so that time had worn on imperceptibly till it was past mid-day. The perfect blue of the sky was of such a deep and polished luminance that it suggested a dome of bright burning metal rather than air, from which the vertical light-rays darted, sharp as needles, plunging their hot points smartingly into the flesh. Jerusalem lay staring up at the brilliant glare, its low white houses looking almost brittle in the blistering flames of noon,—here and there tall palms shot up their slender brown stems and tufts of dusty green against the glassy dazzle of the clear ether,—and, hanging over the roofs of some of the best-built dwellings, the large loose leaves of the fig-trees lolled lazily, spreading wide and displaying on their branches, ripe fruit ready to break into crimson pulp at a touch. Full in the blaze of the sunshine the splendid Temple of Solomon on Mount Moriah glistened like a huge jewel, its columns and porticoes defined with micro-scopical distinctness and clearly visible from every quarter of the city,—while at certain glimmering points of distance the monotonous outlines of buildings

and street corners were relieved by the pink flush of
cactus-flowers and the grey-green of olive-boughs.
Over all the scene there brooded a threatening stillness as of pent-up thunder,—and this heavy calm
of the upper air presented itself in singular opposition
to the tumultuous roaring of the crowd below, whose
savage irritability and impatience were sensibly increased by the parching dryness of the atmosphere.
Pouring through the streets in a fever of excitement
that rose higher with every onward step, the heat
and fatigue of their march seemed to swell their fury
rather than diminish it, and they bellowed like wild
beasts as they scrambled, pushed and tore along, each
man ravenously eager to be among the first to arrive
at the place of execution.   And by and by, when the
soldiers began to halt at various wine-shops on their
way to quench the devouring thirst induced by the
choking dust and the stifling weather, the multitude
were not slow in following their example.   Drink was
purchased and passed about freely in cups and flagons,
and its effect was soon seen.   Disorderly groups of
men and women began to dance and sing,—some
pretended to preach,—others to prophesy,—one of
the roughs offered a goblet of wine to Simon of
Cyrene, and because he steadily refused it, dashed it
violently on the Cross he carried.   The red liquid
trickled off the wood like blood, and the fellow who
had cast it there, gave a tipsy yell of laughter.

'Lo 'tis baptized!' he cried to the applauding
mob,—'With a better baptism than that of headless
John!'

His dissolute companions roared their appreciation
of the jest, and the discordant hubbub grew more
and more deafening.   With that curious fickleness
common to crowds, every one seemed to have forgotten Barabbas for whose release they had so
recently and eagerly clamoured.   They were evidently

not aware of his presence among them,—probably
they did not recognise him, clad as he was in sober
and well-ordered apparel. He was in the thick of
the press however, and watched the coarse half-
drunken antics of those around him with a pained
and meditative gravity. Occasionally his eyes grew
restless and wandered over the heaving mass of
people in troubled search, as though looking for
something lost and incalculably precious. Melchior,
always beside him, observed this and smiled somewhat satirically.

'She is not there,'—he said—'Thinkest thou she
would mingle with this vulgar swarm? Nay, nay!
She will come, even as the high-priests will come,
by private by-ways,—perchance the excellent
Caiaphas himself will bring her.'

'Caiaphas!' echoed Barabbas doubtfully—'What
knoweth she of Caiaphas?'

'Much!' replied Melchior. 'His wife is one of her
friends elect. Have I not told thee, thou simple-
souled barbarian, to remember that thou hast been
lost to the world for eighteen months? To a woman
'tis an ample leisure wherein to work mischief! Nay,
be not wrathful!—'tis my alien way of speech, and I
am willing to believe thy maiden a paragon of all the
virtues till '——

'Till what?' demanded Barabbas suspiciously.

'Till it is proved otherwise!' said Melchior. 'And
that she is beauteous is beyond all question,—and
beauty is all that the soul of a man desireth.
Nevertheless, as I told thee a while agone, 'twas her
brother that betrayed the "Nazarene."'

'I marvel at it!' murmured Barabbas—'Judas was
ever of an open candid nature.'

'Thou didst know him well?' questioned Melchior
with one of his keen looks.

'Not well, but sufficiently'—and Barabbas flushed

a shamed red as he spoke—'He was one of my fellow-workers in the house of Shadeen,—the merchant I told thee of'——

'The Persian dealer in pearls and gold?—Ah!' and Melchior smiled again,—'And, all to please the sister of this so candid Judas, thou didst steal jewels and wert caught in thy theft! Worthy Barabbas! Methinks that for this Judith of thine, thou didst commit all thy sins!'

Barabbas lowered his eyes.

'She craved for gems,'—he said, in the tone of one proffering suitable excuse,—'And I took a necklet of pure pearls. They were suited to her maidenhood, and seemed to me better placed round her soft dove's throat than in the musty coffer of Shadeen.'

'Truly a notable reason for robbing thy employer! And thy plea for the right to commit murder was equally simple,—Gabrias the Pharisee slandered the fair one, and thou with a knife-thrust didst silence his evil tongue! So! To speak honestly 'tis this Judith Iscariot is the cause of all thy sufferings and thy imprisonment and yet—thou lovest her!'

'If thou hast seen her'—murmured Barabbas with a sigh.

'I have!' returned Melchior tranquilly—'She is willing to be seen! Is she not the unrivalled beauty of the city, and wherefore should she be chary of her charms? They will not last for ever; best flourish them abroad while yet they are fresh and fair! Nevertheless they have made of thee both thief and murderer.'

Barabbas did not attempt to contradict the truth of this pitiless statement.

'And if all were known'—pursued Melchior,—'the sedition in which thou wert concerned perchance arose from her persuasion?'

'No, no!' averred Barabbas quickly—'There were

many reasons. We are under tyranny; not so much
from Rome as from our own people who assist to
make the laws. The priests and the Pharisees rule
us, and many are the abuses of authority. The poor
are oppressed,—the wronged are never righted. Now
I have read many a Greek and Roman scroll,—and
have even striven to study somewhat of the wisdom
of the Egyptians, and I have the gifts of memory and
ready speech, so that I can, if needful, address a
multitude. I fell in with some of the disaffected, and
gave them my service in their cause,—I know not how
it chanced,—but surely there is a craving for freedom
in the breast of every man?—and we,—we are not free.'

'Patience! ye shall have wondrous liberty ere long!'
said Melchior, a dark look flashing from his eyes—
'For the time is coming when the children of Israel
shall rule the land with rods of iron! The chink of
coin shall be the voice of their authority, and yonder
thorn-crowned Spirit will have lived on earth in vain
for those who love gold more than life. The triumph
of the Jews is yet to be! Long have they been the
captive and the conquered,—but they shall make
captives in their turn, and conquer the mightiest
kings. By fraud, by falsehood, by cunning, by
worldly-wisdom, by usury, by every poisoned arrow
in Satan's quiver they shall rule! Even thy name,
Barabbas, shall serve them as a leading title; 'tis *thou*
shalt be "King of the Jews" as far as this world holds,—
for He who goeth before us is King of a wider nation
—a nation of immortal spirits over whom gold has
no power!'

Barabbas gazed at him in awe, understanding little
of what he meant, but chilled by the stern tone of his
voice, which seemed to have within it a jarring note
of menace and warning.

'What nation dost thou speak of'—he murmured,—
'What world'——

'What world?' repeated Melchior,—'No single world, but a thousand million worlds! There, far above us'—and he pointed to the dazzling sky, 'is the azure veil which hides their courses and muffles their music,—but they are existent facts, not dreamer's fancies,—huge spheres, vast systems, sweeping onward in their appointed ways, rich with melody, brimming with life, rounded with light, and yonder Man of despised Nazareth, walking to His death, knows the secrets of them all!'

Stricken with a sudden terror, Barabbas stopped abruptly and caught the impassioned speaker by the arm.

'What sayest thou?' he gasped—'Art thou mad? Or hast thou too, beheld the Vision? For I have thought strange and fearful things since I looked upon His face and saw— Nay, good Melchior, why should this crime be visited upon Judæa? Let me harangue the people,—perchance it is not yet too late for rescue!'

'Rescue!' echoed Melchior—'Rescue a lamb from wolves,—a fawn from tigers,—or more difficult still a Faith from priestcraft! Let be, thou rash son of blinded passion, let be! What is designed must be accomplished.'

He was silent for a little space, and seemed absorbed in thought. Barabbas walked beside him, silent too, but full of an inexplicable horror and fear. The surging mob howled and screamed around them,—their ears were for the moment deaf to outer things. Presently Melchior looked up and the amber gleam in his eyes glittered strangely, as he said—

'And Judas,—Judas Iscariot, thou sayest, was of a simple nature?'

'He seemed so when I knew him'—answered Barabbas with an effort, for his thoughts were in a tangle of distress and perplexity—'He was notable for truth and conscientiousness, — he was much

7

trusted; he kept the books of Shadeen. At times
he had wild notions of reform,—he resented tyranny,
and loathed the priests. Yea, so much did he loathe
them that he never would have entered the syna-
gogue, had it not been to please his father, and more
specially Judith, his only sister whom he loved. So
much he once told me. One day he left the city in
haste and secrecy,—none knew whither he went,—
and after that '——

'After that thou didst steal Shadeen's pearls for
thy love and slay thy love's slanderer,'—finished his
companion serenely, 'and thou wert plunged in
prison for thy follies ; and narrowly hast thou escaped
being crucified this day.'

Barabbas looked up, his black eyes firing with a
sudden ardour.

'I would have died willingly to save yon kingly
Man !' he said impulsively.

Melchior regarded him steadily, and his own eyes
softened.

'Breaker of the law, thief and murderer as thou
art convicted of being,' he said, 'thou hast something
noble in thy nature after all ! May it count to thy
good hereafter ! And of Judas I can tell thee somewhat. When he departed secretly from Jerusalem,
he journeyed to the borders of the Sea of Galilee, and
there did join himself in company with the Prophet
of Nazareth and His other disciples. He wandered
with Him throughout the land,—I myself saw him
near Capernaum, and he was ever foremost in service
to his Master. Now, here in Jerusalem last night,
he gave Him up to the guard,—and lo, the name of
"Judas" from henceforth will stand for "traitor" to
the end of time !'

Barabbas shuddered, though he could not have
told why.

'Doth Judith know of this?' he asked.

A fleeting cold smile hovered on Melchior's lips.

'Judith knoweth much,—but not all. She hath not seen her brother since yesterday at sundown.'

'Then, hath he fled the city?'

Melchior looked at him strangely for a moment. Then he answered—

'Yea, he hath fled.'

'And those others who followed the Nazarene,' inquired Barabbas eagerly—'Where are they?'

'They have fled also'—returned Melchior. 'What else should they do? Is it not natural and human to forsake the fallen?'

'They are cowards all!' exclaimed Barabbas hotly.

'Nay!' replied Melchior—'They are—men!'

And noting his companion's pained expression he added,—

'Knowest thou not that cowards and men are one and the same thing, most excellent Barabbas? Didst ever philosophise? If not, why didst thou read Greek and Roman scrolls and puzzle thy brain with the subtle wisdom of Egypt? No man was ever persistently heroic, in small matters as well as great,—and famous deeds are ever done on impulse. Study thyself,—note thine own height and breadth, —thou hast so much bone and muscle and sinew,— 'tis a goodly frame, well knit together, and to all intents and purposes thou art Man. Nevertheless a glance from a woman's eyes, a smile on a woman's mouth, a word of persuasion or suggestion from a woman's tongue, can make thee steal and commit murder. Wherefore thou, Man, art also Coward. Too proud to rob, too merciful to slay,—this would be courage, and more than is in man. For men are pigmies,—they scuttle away in droves before a storm or the tremor of an earthquake,—they are afraid for their lives. And what *are* their lives? The lives of

motes in a sunbeam,—of gnats in a mist of miasma,
—nothing more. And they will never be anything
more, till they learn how to make them valuable.
And that lesson will never be mastered save by the
few.'

Barabbas sighed.

'Verily thou dost love to repeat the tale of my
sins'—he said—'Maybe thou dost think I cannot
hear it too often. And now thou callest me coward!
yet I may not be angered with thee, seeing thou
art a stranger, and I, despite the law's release, am
still no more than a criminal,—wherefore, because
thou seemest wise and of singular powers, I forbear
with thy reproaches. But 'tis not too late to learn
the lesson thou dost speak of, and methinks even I
may make my recovered life of value?'

'Truly thou mayest'—responded Melchior—'For
if thou so dost choose, not all the powers of heaven
and earth can hinder thee. But 'tis a business none
can guide thee in. Life is a talisman, dropped freely
into thy bosom, but the fitting use of the magic gift
must be discovered by thyself alone.'

At that moment the moving crowd came to a sudden
abrupt halt. Loud cries and exclamations were heard.

'He will die ere he is crucified!'

'Lo! he faints by the way!'

'If he can walk no more, bind him with ropes
and drag him to Calvary!'

'Bid Simon carry him as well as the Cross!'

'Support him, ye lazy ruffians!' cried a woman
in the crowd,—'Will ye have Cæsar told that the
Jews are nothing but barbarians?'

The clamour grew louder, and the excited mob
rolled back upon itself with a force that was dangerous to life and limb. People fell and were trampled
or bruised, — children screamed; and for a few
moments the confusion was terrific.

'Now would be the time to attempt a rescue!' muttered Barabbas, with some excitement, clenching his fists as though in eagerness to begin the fray.

Melchior laid a restraining hand on his arm.

'As well try to pluck the sun out of heaven!' he said passionately—'Control thyself, rash fool! Thou canst not rescue One for whom death is the divine fulness of life! Press forward with me quickly,—and we shall discover the cause of this new delay,—but say no word, and raise not a hand in opposition to Destiny. Wait till the end!'

XII

WITH these words, and still holding Barabbas firmly by the arm, he plunged into the thickest part of the crowd, which appeared to yield and give mysterious way to his passage,—and presently reached a place of standing-room where it was possible to see what had occasioned the halt and uproar. All the noise and fury surged round the grand figure of the 'Nazarene,' who stood erect as ever, but nevertheless seemed even in that upright position to have suddenly lost consciousness. His face had an unearthly pallor and His eyes were closed, —and it appeared to the soldiers and people as if Death had laid a merciful hand upon Him ere there was time to torture His life. In response to sundry calls and shouts for water, or some other cool beverage to rouse the apparently swooning Captive, a man came out of the dark interior of his dwelling with a goblet containing wine mingled with myrrh, and handed it to the centurion in charge. Petronius, with a strange sinking at the heart and something of remorse and pity, advanced and lifted it to the lips of the Divine Sufferer, who as the cold rim of the cup touched Him, opened His starry eyes and smiled. The infinite beauty of that smile and its pathetic tenderness,— the vast pardon and sublime patience it expressed, seemed all at once to flash a sudden mysterious light of comprehension into the hearts of the cruel multitude, for, as if struck by a spell, their cries and murmurings ceased, and every head was turned towards the great Radiance which shone upon them with such intense and undefinable glory. Petronius staggered back, chilled with a vague horror, — he returned the cup of wine and myrrh to the man who had offered it,—the 'Nazarene' had not tasted it,— He had merely expressed His silent acknowledgment by that luminous and exquisite smile. And strangely awful did it suddenly seem to the bluff centurion that such an One as He should express gratitude to any man, even by a glance, — though why it appeared unnatural, he, Petronius, could not tell. Meanwhile, some of the women pressing closer and gazing full into the calm fair face of the Condemned, were touched into awe and admiration, and began to utter exclamations of regret and compassion,—others, more emotional, and encouraged by at last hearing an unmistakable murmur of sympathy ripple wave-like through the throng, broke into loud weeping, and beat their breasts with frenzied gesticulations of mourning and despair.

'They will change their minds, these Jews,'—said one of the soldiers sullenly, aside to Petronius—'With all these wailings and halts by the way, our work will never be done. Best press on quickly.'

'Hold thy peace!' retorted Petronius angrily— 'Seest thou not the Man faints with fatigue and maybe with the pain of the scourging? Let him pause a while.'

But He of whom they spoke had already recovered Himself. His lips parted a little, — they trembled and were dewy, as though some heavenly restorative had just touched them. The faint colour flowed back to His face, and He looked dreamily about Him, like a strayed Angel who scarcely recognises the sphere into which it has wandered. The weeping women

gathered near Him timidly, some carrying infants in
their arms, and, undeterred by the frowns of the
soldiers, ventured to touch His garments. One
young matron, a woman of Rome, lifted a small fair-
haired nursling close up to Him that He might look
at it,—the little one stretched out its dimpled arms
and tried to clutch first the crown of thorns, and then
the glittering golden hair. The sweet encourage-
ment and strong tenderness of expression with which
the Divine Immortal met the child's laughing eyes
and innocently attempted caresses, melted the
mother's heart, and she gave way to uncontrollable
sobbing, clasping her loved and lovely treasure close,
and letting her tears rain on its nestling head. The
other women round her, sympathetically infected by
her example, renewed their lamentations with such
hysterical passion that presently the gradual mutterings of impatience and discontent that had for some
minutes proceeded from the male portion of the crowd,
swelled into loud remonstrance and indignation.

'What fools are women!' 'Press forward!' 'We
shall have these whimpering souls preventing the
law's fulfilment!' 'Why delay thus?'

But these angry outcries were of little avail, and
the women still wept and clustered about the
'Nazarene,' till He Himself turned His eyes upon
them with a look of love and invincible command
which like a charm suddenly hushed their clamour.
At the same moment, a low voice, rendered faint
with weariness, dropped on their ears melodiously
like a sweet and infinitely sad song:

'*Daughters of Jerusalem, weep not for me, but weep
for yourselves and for your children!*' Here a deep
sigh interrupted speech; then the mellow accents
gathered strength and solemnity· '*For behold the
days are coming in the which they shall say, Blessed
are the barren, and the wombs that never bare, and the*

breasts which never gave suck. Then shall they begin to say to the mountains, Fall on us! and to the hills, Cover us!'

The rich voice faltered for a moment, and the beautiful eyes of the captive 'King' filled with a deep meditative pity as He added ;—'*For if they do these things in a green tree, what shall be done in the dry?'*

The listening women looked up at Him in tearful astonishment, quieted, yet understanding nothing of His words. The last sentence seemed to them particularly vague and meaningless,—they could not comprehend that He who thus spoke to them was thinking of the whole world merely as '*a green tree*' or a planet in its prime, and that He foresaw little but sorrow from the wilful disbelief and disobedience of its inhabitants when it should become old and like the sapless tree, '*dry.*' Dry of faith, dry of love, dry of all sweet, pure, holy and unselfish emotion,—a mere withered husk of a world ready to be scattered among the star-dust of the Universe, having failed to obey its Maker's will, or to accomplish its nobler destiny. Such premonitory signs are given to thinkers and philosophers alone,—the majority of men have no time and less inclination to note or accept them. There is time to eat, time to steal, time to lie, time to murder, time to become a degradation to the very name of Man ;—but there is no time to pause and consider that after all our petty labours and selfish ambitions, this star on which we live belongs, not to us, but to God, and that if He but willed it so, it could be blotted out of space in a second and never be missed, save perhaps for the one singular distinction that the Divine Christ dwelling upon it from birth to death, has made it sacred.

None among the Jewish populace that morning were able to imagine the vast wonder and mystery investing the sublime Figure which moved amongst

them with such tranquil dignity and resignation,—
none could foresee the tremendous results which were
destined to spring from the mere fact of His existence
upon earth. All that they saw was a Man of extraordinary physical beauty, who for bold and open
teaching of new doctrines pronounced by the priests
to be blasphemous, was being led to His death.
Thrust violently back by the guards, the frightened
group of women who had wept for His sufferings, got
scattered among the crowd, and, drifting hither and
thither like blown leaves in a storm, forgot their
tears in their anxiety to protect their children from
the reckless pushing and buffeting of the onward
swarming rabble. The disorder was increased by the
terrified starting and plunging of horses and mules
that got entangled in the crowd during the progress
of the procession through the narrow and tortuous
streets,—but at last one sharp turn in the road
brought them in full view of Calvary. The people
set up a wild unanimous shout,—and Simon of Cyrene
carrying the Cross looked up startled and pained by
the discordant roar. For he had been lost in a dream.
Unconscious of the weight he bore, he had seemed to
himself to walk on air. He had spoken no word,
though many around him had mocked him and striven
to provoke him by insolent jests and jeers,—he was
afraid to utter a sound lest he should disturb and
dispel the strange and delicious emotion he experi-
enced,—emotion which he could not explain, but
which kept him in a state of bewildered wonderment
and ecstasy. There was music everywhere about
him,—high above the mutterings and murmurings of
the populace, he heard mysterious throbs of melody
as of harps struck by the air,—the hard stones of the
road were soft as velvet to his sandalled feet,—the
Cross he carried seemed scented with the myrtle and
the rose,—and there was no more weight in it than in

a gathered palm-leaf plucked as a symbol of victory.
He remembered how in his youth he had once carried
the baby son of a king on his shoulders down one of
the Cyrenian hills to the edge of the sea,—and the
child, pleased with the swiftness and ease of its
journey, had waved aloft a branch of vine in sign of
triumph and joy. The burden of the Cross was no
heavier than that of the laughing child and tossing
vine! But now,—now the blissful journey must end,
—the rude cries of the savage multitude aroused him
from his reverie,—the harp-like melodies around him
rippled away into minor echoes of deep sadness,—and
as his eyes beheld the hill of Calvary, he, for the first
time since he began his march, felt weary unto death.
He had never in all his years of life known such
happiness as while carrying the Cross of Him who
was soon to be nailed upon it; but now the time had
come when he must lay it down, and take up the far
more weighty burdens of the world and its low
material claims. Why not die here, he thought
vaguely, with the Man whose radiant head gleamed
before him like the sun in heaven? Surely it would
be well, since here, at Calvary, life seemed to have
a sweet and fitting end! He was only a barbarian,
uninstructed and ignorant of heavenly things,—he
could not analyse what he felt or reason out his unfamiliar sensations, but some singular change had
been wrought in him, since he lifted up the Cross,—
thus much he knew,—thus much he realised ;—the
rest was mere wonder and worship.

As the multitude poured itself towards the place of
execution, a party of horsemen dashed through a
side-street and careered up the hill at full gallop, the
hoofs of their spirited steeds tearing up and scattering
morsels of the sun-baked turf like dust in the air as
they passed. They were Roman nobles, visitors to
Jerusalem, who hearing of what was about to take

place, had come out to see this singular Jewish festival of blood. After them followed another group of persons, on foot, and glittering in raiment of various costly hues,—these were Caiaphas, Annas and many of the members of the Sanhedrim, accompanied by a select number of the retinue of their various households. Meanwhile Barabbas was being guarded and guided forward by the astute Melchior, who with wonderful dexterity and composure, piloted him through the thickest of the crush and brought him to a clear space at the foot of the hill. Just as they reached the spot, several richly-attired women, some of them veiled, came out of the shady avenues of a private garden close by and began the ascent at a slow and sauntering pace. They were laughing and talking gaily among themselves; one of them, the tallest, walked with a distinctive air of haughtiness and a swaying suppleness of movement,—she had a brilliant flame-coloured mantle thrown over her head and shoulders.

'Lo there!' whispered Melchior, grasping Barabbas firmly by the arm to keep him prisoner—'Yonder she goes! Seest thou not yon poppy-hued gala garb? 'Tis the silken sheath of the flower whose perfume drives thee mad!—the dove-like desirer of stolen pearls!—the purest and fairest virgin in Judæa, Judith Iscariot!'

With a fierce cry and fiercer oath, Barabbas strove to wrench himself from his companion's hold.

'Release me!' he gasped—'Detain me not thus, or by my soul, I will slay thee!'

His efforts were in vain; Melchior's hand, though light, was firm as iron and never yielded, and Melchior's eyes, flashing fire, yet cold as ice in expression, rested on the heated angry face of the man beside him, unswervingly and with a chill disdain.

'Thou infatuated fool!' he said slowly—'Thou

misguided barbarian! *Thou* wilt slay *me?* "By thy soul" thou wilt? Swear not by thy soul, good ruffian, for thou hast one, strange as it doth seem! 'Tis the only positive thing about thee, wherefore take not its name in vain, else it may visit vengeance on thee! Judgest thou me as easy to kill as a Pharisee? Thou art in serious error! The steel of thy knife would melt in my flesh,—thy hands would fall withered and benumbed didst thou presume to lay them violently upon me! Be warned in time, and pervert not my friendship, for believe me thou wilt need it presently.'

Barabbas looked at him in wild appeal,—a frozen weight seemed to have fallen on his heart, and a sense of being mastered and compelled, vexed his impatient spirit. But he was powerless,—he had, on a mere sudden impulse, put himself, he knew not why, under the control of this stranger,—he had only himself to blame if now his own will seemed paralysed and impotent. He ceased struggling, and cast a longing glance after the flame-coloured mantle that now appeared to be floating lightly up the hill of Calvary like a stray cactus-petal on the air.

'Thou knowest not,' he muttered—'thou canst not know how I have hungered for her face'——

'And thou shalt feed on it ere long'—rejoined Melchior sarcastically,—'And may it quell thy vulgar appetite! But assume at least the appearance of a man,—betray not thyself before her maidens,—they will but scoff at thee. Moreover, bethink thee thou art here as witness of a death,—a death far greater than all love!'

Barabbas sighed, and his head drooped dejectedly on his breast. His strong harsh features were convulsed with passion,—but the strange force exercised over him by his companion was too subtle for resistance. Melchior watched him keenly for a moment ere he spoke again,—then he said more gently, but with earnestness and solemnity—

'Lo, they ascend Calvary! Seest thou not the Condemned and His guards are already half way up the hill? Come, let us follow;—thou shalt behold the world agonised and the sun fade in heaven!— thou shalt hear the conscious thunder roar out wrath at this symbolic slaughter of the Divine in Man! No worse murder was ever wrought,—none more truly representative of humanity!—and from henceforth the earth rolls on its appointed way in a mist of blood,—saved, may be, but stained!—stained and marked with the Cross,—for ever!'

XIII

BARABBAS trembled as he heard. Full of apprehensive trouble and dreary foreboding, he followed his inscrutable new acquaintance. Some strange inward instinct told him that there was a terrible truth in Melchior's words,—though why a stranger and alien to Judæa should know more concerning the mystic 'Nazarene' than the Jews themselves was a problem he could not fathom. Nevertheless he began the brief ascent of Calvary with a sinking heart, and a sensation that was very like despair. He felt that something tremendous and almost incomprehensible was about to be consummated, and that on the children of Israel for evermore would rest the curse invoked by themselves. Could God Himself alter the deliberately self-chosen fate of a man or a nation? No! Even the depraved and ill-taught Barabbas was mentally conscious of the awful yet divine immutability of Free-will.

The dry turf crackled beneath the tread as though it were on fire, for the heat was more than ever overpoweringly intense. Time had worn on till it was nearly three o'clock in the afternoon, and the broad unshadowed glare of the sun streamed pitilessly down upon the hill of execution, which now presented the appearance of a huge hive covered thickly with thousands of swarming, buzzing bees.

The crowd had broken up on all sides, each section
of it striving to attain the best point of view from
whence to watch the progress of the dire tragedy
about to be enacted. The fatal eminence sloped
upward very gently, and on cooler days the climb
would have scarcely been perceptible, but at this
fierce hour, when all the world seemed staring and
aflame with wonder, the way appeared difficult and
long. Melchior and Barabbas however, walking side
by side, managed to keep up a moderately swift and
even pace, despite the vindictive blaze and dazzle of
the sky, and never paused to take breath till, as they
neared the summit, they came upon a little group
of women surrounding the unconscious form of one
of their companions. Barabbas, with a wild idea
that his Judith might be amongst them, sprang
eagerly forward, and this time Melchior let him go.
But he was quickly disappointed,—no silken-robed
beauty was there,—they were all poor, footsore, sad-
faced, ill-clad creatures, some of whom were silently
weeping, while only one of them, who seemed, by her
singular dignity of bearing, to be of a higher rank, stood
apart,—but she was closely veiled, so that her features
were not visible. Their whole attention was centred
on the woman who had swooned, and she appeared,
from her exterior condition, to be the poorest of
them all. Clothed only in a rough garment of
coarse grey linen bound under her bosom with a
hempen girdle, she lay on the ground where she had
suddenly fallen, like one newly dead, — and the
piteous still loveliness of her was such, that Barabbas,
though his wild soul mirrored another and far more
brilliant face, could not help but be moved to compassion, as he bent forward and saw her thus prone
and senseless. The chief glory that distinguished
her was her hair,—it had come unbound, and rippled
about her in lavish waves of warm yet pale gold,—

her features were softly rounded and delicate like those of a child, and the thick lashes that fringed the closed eyes, being more darkly tinted than the hair, cast a shadow beneath, suggestive of pain and the shedding of many tears.

'What aileth her?' asked Barabbas gently.

One or two of the women eyed him doubtfully but offered no reply. Melchior had approached to within a certain distance of the group, and there he waited. Barabbas beckoned him, but seeing he did not stir, went hastily up to him.

'Shall we not be of some service here?' he demanded—''Tis a wondrous fair virgin whom sorrow or pain hath surely overcome.'

'Do as it seemeth unto thee well,'—responded Melchior quietly, looking him full in the face as he spoke; 'nevertheless thou must be advised in this matter. Yon "wondrous fair virgin," as thou callest her, is but a woman of ill-fame,—a golden-haired wanton of the city ways, called Mary Magdalene.'

Barabbas started as if he had been stung. A dark frown gathered on his brows.

'Mary Magdalene!' he muttered—'Of a truth she is a sinner! I have heard sundry evil things of her,—yet of myself I would not be merciless,—I could not stone a woman, ... but if to-day I see and speak with Judith'——

'Enough!' interrupted Melchior disdainfully—'I understand thee! Thou would'st not sully thyself, good thief, with even so much as a look from a wanton, Judith being pure as heaven and Mary black as hell! Leave her where she lies, O thou moralising murderer,—thou true type of the men who make such women!—leave her to the ministrations of her own sex. She whom thou, assassin, dost scorn, hath been brought to penitence and pardoned by Him who dieth presently, yet what of that? 'Tis naught, 'tis

8

naught!—for He must be crucified, but *thou* canst live!—O wondrous world that thus pronounceth equity! Come, let us onward!'

Barabbas listened, sullenly ashamed.

'If she be penitent 'tis well'—he muttered—'but why then goest thou not thyself to her?'

A sudden gravity clouded the ironical glitter in Melchior's eyes.

'Why?' he echoed pensively,—then after a pause, 'Were I to tell thee truly why, thou would'st learn more than is yet fitting to thy nature. Let it suffice to thee to know that among those women there is One, whom I may not venture to approach save in worship,—for where she treads is holy ground! For her sake from henceforth, Woman is made Queen!— nay, look not thus strangely!—thou shalt hear more of this anon.'

He resumed his walk sedately, and Barabbas more and more troubled and perplexed, gave a disquieted glance backward over his shoulder at the group now left behind. He saw that the fainting Magdalene had revived sufficiently to be lifted partially to her feet,—and he caught the flash of the dazzling sunlight on the falling masses of her luxuriant hair. Then he turned his eyes away, and bent his looks downward to the ground, and a silence fell between him and Melchior. All at once a shriek of agony tore the air into sharp echoes, followed by another and yet another. Barabbas stopped, his blood freezing at the hideous outcry. Unable to speak, he gazed at his companion in affrighted inquiry.

''Tis the first taste of pain such as thou mightest this day and at this moment have suffered,' said Melchior, answering his look—'They are nailing down two thieves. Hearest thou not the clang of the hammers? A few paces more and we shall see the work.'

They quickened their steps, and in a couple of
minutes reached the summit of the hill. There they
found themselves in full view of the terrible scene of
execution,—a pageant of such tremendous import,
such sublime horror, that the imagination of man
can scarcely grasp it,—scarcely realise the consum-
mate bitterness of the awful and immortal tragedy.
The multitude had formed into a complete ring,
circling unbrokenly round the crest of Calvary,—
while the soldiery had divided into two lines, one
keeping to the right, the other to the left. At a
signal from the centurion, Simon of Cyrene laid down
with tender and lingering reluctance the great Cross
he had so lightly carried,—and as he did so, the Man
of Nazareth, moving tranquilly to the spot indicated
to Him by His guards, took up His position beside
the intended instrument of His death, and there
waited patiently for the accomplishment of His fate.
The executioners were already busily occupied with
part of their dreadful task,—for, at the crafty suggestion of Caiaphas, the two thieves who had been
brought out from the prison that morning were nailed
on their respective crosses first. This was to satisfy
the refined cruelty of the Jewish priests, who by this
means sought to overpower the 'Nazarene' with
terror, by forcing Him to witness the agonies of those
who were destined to suffer in His sacred company.
But herein the bloodthirsty chiefs of the Sanhedrim
were doomed to disappointment. No shadow of fear
blanched the serene visage of the Divine,—not a
tremor of horror or anxiety quivered through that
stately frame of heroic stature and perfect mould.
He stood erect, as a king of a thousand worlds might
stand, conscious of power and glory,—His tall white-
robed figure was fully outlined against the burning
sky, and seemed to have gathered from the sun-rays
a dazzling luminance of its own,—every prickly point

in His crown of thorns glistened as with drops of
dew,—His fair calm face shone with a beauty not of
mortals,—and so lightly did His sandalled feet seem
poised on the hot and arid soil beneath Him, that He
scarcely appeared to touch the earth more than a
sunlit cloud may do ere rising again into its native
ether. The land, the sky, the air, the sun, all seemed
to be a part of Himself and to share mysteriously in
the knowledge of His presence ; had He spoken one
word,—one word of thunderous command, it would
have shaken the Universe! But with that inward
force known only to God and the angels, He held
His peace,—and His radiant eyes in their poetic
wistfulness and wonder, seemed saying silently—'I
go to lift the curtain from this Death, which all My
foolish creatures fear! I pass through torturing pain
to give weak human nature courage! And I descend
into the grave as Man, to prove that Man, though
seeming dead, shall rise to life again!'

Meanwhile the shrieks and cries that had startled
Barabbas were growing louder and wilder. They
all proceeded from one of the doomed thieves,—the
other was silent. With a mingling of morbid curiosity and nervous dread, Barabbas went shrinkingly
towards the spot where the executioners were at
work, and gazing at the distorted features of the
struggling criminal gave an irrepressible cry of
amazement.

'Hanan!'

Hanan indeed it was, his former fellow-prisoner,
with whom he had fought through iron bars the
previous night, and whom he had left yelling after
him that very morning. Hearing Barabbas speak his
name, the wretched man turned his protruding eyes
round with a hideous expression of rage and envy.

'*Thou*,—Barabbas! *Thou*,—free? Dog! Accursed
devil! What evil conspiracy hast thou worked in

to get thyself released and me condemned? Through thee I sinned!—through thee have I come to this! Coward! I spit on thee! Justice!—I will have justice! Thou lying hypocrite! Didst thou not swear to stand by thy friends? Let be, ye brutes!' and with a yell he tore his arm away from the men who had seized it to nail it against the left-hand beam of the cross on which he was stretched—'Thou, thou Barabbas, art thief as well as I—thou art worse than I, for thou art murderer! Come thou hither and be tormented in my stead! This morning thou didst leave me in my cell starved and athirst,—and lo, they came and brought me forth to die,—while thou art here, pranked out in soft attire, free—free! Thou ruffian! And this is Rome's justice for the Jews! Ah!'—and he screamed furiously, as two or three soldiers beckoned forward by the executioners came and by force tied his arms with strong rope to the cross-beams of the instrument of death, while the great sharp nails were driven remorselessly through the centre of his palms,—'Take ye Barabbas and crucify him!' he yelled,—'He murdered Gabrias, —he stole the jewels of Shadeen,—he it is who stirreth up sedition in the city,—bring out another cross for Barabbas!—let Barabbas die'——

Blood sprang to his mouth, choking his utterance, —his face grew dusky purple with agony and suffocation. The soldiers laughed.

'Thou cowardly dog!' said one of them—'Die like a man, if there be any manhood in a Jew. A Roman would scorn to make such outcry. As for Barabbas, he is set free by law and pardoned.'

Hanan heard, and his eyes rolled horribly with a delirious glare.

'Pardoned—pardoned!' he muttered thickly— 'May all the curses of deepest hell be on thee and thy wanton'——

But his sentence was left unfinished, for at that moment his cross was raised and set upright in the socket prepared for it in the ground,—and the blistering sun blazed down upon his bare head and naked body like an opened furnace-fire. He twisted and writhed in vain,—in his indescribable torture he would have torn his hands from the nails which pierced them, had they not been too tightly bound for such an effort. Most awful it was to look upon him hanging thus, with the anguished blood blackening in his veins and swelling his straining muscles,—and Barabbas turned away his eyes, sick and shuddering.

'Do they all suffer like that?' he asked of Melchior falteringly.

'All who are made of clay and clay only, suffer thus'—responded Melchior, eyeing the tormented criminal with an air of scientific coldness,—'He has had his chance in this world and lost it. None but himself can be blamed for his present condition.'

'Wilt thou apply such moralising to the Nazarene?' demanded Barabbas half indignantly.

Melchior lifted his eyes for an instant to the sky as though he saw some wonder there.

'Ay! Even to the Nazarene!' he said softly— 'He also hath had His Way, and chosen His condition,—and unto Him be the glory hereafter! Time is His slave,—and Destiny His footstool, and His Cross the safety of Humanity!'

'Nay, if such be thy thought of Him'—murmured Barabbas, shaken to his very soul by a trembling awe he could not explain, 'were it not well to speak with Him ere He dies?—to crave a blessing'——

'His blessing is not for me, but all'—interrupted Melhior with solemnity—'And I have spoken with Him,—long ago, when His life on earth was young. But now, 'tis not a time for words,—'tis a time for vigilance and prayer;—watch thou therefore with me, and hold thy peace,—this is but the beginning of wonders.'

Just then the executioners finished nailing the second thief to his cross. This man made no resistance and scarce an outcry. Once only, as his feet were pierced by the huge nail that was roughly hammered through them, he gave vent to an irresistible faint shriek of pain,—but afterwards, with an almost superhuman effort he controlled himself, and only moaned a little now and then. His eyes turned constantly towards the 'Nazarene'—and he seemed to derive ease and satisfaction from merely looking in that direction. There was much renewed excitement and stir among the thronging people as they saw the second cross about to be set up, for they judged that but little time would now elapse before the crowning act of the appalling drama,—the crucifixion of Him whom they accused of blasphemy because 'He made Himself the Son of God.' And in the restless surging to and fro of the mob, Barabbas suddenly spied standing somewhat apart, a knot of women whose costly raiment, adorned with jewels, bespoke them of higher wealth and rank than ordinary,—and among them one dazzlingly fair face shone forth like a star amid flame, for the hair which clustered above it was of a red-gold lustre, and the mantle flung about it had the glowing tint of fire. One devouring eager look, and Barabbas, forgetting all fear, warning, or prophecy, fled like a madman towards that flashing danger-signal of a beauty that seemed to burn the very air encompassing it,—and with wild eyes, outstretched hands and breathless utterance he cried,—

'Judith!'

XIV

SHE whom he thus called upon turned towards him as he came with a haughty air of offence and inquiry,—and the marvellous loveliness of her as she fully confronted him, checked his impetuous haste and held him, as it had often done before, tongue-tied, bewildered and unmanned. Nothing more beautiful in the shape of woman could be imagined than she,—her fairness was of that rare and subtle type which in all ages has overwhelmed reason, blinded judgment, and played havoc with the passions of men. Well did she know her own surpassing charm,—and thoroughly did she estimate the value of her fatal power to lure and rouse and torture all whom she made the victims of her almost resistless attraction. She was Judith Iscariot,—only daughter of one of the strictest and most respected members of the Pharisaical sect in Jerusalem,—and by birth and breeding she should have been the most sanctimonious and reserved of maidens,—but in her case, nature had outstepped education. Nature, in a picturesque mood, had done wondrous things for her,—things that in the ordinary opinion of humankind, generally outweigh virtue and the cleanness of the soul in the sight of Heaven. To Nature therefore the blame was due, for having cast the red glow of a stormy sunset into the bronze-gold of her hair,—for having melted the blackness of night and the fire of stars together and set their mingled darkness and dazzle floating liquidly in her eyes,—for having bruised the crimson heart of the pomegranate-buds and made her lips the colour of the perfect flower,—and for having taken the delicate cream and pink of early almond blossoms and fixed this soft flushing of the Spring's life-blood in the colouring of her radiant face. Small cause for wonder was there in the fact that her beauty conquered all who came within its radius;—even her rigid father himself grew lax, weak and without authority as far as she was concerned, and blinded by the excess of his parental pride in her perfections, had gradually become the merest tool in her hands. How then could Barabbas, the criminal Barabbas, feel himself other than the most abject of slaves in such a dazzling presence! A beaten hound, a chidden child were firmer of resolution than he, when the chill yet lustrous glance he loved fell on him like a star-beam flashing from a frosty sky and set his strong nerves trembling.

'Judith!' he exclaimed again,—and then stopped, discouraged, for her large eyes, cold as the inner silence of the sea, surveyed him freezingly as though he were some insolently obtrusive stranger.

'Judith!' he faltered appealingly—'Surely thou dost know me,—me, Barabbas?'

A sudden light of comprehension swept away the proud annoyance of her look,—her red lips parted a little, showing the even small white teeth within,—then a glimmer of amusement illumined her features, wakening dimples at the curves of her mouth and lifting the delicately pencilled corners of her eyebrows,—then she broke into a soft peal of careless, vibrating laughter.

'Thou, Barabbas?' she said, and laughed once more,—'Thou? Nay, 'tis not possible! Barabbas was of late in prison, and of a truth he could not steal from thence such purple raiment and solemnly sedate expression as thou wearest! Thou canst not be Barabbas,—for scarce two hours agone I saw him standing before Pilate, unclad, and foul as wolves and leopards are!—yet verily he seemed a nobler man than thou!'

Again she gave vent to her silvery mocking mirth, and her eyes flung him a glittering challenge of disdain and scorn. He, however, had recovered partial control of his emotions, and met her taunting gaze steadfastly and with something of sadness,—his dark face had grown very pale,—and all the warmth and rapture had died out of his voice when he spoke again.

'I am Barabbas'—he repeated quietly—'And thou, Judith, dost know it. Have I not suffered for thy sake?—and wilt thou still mock at me?'

She glanced him up and down with an air of mingled derision and pity.

'I do not mock at thee, fool!—thou dreamest! How darest thou say thou hast suffered for my sake? I will have thee scourged for thy presumption! What has the daughter of Iscariot to do with thee, thou malefactor? Thou dost forget thy crimes too easily!'

'Judith!' he muttered, his pale features growing paler, and his hands clenching themselves in an involuntary movement of desperate despair,—'Bethink thee of thy words! Remember the old days, . . . have pity'——

She cut short his hesitating speech by an offended gesture, and turning to the women who stood near, exclaimed derisively,

'Lo, maidens, 'tis Barabbas! Remember ye him who was ever wont to pass by the well in our palm-tree nook in his goings and comings to and from the house of Shadeen?—how he would linger with us till

sunset, wasting his time in idle words and rumours
of the town, when of a truth he should have been
better employed in useful errandry. 'Tis the same
knave who knotted for me the silken hammock on
the fig-tree boughs in my father's garden,—and for
Aglaie, yonder simpering Greek girl of mine, he once
pulled down a flower that blossomed too high for
her to reach. 'Twas all the service he ever did for
us, methinks!—yet he hath become of a most
excellent pride in prison!—the unexpected freedom
given him by the people's vote hath puffed him out
with singular vanities! Would ye have known him,
maidens, clad thus in purple, and of so decorous a
demeanour? As I live, he would have adorned a
cross most fittingly!—'twere pity he were not nailed
beside the Nazarene!'

The women to whom she spoke laughed carelessly
to please her, — but one or two of them seemed
sorry for Barabbas, and glanced at him kindly and
with a certain pity. He meanwhile showed no anger
or impatience at the scoffing words of his beautiful
tormentor, but simply looked her straight in the eyes,
questioningly and sorrowfully. A deeper flush
coloured her fair cheeks,—she was evidently troubled
by the steadfastness of his gaze, — and, noting this
momentary embarrassment of hers, he seized his
opportunity and made a resolute step towards her,
catching her hand in his own.

'Is this thy welcome, Judith?' he said in a passionate whisper—'Hast thou no thought of what my
long long misery has been apart from thee? Deny it
as thou wilt, I sinned for thy sake and suffered for thy
sake!—and 'twas this thought and this alone that
made my suffering less hard to bear. Mock me.
reject me, thou canst not hinder me from loving
thee! Slay me, if it give thee pleasure, with the
jewelled dagger hanging at thy girdle, I shall die

happy at thy feet,—loving thee to the last, thou cruel virgin of my soul!'

His voice in its very whisper thrilled with the strange music that love can give to the roughest tones,—his black eyes burned with ardour,—and his lips trembled in their eloquent appeal. She heard,—and a slow smile smoothed away the disdain in her face; he had grasped her left hand in his and she did not withdraw it. But with her right she felt for the dagger he spoke of,—it was the merest toy weapon set in a jewelled sheath,—yet sharp and strong enough to kill. Moved by capricious impulse she suddenly drew forth the blade and pointed it at his breast. He did not flinch,—nor did he for a second remove his eyes from the adoring contemplation of her perfect loveliness. For a moment she remained thus,—the weapon uplifted,—the radiant smile playing round her mouth like a sunbeam playing round a flower,—then, laughing outright and joyously, she thrust back the dagger in its sheath.

'For this time I will let thee live'—she said with an imperial air of condescension—'The feast of death to-day hath sufficient material in the traitorous Nazarene and yonder rascal thieves. Only I pray thee loosen my wrist from thy rough grasp, else I must hate thee. Lo, thou hast bruised me, fool!—so rude a touch deserves no pardon!'

Her delicate dark brows contracted petulantly. Barabbas gazed remorsefully at the red dents his fingers had made on the velvet softness of her hand, adorned with a few great jewels glistening star-like,—but he said no word,—his heart was beating too painfully and quickly for speech. She, meanwhile, examined minutely the offending marks,—then suddenly raising her eyes with an indescribable witchery of glance and smile, she said,

'Gabrias would have kissed it!'

Had the ground opened beneath his feet,—had a lightning-bolt sped from heaven, Barabbas could not have been more amazed and appalled. Gabrias! The sleek, sanctimonious and false-tongued Pharisee whom he slew and for whose murder he had been cast into prison! She—Judith—spoke of him thus,—and now! With his brain in a whirl and a violent fury beginning to stir in his blood, he stared at her, his face livid, his eyes blazing.

'Gabrias!' he muttered thickly — 'What sayest thou?—Gabrias '——

But ere he could finish his incoherent sentence there came a sudden ugly forward rush of the mob, who, growing impatient of restriction, sought to break the line of the soldiery in order to see more clearly the preparations for the death of the 'Nazarene' which were now about to commence. There ensued a great noise and calling to order, and a motley scene of confusion, during which a company of imposingly attired personages advanced to the spot where Judith and her women stood, and took up their position there. Among them was the high-priest Caiaphas, whose severely intellectual countenance darkened with wrath as he caught sight of Barabbas.

'What doest thou here, dog?' he demanded, approaching and addressing him in a fierce whisper—'Did I not warn thee? Get thee hence! The law's release hath not made thee clean of sin,—thou shalt not mingle with the reputable and godly in the land. Get thee hence, I say, or I will make thee accursed in all men's sight,—yea, even as a leper is accursed!'

His tall form quivered,—and he raised his arm with a gesture of stern menace. Barabbas, pale to the lips, half breathless and giddy with the sickening sensations of doubt and horror which Judith had so unexpectedly raised in his soul, met his cold eyes unflinchingly.

'Thou insolent priest!' he said—'Threaten thy curses to those who fear them,—but I, Barabbas, defy thee! Wherefore should'st thou, liar and hypocrite, sun thyself in the smile of the maiden Iscariot, and I, her friend in olden days, be by thy mandate debarred her company? Verily there is a light beginning to dawn on my foolish and long-darkened brain,—verily I do perceive wherein my trust has been betrayed! I read thy thoughts, thou evil-minded and bloodthirsty Caiaphas! As in a vision vouchsafed in the silence of the night I see the measure of thy plotting! Look to thyself!—for 'tis not Judas, but *thou* who hast brought to this death the innocent Nazarene, — thou and thy tyrannous craft! Look to thyself,—for as God liveth there is a vengeance waiting for thee and thine!'

He spoke at random, hardly conscious of what he said, but carried away by a force and fervour not his own, which made him tremble. Caiaphas retreated, staring at him in dumb rage and amazement,—Judith listening, laughed.

'He hath turned prophet also!' she exclaimed mirthfully—'Let him be crucified!'

Her malicious and cruel suggestion fell on unheeding ears, for just then there was another rush and outcry from the mob, and another futile struggle with the soldiers. Barabbas was compelled to fight with the rest of the reckless crowd for a footing,—and, in the midst of the crush, a strong hand suddenly caught and plucked him as it were out of chaos. Melchior confronted him,—there was a solemn tender look in his eyes,—the ordinary cold composure of his features was softened by deep emotion.

'Thou poor rash sinner!' he said, but with great gentleness—'Thou hast had the first blow on thy credulous man's heart,—the first blight on thy erring man's passions! Stay thou now with me, and ache in silence; let the world and its ways sink out of thy sight and memory for a space,—and if thy soul doth crave for Love, come hither and behold it in all its great supernal glory, slain to appease the ravening hate of man!'

His voice, usually so calm, shook as though tears were threatening to overcome it—and Barabbas, troubled, oppressed and smarting with his own sense of wrong, yielded to his touch passively, moved by his words to a certain awe and self-surrender. Lifting his anguished eyes he looked fixedly at his companion,—

'Tell me the truth now if thou knowest it,' he said in hoarse accents that were almost inaudible—'She is false?—yet no! Do not speak! I could not bear it! Let me die rather than lose my faith!'

Melchior made no reply, but simply attended to the difficult business of pushing and pulling him through the crowd, till they managed at last to find an open spot almost immediately opposite the crosses of the two thieves, who by this time were gasping aloud in the agonies of heat and suffocation, their strained limbs visibly quivering. The men of death were all gathered closely round the tall white figure of the 'Nazarene,'—they were stripping Him of His garments. Meanwhile, Petronius the centurion stood by, watching the process and leaning meditatively on his drawn sword.

'Pilate is crazed!' said an officer, approaching him with a huge parchment scroll—'Lo, what he hath inscribed to be nailed above the cross of the prophet from Galilee!'

Petronius took the scroll and spreading it out, read it slowly and with labour, for he had little scholarship. Three times over were the same words written, in Greek, in Latin, and in Hebrew,—

'JESUS OF NAZARETH,
KING OF THE JEWS.'

'Where see ye any madness in our governor?' demanded Petronius,—'There is naught of such import in the superscription.'

'Nay, but there is,'—persisted the man who had brought it—'And so it was pointed out, for Caiaphas spake unto Pilate thus—" *Write not, King of the Jews, but that he said, I am King of the Jews!* " And Pilate, being but newly recovered from his well-nigh deadly swoon, was wroth with Caiaphas, and answered him in haste, saying—" *What I have written, I have written!* " And of a truth they parted ill friends.'

Petronius said no more,—but glanced at the inscription again, and then, advancing, gave it to one of the executioners. This man, grimy and savage-featured, surveyed it with an admiring leer, and flattening it out, began to nail it at once to the top of the great Cross which still lay on the ground where Simon of Cyrene had left it, waiting for its Divine occupant. With a few deft blows he soon fixed it firmly in position, and satisfied with its prominent appearance, he read it with the tardy pains of a child learning its first alphabet. Tracking out each letter with his blood-stained finger, he gradually unsolved for himself the mystic words that have since resounded through the whole civilised world, and muttered them beneath his breath with a mingling of dull wonder and scorn,—

'JESUS OF NAZARETH,
KING OF THE JEWS.'

XV

THE scene had now assumed a wonderful and terrible picturesqueness. The populace, finding that sudden rushes were of no avail to break the firm line of the Roman soldiery, remained wedged together in a sullen heated mass, watching the proceedings in morose silence. There were a few detached groups standing apart from the actual multitude, evidently by permission of the authorities, —one being composed of the poorly-clad women whom Barabbas had seen and spoken to on the way up the hill, and even at the distance he was he could see the golden gleam of the Magdalen's hair, though her face was buried in her hands. And,—for the distraction of his peace, — he could also see the supple form of Judith Iscariot, wrapped in her flame-coloured mantle, and looking like a tall poppy-flower blossoming in the sun,—the stately Caiaphas stood beside her, with other men of note and position in the city of Jerusalem,—one or two of the stranger Roman nobles had descended from their horses, and were eagerly bending towards her in courtly salutation. Barabbas gazed at her and grew sick at heart, —a horrible disillusion and disappointment crushed his spirit and filled him with a silent rage of pain, an intolerable agony of despair. All at once the ground rocked beneath his feet like a wave of the

9

sea,—he staggered and would have fallen had not
his friend Melchior held him up.

'What is it?' he muttered, but Melchior replied
not. He was looking at the soldiers, who had also
felt the sudden billowy movement of the earth on
which they stood, but who, trained to a wooden
impassiveness, only glanced at one another inquiringly for a second, and then resumed their stiff
attitude and immobility of expression. The ground
steadied itself as swiftly as it had trembled, and the
populace, in their intense excitement, had evidently
failed to note its momentary undulation.

Presently a loud roar of ferocious delight went up
from the mob,—the executioners had stripped the
Condemned of His garments, — and, pleased with
the texture and softness of their material, were now
casting lots for their possession. They disputed
loudly and angrily, the chief contention raging over
the question as to who should have the upper robe
or mantle, which was made of pure white wool, woven
smoothly throughout from top to hem without seam.
Throwing it from hand to hand, they examined the
fleecy fabric with covetous eagerness, making clamorous and conflicting assertions as to its actual
monetary value, much as the relatives of a dead
man squabble over the division of his poor earthly
property. And in the meantime, while they argued
hotly together and lost patience one with the other,
the immortal 'Nazarene' stood ungarmented, await-
ing their cruel pleasure. His grand Figure shone
white as polished alabaster in the brilliant sun,—an
inward luminance gleamed like fire through the
azure branches of His veins and the spotless purity
of His flesh ; His arms had been unbound, and with
an air of mingled relief and weariness He stretched
them forth as one conscious of pleasant freedom, and
the shadow of their whiteness fell on the dull brown

earth like a reflection of the Cross on which He was
so soon to perish. And when He allowed them to
drop again gently and languidly at His sides, that
shadow seemed yet to stay upon the ground, and
deepen and darken. No clouds were in the sky;
the sun was at full dazzle and splendour,—nevertheless that mysterious stain widened and spread slowly,
as though some sudden moisture beneath the soil
were gradually rising to an overflow. Barabbas
noticed it,—he saw too that Melchior observed the
same phenomenon, but neither of them spoke. For
the interest and horror of the Divine drama were now
culminating to their supremest point;—the casting
of lots for the garments of the Condemned was over,
—and each man was apparently satisfied with his
share of the spoil. The chief executioner, not without
a touch of pity in his rough face, approached the
'Nazarene,' and instead of using force as he had
been compelled to do in the case of the crucified
malefactors, bade Him, in a low tone, take His place
upon the Cross without offering useless resistance to
the law. The terrible mandate was obeyed instantly
and unhesitatingly. With perfect calmness and the
serene ease of one who, being tired, is glad to rest,
the Ruler of the Worlds laid Himself down within
the waiting arms of Death. As peacefully as a weary
traveller might stretch himself upon a couch of
softest luxury, so did the Conqueror of Time stretch
out His glorious limbs upon the knotty wooden
beams of torture, with sublime readiness and unconquerable patience. Had He spoken at that thrilling
moment, He might have said—'Even so, O children
of My Father, lay yourselves down upon the rack of
the world's misprisal and contempt! If ye would
win a force divine, stretch out your limbs in readiness
to be pierced by the nails that shall be driven into
them by friends and foes! Wear ye the crown of

thorns till the blood starts from your aching brows,
—be stripped bare to the malicious gaze of sensuality
and sin! Let them think that they have tortured
you, slain you, buried you,—hidden you out of sight
and out of mind! Then arise, O ye children of My
Father,—arise on the wings of the morning, full-filled
with power!—power living, everlasting and triumphant!—for ye shall see the world at your feet and all
heaven opened above you; the circling universe
shall ring with the music of your names and the
story of your faithfulness, and sphere upon sphere
of angels shall rejoice with you in glory! For
behold, from this day henceforth, I and those whom
I call Mine shall alter Death to Life, and Life to
Immortality!'

But no words such as these were uttered: the
Divine lips were fast closed, and mute as heaven
itself. But from the watching crowd there went up
a faint murmur of irrepressible admiration for the
tranquil heroism with which the young 'Prophet of
Galilee' accepted His fate, as well as for the singularly
sculptural beauty and resignation of His attitude.
The executioners approached Him with a certain awe
and timorousness.

'One would think him made of marble,' muttered
one, pausing, hammer in hand.

'Marble doth not bleed, thou fool!' said his fellow,
harshly, yet with an angry consciousness that he too
felt a tremor of fear and repugnance at the work
about to be done.

The other men were silent.

The select and richly-attired company of those
influential or wealthy persons who were standing
immediately round the high-priest Caiaphas, now
advanced a little,—and Judith Iscariot, radiant as a
sun-flash embodied in woman's shape, leaned forward
eagerly with the pleased smile of a child who is

promised some rare and mirthful gala show. Her
brilliant dark eyes roved indifferently and coldly over
the outstretched Form upon the Cross,—her jewelled
vest rose and fell lightly with the gradual excited
quickening of her breath. She looked,—but she did
not speak,—she seemed to gloat silently upon the
prospect of the blood-shedding and torture soon to
ensue. And from the opposite side to that on which
she stood, there suddenly emerged another woman,
young and fair as she, though worn with weeping,—a
woman whose wild white face was like that of some
beautiful sad angel in torment. Throwing up her
hands in a dumb frenzy of protest and appeal, she
ran unsteadily forward a few steps, then stopped and
fell on her knees, covering her anguished features in
the loosened shower of her golden hair with a low
shuddering cry. None out of the assembled throng
went to offer her comfort or assistance,—people peered
curiously at her over each other's shoulders, exchanging a few side-looks of derision and contempt,—but
not a soul approached her save one,—one of her own
sex, who was closely veiled, and who, advancing with
a light yet queenly tread, knelt down beside her, and
passing one arm around her, laid her forlorn fair head
against her breast and so quietly remained. Judith
Iscariot, lifting her ringed hand to her eyes to shade
them from the sun's glare, gazed at that kneeling
group of two with haughty disgust and scorn.

'Lo, the sinners with whom this madman of Galilee
consorted!' she exclaimed to Caiaphas—'Yonder
yellow-haired vileness is the Magdalen,—she should
be stoned from hence!'

'Yea verily she should be stoned from any place
where thou dost pass, fair Judith!' said Caiaphas
deferentially, yet with the shadow of a sneer on his
thin pale lips—'Evil company should be far distant
from thee, and for this cause did I just lately chase

the insolent Barabbas from thy presence. But concerning this woman Magdalen, yonder matron who doth thus embrace her, cannot immediately be spoken with or banished from this place, for 'tis the Mother of the Galilean. She hath come hither to behold him die. Were we to visit her with harshness, or deny and deprive her of her privilege to watch this death and make fitting lament thereon, she, and the women she elects as friends,—the populace would raise an outcry against us, and most justly. For law must ever go hand in hand with mercy. Have patience then, good Judith, till the end,—though of a truth I crave to know why thou hast ventured hither if thou art offended at the sight of sinners? In such a multitude as this thou canst not hope to find all virtuous!'

Something sarcastic in the tone of his voice called up a sudden red flush on Judith's cheeks,—but her eyes grew cold and hard as a midnight frost.

'I,—like the mother of the Nazarene, have come to see him die!' she said with a cruel smile,—'She will watch his torture with tears doubtless,—but I, with laughter! His agony will be my joy! For I hate him,—I hate him! He hath cast dissension in our house,—he hath turned my brother's heart from mine, and made of him a slave to his fanatic doctrine. For look you, what happier man was there than Judas, beloved of my father, and dear to me beyond all earthly countings, till in an evil hour he was ensnared from home by idle rumours of the power of this boastful prophet of Galilee? What needed we of any new religion,—we who served the God of Abraham, of Isaac and of Jacob, and who had followed the teachings of the law from our youth up till now? Is it not a shame to speak it, a shame to think it, that Judas, well-born and comely of countenance, my father's only son and heir, hath actually wandered in vagabondage across the land with this carpenter's son of Nazareth, dwelling among common fisher-folk, visiting the unclean and leprous poor, eating the husks of want instead of the bread of plenty,—deserting his home, forsaking me, his sister, and disobeying his father's command, all for the sake of this impostor who hath at last been found guilty of blasphemy and condemned to his long-deserved death. Judge how I hate the traitor! Ay, with a hate surpassing any love! I rose betimes this morning to be the witness of his trial,—when the mob were inclined to pity, I whispered words that roused them anew to wrath,—'twas I who gave the keynote "Crucify him!"—didst thou not mark how readily the chorus answered?'

Caiaphas looked down a trifle uneasily, then up again.

'Yea, I did mark it,'—he said softly—'And that I heard and knew thy voice is no matter for surprise, seeing that it was a strain of music amid much discord. And freely do I sympathise with thy sorrow concerning Judas,—thy brother was ever thy dear and favourite companion, and this Galilean miracle-monger hath brought him naught save ruin. He hath fled the city, they say. Knowest thou whither?'

A vague anxiety shadowed the beautiful face he watched so narrowly.

'Nay, not I,' she answered, and her accents trembled, 'Last night he came to me, — 'twas after he had led the guards to the garden of Gethsemane where they captured the Nazarene,—and like a madman, he called down curses upon himself and me. He was distraught, — I knew him not, — he raged and swore. I strove to calm him,—he thrust me from him,—I called him by every endearing name, but he was as one deaf to affection or to reason ;—I bade him think of our dead mother, how she loved him,—

he shrieked at me as though I had plunged a dagger in his heart. Our father besought him with tears to remember all the claims of family and duty, but still he raved and beat his breast, crying aloud "I have sinned! I have sinned! The weight of heaven and earth crushes my soul—the innocent blood is red upon my hands! I have sinned! I have sinned!" Then with a sudden violence he flung us from him, and rushed furiously from our dwelling out into the night. I followed him fast, hoping to stay him ere he could have left our garden,—but his was a crazed speed,—I found him not. The moon was shining and the air was still,—but he had gone,—and since then I have not seen him.'

Two tears quivered on her silky lashes and fell among the jewels at her breast. A gathering trouble darkened the high-priest's countenance.

''Tis strange,' he muttered—''Tis very strange! He hath fulfilled a duty to the laws of his people, and now, when all is done, he should rejoice and not lament. Nevertheless, be sure his humour is but temporarily distracted, though I recognise the actual cause thou hast for sisterly misgiving. Yet take thou comfort in believing all is well,—and let thy thirst of vengeance now be satisfied, for see, they do begin to nail the malefactor down.'

He spoke thus, partly to divert Judith's thoughts from anxiety on her brother's account, and partly because just then he saw Petronius the centurion give the fatal signal. Petronius had in truth purposely delayed this act till the last possible moment, and now, when he was finally compelled to lift his gauntleted hand in sign that the terrible work of torture should commence, he caught, for the further inward distress and remorse of his mind, a sudden look from the patient, upturned, Divine eyes. Such eyes!—shining like twin stars beneath the grand

supernal brows, round which the rose-thorns pressed
their piercing circlet,—eyes alit with some supreme
inscrutable secret spell that had the power to shake
the spirit of the strongest man. Petronius could not
bear those eyes,—their lustrous purity and courage
were too much for his composure,—and trembling
from head to foot with an almost womanish nervousness, he turned abruptly away. The murmuring
noise of the vast expectant multitude died off
gradually like the retreating surge of a distant sea,
—a profound silence reigned,—and the hot move-
lessness of the air grew more and more weightily
intensified. The executioners having received their
commands, and overcoming their momentary hesitation, gathered in a rough half-nude group around the
Cross whereon lay unresistingly the Wonder of the
Ages, and knelt to their hideous task, their muscular
brown arms, grimy with dust and stained already
with splashes of blood from the crucifying of the two
thieves, contrasting strangely with the dazzling whiteness of the Figure before them. They paused a
moment, holding the huge long-pointed nails aloft ;
. . . would this Man of Nazareth struggle ?—would
it be needful to rope His limbs to the wooden beams
as they had done to the other two condemned?
With the fierce scrutiny of those accustomed to
signs of rebellion in the tortured, they studied their
passive Captive, . . . not a quiver stirred the firmly
composed limbs, . . . not a shade of anxiety or
emotion troubled the fair face, . . . while the eyes,
rolled up to the blinding splendour of the sky, were
gravely thoughtful and full of peace. No bonds
were needed here ;—the Galilean was of marvellously
heroic mould,—and every hardened torturer around
Him, silently in his heart of hearts recognised and
respected the fact. Without further parley they
commenced their work, . . . and the startled earth,

affrighted, groaned aloud in cavernous echoes as the cruel hammers heavily rose and fell, clanging out the tocsin of a God's death and a world's redemption. And at the self-same moment, up to the far star-girdled Throne of the Eternal, sped the tender low-breathed supplication of the dying Well-Beloved,

'*Father, forgive them, for they know not what they do!*'

XVI

A DREADFUL hush of horror reigned. The stirless heat of the atmosphere felt as heavy to the senses as an overhanging solid mass of burning iron. The forces of Nature seemed paralysed, as though some sudden shock had been dealt at the core of life, or as though the rolling world had paused, palpitating for breath in its pacing round the sun. Not a sound broke the oppressive stillness save the dull reverberation of the hammers at their deadly business,—for the vast human multitude stood dumb, sullenly watching the working of their will, yet moved by a vague remorse and an equally vague terror. Not one among them would have dared to suggest at this late hour any mercy for the Victim ; they, the people, had desired this thing, and their desire was being accomplished. All being carried out as they wished, they could not well complain, nor could they recall their own decision. But there was something unnatural and ghastly in the scene,—a chill sense of nameless desolation began to creep upon the air,—and while each man and woman present strained both body and sight to see the fine fair limbs of the 'Galilean' pierced through and fastened to the torture-tree, they were all conscious of fear ; fear of what or of whom, none could have truly told,—nevertheless fear dominated and daunted the spirits of every one. And it was this unconfessed

inexplicable alarm that kept them silent,—so that
not even a whispered 'Alas!' escaped from any pitying voice when the beauteously arched, delicate feet
of the Divine Sufferer were roughly seized, crossed
over and held in position by one executioner, while
another placed the nail in the nerve-centres of the
tender flesh.   A third callous ruffian dealt the
measured blows which drove in the thick, sharp iron
prong with a slow force calculated to double and
treble the exquisite agony of lingering martyrdom,—
and swiftly the hurt veins rebelled against their wrong
in bursting jets of innocent blood.   The crimson stain
welled up and made a piteous rose on the torn skin's
whiteness, but He who was thus wounded, stirred not
at all, nor uttered a cry.   His human flesh mutely
complained of human injustice in those reproachful
red life-drops ; but the indomitable Spirit that dwelt
within that flesh made light of merely mortal torment,
and was already seizing Death in the grasp of victory.
And the feet that had borne their Owner into dreary,
forsaken ways where the poor and the outcast dwell
in sorrow,—that had lightly paused among the 'lilies
of the field' while such sweet words were spoken as
made these simple flowers talismans of grace for ever,
—that had moved softly and tenderly through the
fields of corn and gardens of olive, and villages and
towns alike, carrying consolation to the sad, hope to
the lost, strength to the weak,—now throbbed and
ached and bled in anguish for man's ingratitude,
man's forgetfulness, man's abhorrence of the truth, and
suicidal doubt of God.   How easy it is to hate! . . .
how difficult to love, as Love demands! . . . Many
assembled there on Calvary that never-to-be-forgotten
day, had listened to the fearless and holy teaching of
Him whose torment they now coldly watched, when
in the fields, on the hills, or by the reverent sea, He
had taught them the startling new lesson that '*God*

is a Spirit; and they that worship Him must worship Him in Spirit and in Truth.' No savage ' Jehovah-Jireh,' craving for murder and thirsting for vengeance was the supreme Creator, but a Father,—a loving Father, of whom this youthful Prophet with the heaven-lit eyes had said—' *Fear not, little flock!—it is your Father's good pleasure to give you the Kingdom!'* He,—this Man upon the Cross,—had on one memorable morning, gathered about Him a crowd of the fallen and sick and poor and disconsolate, and with a tender smile as radiant as the summer sunshine, had said—' *Come unto Me, all ye that are weary and heavy-laden, and I will give you rest!'* . . . And they had come,—those heart-broken and agonised of the earth, —they had knelt and wept at His feet,—they had kissed His garments and the ground on which He trod,—they had placed their little children in His arms, and had told Him all their sorrows. And He had laid His hands upon them in blessing,—those fair white hands of mystic power and healing, which dispensed naught but good,—but which now, palms outward, were fastened to the death-rack, . . . a symbolic token of the world's reward to all its noblest souls! . . . The blood oozed slowly and reluctantly from those hands, but, as was usual in the dolours of crucifixion, gathered itself painfully in the outstretched arms,—swelling the veins and knotting the muscles,— though as yet the terrible ordeal had not reached its height, for the Cross had still to be lifted. For that tremendous uplifting the whole universe waited,—for that, the very heavens were at pause and the angels stricken dumb!

The executioners having finished the first part of their task, now beckoned the centurion to step forward and see for himself that the nails in the Victim's body were secure, so that he might be able to certify to the authorities that the law had been adequately

fulfilled. With a sickening heart, Petronius obeyed
the signal. But his sight was dazzled,—his brain
reeled,—there was a choking dryness in his throat,
and he could not speak a word. Yet this time the
Man of Sorrows never looked at him,—the Divine
orbs of light and genius were turned to heaven alone,
as though absorbing the fiery glory of the sun. And,
—was it fancy, or some delusion of his own sense of
vision that suddenly gave him the impression of an
approaching darkness in the sky?—as if indeed the
sun were losing lustre? He rubbed his eyes and
gazed dubiously about,—surely a mysterious shadow
as of outspread wings rested on the landscape! Were
the people,—were the soldiers conscious of this?
Apparently not. Their attention was concentrated
on the work of death,—and there was a general eager
forward movement of the crowd to see the Cross set
up. As Petronius, dazed and bewildered, stepped
back, the executioners, six in all, men of sinewy and
powerful build, bent themselves energetically to the
completion of their work, . . . in vain! Their united
forces could not raise the world's Eternal Symbol one
inch from the ground! They struggled and dragged
at it, the sweat pouring from their brows,—but its
priceless freight of Godhead, Majesty and Love
resisted all their efforts.

'I said he was a Hercules,' growled the chief man,
wringing the perspiration from his rough beard,—
'The Cross itself is of uncommon size, and he upon
it hath the mould of heroes. What, Simon! Simon
of Cyrene! Art thou there?'

The crowd moved and murmured, and made way,—
and Simon, thus apostrophised, came slowly to the front.

'What need ye more of me?' he demanded sullenly,
'Think ye I will aid in murder?'

'Thou Libyan ass!' retorted the executioner—'Who
talks of murder? This is the law's work, not ours.

Lend us thy brawny arms a minute's space,—thou art made in a giant's shape, and should'st have a giant's force withal. An' thou wilt not '—he added in a lower tone—'we must use greater roughness.'

Simon hesitated,—then, as if inwardly compelled, advanced submissively to the foot of the Cross. His eyes were cast down, and he bit his lips to hide their nervous trembling.

' Lift ye all together the upper beams '—he said softly to the executioners, hushing his voice like one who speaks in rapture or in reverence—' I will support the end.'

They stared amazedly,—he was voluntarily choosing the greater weight which would inevitably be his to bear directly the Cross was raised. But they offered no opposition. Stronger than any lion he was known to be,—let him test his strength now, for here was his opportunity! So they thought as they went in the direction he indicated,—three men to the right and three to the left. The excitement of the people was now intense,—so passionately absorbed indeed had it become, that none seemed to be aware of a singular circumstance that with each moment grew more pronounced and evident,—this was the solemn spreading of a semi-darkness which, like advancing twilight, began gradually to blot out all the brilliant blue of the afternoon skies. It came on stealthily and almost imperceptibly,—but the crowd saw nothing as yet, . . . nothing but the huge bronzed figure of Simon stooping to lift the Crucified. Tenderly, and with a strange air of humiliation, the rough-featured black-browed Cyrenian laid hands upon the Cross once more,—the Cross he had so lightly borne to Calvary, —and grasping it firmly, drew it up ; up by slow and sure degrees, till the pierced and bleeding feet of the Christ came close against his straining breast, . . . inch by inch, with panting breath and an ardent force

that was more like love than cruelty, he lifted it
higher and higher from the ground, the executioners
holding and guiding the transverse beams upward till
these were beyond their reach,—and Simon alone,
with wildly beating heart and muscles stretched nigh
to breaking, supported for one lightning instant the
world's Redeemer in his arms! He staggered and
groaned,—the blood rushed to his face and the veins
in his forehead swelled, . . . but he held his ground
for that one terrific moment, . . . then, . . . a dozen
men rushed excitedly to his assistance, and with their
aid, the great Cross, with the greatest Love transfixed
upon it, was thrust into the deep socket dug for its
reception on the summit of the hill. It fell in with a
thudding reverberation as though its end had struck
the very centre of the earth,—and trembling to and
fro for a few seconds like a tree shaken by a storm-
wind, was soon perfectly still, fixed steadily upright
between the two already crucified thieves, who though
dying fast, were not yet dead. Salvation's Symbol
stood declared ;—and Simon of Cyrene, having done
all he was needed to do, retreated slowly with
faltering steps and swimming brain, conscious only of
one thing,—that the blood of the Victim had stained
his breast, and that the stain seemed to burn his flesh
like fire. He folded his garment over it to hide it,
as though it were a magic talisman which must for
safety's sake be well concealed ; it gave him pain as
much as if he had himself been wounded, . . . and
yet . . . it was a pang that thrilled and warmed his
soul ! He saw nothing,—the earth appeared to eddy
round him like a wave,—but he stumbled on blindly,
heedless of whither he went, and forcing his way
through the crowd that gaped at him in wonderment,
the while he muttered from time to time under his
breath the words of the inscription above the head of
the Divine Martyr,

'JESUS OF NAZARETH, KING OF THE JEWS!'
And now, the Cross being openly set up, and the
slow devourings of death having commenced upon
the sinless Sacrifice, a long wild shout of savage
exultation arose from the multitude,—a shout that
rang in harsh hoarse echoes over the hill, through the
low-lying gardens beyond, and away as it seemed to
the summit of Mount Moriah, where over Solomon's
glistening Temple, a cloud as of dust or smoke, hung
like a warning of storm and fire. And the barbaric
human clamour as it mutteringly died away, was
suddenly taken up and all unexpectedly answered by
a grander uproar,—a deep, threatening boom of far-
off thunder. In circling tones and semi-tones of
wrath it volleyed through the skies,—and, startled by
the sound, the people, roused for the first time from
their morbid engrossment in the work of cruel torture
and blood-shedding, looked up and saw that the
heavens were growing dark and that the sun was
nearly covered by an inky black cloud, from which
its rim peered feebly like a glimmering half-moon.
Against the background of that obscured sun and
sable cloud, the Cross stood clear, the outstretched
Figure on it, looking, in that livid murkiness, whiter
than a shape of snow,—and the multitude silenced
anew by some strange terror, watched and listened,—
chained in their thousands to the one spot by mingled
fear and fascination. Afraid to move they knew not
why, and waiting for they knew not what, they gazed
all with one accord at the huge Cross and its em-
blazoned Glory, suspended between them and the
pallidly vanishing sun, — and murmured to one
another vaguely between-whiles of storm and rain,—
there would be a heavy shower, they said,—good for
the land and cooling to the air. But they spoke at
random,—their thoughts were not with their words,
and their minds were ill at ease. For the omnipresent

10

spirit of fear, like a chill wind, breathed upon their nerves, lifting the very hair of their flesh, and causing their limbs to tremble. And ever the skies darkened; and ever, with scarce a moment's pause, the gathering thunders rolled.

XVII

DEEPER and deeper drooped the dull grey gloom, like a curtain falling slowly and impenetrably over all things. The strange stillness of the multitude, . . . the heavy breathlessness of the air, . . . and the appalling effect of the three crosses with the tortured figures on them, standing out against the lurid storm-light, were sufficient to inspire a sense of awe and dread in the mind of the most hardened and callous beholder. The booming thunder swinging to and fro in the clouds resembled the sepulchral sound of an iron-tongued funeral bell, half muffled, half clamant, . . . and presently the landscape took upon itself a spectral look, as of being a dream scene unsubstantially formed of flitting vapour. The circling line of the Roman soldiery appeared to lessen to the merest thread of gleaming steel,—the serried ranks of the populace merged into a confused, apparently intangible blur, —and in the singular flitting and wavering of light and shade, it happened that at last only the one central Cross became pre-eminently visible. Outlined with impressive distinctness, it suddenly seemed to assume gigantic proportions, stretching interminably as it were to east and west, up to heaven and down to earth, while behind the head of the Divine Crucified a golden peak of the veiled sun shone like the suggestion of a new world bursting into being.

One instant this weird glamour lasted, . . . and then
a blue blaze of lightning cut up the sky into shreds
and bars, followed instantaneously by a terrific clap
of thunder. Men grew pale, . . . women screamed ;
even the soldiers lost their wonted composure,
and looked at each other in doubting and superstitious dread. For they had their gods, these rough
untutored men, — they believed in the angers of
Jupiter,—and if the fierce god's chariot-wheels were
rattling through the far empyrean thus furiously,
surely his wrath would soon exceed all bounds !
And could it be because the 'Nazarene' was crucified? Their darkening countenances, full of apprehension, expressed their thoughts, and the high-priest
Caiaphas, quick to detect the least hint of a change
in the popular sentiment, became uneasy. This
storm commencing at the very moment of the
crucifixion, might so impress and terrify the ignorant
rabble, that they might imagine the death of the
Galilean Prophet was being visited on them by the
powers of heaven, — and possibly might insist on
having Him taken down from the Cross after all.
He imparted his politic fears to Judith Iscariot in a
whisper,—she too had grown pale at the loud threat
of the gathering storm, and was not without a nervous
sense of alarm,—but she was prouder than most of
her sex, and scorned to outwardly show any misgiving, whatever she inwardly felt. And while
Caiaphas yet murmured discreetly in her ear, a
sudden glow as of fire was flung upon Calvary,—the
sable mask of cloud slid from the sun,—and wide
rays of light, tinged with a singular redness like that
of an out-breaking volcano, blazed forth brilliantly
over the hill. Cheered by the splendour, the people
threw off, in part, their vague terrors,—their faces
brightened,—and Caiaphas profiting by his opportunity, stepped out in full view of the crowd, and

advanced majestically towards the Cross from which
the 'King of the Jews' looked down upon him.
Lifting his hand to shade his eyes from the crimson
glare which haloed with a burning ring the outstretched patient Figure, he exclaimed in clear loud
accents—'*Thou that destroyest the temple and buildest
it in three days, save thyself and come down from the
cross!*'

The multitude heard, and roared applause and
laughter. Even the grim soldiers smiled — for,
thought they, if the Man of Galilee were a true
miracle-worker, He could never have a better opportunity for displaying His powers than now. Caiaphas
smiled proudly,—he had struck the right note, and
had distracted the attention of the mob from their
personal alarms of the storm, to renewed interest in
the cruelty that was being enacted. Still standing
before the Cross, he studied with placid pitilessness
every outline of the perfect Human Shape in which
Divine Glory was concealed,—and watched with the
scientific interest of a merciless torturer the gradual
welling up and slow dropping of blood from the
wounded hands and feet, — the pained, patient
struggling of the quickened breath,—the pale parted
lips,—the wearily-drooping, half-closed eyes. Annas,
sleek and sly, with an air of hypocritical forbearance
and compassion, approached also, and looked up at
the same piteous spectacle. Then, rubbing his hands
gently together, he said softly, yet distinctly—

'*He saved others,—himself he cannot save! If he
be the King of Israel, let him now come down from the
cross, and we will believe him!*'

The dying thief Hanan, now in the last stage of
his agony, caught these words, and twisting himself
fiercely forward, muttered groans and hideous curses.
His neck swelled,—his tongue protruded,—and the
frightful effort he made to speak distorted his whole

repulsive countenance, while his body, agitated by muscular twitchings, violently shook the cross on which he was roped and nailed.

'Thou blasphemer!' he gasped at last, rolling his fierce eyes round, and fixing them on the fair thorn-crowned Head that with every moment drooped lower and lower,—'Well it is that thou should'st die, . . . yet willingly would I have seen Barabbas nailed where thou art! Nevertheless thou art a false and evil prophet,—*if thou be the Christ, save thyself and us!*'

The other crucified malefactor, close upon his end, and panting out his life in broken breaths of anguish, suddenly writhed himself upward against his cross, and forced himself to lift his heavy head.

'Hanan!' he muttered hoarsely, '*Dost thou not fear God? . . . Seeing thou art in the same condemnation?*' He broke off, struggling against the suffocation in his throat, then continued to murmur incoherently,—'*And we indeed justly, . . . for we receive the due reward of our deeds, . . . but this Man hath done nothing amiss.*'

Again he stopped. All at once a great wonder, rapture and expectation flashed into his livid face and lightened his glazing eyes. He uttered a loud cry, turning himself with all his strength towards the silent Christ.

'*Lord . . . Lord*' . . . he stammered feebly, '*Remember me . . . when . . . Thou comest . . . into . . . Thy Kingdom!*'

Slowly,—with aching difficulty, but with unconquerably tender patience, the Divine Head was gently raised,—the lustrous suffering eyes bent their everlasting love upon him,—and a low voice, hushed and sad, yet ever musical, responded,—

'*Verily I say unto thee,—This day shalt thou be with Me in Paradise!*'

And as the wondrous promise reached his ears, the tortured and repenting sinner smiled,—the anguish passed away from his features, leaving them smooth and calm,—and with one faint groan his head fell heavily forward on his chest, . . . his limbs ceased trembling, . . . he was dead. Hanan still lingered in the throes of reluctant dissolution,—his awful struggle having become a mere savage revolt of material nature, from which the strongest turned away their eyes, shuddering.

Another reverberating crash of thunder bellowed through the sky; this time the earth rocked in answer, and the people were seized anew with dread. Caiaphas, self-possessed and full of dignity, still held his ground, ready to face and quell any fresh super-stitious alarms, inviting by his very attitude as it were, all the world to bear witness to the justice of the law's condemnation. Pointing upward to the Cross, he cried aloud,—

'*He trusted in God! Let Him deliver him now if He will have him; for he said, I am the Son of God!*'

But the multitude were not so ready to respond as before,—they were troubled by forebodings and fears which they could not explain,—and their eyes were not so much fixed on the crucified 'Nazarene' as on the sun behind Him,—the sun which now looked like a strange new planet coloured a blackish red. They were also noting the conduct of a small brown bird, which had settled on the Cross, and was now desper-ately plucking with its tiny beak at the crown of thorns that circled the bleeding brows of the 'King.' A soldier threw a stone at it,—it flew away, but swiftly returned to resume its singular, self-appointed task. Again and again it was driven off,—and again and again it came back fearlessly, fluttering round the shining Head of the Christ, and striving, as it

seemed, to tear off the thorny coronal. Its feeble
but heroic efforts were rewarded by one upward
glance from the loving eyes of the Beloved,—and
then the innocent feathered creature, mournfully
chirping, flew away for the last time, its downy
breast torn and stained with blood, but otherwise
uninjured.

This trifling incident gave a singular emotion of
pleasure to the crowd. They found something
touching and dramatic in it,—and the bird's wound
of love elicited far more sympathy than the speechless
and supernal sorrows of the Man Divine. Compassion and interest for birds and animals and creeping
things of the wood and field often distinguish the
otherwise selfish and cold-hearted ; and many a man
has been known to love a dog when in human
relationships he would willingly slander his friend or
slay his brother.

Again a shaft of lightning flashed through the
heavens, followed by a lion-like hungry roar of
thunder, and many of the people began to move to
and fro troublously, and turn their eyes from the hill
city-wards in alarm and anxiety. All at once in the
full red glare of the volcanic sun Judith Iscariot ran
forward excitedly, her flame-coloured mantle falling
away from her tawny gold tresses, her lips parted in
a smile, her glowing exquisite face upturned, and the
jewels on her attire gleaming with lurid sparks like
the changing hues of a serpent's throat. Lifting up
her round white arm, ablaze with gems from wrist
to shoulder, she pointed derisively at the dying
Christ and laughed,— then making an arch of her
two hands above her mouth so that her voice
might carry to its farthest, she cried aloud to Him
mockingly,—

'*If thou be the Son of God, come down from the
Cross!*'

The words rang out with vibrating distinctness, clear as a bell, and Barabbas, though he was at some distance off, heard them, and saw that it was Judith who spoke. Moved to an unspeakable horror and dismay, he rushed towards her, scarcely knowing what he did, but full of the idea that he must stop her cruel, unwomanly gibing,—must drag her away, by sheer force if necessary, from the position she had taken up below the Cross. Her beautiful figure standing there looked strange and devilish,—her red mantle caught blood-like gleams from the red sun,—above her the tortured limbs of the God-Man shone marble white and almost luminous, while His dreamful face drooped downward, now had upon it a stern shadow like the solemn unspoken pronouncement of an eternal reproach and doom. And the radiant mirthful malice of the woman's eyes flashed up at that austerely sublime countenance in light scorn and ridicule, as with shriller yet still silver-sounding utterance she cried again,—

'Hearest thou me, thou boaster and blasphemer? *If thou be the Son of God, come down from the Cross!*'

As the wicked taunt left her lips for the second time, a twisted and broken flash of lightning descended from heaven like the flaming portion of a destroyed planet, and striking straight across the scarlet ball of the sun, seemed literally to set the Cross on fire. Blazing from end to end of its transverse beams in a flare of blue and amber, it poured lurid reflections on all sides, illumining with dreadful distinctness the pallid shape of the Man of Sorrows for one ghastly instant, and then vanished, chased into retreat by such a deafening clatter and clash of thunder as seemed to split a thousand rolling worlds in heaven. At the same moment the earth heaved up, and appeared to stagger like a ship in a wild sea, ... and with a sudden downward swoop as of some colossal eagle, dense darkness fell,—impenetrable, sooty darkness, that in one breath of time blotted out the face of nature and made of the summer-flowering land a blind black chaos.

XVIII

SHRIEKS and groans,—confusion and clamour,—
wild shouts for help,—wilder cries for light,—
and the bewildering, maddening knowledge that
numbers of reckless terrified human beings were
rushing hither and thither, unseeingly and distractedly,
—these were the first results of that abrupt descent
of black night in bright day. 'Light! Give us
light, O God!' wailed a woman's voice, piercing
through the dismal dark; and the frantic appeal,
'Light! light!' was re-echoed a thousand times by
the miserable, desperate, wholly panic-stricken crowd.
To and fro wandered straggling swarms of men and
women, touching each other, grasping each other,
but unable to discern the faintest outline of each
other's forms or features. Some sought to grope
their way down the hill, back to the city,—some
wrestled furiously with opposing groups of persons in
their path,—others, more timorous, stayed where they
were, weeping, shrieking, striking their breasts and
repeating monotonously, 'Light,—light! O God of
our fathers, give us light!'

But no answer to their supplications came from the
sable pall that solemnly loomed above them, for now
not even the lightning threw a chance spear across
the clouds, though with incessant, unappeased ferocity
the thunder roared, or rolling to a distance muttered

and snarled. A soldier of more self-possession and
sense than his fellows managed after a little while to
strike a light from flint and steel, and as soon as the
red spark shone, a hundred hands held out to him
twigs and branches that they might be set on fire and
so create a blazing luminance within the heavy gloom.
But scarcely had a branch or two been kindled, when
such a shriek went up from those on the edge of the
crowd as froze the blood to hear.

'The faces of the dead!' they cried—'The dead
are there,—there, in the darkness! Shut them out!
Shut them out! They are all dead men!'

This mad outcry was followed by the screams of
women, mingled with hysterical bursts of laughter
and weeping, many persons flinging themselves face
forward on the ground in veritable agonies of terror,
—and the soldier who had struck the light dropped
his implements, paralysed and aghast. The kindled
branches fell and sputtered out,—and again the unnatural midnight reigned, supreme, impermeable.
There was no order left; the soldiery were scattered;
the mob were separated into lost and wandering
sections; and 'Light! light!' was the universal
moan. Truly, in that sepulchral blackness, they were
'the lost sheep of the house of Israel,' ignorantly and
foolishly clamouring for 'light!' when the one and
only Light of the World was passing through the
'Valley of the Shadow,' and all Nature in the great
name of God, was bound to go with Him! The
atmosphere lost colour, — the clouds thundered,—
earth trembled,—the voices of birds and animals were
mute,—the trees had ceased to whisper their leafy
loves and confidences,—the streams stopped in their
silver-sounding flow,—the sun covered its burning
face,—the winds paused on their swift wings,—and
only Man asserted, with puny groans and tears, his
personal cowardice and cruelty in the presence of the

Eternal. But at this awful moment the powers of heaven were deaf to his complaining, and his craven cries for help were vain. Our shuddering planet, stricken with vast awe and wonder to its very centre, felt with its suffering Redeemer the pangs of dissolution, and voluntarily veiled itself in the deep shadow of death,—a shadow that was soon to be lifted and gloriously transformed into light and life immortal !

The heavy moments throbbed away,—moments that seemed long as hours,—and no little gleaming rift broke the settled and deepening blackness over Calvary. Many of the people, giving way to despair, cast themselves down in the dust and wept like querulous children, — others huddled themselves together in seated groups, stunned by fright into silence, — a few howled and swore continuously,— and all the conflicting noises merging together, suggested the wailing of lost beings in spiritual torment. All at once the strong voice of the high-priest Caiaphas, hoarse with fear, struck through the gloom.

' People of Jerusalem !' he cried—' Kneel and pray ! Fall down before the God of Abraham, of Isaac and of Jacob, and entreat Him that this visitation of storm and earthquake be removed from us ! Jehovah hath never deserted His children, nor will He desert them now, though it hath pleased Him to afflict us with the thunders of His wrath ! Be not afraid, O ye chosen people of the Lord, but call upon Him with heart and voice to deliver us from this darkness ! For we have brought His indignation upon ourselves, inasmuch as we have suffered the false prophet of Galilee to take His Holy Name in vain, and He doth show us by His lightnings the fiery letter of His just displeasure. And whereas these shadows that encompass us are filled perchance with evil spirits who come to claim the soul of the boastful and blasphemous Nazarene, I say unto ye all, cover yourselves and pray to the God of your fathers, O sons and daughters of Jerusalem, that He may no longer be offended,—that He may hear your supplications in the time of trouble, and bring you out of danger into peace!'

His exhortation, though pronounced in tremulous tones, was heard distinctly, and had the desired effect. With one accord the multitude fell on their knees, and in the thickening shadows that enveloped them began to pray as they were told,—some silently, some aloud. Strange it was to hear the divers contrasting petitions that now went muttering up to the invisible Unknown ;—Latin tongues against Hebrew and Greek,—appeals to Jupiter, Mercury, Diana and Apollo, mingling with the melancholy chant and murmur of the Jews.

'Our God, God of our fathers, let our prayer come before Thee! Hide not Thyself from our supplication! We have sinned,—we have turned aside from Thy judgments, And it hath profited us naught! Remember us, O God, and be merciful! Consume us not with Thy just displeasure! Be merciful and mindful of us for blessing! Save us unto life! By Thy promise of salvation and mercy, Spare us and be gracious unto us, O God!'

And while they stammered out the broken phrases, half in hope, half in fear, the thunder, gathering itself together like an army of war - horses and chariots, for sole reply crashed down upon them in the pitchy darkness with a fulminating ferocity so relentless and awful, that the voices of all the people, Jews and aliens alike, died away in one long quavering, helpless human wail. Their prayers sank to affrighted whispers,—and the thunder still pelting in angry thuds through the dense air, was as the voice of God, pronouncing vast and unimaginable things.

Meanwhile, as already described, Barabbas had rushed towards Judith Iscariot just as the darkness fell,—and when the blinding vapours enveloped him he still kept on his course, striking out both arms as he ran that they might come first in contact with the woman he loved. He had calculated his distance well, — for presently, his outstretched hands, groping heedfully up and down in the sombre murk, touched a head that came to about the level of his knee,—then folds of silk, — then the outline of a figure that was huddled up on the ground quite motionless.

'Judith!—Judith!' he whispered—'Speak! Is it thou?'

No answer came. He stooped and felt the crouching form; here and there he touched jewels,—and then he remembered she had worn a dagger at her girdle. Cautiously passing his arms about, he found the toy weapon hanging from the waist of this invisible woman-shape, and realised, with a thrill of comfort, that he was right,—it was Judith he touched, —but she had evidently fainted from terror. He caught her, clasped her, lifted her up, and supported her against his breast, his heart beating with mingled despair and joy. Chafing her cold hands, he looked desperately into the dense obscurity, wondering whether he could move from the spot without stumbling against one at least of those three terrible crosses which he knew must be very near. For Judith had stood directly beneath that on which the wondrous 'Nazarene' was even now slowly dying, and she would scarcely have had time to move more than a few steps away when the black eclipse had drowned all things from sight. He, Barabbas, might at this moment be within an arm's

length of that strange 'King' whose crown was of
thorns,—an awful and awe-inspiring idea that filled
him with horror. For, to be near that mysterious
Man of Nazareth,—to know that he might almost
touch His pierced and bleeding feet,—to feel perchance, in the horrid gloom, the sublime and mystic
sorrow of His eyes,—to hear the parting struggle of
His breath,—this would be too difficult, too harrow-
ing, too overwhelming for the endurance or fortitude
of one who knew himself to be the guilty sinner that
should have suffered in the place of the Innocent and
Holy. Seeking thus to account to his own mind for
the tempestuous emotions which beset him, Barabbas
moved cautiously backward, not forward, bearing in his
recollection the exact spot in which he had seen Judith
standing ere the black mists fell ; and, clasping her
firmly, he retreated inch by inch, till he thought he
was far enough removed from that superhuman Symbol
which made its unseen Presence all-dominant even in
the darkness. Then he stopped, touching with gentle
fingers the soft scented hair that lay against his
breast, while he tried to realise his position. How
many a time he would have given his life to have
held Judith thus familiarly close to his heart !—but
now,—now there was something dreary, weird and
terrible, in what, under other circumstances, would
have been unspeakable rapture. Impossible, in this
black chaos, to see the features or the form of her
whom he embraced ; only by touch he knew her ;
and a faint chill ran through him as he supported
the yielding supple shape of her in his arms ;—her
silken robe, her perfumed hair,—the cold contact
of the gems about her,—these trifles repelled him
strangely, and a sense of something sinful oppressed
his soul. Sin and he were old friends,—they had
rioted together through many a tangle of headstrong
passion,—why should he recoil at Sin's suggestions

now? He could not tell,—but so it was ;—and his brain swam with a nameless giddy horror, even while he ventured, trembling, to kiss the unseen lips of the creature he had but lately entirely loved, and now partly loathed.

And,—as he kissed her she stirred,—her body quivered in his hold,—consciousness returned, and in a moment or two she lifted herself upright. Sighing heavily, she murmured like one in a dream—

'Is it thou, Caiaphas?'

A fierce pang contracted the heart of the un-happy man who loved her,—he staggered, and almost let her fall from his embrace. Then, controlling his voice with an effort, he answered hoarsely—

'Nay,—it is I,—Barabbas.'

'Thou!' and she flung one arm about his neck and held him thus entwined—'Thou wert ever brave and manful!—save me, my love, save me! Take me out of this darkness,—there must be light in the city,—and thou art fearless and skilful enough to find a way down this accursèd hill.'

'I cannot, Judith!' he answered, his whole frame trembling at the touch of her soft caressing arm,— 'The world is plunged in an impenetrable night,— storm and upheaval threaten the land,—the city itself is blotted out from view. The people are at prayer; none dare move without danger,—there is no help for it but to wait, here where we are, till the light cometh.'

'What, thou art coward after all!' exclaimed Judith, shaking herself free from his clasp—'Thou fool! In the city, lamps can be lit, and fires kindled, and we be spared some measure of this gloom. If thou wert brave,—and more than all, if thou didst love me,—thou would'st arouse thy will, thy strength,

11

thy courage,—thou would'st lead me safely through this darkness as only love can lead,—but thou art like all men, selfish and afraid!'

'Afraid! Judith!' His chest heaved,—his limbs quivered. 'Thou dost wrong me!—full well thou knowest thou dost wrong me!'

'Prove it then!' said Judith eagerly, flinging herself against him and putting both arms round his neck confidingly—'Lo, I trust thee more than any man! Lead me from hence; we will move slowly and with care,—thou shalt hold me near thy heart, —the path is straight adown the hill,—the crosses of the criminals are at the summit, as thou knowest, and if we trace the homeward track from here surely it will be easy to feel the way.'

'What of the multitude?' said Barabbas—'Thou knowest not, Judith, how wildly they are scattered, —how in their straying numbers they do obstruct the ground at every turn,—and it is as though one walked at the bottom of the sea at midnight, without the shine of moon or stars.'

'Nevertheless, if thou lovest me, thou wilt lead me,'—repeated Judith imperatively. 'But thou dost not love me!'

'I do not love thee! I!' Barabbas paused,—then caught the twining arms from about his neck and held them hard. 'So well do I love thee, Judith, that, if thou playest me false, I can hate thee! 'Tis thou that art of dubious mind in love. I have loved only thee; but thou, perchance, since I was chained in prison, hast loved others. Is it not so? Speak!'

For all answer she clung about his neck again and began to weep complainingly.

'Ah, cruel Barabbas!' she wailed to him between her sobs,—'Thou standest here in this darkness, prating of love while death doth threaten us. Lead me away, I tell thee,—take me homeward,—and thou shalt have thy reward. Thou wilt not move from this accursed place which hath been darkened and confused by the evil spells of the Nazarene,—thou wilt let me perish here, because thou dost prize thine own life more than mine!'

'Judith! Judith!' cried Barabbas in agony—'Thou dost break my heart,—thou dost torture my soul! Beware how thou speakest of the dying Prophet of Galilee,—for thou didst taunt Him in His pain,— and this darkness fell upon us when thy cruel words were spoken! Come,—if thou must come; but remember there is neither sight nor sense nor order in the scattered multitude through which we must fight our passage,—'twere safer to remain here,—together, —and pray.'

'I will not pray to God so long as He doth wantonly afflict us!' cried Judith loudly and imperiously—'Let Him strike slaves with fear,—I am not one to be so commanded! An' thou wilt not help me, I will help myself; I will stay no longer here to be slain by the tempest, when with courage I might reach a place of safety.'

She moved a step away,—Barabbas caught her mantle.

'Be it as thou wilt!' he said, driven to desperation by her words,—'Only let me hold thee thus,'—and he placed one arm firmly round her,—'Now measure each pace heedfully,—walk warily lest thou stumble over some swooning human creature,—and with thy hands feel the air as thou goest, for there are many dangers.'

As he thus yielded to her persuasions, she nestled against him caressingly, and lifted her face to his. In the gloom their lips met, and Barabbas, thrilled through every pulse of his being by that voluntary kiss of love, forgot his doubts, his suspicions, his sorrows, his supernatural forebodings and fears, and moved on with her through the darkness as a lost and doomed lover might move with his soul's ruin through the black depths of hell.

XIX

SLOWLY and cautiously they groped their way along, and for two or three yards met with no obstacle. Judith was triumphant, and with every advancing step she took, began to feel more and more secure.

'Did I not tell thee how it would be?' she said exultingly, as she clung close to Barabbas,—'Danger flies from the brave-hearted, and ere we know it, we shall find ourselves at the foot of the hill.'

'And then'— murmured Barabbas dubiously.

'Then, doubt not but that we shall discover light and guidance. And I will take thee to my father's house, and tell him thou hast aided in my rescue, and he will remember that thou hast been freed from prison by the people's vote, and he will overlook thy past, and receive thee with honour. Will that not satisfy thee and make thee proud?'

He shuddered and sighed heavily.

'Alas, Judith, honour and I are for ever parted, and I shall never be proud of aught in this world again! There is a sorrow on my heart too heavy for me to lift,—perchance 'tis my love for thee,—perchance 'tis the weight of mine own folly and wickedness; but be the burden what it may, I am stricken by a grief that will not vent itself in words. For 'tis I, Judith, I

who should have died to-day, instead of the holy
"Nazarene"!'

She gave an exclamation of contempt, and
laughed.

'Callest thou him holy?' she cried derisively—
'Then thou art mad!—or thou hast a devil! A malefactor, a deceiver, a trickster, a blasphemer,—and
holy!'

Another light laugh rippled from her lips, but was
quickly muffled, for Barabbas laid his hands upon her
mouth.

'Hush,—hush!' he muttered,—'Be pitiful! Some
one is weeping, . . . out there in the gloom!
Hush!'

She struggled with him angrily, and twisted herself
out of his hold.

'What do I care who weeps or laughs?' she exclaimed,—'Why dost thou pause? Art stricken
motionless?'

But Barabbas replied not. He was listening to a
melancholy sobbing sound that trembled through the
darkness,—the sorrowing clamour of a woman's
breaking heart,—and a strange anguish oppressed
him.

'Come!' cried Judith.

He roused himself with an effort.

'I can go no further with thee, Judith,'—he said
sadly,—'Something,—I know not what,—drags me
back. I am giddy,—faint,—I cannot move!'

'Coward!' she exclaimed—'Farewell then! I go
on without thee.'

She sprang forward—but he caught at her robe
and detained her.

'Nay,—have patience,—wait but a moment'—he
implored in tones that were hoarse and unsteady—'I
will force my steps on with thee, even if I die. I have
sinned for thy sake in the past—it matters little if I

sin again. But from my soul I do beseech thee that thou say no more evil of the " Nazarene " !'

'What art thou, that thou should'st so command me?' she demanded contemptuously,—'And what has the " Nazarene " to do with thee, save that he was sentenced to death instead of thee? Thou weak slave! Thou, who didst steal pearls only because I said I loved such trinkets!—oh, worthy Barabbas, to perjure thyself for a woman's whim! —thou, who didst slay Gabrias because he loved me!'

'Judith!' A sudden access of fury heated his blood,—and seizing her in both arms roughly he held her as in a vice. 'This is no time for folly,—and whether this darkness be of heaven or hell, thou darest not swear falsely with death so close about us! Take heed of me! for if thou liest I will slay thee! Callest thou me weak? Nay, I am strong,—strong to love and strong to hate, and as evil in mind and passion as any man! I will know the truth of thee, Judith, before I move, or let thee move another inch from hence! Gabrias loved thee, thou sayest, —come, confess!—didst thou, in thy turn, love Gabrias?'

She writhed herself to and fro in his grasp rebelliously.

'I love no man!' she cried in defiance and anger. 'All men love *me!* Am I not the fairest woman in Judæa?—and thou speakest to me of one lover—one! And thou would'st be that one thyself? O fool! What aileth thee? Lo, thou hast me here in thine arms,—thou canst take thy fill of kisses an' thou wilt,—I care naught, so long as thou dost not linger on this midnight way. I offer thee my lips,—I am thy sole companion for a little space,—be grateful and content that thou hast so much. Gabrias loved me, I tell thee,—with passion, yet guardedly,—but now there are many greater than he who love me, and who have not his skill to hide their thought'——

'Such as the high-priest Caiaphas!' interrupted Barabbas in choked, fierce accents.

She gave a little low laugh of triumph and malice commingled.

'Come!' she said, disdaining to refute his suggestion,—'Come, and trouble not thyself concerning others, when for this hour at least I am all thine. Rejoice in the advantage this darkness gives thee,—lo, I repel thee not!—only come, and waste no more precious time in foolish questioning.'

He loosened his arms abruptly from about her, and stood motionless.

'Come!' she cried again.

He gave her no response.

She rushed at him and clutched him by his mantle, putting up her soft face to his, and showering light kisses on his lips and throat.

'Barabbas, come!' she clamoured in his ears—'Lead me onward!—thou shalt have love enough for many days!'

He thrust her away from him loathingly.

'Get thee hence!' he cried,—'Fairest woman of Judæa, as thou callest thyself and as thou art, tempt me no more, lest in these hellish vapours I murder thee! Yea, even as I murdered Gabrias! Had I thought his boast of thee was true, *he* should have lived, and *thou* should'st have been slain! Get thee hence, thou ruin of men!—get thee hence,—alone! I will not go with thee!—I tear the love of thee from out my heart, and if I ever suffer thy fair false face to haunt my memory, may Heaven curse my soul! I take shame upon myself that I did ever love thee, thou evil snare!—deceive others as thou wilt, thou shalt deceive Barabbas no more!'

Again she laughed, a silvery mocking laugh, and

like some soft lithe snake, twined herself fawningly about him.

'No more?' she queried in dulcet whispers—'Thou wilt not be deceived, thou poor Barabbas?—thou wilt not be caressed?—thou wilt no longer be my slave? Alas, thou canst not help thyself, good fool!—I feel thee tremble,—I hear thee sigh!—come,—come!' and she pulled him persuasively by the arm,—'Come! —and perchance thou shalt have a victory thou dreamest not of!'

For one dizzy moment he half yielded, and suffered himself to be dragged forward a few paces like a man in a dull stupor of fever or delirium,—then, the overpowering emotion he had felt before came upon him with tenfold force, and again he stopped.

'No!' he exclaimed—'No, I will not! I cannot! No more, no more! I will go no further!'

'Die then, fool, in thy folly!' she cried, and bounded away from him into the gloom. Hardly had she disappeared, when a monster clap of thunder burst the sky, and a ball of fire fell to earth, hissing its way through the darkness like a breaking bomb. At the same instant, with subterranean swirl and rumble the ground yawned asunder in a wide chasm, from which arose serpentine twists of fiery vapour and forked tongues of flame. Paralysed with horror, Barabbas stared distractedly at this terrific phenomenon, and as he looked, saw the lately vanished Judith made suddenly visible in a glory of volcanic splendour. Her figure, brilliantly lighted up by the fierce red glow, was on the very edge of the hideous chasm, and appeared to blaze there like a spirit of fire. Had she gone one step further, she would have been engulfed within its depths,—as it was she had escaped by a miracle. For one moment Barabbas beheld her thus, a glittering phantom as she seemed, surrounded by dense pyramids of smoke and jets of flame,—then, with another underground roar and trembling the ghastly light was quenched, and blackness closed in again, — impenetrable blackness, in which nothing could be seen, and nothing heard, save the shrieks and groans of the people.

XX

THE panic was now universal and uncontrollable. Crowds of frantic creatures, struggling, screaming, weeping, and fighting invisibly with one another, rushed madly up and down in the darkness, flinging themselves forward and backward like the swirling waves of a sea. The murky air resounded with yells and curses,—now and then a peal of hideous laughter rang out, and sometimes a piercing scream of pain or terror, while under all these louder and more desperate noises ran the monotonous murmuring of prayer. The impression and expectation of renewed disaster burdened the minds of all; the shuddering trouble of the earth had terrified the boldest, and many were in momentary dread that the whole hill of Calvary would crumble beneath them and swallow them up in an abyss of fire. Barabbas stood still where Judith had left him,—his limbs quivering, and a cold sweat breaking out over all his body,—yet he was not so much conscious of fear as of horror,—horror and shame of himself and of the whole world. An ineffaceable guilt seemed branded on mankind,—though how this conviction was borne in upon him he could not tell. Presently, determining to move, he began to retrace his steps cautiously backward, wondering, with a sinking heart, whether Judith had still gone on. She must have realised her danger; she would never

have proceeded further, knowing of that frightful rent
in the ground, into which, in her wilful recklessness,
she had so nearly plunged.   Once he called 'Judith!'
loudly, but there was no response.

Stumbling along in doubt and dread, his foot
suddenly came in contact with a figure lying prone,
and stooping to trace its outline, he touched cold
steel.

'Take heed, whosoe'er thou art,' said a smothered
voice, 'and wound not thyself against my sword-edge.
I am Petronius.'

'Dost thou find safety here, soldier?' inquired
Barabbas tremulously—'Knowest thou where thou
art in this darkness?'

'I have not moved from hence'—replied Petronius;
'I was struck as by a shock from heaven, and
I have stayed as I fell. What would it avail me
to wander up and down? Moreover, such as I am,
die at their post, if die they must,—and my post is
here, close by the Cross of the "Nazarene."'

Barabbas shuddered, and his blood grew cold in
his veins.

'Is He dead?' he asked in hushed awed accents.

'Nay, He breathes yet'—replied the centurion
with equal emotion,—'And,—He suffers!'

Yielding to an overwhelming impulse of passion
and pain, Barabbas groped his way on a few steps,
and then, halting, stretched out his hands.

'Where art Thou?' he muttered faintly —'O
Thou who diest in my wretched stead, where art
Thou?'

He listened, but caught no sound save that of
sobbing.

Keeping his hands extended, he felt the dense air
up and down.

'Who is it that weeps?' he asked, softening his
voice to its gentlest tone—'Speak to me, I beseech

thee!—whether man or woman, speak! for behold I am a sinner and sorrowful as thou!'

A long, low gasping sigh quivered through the gloom,—a sigh of patient pain; and Barabbas, knowing instinctively Who it was that thus expressed His human sense of torture, was seized by an agony he could not quell.

'Where art thou?' he implored again in indescribable anxiety—'I cannot feel thee,—I cannot find thee! Darkness covers the world and I am lost within it! Thy sufferings, Nazarene, exceed all speech, yet, evil man as I am, I swear my heart is ready to break with thine!'

And as he thus spoke involuntarily and incoherently, he flung himself on his knees, and scalding tears rushed to his eyes. A trembling hand touched him,—a woman's hand.

'Hush!' whispered a broken voice in the gloom— 'Thou poor, self-tormented sinner, calm thyself, and pray! Fear not; count not up thy transgressions, for were they more numerous than the grains of sand in the desert, thy tears and sorrows here should win thy pardon. Kneel with us, if thou wilt, and watch; for the end approaches,—the shadows are passing, and light is near.'

'If this be so,' said Barabbas, gently detaining the small hand that touched him—'Why dost thou still continue to weep? Who art thou that art so prodigal of tears?'

'Naught but woman,'—answered the sweet whispering voice—'And as woman I weep,—for the great Love's wrong!'

She withdrew her hand from his clasp,—and he remained where he was beside her, quietly kneeling. Conscious of the nearness of the Cross of the 'Nazarene' and of those who were grouped about it, he felt no longer alone,—but the weight of the

mysterious sorrow he carried within himself per-
ceptibly increased. It oppressed his heart and
bewildered his brain,—the darkness seemed to
encircle him with an almost palpable density,—and
he began to consider vaguely that it would be well
for him, if he too might die on Calvary with that
mystic 'King' whose personality had exercised so
great a fascination over him. What had he to live
for? Nothing. He was outcast through his own
wickedness, and as the memory of his sins clouded his
mind he grew appalled at the evil in his own nature.
His crimes of theft and murder were the results of his
blind passion for Judith Iscariot,—and this blind
passion now seemed to him the worst crime of all.
For this his name and honour were gone,—for this
he had become a monster of iniquity in his own sight.
Yet,—strange to say, only that very morning, he had
not thought himself so vile. Between the hours of
his being brought before Pilate, and now,—when he
knelt in this supernatural darkness before the unseen
dying 'Man of Nazareth,' an age seemed to have
passed,—a cycle of time burdened with histories,—
histories of the soul and secret conscience, which are
of more weight in God's countings than the histories
of empires. The people had released him,—they had
hailed him, the liberated thief and murderer, with
acclamations,—true!—but what was all this popular
clamour worth, when in his own heart he knew himself to be guilty of the utmost worst that could be
done to him? Oh, the horrible, horrible burden of
recognised sin!—the dragging leaden weight that
ties the immortal spirit down to grossness and
materialism, when it would fain wing its way to the
highest attainment!—the crushing consciousness of
being driven back into darkness out of light supernal!
of being thrust away, as it were, with loathing, out of
the sight and knowledge of the Divine! This was a

part of the anguish of Barabbas,—a mental anguish he had never felt till now,—and this was why he almost envied his former comrade Hanan for having been elected to die in the companionship of the 'Nazarene.' All these thoughts of his were purely instinctive; he could not reason out his emotions, because they were unlike himself and new to him. Nevertheless, if he uttered a prayer at all while kneeling in that solemn gloom, it was for death, not life.

And now, all suddenly through the heavy murk, a muffled clangour stirred the air,—the tolling of great bells and smaller chimes from the city. Swinging and jangling, they made themselves heard distinctly for the first time since the darkness fell over the land,—a sign that the atmosphere was growing clearer. They were ringing out the hour of sunset, though no sun was visible. And, as they rang, Barabbas felt that some one near him moved softly among the shadows, and stood upright. He strove to discern the outline of that risen shape, and presently, to his intense amazement, saw a pale light begin to radiate through the vapours and gradually weave a faintly luminous halo round the majestic form of a Woman, whose face, divinely beautiful, supremely sad, shone forth from the darkness like a star, and whose clasped hands were stretched towards the great invisible Cross in an attitude of yearning and prayer. And the bells rang and the light widened, and in two or three moments more, a jagged rift of dusky red opened in the black sky. Broadening slowly, it spread a crimson circle in the heavens immediately behind the summit of the Cross of the 'Nazarene;'—first casting ruddy flashes on the inscribed letters, 'Jesus of Nazareth, King of the Jews,' and then illumining with a flame-like glow the grand thorn-crowned head of the Crucified. Ah, what sublime, unspeakable, mystic agony was

written now upon that face Divine! Horror of the
world's sin,—pity for the world's woe,—love for the
world's poor creatures,—and the passionate God's
yearning for the world's pardon and better hope of
heaven,—all these great selfless thoughts were seen
in the indescribably beautiful expression of the pallid
features, the upward straining eyes,—the quivering,
tender lips;—and Barabbas, staring at the wondrous
sight, felt as though his very soul and body must melt
and be dissolved in tears for such a kingly Sorrow!
The blood-red cleft in the sky lengthened,—and,
presently, shooting forth arrowy beams as of fire,
showed a strange and solemn spectacle. For as far
as eye could see in the lurid storm-light, the whole
multitude of the people upon Calvary were discovered
kneeling before the Cross of Christ! All faces were
turned towards the dying Saviour; in trouble, in fear
and desperation, every human creature there had
fallen unknowingly before their only Rescue whose
name was Love!—and, as the darkness broke up and
parted in long wavy lines, the widening radiance of
the heavens revealed what seemed to be a worshipping
world! . . . But only for an instant,—for with the
gathering, growing light, came the rush of every-day
life and movement,—the prostrate crowd leaped up
with shouts of joy, glad exclamations of relief and
laughter,—danger was over,—death no longer seemed
imminent,—and as a natural result, God was forgotten.
The thunder still growled heavily, but its echoes were
rolling off into the far distance. And while the
people grew more and more animated, scattering
themselves in every direction, finding and embracing
their friends and narrating their past fears, Barabbas
rose also from his knees, wondering, awed and afraid.
Directly facing him was the Cross of the 'Nazarene,'
—but, beside him was—the Magdalen! With her he
had knelt in the deep darkness,—it must have been

her hand that had touched him,—it must have been her voice that had so gently soothed him. He trembled; she was a woman of many sins,—yet was she—was she so much worse than—than Judith? His soul sickened as this comparison crossed his mind; yet, loathe it as he might, it still forced itself upon his attention. Judith Iscariot, beautiful, imperious, and triumphant in the secrecy of undiscovered sin,—Mary Magdalene, beautiful also, but broken-hearted, humbled to the dust of contempt, openly shamed,—and—penitent. Which of the twain deserved the greater condemnation?

A deep sigh broke from his lips,—a sigh that was almost a groan; an evil man himself, what right had he to judge of evil women! Just then the Magdalen raised her tear-wet eyes and looked at him,—her luxuriant hair fell about her like a golden veil,—her mouth quivered as though she were about to speak, —but as she met his sternly meditative gaze, she recoiled, and hiding her face in the folds of her mantle, dragged herself nearer to the foot of the Cross, and crouched there, motionless. And the other woman,— she for whom, as Barabbas imagined, the welcome light had been kindled in the beginning,—what of her? She no longer stood erect as when the bells had rung,—she had fallen once more upon her knees, and her face, too, was hidden.

Suddenly a voice, pulsating with keenest anguish, yet sweet and resonant, pealed through the air:

'*Eli, Eli, lama sabacthani!*'

With one accord the moving populace all came to an abrupt halt, and every eye was turned towards the central Cross from whence these thrilling accents rang. Bars of gold were in the sky,—and now, the long-vanished sun, red as a world on fire, showed itself in round splendour above the summit of Calvary.

12

'*Eli, Eli, lama sabacthani!*' cried the rich agonised voice again, and the penetrating appeal, piercing aloft, was caught up in the breaking clouds and lost in answering thunder.

'*He calleth for Elias!*' exclaimed a man, one of those in the front rank of the crowd that was now pressing itself towards the Cross in morbid curiosity, —'*Let us see whether Elias will come to take him down!*'

And he laughed derisively.

Meanwhile Petronius, the centurion, looked up,— and saw that the last great agony of death was on the 'Nazarene.' Death in the bloom of life,—death, when every strong human nerve and sinew and drop of blood most potently rebelled at such premature dissolution,—death in a torture more hideous than imagination can depict or speech describe,—this was the fate that now darkly descended upon divinest Purity, divinest Love! Terrible shudderings ran through the firm, heroically moulded Man's frame,— the beautiful eyes were rolled up and fixed,—the lips were parted, and the struggling breath panted forth in short quick gasps. The fiery gold radiance of the heavens spread itself out in wider glory,—the sun was sinking rapidly. Moved by an impulse of compassion, Petronius whispered to a soldier standing by, who, obeying his officer's suggestion, dipped a sponge in vinegar and placing it on a tall reed, lifted it to the lips of the immortal Sufferer, with the intention of moistening the parched tongue and reviving the swooning senses. But there was no sign that He was conscious,—and while the soldier still endeavoured to pass the sponge gently over the bleeding brows to cool and comfort the torn and aching flesh, the sleek priest Annas stepped forward from amongst the people and interfered.

'*Let be,—let be!*' said he suavely, and with a meek

smile,—'*Let us see whether Elias will come to save him!*'

The crowd murmured approval,—the soldier dropped the reed, and glancing at Petronius, drew back and stood apart. Petronius frowned heavily, and surveyed the portly priest with all a martial Roman's anger and disdain; then he raised his eyes again, sorrowfully and remorsefully, to the tortured figure of the Crucified. Harder and faster came the panting breath; and, by some inexplicable instinct all the soldiers and as many of the multitude as could get near, gathered together in solemn silence, and stared up as though fascinated by some mystic spell, at the last fierce struggle between that pure Body and divine Spirit. The sun was disappearing,—and from its falling disc, huge beams rose up on every side, driving all the black and thunderous clouds in the direction of Jerusalem, where they hung darkening over the city and Solomon's Temple. Suddenly the difficult breathing of the 'Nazarene' ceased; a marvellous luminance fell on the upturned face,—the lips that had been parted in gasping agony closed in a dreamy smile of perfect peace,—and a flaming golden glory, wing-shaped and splendid, woven as it seemed out of all the varying hues of both storm and sunset, spread itself on either side of the Cross. Upward, to the topmost visible height of heaven these giant cloud-pinions towered plume-wise, and between them, and behind the dying Christ, the sun, now sunk to a half-circle, glittered like an enormous jewelled monstrance for the Host in some cathedral of air. In the midst of this ethereal radiance the pale face of the world's Redeemer shone forth, rapt and transfigured by mysterious ecstasy,—and His voice, faint, solemn, but melodious as music itself, thrilled softly through the light and silence:

'*Father! Into Thy hands ... I commend—My Spirit!*'

As the words were uttered, Petronius and the soldier who had proffered the vinegar, exchanged a glance,— a rapid glance of mutual suggestion and understanding. With assumed roughness and impatience, the soldier raised his spear and deliberately thrust it deep into the side of the dying 'Nazarene.' A stream of blood gushed out, mingled with water ; and the man whose merciful desire to put an end to torture had thus impelled him to pierce the delicate flesh, sprang back, vaguely affrighted at what he had done. For, with the sharp shock of the blow, the thorn-crowned Head drooped suddenly,—the eyes that had been turned to heaven now looked down, . . . down, for the last time to earth, . . . and rested upon the watching crowd with such an unspeakable passion of pity, love and yearning, that all the people were silent, stricken with something like shame as well as awe. Never again in all the centuries to come would such a Love look down upon Humanity !—never again would the erring world receive such a sublime Forgiveness !—such a tender parting Benediction ! The wondrous smile still lingered on the pale lips,—a light more glorious than all the sunshine that ever fell on earth illumined the divinely beautiful features. One last, lingering, compassionate gaze,—the clear, searching, consciously supernal gaze of an immortal God bidding farewell for ever to mortality, and then, . . . with an exulting sweetness and solemnity, the final words were uttered :

'*It is finished !*'

The fair head fell forward heavily on the chest,— the tortured limbs quivered once . . . twice . . . and then were still ! Death had apparently claimed its own,—and no sign was given to show that Death itself was mastered. All was over ;—God's Message had been given, and God's Messenger slain. The law was satisfied with its own justice ! A god could not have died, — but He who had been called the 'Son of God' was dead! It was 'finished;' — the winged glory in the skies folded itself up and fled away; and like a torch inverted, the red sun dropped into the night.

XXI

A BRIEF pause ensued. The solemn hush that
even in a callous crowd invariably attends the
actual presence of death reigned unbroken for a while,
—then one man moved, another spoke, the spell of
silence gave way to noise and general activity, and
the people began to disperse hastily, eager to get
back safely to their homes before the deepening night
entirely closed in. Some compassion was expressed
for the women who were crouched at the foot of the
' Nazarene's ' Cross,—but no one went near them, or
endeavoured to rouse them from their forlorn attitudes.
Barabbas had, unconsciously to himself, recoiled from
the horror of beholding the Divine death-agony, and
now stood apart, his eyes fixed on the ground and
his tired body quivering in every limb. The populace
appeared to have forgotten him,—they drifted past
him in shoals, talking, laughing, and seemingly no
longer seriously oppressed by the recollection of the
terrifying events of the afternoon. The three crosses
stood out black against the darkening sky;—the
executioners were beginning to take down the body
of Hanan, in which a few wretched gasps of life still
lingered. Looking from right to left, Barabbas could
see no face familiar to him,—the high-priests Caiaphas
and Annas had disappeared,—there was no sign of
Judith Iscariot anywhere, and he could not even

perceive the striking and quaintly garbed figure
of his mysterious acquaintance Melchior. The
only person he recognised was Petronius the
centurion, who was still at his post by the central
Cross, and who by his passive attitude and
downcast eyes appeared to be absorbed in melancholy meditation. Barabbas approached him, and
saw that his rough bearded face was wet with
tears.

'*Truly*,' he muttered beneath his breath as he
thrust his sword of office back into its scabbard—
'*Truly this Man was the Son of God!*'

Barabbas caught the words, and stared at him in
questioning terror.

'Thinkest thou so?' he faltered—'Then . . . what
shall be done to those who have slain Him?'

'I know not,'—answered Petronius,—'I am an
ignorant fool. But perchance no more ignorant than
they who did prefer thy life, Barabbas, to the life of
the "Nazarene." Nay, look not so heavily!—thou art
not to blame,—'twas not thy choosing. 'Twas not
even the people's choosing—'twas the priests' will!
A curse on priests, say I !—they have worked all the
evil in the world from the beginning, blaspheming
the names of the Divine to serve their ends. This
Crucified Man was against priestcraft,—hence His
doom. But I tell thee this same "King of the Jews,"
as they called Him, was diviner than any of the gods
I wot of,—and mark me!—we have not seen or heard
the last of Him!'

He turned away with a kind of fierce impatience
and shame of his own emotion, and resumed his duty,
that of superintending the taking down of the three
crucified bodies from their respective trees of torture.
Barabbas sighed, and stood looking on, pained and
irresolute. The shadows of night darkened swiftly,—
and the figure of the dead Christ above him seemed

strange and spectral,—pathetic in its helplessness,—
yet . . . after all,—a beautiful lifeless body,—and . . .
nothing more! A sense of bitter disappointment
stole over him. He now realised that throughout
the whole of the terrible tragedy, he had, unconsciously to himself, believed it impossible for the
wondrous 'Man of Nazareth' to die. The impression
had been firmly fixed in his mind, he knew not how,
that at the last moment, some miracle would be
enacted in the presence of the whole multitude;—
that either the Cross itself would refuse to hold its
burden,—or that some divinely potent messenger
from heaven, whose heralds had been the storm
and earthquake, would suddenly descend in glory
and proclaim the suffering 'Prophet' as the true
Messiah. Surely if He had been indeed the 'Son
of God,' as Petronius said, His power would
have been thus declared! To Barabbas the present end of things seemed inadequate. Death
was the ordinary fate of men; he would have
had the kingly 'Nazarene' escape the common lot.
And while he pondered the bewildering problem,
half in vexation, half in sorrow, a voice said softly
in his ear,—

'*It is finished!*'

He started, and turned to behold his friend, the
mystic Melchior, whose dark features were ghastly
with a great pallor, but who nevertheless forced a
grave and kindly smile as he repeated,—

'*It is finished!* Didst thou not also, with all the
rest of the world, receive that marvellous assurance?
Henceforth there will be no true man alive who fears
to die! Come; we have no more to do here;—our
presence is somewhat of a sacrilege. Leave the dead
Christ to the tears and lamentations of the women
who loved Him. We men have done our part; we
have murdered Him!'

He drew Barabbas away, despite his expressed reluctance.

'I tell thee,' he said—'thou shalt see this Wonder of the Ages again at an hour thou dreamest not of. Meantime, come with me, and hesitate no more to follow out thy destiny.'

'My destiny!' echoed Barabbas—'Stranger, thou dost mock me! If thou hast any mystic power, read my soul, and measure its misery. I have no destiny save despair.'

'Despair is a blank prospect'—said his companion tranquilly, 'Nevertheless because a woman is false and thy soul is weak, thou needest not at once make bosom-friends with desperation. Didst thou discover thy Judith in the darkness?'

The sombre eyes of Barabbas flashed with mingled wrath and anguish as he answered,

'Ay,—I found her,—and,—I lost her!'

'Never was loss so fraught with gain!'—said Melchior—'I saw her, when the light began to pierce the storm-clouds, hurrying swiftly down the hill citywards.'

'Then she is safe!' exclaimed Barabbas, unable to conceal the joy he felt at this news.

'Truly she is,—or she should be,' responded Melchior; 'She had most excellent saintly protection. The high-priest Caiaphas was with her.'

Barabbas uttered a fierce oath and clenched his fist. Melchior observed him attentively.

'Methinks thou art still in her toils,' he said—'Untutored savage as thou art, thou canst not master thy ruffian passions. Nevertheless I will yet have patience with thee.'

'*Thou* wilt have patience with me!' muttered Barabbas with irritation,—'*Thou* wilt! Nay, but who art thou, and what hast thou to do with me, now or at any future time?'

'What have I to do with thee?' repeated Melchior—
'Why—nothing! Only this. That being studiously
inclined, I make thee an object of my study. Thou
art an emblem of thy race in days to come,
Barabbas;—as I before told thee, thou art as much
the symbol of the Israelites as yonder crucified
"Nazarene" is the symbol of a new faith and civilisa-
tion. Did I not say to thee a while ago that
thou, and not He, must be from henceforth "King
of the Jews"?'

'I understand thee not,' said Barabbas wearily—
'Thou wilt ever speak in parables!'

''Tis the custom of the East'—answered Melchior
composedly,—'And I will read thee the parable of
thyself at some more fitting time. At present the
night is close upon us, and there is yet much to be
done for the world's wonderment, . . . stay!—whom
have we here?'

He stopped abruptly, holding Barabbas back by
the arm. They had nearly stumbled over the
prostrate form of a man who was stretched out on the
turf, face downward, giving no other sign of life save
a convulsive clutching movement of his hands.
Melchior bent over him and tried to raise him, but
his limbs were so rigidly extended that he appeared
to be positively nailed to the ground.

'He is in some fit, or hath the falling-sickness'—
said Barabbas,—'Or he hath been smitten thus with
terror of the earthquake.'

All at once, as they still made efforts to lift him,
the fallen man turned up a ghastly face and stared
at them, as though he saw some hideous and appalling
vision. Tearing up handfuls of the grass and earth
in his restless fingers, he struggled into a kneeling
posture, and still surveyed them with so much wild-
ness and ferocity that they involuntarily drew back,
amazed.

'What will ye do to me?' he muttered hoarsely,—
'What death will ye contrive? Stretch me on a rack
of burning iron,—tear my bones one by one from out
my flesh,—let the poisoned false blood ooze out drop
by drop from my veins,—do all this and ye shall not
punish me as I deserve! There are no ways of
torture left for such an one as I am!' And with
a frightful cry he suddenly leaped erect. 'Coward,
coward, coward!' he shrieked, tossing his arms wildly
in the air. 'Coward! Brand it on the face of
heaven!—the only name left to me—coward! False,
treacherous coward! Write it on stone,—post it up
in every city,—shout it in the streets—tell all the
world of me,—me, the wretched and accursed man,—
the follower of the Christ,—the faithless servant who
denied his Master!'

With another terrible cry, he again flung himself
on the ground, and throwing his arms over his head,
wept aloud in all the fierce abandonment of a strong
man's utter misery.

Melchior and Barabbas stood beside him, silent.
At last Melchior spoke.

'If thou art Peter'— he began.

'Oh, that I were not!' cried the unhappy man—
'Oh, that I were anything in the world,—a dog,
a stone, a clod of earth,— anything but myself!
Look you, what is a man worth, who, in the hour of
trial, deserts his friend? And such a Friend!—a
King — a God!' Tears choked his voice for a
moment's space; then raising his forlorn head, he
looked piteously at his interlocutors. 'Ye are
strangers to me'—he said—'Why do ye stand there
pitying? Ye know naught of what has chanced
concerning the Man of Nazareth.'

'We know all,' — replied Melchior with grave
gentleness—'And for the "Nazarene," grieve not,
inasmuch as His sorrows are over,—He is dead.'

'Ye know naught—naught of the truth!' cried Peter despairingly—'That He is dead is manifest, for the world is dark as hell without Him! Yea, He is dead;—but ye know not how His death was wrought! I watched Him die;—afar off I stood,—always afar off!—afraid to approach Him,—afraid to seek His pardon,—afraid of His goodness,—afraid of my wickedness. Last night He looked at me,—looked at me straightly when I spoke a lie. Three times did I falsely swear I never knew Him,—and He,—He said no word, but only looked and gently smiled. Why, oh, why'—moaned the miserable man, breaking into tears again,—'why, when I denied His friendship did He not slay me?—why did not the earth then open and swallow me in fire! Nay, there was no quick vengeance taken,—only that one look of His,—that look of pity and of love!—O God, O God! I feel those heavenly Eyes upon me now, searching the secrets of my soul!'

Weeping, he hid his face,—his wretchedness was so complete and crushing that the hardest and most unpitying heart in the world would have been moved to compassion for such bitter and remorseful agony. Barabbas, inclined to despise him at first for the confession of his base cowardice, relented somewhat at the sight of so much desperation, and there was a certain touch of tenderness in the austerity of Melchior's manner, as with a few earnest words he persuaded the sorrowing disciple to rise and lean upon his arm.

'What is past is past,'—he said gravely—'Thou canst never undo, Peter, what thou hast done,—and this falsehood of thine must needs be chronicled for all time as a token to prove a truth,—the awful truth that often by one act, one word, man makes his destiny. Alas for thee, Peter, that thou too must serve as symbol! A symbol of error,—for on thy

one lie, self-serving men will build a fabric of lies in
which the Master whom thou hast denied will have
no part. I know thy remorse is great as thy sin,
—yet not even remorse can change the law,—for
every deed, good or evil, that is done in this world,
works out its own inexorable result. Nevertheless thou hast not erred so wickedly as thy fellow,
Judas.'

'Nay, but he could die!' cried Peter, turning his wild white face to the dark heavens—
'Judas could die!—but I, coward as I am, live
on!'

Barabbas started violently.

'Die!' he exclaimed, 'What sayest thou? Judas?
Judas Iscariot?—He is not dead?'

Peter threw up his arms with a frenzied gesture of
despair.

'Not dead?—not dead?'—he echoed shrilly—'If
ye do not believe me, come and see! Come! Down
by Gethsemane ye will find him,—outside the garden,
in a dark hollow sloping downward like a grave,—
under the thickest shadows of the olive-trees, and
close to the spot where he betrayed the Master.
There ye shall behold him!' and his agonised voice
sank to a shuddering whisper; 'His body hangs
from a gnarled leafless branch like some untimely
fruit of hell,—some monstrous birth of devils!—
the very air seems poisoned by his livid corpse!
Horrible! . . . horrible! . . . ye know not how he
looks, . . . dead, . . . and swinging from the leafless bough! He slew himself thus last night rather
than face this day,—would to God I had done
likewise'!—so should I have been even as he, cold,
stiff, and free from torturing memory these many
hours!'

Overwhelmed by this new and unexpected horror,
Barabbas felt as though the earth were giving way

beneath him,—he staggered, and would have fallen
had not Melchior caught him by the arm.

'Judith!' he gasped hoarsely—'Judith!—her
brother—dead—and self-slain! How will she
bear it! Oh, my God, my God! who will tell
her?'

Peter heard the muttered words, and gave vent to
a bitter cry of misery and fury.

'Who will tell her?' he shrieked—'I will! I will
confront the fiend in woman's shape,—the mocking,
smiling, sweet-voiced, damnëd devil who lured us on
to treachery! Judith, sayest thou? Bring me to
her,—confront me with her, and I will blazon forth
the truth! I will rend heaven asunder with mine
accusation!'

He shook his clenched hands aloft, and for the
moment his grief-stricken face took upon itself a
grandeur and sublimity of wrath that was almost
superhuman.

'Who will tell her?' he repeated—'Not only I, but
the slain Judas himself will tell her!—his fixed and
glassy eyes will brand their curse upon her,—his stark
dead body will lay its weight upon her life,—his
dumb mouth will utter speechless oracles of vengeance! Accursed be her name for ever!—she knew,—
she knew—how weak men are,—how blind, how mad,
how fooled and frenzied by a woman's beauty,—she
traded on her brother's tenderness, and with the
witchery of her tongue she did beguile even me! Do
I excuse mine own great wickedness?—Nay, for my
fault was not of her persuasion, and I am in my own
sight viler than any sinner that breathes,—but I say
she knew, as evil women all do know, the miserable
weakness of mankind, and knowing it, she had no
mercy! 'Tis she hath brought her brother to his
death,— for 'twas her subtle seeming-true persuasion that did work upon his mind and lead him

to betray the Master! Yea, 'twas even thus!—and
I will tell her so!—I will not shrink!—God
grant that every word I speak may be as a
dagger in her false, false heart to stab and torture
her for ever!'

His features were transfigured by strange fervour,—
a solemn passion, austere and menacing, glowed in his
anguished eyes, and Barabbas, with a wild gesture of
entreaty cried aloud,

'Man, undo thy curse! She is but a woman—and
—I loved her!'

Peter looked at him with a distracted, dreary
smile.

'Loved her! Who art thou that speakest of
love in these days of death? Lo you, there is no
love left in all the world,—'tis crucified! Loved
her, thou sayest? Then come and see her work,
—come!—'tis a brave testimony of true love!—
come!'

He beckoned them mysteriously, and began to run
before them. . . . Melchior stopped him.

'Where dost thou hasten, Peter?' he said gently.
'Thou art distraught with sorrow,—whither would'st
thou have us follow thee?'

'To Gethsemane!' replied Peter, with a terrible
look—'To Gethsemane,—but not inside the garden!
No—no!—for there He, the Elect of God, the Messenger of Heaven, last night prayed alone,—and we,
we His disciples, did we pray also? Nay—we slept!'
and he broke into a discordant peal of delirious
laughter—'We, being men, could find naught better
to do than sleep! More senseless than the clods of
earth on which we lay, we slumbered heavily inert,
dead to our Master's presence, deaf to His voice!
"Could ye not watch," said He, with soft patience to
us, "with Me one hour?" No, not one hour!—it was
not in us to forget ourselves in His grief, even for that

space of time. We craved for sleep, and took it,—
we could not sacrifice an hour's comfort for His sake!
Why, all heaven was wakeful!—the very leaves and
blades of grass must have found eyes to watch with
Him,—we,—we men only, His friends and followers—
slept! Oh, 'twas brave of us!—'twas passing tender!
Mark ye thus the value of earth's love! we swore we
loved Him,—nevertheless we left Him. When the
guards came suddenly upon us, we all forsook Him
and fled,—I only followed Him, but afar off,—always
afar off! This is what man calls faithfulness!' He
paused, trembling violently, then resumed in impatience and agitation—'Come! not inside Gethsemane, for methinks there are angels there,—but
outside, where Judas waits! He is patient enough
now,—he will not move from thence till he is carried,
—will ye bear him home? Home to his father's
house!—lay him down at his sister's feet, while his
dead eyes stare beyond all life and time out to interminable doom!—Carry him home and lay him down!
—down before her who did wickedly and wantonly
work his ruin,—and let her weep—weep till tears
drown every vestige of her beauty, and yet she shall
never blot from her accursed life the memory of the
evil she hath done!'

'Oh, thou unpitying soul!' cried Barabbas desperately — 'What proof hast thou, thou self-
convicted false disciple, of Judith's wrong-doing?
How hath she merited thy malediction? Thou dost
rave!—thy words are wild and without reason!—
as coward thou didst deny thy Master,—as coward
still thou wilt shift blame upon a woman! How
canst thou judge of her, being thyself admittedly
so vile?'

Peter looked at him in haggard misery.

'Vile truly am I'— he said—'And coward I have
proclaimed myself. But who art thou? If I mistake

not, thou art the people's chosen rescued prisoner,—
Barabbas is thy name. Wert thou not thief and
murderer? Art thou not vile? Art thou not
coward? I reproach thee not for thy sins! Nevertheless I know who roused the baser part of me,—for
every man hath a baser part,—and who did change
the faithful Judas to a traitor. 'Twas subtly done,—
'twas even wise in seeming,—so cunningly contrived
as to appear most truly for the best. Would ye know
how? Then follow me as I bid—and I will tell all
while my heart is full, for if God be merciful to me I
shall not live long ; and I must speak the truth before
I die.'

He was calmer now and his words were more
coherent ; Melchior exchanged a meaning look with
Barabbas, and they both silently prepared to follow
him. As they began to walk forward slowly, a
man, tall, and of singularly stately bearing, brushed
past them in the darkness, and with a murmured
word of apology and salutation pressed on in
evident haste. Peter stopped abruptly, looking after
him.

'Yonder goes Joseph of Arimathea'—he murmured,
straining his eyes through the evening shadows to
watch the swiftly receding figure—'A good man and
a just. In secret he also was one of the Master's
followers. Whither, I wonder, doth he bend his steps
so late?'

He seemed troubled and perplexed ;—Melchior
touched his arm to recall his wandering thoughts. He
started as from a dream, and looked round with a
vague smile. At that moment the moon rose, and
lifting up a silver rim above Calvary, illumined with
sudden ghostly radiance the three crosses on the
summit of the hill. They were empty. With haggard
face and piteous eyes, Peter gazed upwards and
realised that the body of his Lord was taken down

13

from the Cross and no longer visible,—and, covering his face in a fold of his mantle, he turned away and walked on slowly, while his companions following him in pitying silence heard the sound of smothered bitter weeping.

XXII

AT the foot of the hill they stopped.
To the left a tuft of palm-trees towered, and under their spreading fan-like leaves was a well of clear water, with a rough stone bench beside it. The stars were beginning to sparkle thickly in the sky, and the climbing moon already lit the landscape with almost the clearness of day.

Peter uncovered his pallid face and looked awfully around him.

'Here,' he said in trembling accents,—'here the Master sat three days agone. Here did He discourse of marvels,—of the end of this world and of the glory of the world to come, and flashing upon us His eyes full of strange light and fire, He said, "*Heaven and earth shall pass away, but My words shall not pass away!*" Here,—only three days agone!'

He sighed heavily, and moving feebly to the stone bench, sank down upon it, shuddering.

'Bear with me, sirs, a while'—he murmured faintly; 'there is a mist before my sight, and I must rest ere I can walk further. Would ye not think me stricken old?—yet I am young—younger by two years than He who died to-day. Yea, we were all in the prime of youth and strength, we who

followed Him,—and we should by very ardour of
our blood have had some courage,—yet were we as
weak and cowardly as though we had been dotards
in the depth of age!'

His two companions said nothing. Barabbas,
preoccupied with thoughts too wretched for utterance, sat down wearily on the projecting edge of
the well, and stared darkly into the still water where
a few stars were glitteringly reflected; Melchior
stood, leaning slightly against one of the tall slim
palm-tree stems, his picturesque saffron-hued garments appearing white in the early brilliance of the
moon, and his dark features sternly composed and
attentive. To him Peter turned his restless, weary
eyes.

'Thou art of Egypt surely?' he said—'Thou hast
the manner born of the land where men do chronicle
the histories of life and time?'

Melchior met his questioning gaze tranquilly.

'Trouble not thy mind concerning me, thou
forlorn disciple of the God!' he answered—'Whence
I come or whither I go is of no more purport than
the tossing hither and thither of a grain of dust or
sand. Henceforward let no man set value on himself, since the Divine hath condescended to be
humiliated even unto death.'

Peter scrutinised him yet more closely.

'Wert thou also His disciple?' he asked.

'As well inquire of me whether I feel the warmth
and see the glory of the sun!'—responded Melchior—
'Those of my race and calling have known of Him
these thousand years and waited for His coming.
Nevertheless, touching these mysteries they are not
for thy nation, Peter, nor for thy time,—wherefore
I pray thee, if thou desirest to have speech with us
on any matter, let it be now, and concern not thy

mind with the creed of one who is, and ever will be, a stranger to Judæa.'

He spoke gravely, gently, but with an air that repelled inquisitiveness.

Peter still kept his eyes fixed musingly upon him, —then he gave vent to another troubled sigh.

'Be it as thou wilt!' he said—'Yet truly thou dost call to mind the tale I have been told of certain kings that came to worship the Lord at Bethlehem, the night that He was born. 'Twas a strange history! and often have I marvelled how they could have known the very day and hour, . . . moreover there were wise men from the East'—He broke off,—then added hurriedly — 'Wert thou perchance one of these?'

Melchior shook his head slightly, a faint serious smile on his lips.

'Howbeit,' went on Peter with melancholy emotion; 'if thou dost ever write of this day, I pray thee write truly. For methinks the Jews will coin lies to cleanse this day from out the annals of their history.'

'Tis thou should'st write, Peter'—said Melchior with a keen look,—'And in thy chronicle confess thine own great sin.'

'I am no scribe'—replied the disciple sorrowfully; 'I have never learned the skill of letters. But if I ever wrote, thinkest thou I would omit confession of my frailty? Nay!—I would blazon it in words of fire!' He paused with a wild look, then resumed more calmly—'Sir, this will never be. I am an ignorant man, and have no learning save that which He of Nazareth taught, and which I was ever the last to comprehend. Therefore I say, report my story faithfully—and if thou wilt be just, say this of the dead Judas,—that out of vain-glorious pride and love

he did betray his Master,—yea, out of love was born
the sin,—love and not treachery!'

Barabbas turned from his dreary contemplation of
the deep well-water, and fixed his brooding black
eyes upon the speaker, — Melchior still maintained
his attitude of grave and serene attention.

'Judith was treacherous'—continued Peter—'but
not so Judas. Beautiful as he was and young, his
thoughts aspired to good,—his dreams were for the
purification of the world, the happiness of all mankind. He loved the Master,—ay, with a great and
passionate love exceeding all of ours,—and he believed
in His Divinity and worshipped Him. He willingly
resigned home, country and kindred to follow Him,
— and now, having sinned against Him, he hath
given his life as penalty. Can mortal man do more?
God knoweth!'

He stopped again,—his breath came in a short
gasping sigh.

'When we entered Jerusalem a week agone'—he
continued slowly, —'Judas had been long absent
from his father's house, and long estranged from his
one sister whom he loved. Ye know the manner of
our coming to the city?—how the multitude rushed
forth to meet and greet Jesus of Nazareth, and called
Him "King," shouting "Hosannas" and strewing
His path with flowers and branches of the palm?
One who watched the crowd pass by said unto me—
"Why do ye not check this folly? Think ye the
priests will tamely bear the entrance of this Galilean
Prophet as a king? Nay, verily they will slay him
as a traitor!" And when I told these words to
Judas, he smiled right joyously, saying, "What need
we care for priestly malice? Truly our Master is a
King!—the King of Heaven, the King of earth!—
and all the powers of hell itself shall not prevail

against Him!'" Seeing his faith and love were
such, I said no more, though truly my heart misgave
me.'

His eyes dwelt on the ground with an unseeing
dreary pain.

'That night, that very night on which we entered
Jerusalem, Judas went forth to see his sister. Oft
had he spoken of her fairness,—of the wonder of
her beauty, which, he would swear, was gorgeous
as the radiance of roses in the sun. He meant to
bring her to the Master's feet,—to tell her of His
teachings, His miracles, His wondrous tenderness
and love for all that were in sickness or in sorrow.
Light-hearted as a boy, he left us on this errand,—
but when he returned to us again, he was no more
the same. Sitting apart from us gloomy and absorbed in thought, oft-times I saw him gazing at our
Lord with a strange grief and yearning in his eyes
as though he sought to pierce the depth of some
great mystery. The days went on, till two evenings
before we shared with our Master the supper of the
Passover. Then Judas came to me, and taking me
aside, unburdened all his secret mind.'

Here Peter newly smitten by remorse and despair
gave an eloquent gesture half of wrath, half of
suffering.

'Heaven be my witness!' he cried—'that when I
heard his plan I thought it would be well! I thought
that all the world would see we had not worshipped
the Divine Man in vain! Pride in His glory, love
for His Name, and ignorance of destiny,—these were
the sins of Judas Iscariot,—but there was no malice
in him, that I swear! The wretched youth's ambition
for his Master was his ruin — but of us separate
twain I was the faithless one!—Judas, even in his
fault, was nevertheless faithful! Dost thou hear me,

thou silent dreamer out of Egypt?' and he flashed
a wild glance at the quiet Melchior; 'Dost thou hear?
Write it if thou wilt on granite tablets in thy mystic
land of the moon,—for I will have it known! Judas
was faithful, I say!—and he loved the Lord better
than any one of us all!'

'I hear thy words, Peter'—said Melchior gently—
'and I shall remember their purport.'

Calmed by the soft reply, the unhappy disciple
recovered in part his self-possession, and went on
with the coherent sequence of his narrative.

'Yea, in all things Judas was faithful. When he
came first to confide in me, he told me that the chief
priests and elders of the city were full of wrath and
fear at the sway our Master had obtained over the
minds of the people, and that they sought some
excuse to kill Him. "Then let us away," said I.
"Let us return unto the mountains, and the shores
of Galilee, where our beloved Lord can teach His
followers, unmolested, and at liberty." "Nay!" returned Judas in a voice of triumph—"Knowest thou
not that if His words be true, our Lord can never
die? Wherefore, why should we be driven from the
city as though we were affrighted concerning His
safety? Hear first what my sister Judith saith."
And I did hear.'

Barabbas looked up, his eyes gleaming with anxiety
and foreboding. Peter met his gaze mournfully.

'She—Judith—so I learned,—had welcomed her
errant brother with such tenderness as moved his
heart. She reproached him not at all, but listened
with a patient interest to the story of his wanderings.
Then she most gently said she doubted not the
truth of the Divinity dwelling within the famous
"Nazarene," but surely, she argued, it were not un-
reasonable to ask that such Divinity be proved?

Whereat Judas, troubled in spirit, replied—"Verily it hath been proved oftentimes by many marvellous miracles." "Not in Jerusalem,—not to the priests and rulers"—answered Judith. "For they believe nothing of thy Prophet of Galilee, save that He is a false blasphemer, a malcontent and traitor. Nevertheless if He be of supreme omnipotence as thou dost say, Judas, 'tis thou canst make Him seize at once the mastery of the world,—and thus how grandly thou wilt prove thy love!" Judas, entranced at the boldness of this thought, bade her tell him how such glory for his Lord might speedily be won. "Never was task more easy"—she replied—"Resign Him to the law,—betray Him to the priests! Then will He avow His godhead with all the majesty of Heaven! We shall acclaim Him as the true Messiah,—and not we alone, but every nation of the earth must worship Him! For bethink thee, dearest brother, if He be indeed Divine, He cannot be slain by any earthly foe!" This,' continued Peter, ' is what Judas told me of his sister's word. And, at the time, it seemed both wise and just. For why should our great Lord suffer poverty and pain when empires could be His? Why should He wander homeless through the world, when all the palaces of earth should open to His coming? So Judas thought,—and I thought with him,—for the Master being in all things glorious, we saw no wrong in striving to make His glory manifest.'

'Nature's symbols are hard to read, Peter,' said Melchior suddenly—'And of a truth thou canst not comprehend their mystic lettering! What glory has ever yet been rendered "manifest" except through suffering? How could'st thou think to fit the tawdry splendours of earthly kingdoms to the embodied Spirit of the Divine? What throned and jewelled potentate hath ever lifted from the world a portion of its weight of sin? What name applauded by the people, hath ever yet bestowed salvation on a living soul? Lo, the very prophets of thy race have prophesied to thee in vain,—and to thy scared wits the oldest oracles lack meaning! Did not thy Master tell thee of His fate, and could'st thou not believe even Him?'

Peter grew very pale, and his head drooped on his breast.

'Yea, He did tell me'—he answered sorrowfully—'And I rebuked Him! I! I said—"This shall not be." And with all the wrath of a wronged King He turned upon me, saying "*Get thee behind Me, Satan! —for thou savourest not the things that be of God, but the things that be of men.*" And I fell back from Him affrighted, and was sore at heart all day!'

Melchior left his position by the palm-tree, and advancing, laid one hand on the disciple's arm.

'And thou could'st not realise, weak soul, these "things that be of God"?' he queried gravely—'Thou could'st not detach thy thoughts from earth? earth's paltry power and foolish flaunting ostentation? Alas for thee and those that take thee for a guide! for verily this fatal clinging of thy soul to things *temporal* shall warp thy way for ever and taint thy mission!'

Peter rose from his seat gazing at the speaker in wonder and dread. The moonlight fell on both their faces;—Melchior's was calm, stern and resolved,—Peter's expressed the deepest agitation.

'In God's name who art thou?' he asked apprehensively—'By whose authority dost thou prophesy concerning me?'

Melchior answered not.

'None shall take *me* for guide!' went on Peter

more excitedly—'For do I not confess myself a faulty man and spiritless? Moreover I am subject to temptations'—and he shuddered—'temptations many and grievous. Lo, the Master knew this of me,—for last night—only last night He said unto me—"*Simon, Simon, Satan hath desired to have thee that he may sift thee even as wheat. But I have prayed for thee that thy faith fail not*"'——

'And neither shall it fail!' interrupted Melchior solemnly—'By faith alone the fabric raised upon thy name shall live! Nevertheless thy cowardice and fears shall live on also, and thy lie shall be the seed from whence shall grow harvests of error! The law of compensation weighs on thee even as on every man, and thy one negation, Petrus, shall be the cause of many!'

Peter looked at the dark inscrutable countenance that confronted him, and lifted his hands as though to ward off some menacing destiny. He trembled violently.

'Strange prophet, thou dost fill my soul with terrors!' he faltered—'What have I to do with those that shall come after me? Surely when these days are remembered, so will my sin be known and evermore accursed,—and who would raise a fabric, as thou sayest, on the memory of a lie? Nay, nay!—prophesy if thou wilt, good or evil, an' thou must needs prophesy—but not here—not in this place where the Master sat so lately. It is as though He heard us—there is something of His presence in the air!'

He cast a timorous glance up and down, and then began to walk forward feebly yet hurriedly. They all three paced along the moonlit road, Barabbas casting many a dubious side-look at the worn and troubled face of the disciple.

'Strange that this man could have denied his Master!' he thought with passionate scorn—'And I,—base sinner as I am, having but seen that Master once, would willingly have died for Him had it been possible! If all His followers are of such coward stuff as this, surely the history of this day, if left to them, will be but a perverted chronicle!'

Meanwhile, after a heavy pause, Peter resumed his interrupted narrative.

'When Judas told me of his sister's words, me-thought I saw new light break in upon our lives. The world would be a paradise,—all men would be united in love and brotherhood if once the God on earth were openly revealed! Yet out of fear I hesi-tated to pronounce a judgment; and seeing this, Judas persuaded me to go with him to Judith and hear her speak upon the matter. So, he said, I should be better skilled to reason without haste or prejudice.'

Here he threw up his hands with a wild gesture.

'Would I had never seen her!' he cried—'In what a fair disguise the fiend did come to tempt my soul! I took her for an angel of good counsel!—her beauty, her mild voice, her sweet persuasions, her seeming-wise suggestions, oh, they made havoc of my better thoughts! She stood before us in her father's garden, clothed softly in pure white, a very spirit of gentleness and quietude, speaking full soberly and with most excellent justice as I deemed. "Truly I doubt not that this Lord of thine is very God," she said—"Nevertheless as the rulers of the city believe Him naught but human perjurer and traitor, ye who love Him should compel Him to declare His glory. For if He be not, as He saith, Divine, ye do wrong to follow a deceiver. Surely this thing is plain? If

He be God, we all will worship Him; if He be man only, why then ye are but blindly led astray, and made as fools by trickery." Thus did she speak, and I believed her,—her words seemed full of truth and justice,—she was right, I said,—our Master was Divine, and He should prove it! Smiling, she bowed her head and left us,—and Judas, turning on me, cried—"Now, Simon Peter, what thinkest thou?" And I answering, said "Do as it seemeth well unto thee, Judas! Our Lord is Lord of the whole heaven and earth, and none can injure Him or take away His glory!"'

Pausing again, he looked upward with a sad, wild anguish, the pale moonbeams falling coldly on his tear-worn, rugged countenance.

'What counsel could I give?' he exclaimed, as though he were defending himself to some unseen listener in the starry skies—'What did I know? I had no key to heaven's mysteries! A poor unlearned fisherman, casting my nets by Galilee, was I, when He, the Marvellous One, came suddenly upon me, and with a lightning-glance of power said "*Follow Me!*" Andrew, my brother, was with me, and he will testify of this,—that we were ignorant and stricken by poverty, and all we knew and felt was that this Jesus of Nazareth must be obeyed,—that we were bound by some mysterious influence to follow where He led,— that home and kindred were as nought to us, compared with one smile, one searching look from Him! In beauty, in majesty, in high command a very King He seemed; why, why should not the world have known it? It seemed but natural,—it seemed but just, —and last night, when Judas rose from supper and went out, I knew whither he had gone! I knew—I knew!' He shuddered and groaned, — then with a savage gesture cried—'A curse on woman! Through her

came sin and death !—through her is hell created !—
through her is now betrayed the Holy One of God !
Accursëd may she be for ever !—and cursëd be all
men who love her perishable beauty, and trust her
treacherous soul ! '

His white face became contorted with fury ;—
Melchior surveyed him with calm compassion.

' Thy curses are in vain, Petrus,'—he said—' They do
but sound on deaf and empty air. He who curses
woman or despises her, must henceforth be himself
despisëd and accursëd. For now by woman's purity
is the whole world redeemed,—by woman's tenderness
and patience the cords of everlasting love are tied
between this earth and highest heaven ! Truly the
language of symbols is hid from thee, if thou canst
curse woman, remembering that of woman thy
Master was born into the world ! Were there a
million treacherous women meriting thy curse, it
matters little,—for from henceforward Womanhood
is rendered sacred in the sight of the Eternal,
through Her whom now we call the Mother of the
" Nazarene "!'

He paused,—then added, ' Moreover, thou canst
not fasten the betrayal of thy Lord on Judith Iscariot.
Partly she was to blame,—yet she was but a tool in
the hands of the true arch-traitor. If ye would track
treachery home to its very source, search for it where
it hath its chief abiding-place,—in the dens of priestcraft and tyranny,—among the seeming holy, the
seeming sanctified,—they with whom lies are part of
sacred office ! '

Barabbas started.

' 'Twas Caiaphas ?' he cried excitedly—' Tell me—
such news will be some comfort to my soul — 'twas
Caiaphas who first did scheme this murder of the
Christ ?'

Melchior looked at him steadily.

'Even so'—he said—''Twas Caiaphas. What would'st thou? 'Tis ever, and 'twill ever be, a self-professing Priest of the Divine who crucifies Divinity!'

XXIII

AS he spoke a faint wind stirred the shrubs and trees on either side of the road like an assenting sigh from some wandering spirit. The disciple Peter stared upon him in troubled and vague amazement.

'How could it be Caiaphas?' he asked—'True it is that Judas went to Caiaphas, but not till he had himself resolved upon the deed he meant to do.'

'Thou knowest not each private detail of this history, Petrus'—answered Melchior,—'And as thou knowest not all, neither will they who come after thee ever know. Hast thou not heard of love existing between man and woman,—or if not love, a passion passing by that name, which hath made many strange annals in history? Even such passion has there been 'twixt haughty Caiaphas and wanton Judith,— nay, thou misguided Barabbas, wince not nor groan —'tis true! To her the sensual priest confided all his plan; he trained her in the part she had to play,— by his command and in his very words she did persuade and tempt her credulous brother,—yea, even with a seeming excellent purpose in the work, to bring back Judas to his home and the religion of his fathers. Moreover, for her ready help and willingness she did receive much gold from Caiaphas, and jewels and soft raiment, things that such women love far more than virtue. "Trap me the Nazarene, fair Judith," he said, "with such discretion and wise subtilty that it shall seem not my work but thy brother's act of conscience and repentance to his faith and people, and I will give thee whatsoever most thy heart desires." And well did she obey him; as why should she not?—seeing he long hath been her lover.'

Barabbas shrank back trembling. Every instinct in him told him it was the truth he heard, yet he could not bear to have it thus pitilessly thrust upon him. Meanwhile the unhappy Simon Peter wrung his hands together in desperation.

'Nay, who could guess so deep and dastardly a plot!' he cried—'And if thou knewest it, thou fateful stranger, and wert in Jerusalem, why not have given us warning?'

'Of what profit would have been my words?' demanded Melchior with sudden scorn—'Ye would not believe the sayings of your Master,—how then should ye believe me? Ye were and are, the very emblems of mankind, self-seeking, doubting and timorous,—and gloze it over as ye will, ye were all unfaithful and afraid! As for me, 'tis not my creed to strive and turn the course of destiny. I say the priests have killed the Christ; and the great Murder is not yet finished. For they will kill Him spiritually a million times again ere earth shall fully comprehend the glory of His message. Ay!— through the vista of a thousand coming years and more, I see His silent patient Figure stretched upon the Cross, and ever the priests surround Him, driving in the nails!' He paused, and his dark eyes flashed with a strange fierce passion,—then he continued quietly — ''Tis so ordained. Lo, yonder are the shadows of Gethsemane,—if thou hast aught of import more to say of Judas,—it were well to speak it here—and now—ere we go further.'

14

Instinctively he lowered his voice,—and with equal instinctiveness, all three men drew closer together, the moonlight casting lengthened reflections of their draped figures on a smooth piece of sun-dried turf which sloped in undulating lines down towards a thicket of olive-trees, glimmering silver-grey in the near distance. Peter trembled as with icy cold, and looked timorously backward over his shoulder with the manner of one who expects to see some awful presence close behind him.

'Yea,—out of justice to the dead,—out of pure justice'—he muttered faintly—'ye should know all of Judas that my faltering tongue can tell. For of a truth his end is horrible! 'Twas a brave youth, comely and bold, and warm and passionate,—and to die thus alone—down there in the darkness!' . . . Clenching his fists hard, he tried to control his nervous shuddering, and went on, speaking in low troubled tones,—'I said he went to Caiaphas. This was two nights before our last supper with the Lord. He told me all. Caiaphas feigned both anger and indifference. "We have no fear of thy mad fanatic out of Galilee"— he said—"but if thy conscience do reproach thee, Judas, as well it may, for thy desertion of the law and the faith of thine own people, we will not discourage or reject thy service. Yet think not thou canst arrogantly place the Sanhedrim under any personal obligation for thine offered aid,—the priests elect may take no favours from one who hath perversely deserted the holy rites of God, and hath forsaken the following of his fathers. Understand well, we cannot owe thee gratitude; for thou hast severed thyself wilfully from us and hast despised our high authority. Wherefore if now thou art prepared to render up the Man of Galilee, name thine own payment." Now Judas had no thought of this, and being sorely grieved, refused, and went away, stricken at heart.

And to his sister he declared all, and said—" I will not sell the Lord into His glory for base coin." But she made light of the matter and mocked at his scruples. "Thou silly soul, thou dost not sell thy Lord!" she said—"Thou dost merely enter into a legal form of contract, which concerns thee little. 'Tis the Pharisaical rule of honour not to accept unpaid service from one who doth openly reject the faith. Take what they offer thee,—canst thou not use it for the sick and poor? Remember thou art serving thy Master,—thou dost not 'sell' or otherwise betray Him. Thy work prepares Him to avow His glory!—think what a marvel thou wilt thus reveal to all the world! Hesitate not therefore for a mere scribe's formula." Then Judas, thus persuaded, went again to Caiaphas, saying "Truly ye have your laws with which I have naught in common, yet if it must be so, *what will ye give me if I betray Him unto you?*" And straightway they counted from the treasury thirty pieces of silver, which Judas took unwillingly. Alas, alas! If he had only known! Surely this very money was as a blind for Caiaphas, —a seeming legal proof that he was innocent of treachery,—but that, in custom of the law, he paid the voluntary, self-convicted traitor. Who could accuse Caiaphas of cruelty?—of malice?—of intent to murder? Caiaphas was not paid! All things conspired to fix the blame on Judas,—to make him bear alone that awful weight of crime, which heavier than all burdens of despair, hath sunk him now within the depths of hell.'

He pressed his hands upon his forehead for a moment and was silent. Barabbas watched him gloomily, absorbed in his every gesture, his every word,—Melchior's eyes were cast down, and a stern expression shadowed his features, notwithstanding that every incident of the story seemed known to him.

'The end came quickly'—proceeded the disciple, after a sorrowful pause—'All the misery and fury and despair fell upon us in one blow. The haste and anger of the law swept down upon us like a storm which we had neither force nor valour to resist. At the entrance to the garden of Gethsemane, Judas waited, with glare of torches and armed men,—and as the Lord came forth from out of the shadows of the trees, he went to meet Him. Pale with expected triumph, love and fear, he cried "*Hail, Master!*" and kissed Him. And such a silence fell upon us all that methought the very earth had stopped its course, and that all the stars were listening! Now, thought I, will the glory of the God expand!—and even as we saw Him transfigured on the mountain, so will He shine in splendour, mighty and terrible, and overwhelm His enemies as with fire! But He, the Master, changed not in aught, nor spoke; in stillness and in patience He fixed His eyes on Judas for a while—then in low tones He said—"*Friend, wherefore art thou come? Betrayest thou the Son of Man with a kiss?*" And Judas, with a cry of anguish, fell back from Him affrighted, and clutched at my garments, whispering—"Surely I have sinned!—or else He hath deceived us!" Meanwhile the armed guards stood mute as slaves, not offering to touch the Lord, till He, addressing them, said—"*Whom seek ye?*" Then they, abashed, did answer—"Jesus of Nazareth." Whereupon the Master looked upon them straightly, saying "*I am He.*" Then, as though smitten by thunder at these words, they went backward and fell to the ground. And I, foolishly, thought the hour we waited for had come,—for never did such splendour, such dignity and power appear in mortal frame as at that moment glorified our Lord. Again He spoke unto the guard, saying "*Whom seek ye?*" And again they answered trembling, "*Jesus of*

Nazareth." Then said He tranquilly—"*I have told
ye that I am He. If therefore ye seek Me, let these go
their way.*" And turning upon us slowly, He waved
His hand in parting,—a kingly sign of proud and
calm dismissal. Staring upon Him, as though He
were a vision, we retreated from His path, while He
did royally advance and render Himself up to those
who sought Him. And these, in part recovered from
their fear, laid hold on Him and led Him away.
We,—we His disciples gazed after Him a while, then
gazing on each other, raved and wept. "Deceived!
Deceived!" we cried—"He is not God but man!"
And then we fled, each on our separate ways,—and
only I, moved by desire to see the end, followed
the Master afar off, even unto the very house of
Caiaphas.'

Here Peter stopped, overcome by agitation. Tears
sprung to his eyes and choked his voice, but presently
mastering himself with an effort, he said hoarsely,
and in ashamed accents,—

'There I did deny Him! I confess it,—I denied
Him. When the chattering slaves and servants of
the high-priest declared I was His disciple, I swore,
and said "I know not the man!" And after all
'twas true,—'twas true! I knew not the "man,"—
for I had known, or thought that I had known,
the God!'

Melchior raised his piercing dark eyes, and studied
him closely.

'Thus dost thou play the sophist!' he said with
chill disdain—'Thus wilt thou bandy reasons and
excuses for thine own sins and follies! Weak,
cowardly, and moved by the desire of temporal
shows, thou wilt invent pardon for thine own blindness thus for ever! Thou art the perfect emblem
of thy future fame! If thou had'st truly known the
God, thou could'st not have denied Him,—but if

thou wilt speak truth, Petrus, thou never hast believed in Him, save as a possible earthly King, who might in time possess Jerusalem. To that hope thou didst cling,—and of things heavenly thou hadst no comprehension. To possess the earth has ever been thy dream!—maybe thou wilt possess it, thou and thy followers after thee,—but Heaven is far distant from thy ken!' Peter's face flushed, and his eyes glittered with something like anger.

'Thou dost judge me harshly, stranger'—he said. 'Nevertheless perchance thou hast some justice in thy words. Yet surely 'tis not unnatural to look for glory from what is glorious? If God be God, why should He not declare Himself?—if He be ruler of the earth, why should not His sway be absolute and visible?'

'He doth declare Himself—His sway is absolute and visible!' said Melchior,—'But thou art not His medium, Petrus!—nor doth He stoop from highest Heaven to learn earth's laws from thee.'

Peter was silent. Barabbas now looked at him with renewed curiosity,— he was beginning to find out the singular and complex character of the man. Cowardice and dignity, terror and anger, remorse and pride all struggled together in his nature, and even the untutored Barabbas could see that from this timorous disciple anything in the way of shiftiness or subterfuge might be expected, since he was capable of accusing and excusing himself of sin at one and the same time.

'Say what thou wilt' he resumed, with a touch of defiance in his manner—''twas the chagrin and the bitter disappointment of my soul that caused me to deny the "Man." I was aflame with eagerness to hail the God!—'twould have been easy for Him to declare His majesty, and yet, before the minions of the law He held His peace! His silence and His patience maddened me!—and when He passed out with the guard and looked at me, I wept,—not only for my own baseness, but for sheer wretchedness at His refusal to reveal Himself to men. Meanwhile, as He was led away to Pontius Pilate, Judas, furious with despair, rushed into the presence of Caiaphas, and there before him and other of the priests and elders cried aloud—"*I have sinned, in that I have betrayed the innocent blood!*" And they, jeering at him, laughed among themselves, and answered him saying "*What is that to us? See thou to that!*" Whereat he flung down all the silver they had given him on the floor before them and departed,—and as he ran from out the palace like a man distraught, I met and stopped him. "Judas, Judas, whither goest thou?" I cried. He beat me off. "Home! Home!" he shrieked at me—"Home—to *her!*—to the one sister whom I loved, who did persuade my soul to this night's treachery! Let me pass!—for I must curse her ere I die!—her spirit needs must follow mine to yonder beckoning Doom!" And with a frightful force he tore himself from out my grasp, and like a drifting phantom on the wind, was gone!'

Here Peter raised his hands with an eloquent gesture, as though he again saw the vanishing form of the despairing man.

'All through last night,' he continued in hushed accents — 'I sought for him in vain. Round and about Iscariot's house I wandered aimlessly,—I saw none of whom I dared ask news of him,—the fatal garden where together we had speech with Judith, was silent and deserted. Through many streets of the city, and along the road to Bethany I paced wearily, until at last some fateful spirit turned my steps towards Gethsemane. And there,—there at last—I found him!'

He paused,—then suddenly began to walk rapidly.

'Come!' he said, looking backward at Melchior
and Barabbas—'Come! The night advances,—and
he hath passed already many lonely hours! And
not long since the Master said—"*Greater love hath
no man than this,—that a man lay down his life for
his friends.*" Verily Judas hath laid down his life,
—and look you, to die thus in the full prime of
youth, strangled even as a dog that hath run wild,
is horrible!—will't not suffice? 'Twere hard that
Judas should be evermore accursed, seeing that for
his folly he hath paid the utmost penalty, and is, by
his own hand, dead!'

'And thou livest!' said Melchior with a cold
smile—'Thou sayest well, Petrus;—'twere hard that
Judas should be evermore accursed and thou adjudged
a true apostle! Yet such things happen—for the
world loves contrarys and falsifications of history,—
and while perchance it takes a month to spread a
lie, it takes a hundred centuries to prove a truth!'

Peter answered not,—he was pressing on with increasing speed and agitation. All at once he halted,
—the road made an abrupt slope towards a mass of
dense foliage faintly grey in the light of the moon.

'Hush!—hush!' he whispered—'He is dead,—but
there is a strange expression in his eyes,—he looks
as if he heard. One cannot tell,—the dead may hear
for all we know! Tread gently,—yonder is the
garden of Gethsemane, but he is not within it. He
stays outside,—almost upon the very spot where he
did give the Master up to death, meaning to give
Him glory! Come!—we will persuade him to depart
with us,—betwixt us three he shall be gently carried
home,—perchance his sister Judith marvels at his
absence, and waits for his return! How she will
smile upon him when she sees the manner of his
coming!'

And he began to walk forward on tip-toe.

Barabbas grew deadly pale and caught Melchior by the arm. The rugged figure of the disciple went on before them like a dark fluttering shadow, and presently turned aside from the road towards a turfy hollow where a group of ancient olive-trees stretched out their gaunt black branches like spectral arms uplifted to warn intruders back. Pausing at this gloomily frondaged portal, Peter beckoned his companions with a solemn gesture,—then, stooping under the boughs, he passed and disappeared. Hushing their footsteps and rendered silent by the sense of awe, Melchior and Barabbas followed. The hanging foliage drooped over them heavily, and seemed to draw them in and close them out of sight, —and although there was scarcely any wind to move the air, the thick leaves rustled mysteriously like ghostly voices whispering of some awful secret known to them alone—the secret of a tortured soul's remorse, —the indescribable horror of a sinner's death, self-sought in the deeper silence of their sylvan shadows.

XXIV

MEANWHILE the city of Jerusalem was pleasantly astir. Lights twinkled from the windows of every house, and from many an open door and flower-filled garden came the sounds of music and dancing. Those who had been well-nigh dead with fear at the earthquake and the unnatural darkness of the day, were now rejoicing at the safety of themselves and their relations. No more cause for apprehension remained; the night was cloudlessly beautiful, and brilliant with the tranquil glory of the nearly full moon,—and joyous parties of friends assembled together without ceremony to join in merriment and mutual congratulation. The scene on Calvary was the one chief topic of conversation,— every tongue discoursed eloquently upon the heroic death of the 'Nazarene.' All agreed that never was so beautiful a Being seen in mortal mould, or one more brave, or royal of aspect,—nevertheless it was also the general opinion that it was well He was dead. There was no doubt but that He would have been dangerous,—He advanced Himself as a reformer, and His teachings were decidedly set against both the realm's priestcraft and policy. Moreover it was evident that He possessed some strange interior power,—He had genius too, that strong and rare quality which draws after it all the lesser and weaker spirits of men,—it was well and wise that He was crucified! People who had travelled as far as Greece and Rome, shook their heads and spoke profoundly of 'troublesome philosophers,' they who insisted on truth as a leading principle of life, and objected to shams.

'This Galilean was one of their kind'—said a meditative old scribe, standing at his house-door to chat with a passing acquaintance,—'Save that He spoke of a future life and an eternal world, He could say no better and no more than they. Surely there are stories enough of Socrates to fill one's mouth,— he was a man for truth also, and was for ever thus upsetting laws, wherefore they killed him. But he was old, and the "Nazarene" was young,—and death in youth is somewhat piteous. All the same 'tis better so, — for look you, He ran wild with pro- phecy on life eternal. Heaven defend us all, say I, from any other world save this one!—this is enough for any man — and were there yet another to inherit, 'tis certain we are not fitted for it; we die, and there's an end,—no man ever rose from the dead.'

'Hast thou heard it said'—suggested his friend hesitatingly, 'that this same "Nazarene" declared that He would rise again?'

The old scribe smiled contemptuously.

'I have heard many things'—he answered,—'but because I hear, I am not compelled to believe. And of all the follies ever spoken this is the greatest. No doubt the Galilean's followers would steal His body if they could, and swear He had arisen from the dead,—but the high-priest Caiaphas hath had a warning, and he will guard against deception. Trouble not thyself with such rumours,—a dead man, even a prophet of God, is dead for ever.'

And he went in and shut his door, leaving his

acquaintance to go on his way homeward, which that personage did somewhat slowly and thoughtfully.

All the streets of the city were bathed in a silver-clear shower of moonbeams,—the air was balmy and scented with the fragrance of roses and orange-boughs,—groups of youths and maidens sauntered here and there in the cool of the various gardens, laughing, chatting, and now and then lifting up their well-attuned voices in strophes of choral song. Jerusalem basked in the soft radiance of the Eastern night like a fairy city of pleasure, and there was no sign among her joyous people to show that the Redeemer of the world had died for the world's sake that day.

In marked contrast to the animation prevailing in other streets and courts, a great stillness surrounded the house of Pontius Pilate, the Roman governor. The fountain in the outer colonnade alone made music to itself as it tossed up its delicate dust-like spray that fell tinkling back again into the marble basin,—no wandering breeze ruffled the petals of the white roses that clung like little bunches of crumpled silk to the dark walls,—even the thirsty and mono-tonous chirp-chirping of the locusts had ceased. Now and then a servant crossed the court on some errand, with noiseless feet,—and one Roman soldier on guard paced slowly to and fro, his sandals making scarcely any sound as he measured his stately march forward a dozen lengths or so, then backward, then forward again, the drooping pennon on his lifted lance throwing a floating snake-like shadow behind him as he moved. Pilate, since the morning, had been seriously indisposed, and all his retinue were more or less uneasy. Quiet had been enforced upon the household by its haughty and resolute mistress,—and now that night had fallen the deep hush seemed likely to be unbroken till a new day should dawn.

So that when a loud and urgent knocking was heard at the outmost gate, the porter who opened it was almost speechless with indignation and amazement.

'I prithee cease thy rude clamour'—he said, after he had looked out of his loophole of observation and seen that the would-be intruder was a man of distinguished appearance and attire—'Thou canst not enter here with all thy knocking,—the governor is ill and sees no man.'

'Nevertheless I must have speech with him,' responded the visitor—'I do beseech thee, friend, delay me not—my matter presses.'

'I tell thee 'tis not possible'—said the porter—'Would'st have us lose our heads for disobeying orders? Or crucified even as the "Nazarene"?'

'My business doth concern the "Nazarene"'—was the reply, given hurriedly and with evident emotion—'Tell this to one in authority, and say that 'tis Joseph of Arimathea who waits without.'

At these words the porter ceased arguing, and disappeared across the court into the house. Presently he returned, accompanied by a tall slave, wearing a silver chain of office.

'Worthy Counsellor'—said this retainer, respectfully saluting the Arimathean,—'Thou canst not at this late hour have speech with Pilate, who hath been sorely overwrought by the harassments of the day,—but I am commanded by the lady Justitia to say that she will receive thee willingly if indeed thy matter is of the Man of Nazareth.'

'It is—it is'—answered Joseph eagerly—'I do entreat thee, bring me to thy lady straight, for every moment lost doth hinder the fulfilment of mine errand.'

The slave said no more, but signed to the porter to unbar the gate with as little noise as possible.

Then he led the way across the court, gave a word
of explanation to the soldier on guard, and finally
escorted the visitor into an arched vestibule adorned
with flowering plants, and cooled by sparkling jets of
water that ran from carved lions' mouths into a deep
basin of yellow marble.   Here the slave disappeared,
leaving the Arimathean alone.   He paced up and
down with some impatience, full of his own burning
thoughts that chafed at every fresh delay, and he
was violently startled when a grave mellow voice
said close to him,

'What of the Christ? Have ye indeed slain
Him?'

'Lady!' . . . he stammered, and turned to confront
the wife of Pilate, who had silently entered the
vestibule behind him.   For a moment he could find
no words wherewith to answer her,—the steadfastness
of her dark eyes troubled him.   She was beautiful in
a grand and stately way,—her resolute features and
brooding brows expressed more fierceness than
tenderness, and yet her lips quivered with some
deeply suppressed emotion as she spoke again and
said—

'Surely thou art a Jew, and hast had thy share in
this murder?'

With the shock of this bitterly pronounced accusation he recovered his self-possession.

'Noble Justitia, I beseech thee in the name of God
number me not with the evil ones of this misguided
nation!' he answered passionately—'Could I have
saved the heaven-born "Nazarene," surely I would have
given my own life willingly! For I have gathered
profit from His holy doctrine, and am His sworn
disciple, though secretly, for fear of the harshness of
mine own people, who would cast me out from their
midst if they knew the change wrought within my
soul. Moreover I am a man who hath studied the

sayings of the prophets, not lightly but with sober judgment, and do accept all the things that now have chanced to us as fulfilment of the word of God. And most heartily do I render thanks unto the Most High that He hath in His great mercy permitted me to see with mortal eyes His chosen true Messiah!'

'Thou dost then freely acknowledge Him as One Divine?' said Justitia, fixing a searching look upon him.

'Most surely, lady! If ever any god did dwell on earth, 'twas He.'

'Then He lives yet?'

Joseph looked perplexed and troubled.

'Nay! He is dead. Hath He not been crucified?'

'Doth a god die?' asked Justitia, her sombre eyes glittering strangely — 'What power have mortal tortures on immortal spirit? Summon thy reason and think calmly—art sure that He is dead?'

Her words and manner were so solemn and impressive that the Arimathean counsellor was for a moment bewildered and amazed, and knew not what to say. Then, after a doubtful pause, he answered,

'Lady, as far as human eye and sense can judge, life hath verily departed from Him. His body hath been taken down from off the Cross, and for the reason that they found Him dead, they have spared the breaking of His limbs. Whereas the malefactors that were crucified with Him have had their joints twisted and snapt asunder lest haply any spark of pained existence should linger in them yet. But He of Nazareth having perished utterly, and no faint pulse of blood being feebly astir in any portion of His matchless frame, the men of the law have judged it politic and merciful to give His mortal pure remains to her who bore Him,—Mary, His sorrowing Mother, who weeps beside Him now.'

Justitia heard, and her pale resolute face grew paler.

'Is't possible Divinity can perish?' she murmured. Again she looked steadily, searchingly at the thoughtful and earnest countenance of the Arimathean, and added, with a touch of the domineering haughtiness which made her name a terror to her household,— 'Then, Counsellor Joseph, if thy words be true, and the Galilean Prophet be no longer living, what can thine errand be concerning Him?'

''Tis naught but one of simple duty to the noble dead'—he replied quickly, and with anxiety—'I fain would bury the body of the Lord where it may be most reverently shrined and undisturbed. There is a sepulchre newly hewn among the rocks outside the city, not far from Calvary, but going downwards towards Gethsemane,—'twas meant for mine own tomb, for well I know the years advance with me, and only God knoweth how soon I may be called upon to die,—nevertheless if I may lay the body of the Master therein, I shall be well content to be interred in baser ground below Him. We would not have Him sepulchred with common malefactors, — wherefore, noble lady, I seek thy lord the governor's permission to place within this unused burial cave of mine own choosing and purchase, the sacred corpse of One who, to my thinking, was indeed the Christ, albeit He hath been crucified. This is my errand,—and I have sped hither in haste to ask from Pilate his free and favourable consent, which, if it be granted, will make of me a grateful debtor to the gentleness of Rome.'

Justitia smiled darkly at the courteous phrase 'the gentleness of Rome,'—then her fierce brows contracted in a puzzled line.

'Truly I know not how to aid thee, friend,'—she

said after a pause—'I have no power to grant thee this permit,—and my lord is sorely wearied and distempered by strange fancies and—dreams,—unhappy and confusing dreams,'—she repeated slowly and with a slight shudder—'Yet—stay! Wait but one moment,—I will inquire of him his mood,—perchance it may relieve him to have speech with thee.'

Gliding away on her noiseless sandalled feet, her majestic figure in its trailing robes of white glimmered in and out the marble columns of the corridor and rapidly disappeared. Joseph of Arimathea sighed heavily, and stood looking vaguely at the trickling water running from the mouths of the stone lions into the marble-lined hollow in the centre of the vestibule, wondering to himself why his heart had beat so violently, and why his thoughts had been so suddenly troubled when he had been asked the question, 'Art sure that He is dead?' He was not left long alone to indulge in his reflections,—Justitia returned almost as quickly as she had vanished, and pausing at a little distance beckoned to him.

'Pilate will see thee'—she said, as he eagerly obeyed her gesture—'But should'st thou find him wild and wandering in discourse, I pray thee heed him not. And beware how thou dost speak of his distemper to the curious gossips of the city,—I would not have it noised abroad that he hath been all day so far distracted from his usual self'—here her steady voice trembled and her proud eyes filled with sudden tears—'He hath been ill—very ill—and only I have tended him; and notwithstanding he is calmer now, thou must in converse use discretion.'

'Trust me, noble lady'—replied the Arimathean with profound feeling, 'I will most faithfully endeavour that I shall not err in aught, or chafe thy lord with any new displeasure.'

She bent her haughty head, partly in acknowledg-

15

ment of his words, partly to hide the tears that
glittered on her lashes, and, without further parley,
led the way to her husband's private room.   In deep
silence, hushing his footsteps heedfully as he moved,
the Arimathean counsellor followed her.

XXV

PASSING through a narrow passage curtained off from the rest of the house, they entered a long low vaulted apartment brilliantly ablaze with lights. Roman lamps set on iron brackets illuminated every corner that would otherwise have been dark, — waxen torches flamed in every fixed sconce. There was so much flare, and faint smoke from burnt perfumes, that for a moment it was impossible to discern anything clearly, although the wide casement window was set open to the night, and steps led down from it to a closely-walled garden on which the moon poured refreshing showers of silver radiance, eclipsing all the artificial glamour and glare within. And at this casement, extended on a couch, lay Pilate, pallid and inert, with half-closed eyes, and limp hands falling on either side of the silken coverlet spread over him — he had the supine and passive air of a long-ailing, dying man to whom death would be release and blessedness. Joseph of Arimathea could scarcely restrain an exclamation of amazed compassion as he saw him,—but a warning glance from Justitia silenced him, and he repressed his feeling. She meanwhile went up to her husband's couch and knelt beside it.

'The counsellor is here, Pontius'—she said softly—'Hast thou strength to give him audience?'

Pilate opened his eyes widely and stared vaguely at his visitor,—then lifting one hand that trembled in the air with weakness, beckoned him to approach.

'Come nearer,—nearer still'—he murmured with a kind of feeble pettishness,—'Thou hast the look of a shadow yonder,—the room is full of shadows. Thou art Joseph? From that city of the Jews called Arimathea?'

'Even so, my lord'—answered Joseph in subdued accents, noting with pained concern the Roman governor's prostrate and evidently suffering condition.

'And being a Jew, what dost thou seek of me?' went on Pilate, his heavy lids again half closing over his eyes—'Surely I have this day fully satisfied the Israelitish thirst for blood!'

'Most noble governor,' said Joseph, with as careful gentleness and humility as he could command—'Believe me that I am not one of those who forced thee to the deed 'twas evident thy spirit did repudiate and abhor. And albeit thou hast been named a tyrant and a cruel man by the unthinking of my nation, I know thy gentleness, having discovered much of thy good work in deeds of charity among the poor,—therefore I come to beg of thee the Body of the Christ'——

With a sudden excited movement, Pilate dashed aside the silken draperies that covered him, and sat up, nervously clutching his wife's arm.

'The Body of the Christ!' he echoed wildly—'Hearest thou that, Justitia! The Body of the Christ!'

His purple garments fell about him in disordered

folds,—his vest half open, showed his chest heaving agitatedly with his unquiet and irregular breathing,— his eyes grew feverishly luminous, and gleamed with a strange restless light from under the shadow of his tossed and tumbled hair. Joseph, alarmed at his aspect, stood hesitating,—Justitia looked at him, and made him a mute sign to go on and make his appeal quickly.

'Yea, 'tis the Body of the Christ I ask from thee;' he proceeded then, anxiously yet resolvedly—'And verily I would not have troubled thee at this hour, Pilate, but that thou art governor and ruler of the civil laws within Judæa, therefore thou alone canst give me that which hath been slain by law. I fain would lay the sacred corpse within mine own new sepulchre, with all the tears and prayers befitting a great hero dead.'

'Dead?' cried Pilate, fixing a wild stare upon him, 'Already dead? Nay—art thou sure?'

A chill tremor shook the strong nerves of the Arimathean. Here was the same question Justitia had asked him a few minutes since,—and it aroused the same strange trouble in his mind. And while he stood amazed, unable to find words for an immediate response, Pilate sprang erect, tossing his arms up like a man distraught.

'Dead!' he cried again. 'O fools, fools, whose sight is so deceived! No mortal power can slay the "Nazarene,"—He lives and He hath always lived! Yea, from the beginning even unto the end, if any end there be! What?—ye have crucified Him?—ye have seen His flesh pierced, and His blood flow? Ye have touched Him?—ye have seen Him share in mortal labours, mortal woes and mortal needs,—ye have proved Him made of perishable fleshly stuff that ye can torture and destroy?—O poor dim-sighted fools! Lo, ye have done the bravest and most wondrous

deed that ever was inscribed in history,—ye have
crucified a Divine Appearance !—ye have gloated
over the seeming death of the Deathless ! A God
was with us,—wearing apparent mortal vesture, but
those who saw the suffering Man and Man alone,
did only *think* they saw ! I looked beyond,—I,
Pilate,—I beheld '— Here he broke off with a
smothered exclamation, his eyes fixing themselves
alarmedly upon the outer garden bathed in the
full glory of the moon. 'Justitia ! Justitia !' he
cried.

She sprang to him,—and he caught her convulsively
in his arms, drawing her head down against his
bosom, and straining her to his heart with passionate
violence.

Hush !—hush !' he murmured,—' Let us not weep,
— the thing is done, — remorse will not avail.
Accursëd Jews !—they forced my hand,—they, with
their devilish priest, did slay the Man, not I.
"*Ecce Homo !*" I cried to them, — I sought to
make them see even as I saw,—the glory, the
terror, and the wonder,—the radiance of that seeming - human Form, so fine and marvellous, that
methought it would have vanished into ether !
Even as the lightning did He shine ! His flesh was
but a garment, transparent as a mist, through
which one sees the sun ! Nevertheless, let us not
weep despairingly,—tears are but foolish—for He is
not dead—He could not die, although He hath been
crucified. He hath the secret clue of death ;—'tis
a mystery unfathomable, — for what the gods may
mean by this we know not,—and what the world
hath done we know not, — howbeit let the world
look to it, for we are not to blame !' He paused,
caressing with a sort of fierce tenderness the dark
ripples of his wife's luxuriant hair. 'My love !' he
said pityingly—'My poor, tired, anxious heart ! No

more tears, Justitia, I pray thee,—we will forget this day, for truly it concerns us not,—'tis the Jews work,—let the Jews answer for it — for I will not ; neither to Cæsar nor to God! I have said and still will say — *I am innocent of the blood of this just Man !*'

Here, loosening his arms suddenly from around his wife, he raised them with a proud and dignified gesture of protest,—then turning suddenly, and perceiving Joseph of Arimathea where he stood apart, a silent and troubled spectator of the scene, he advanced towards him, and said gently—

' Friend, what seekest thou of me ?'

The Arimathean cast a despairing glance of appeal at Justitia, who, hastily dashing away the tears on her cheeks, and mastering the emotion that betrayed itself in her pale and sorrowful countenance, came to his rescue.

'Dear lord, hast thou forgotten ?' she said gently, as with a guiding movement of her hand she persuaded Pilate to resume his seat upon the couch near the open window—' Thou art not well, and the harassments of thy work have over-wearied thee. This man doth seek the body of the" Nazarene " for burial,—himself he charges with the duties of this office if thou wilt give him thy permit,—grant him his boon, I do beseech thee, and let him go his way, for thou must rest again and sleep — thou hast been sorely tried ! '

Pilate sank heavily among his cushions, looking blankly into nothingness.

' Thou would'st bury the Christ ?' he asked at last, speaking with difficulty, as though his tongue were stiff and refused utterance.

' Such is my one desire, my lord ' — answered Joseph, hopefully now, for Pilate seemed more capable of reason.

'In thine own sepulchre?'

'Even there.'

''Tis large? Will't hold embodied Light and Life, and yet not rive asunder?'

'My lord!'—faltered the Arimathean, in dismay and fear.

Justitia slipped one arm around her husband's neck and said something to him in a soothing whisper. Pilate smiled somewhat piteously, and drawing her hand down to his lips kissed it.

'This gentle lady,—my wife, good sir,—tells me that my thoughts wander, and that I fail to give thee fitting answer. I crave thy pardon, counsellor,—thou art a counsellor, it seems, and therefore no doubt hast patience with the erring, and wisdom for the weak. Thou would'st ensepulchre the "Nazarene"?—the body of the Crucified thou would'st number with dead men?—why then, even so let it be!—Take thou possession of That which thou dost deem a corpse of common clay,—thou hast my leave to honourably inter the same. My leave!' —and he laughed wildly—'My leave to shut within the tomb That which no tomb can hold, no close-barred cave can keep, no time destroy! Go!—do as thou wilt,—do all thou wilt!—thou hast thy boon!'

Relieved from his suspense, and full of gratitude, the Arimathean bowed profoundly to the ground, and was about to retire, when a great noise of disputation was heard in the outer vestibule. Justitia started up from her husband's side in wondering indignation, and was on the point of going forth to inquire the cause of such unseemly disturbance, when the door of the apartment was furiously flung open, and the high-priest Caiaphas burst in, his glistening sacerdotal garments disordered and trailing behind him, and his face livid with passion.

'Thou art a traitor, Pilate!' he exclaimed—'Already dost thou scheme with tricksters for the pretended resurrection of the " Nazarene " !'

XXVI

PILATE rose slowly up and confronted him, Justitia at his side. He was now perfectly calm, and his pale features assumed a cold and repellent dignity.

'Whom callest thou traitor, thou subject of Rome?' he said—'Knowest thou not that though thou art high-priest of the Jewish faith, thou art answerable to Cæsar for insult to his officer?'

Caiaphas stood breathless and trembling with rage.

'Thou also art answerable to Cæsar if thou dost lend thyself to low imposture!' he said—'Dost thou not remember that this vile deceiver out of Galilee who hath been crucified did say "*After three days I will rise again*"? And do I not find thee giving audience to one of His known followers, who oft hath entertained Him and listened to His doctrines? This counsellor'—and he emphasised the term sarcastically, eyeing the unmoved and stately figure of Joseph of Arimathea up and down angrily—'now seeks His body to bury it in a sepulchre, whereof he only hath the seal and secret. And why doth he offer this free service? That he may steal the corpse in the silence of the second night, and make away with it, and then give out a rumour that the Christ is risen! *So shall the last error be worse than the first* with the silly multitude, if his scheme be not prevented.'

Joseph lifted his clear grave eyes and looked full at the speaker.

'I heed not thy wicked accusation, Caiaphas'—he said tranquilly—'Thou knowest it is false, and born from out the fury and suspicion of thy mind. Thy fears do make a coward of thee,—perchance when thou didst find the veil of the Temple rent in the midst this day, and knewest by inquiry that so it had been torn at the very moment of the passing of the soul of the "Nazarene," thou wert shaken with strange terrors that still do haunt and trouble thee! Rally thyself and be ashamed,—for none shall steal the body I have claimed from Pilate,—rest for the dead is granted even by the most unmerciful; and this rest is mine to give to One who, whether human or Divine, was innocent of sin, and died through treachery undeservedly.'

The blood rushed to the high-priest's brows, and he clenched his hands in an effort to keep down his rising wrath.

'Hearest thou that, Pilate?' he exclaimed— 'Sufferest thou this insolence?'

'What insolence?' asked Justitia suddenly—'Tis true the Man of Nazareth had no fault in Him at all, and that ye slew Him out of fear!'

Caiaphas glared at her, his cold eyes sparkling with rage.

'I argue not with women!' he said through his set teeth—'They are not in our counsels, nor have they any right to judgment.'

Justitia smiled. Her full black eyes met his piercing shallow ones with such immeasurable scorn as made him for the moment tremble. Avoiding her glance, he addressed himself once more to Pilate—

'Hear me, thou governor of Judæa under Cæsar,'—
he said—'And weigh thou this matter well lest thou
unheedfully fall beneath the weight of the Imperial
displeasure. Thy Roman soldiery are stricken with
some strange disease, and speak as with the milky
mouths of babes, concerning mercy!—'tis marvellous
to note yon bearded men seized with effeminate
virtue! Wherefore, out of this sudden craze of
mercy they have spared to break the limbs of the
blasphemous "Nazarene," proffering for excuse that
He is dead already. What matter! I would have
had every joint within His body wrenched apart!—
yea, I would have had His very flesh hewn into pieces
after death, if I had had my way!' He paused,
quivering with passion and breathing heavily. Pilate
looked at him with immovable intentness. 'Thy
centurion is at fault'—he continued—'for he it is
who hath, upon his own authority, given the corpse
unto the women who besought it of him, and they
make such a weeping and a lamentation as might
rouse the multitude, an' 'twere not that the hour is
late and night has fully fallen. And with them is
that evil woman of the town, the Magdalen, who
doth defy us to remove the body and place it as it
should be, with the other malefactors, saying that
this man'—and he indicated by a disdainful gesture
the Arimathean counsellor,—'hath sought thy leave
to lay it in his own new tomb with honour. Honour
for a trickster and blasphemer!—If thou dost grant
him this permit, I swear unto thee, Pilate, thou dost
lend thyself unto a scheme of deep-laid cunning
treachery!'

Still Pilate eyed him with the same fixed steadfastness.

'My centurion, thou sayest, is at fault' — he
observed presently in cold meditative accents—'What
centurion?'

'Petronius,—even he who was in charge. I made him accompany me hither. He waits without.'

'Call him, Justitia,'—said Pilate, seating himself upon his couch and assuming an attitude of ceremonious dignity and reserve.

Justitia obeyed, and in answer to her summons the centurion entered, saluted and stood silent.

'The "Nazarene" is dead?' said Pilate, addressing him in the measured tones of judicial inquiry.

'Sir, he hath been dead these two hours and more.'

'Thou art not herein deceived?'—and Pilate smiled strangely as he put the question.

Petronius stared in respectful amazement.

'My lord, we all beheld him die,—and one of us did pierce his side to hasten dissolution.'

'Why didst thou practise mercy thus?'

A troubled look clouded the soldier's honest face.

'Sir, there have been many terrors both in earth and air this day,—and—he seemed a sinless man and of a marvellous courage.'

Pilate turned towards Caiaphas. 'Seest thou the reason of this matter?' he said—'This Petronius is a Roman,—and 'tis in Roman blood to give some reverence to courage. Your Jew is no respecter of heroic virtues,—an' he were, he would not need to pay tribute unto Cæsar!'

The high-priest gave a scornful, half-derisive gesture.

'The very man now crucified, whose heroism thy soldier doth admire, was a Jew,'—he said.

'Not altogether,' interposed Joseph of Arimathea suddenly—'Mary, his mother, was of Egypt.'

Caiaphas sneered.

'And Joseph his father was of Nazareth,'—he said; 'And as the father is, so is the son.'

At these words a singular silence fell upon the group. Justitia grew deadly pale, and leaned on the

corner of her husband's couch for support, — her
breath came and went hurriedly, and she laid one
hand upon her bosom as though to still some teasing
pain. Pilate half rose,—there was a strange light in
his eyes, and he seemed about to speak,—but
apparently on consideration altering his intention he
sat down again, turning so wild a gaze upon Petronius
that that officer was both dismayed and startled.

'Thou hast done well'—he said at last, breaking
the oppressive stillness by an evident effort,—'Mercy
doth well become a stalwart Roman, strong in brute
strength as thou art. I blame thee not in aught!
And thou, great Caiaphas'—here he fixed his eyes
full on the high-priest, 'dost nobly practise sentiments
which best befit thy calling,—revenge, bloodthirstiness and fear! Peace!—snatch not the words from
out my mouth by thy unseemly rage of interruption,
—I know the terror that thou hast of even the dead
body of Him that thou hast slain,—but thou art too
late in thy desire to carry cruelty beyond the grave.
The Arimathean counsellor hath my permit to bury
the "Nazarene" in honour even as he doth desire, in his
own sepulchre newly hewn. But if thou dost suspect
his good intent, and thinkest there is treachery in his
honest service, seal thou the tomb thyself with thine
own mark; and set a watch of as many as thou wilt,
picked men and cautious, to guard the sepulchre till
the third day be past. Thus shall all sides have
justice, — thou, Joseph, and thou, Caiaphas, — and
inasmuch as this Petronius showeth too much mercy,
thou canst choose another centurion than he to head
thy band. More I cannot do to satisfy demand'—
here he broke off with a shuddering sigh of
weariness.

''Tis enough'—said Caiaphas sullenly—'Nevertheless, Pilate, hadst thou been wise, thou would'st have
refused the malefactor's body to this counsellor.'

And he darted an angry and suspicious glance at the Arimathean, who returned his look steadily.

'Hast urged enough against me, Caiaphas?' he said—'Verily, were it not for my race and lineage, I would take shame unto myself this day that I am born a Jew, hearing thee vent such paltry rage and puny fear, and thou the high-priest of the Temple! But I will not bandy words with thee;—I do most readily accept the judgment of our excellent lord the governor, and herewith invite thee to be witness of the burial of the "Nazarene." Thou canst examine the sepulchre within and without to make thyself sure there is no secret passage to serve for thy suspected robbers of the dead. Bring thou thy seals of office, and set a watch both night and day,—I give thee promise that I will not hinder thee.'

Caiaphas bent his head in stiff and haughty acknowledgment, and turned on his heel to leave the apartment, then glancing over his shoulder at the pensive and drooping figure of Pilate, he said with forced pleasantness,

'I wish thee better health, Pilate!'

'I thank thee, priest'—responded Pilate without looking up—'I wish thee better courage!'

With an indifferent nod, Caiaphas was about to leave the room, when, seeing that Petronius the centurion had just saluted the governor and was also departing he stopped him by a gesture.

'Didst thou inquire as I bade thee, concerning young Iscariot?'

'Sir,' answered Petronius gravely—''tis rumoured in the city that Iscariot is dead.'

'Dead!' Caiaphas clutched at him to steady himself, for everything seemed suddenly reeling,—then he repeated again in a hoarse whisper—'Dead!'

For a moment the air around him grew black, and when he recovered his sickening senses, he saw that

Pilate had risen and had come forward with his wife clinging to him, and that both were looking at him in undisguised astonishment, while Joseph of Arimathea was shaking him by the arm.

'What ails thee, Caiaphas?' asked the counsellor,—'Why art thou thus stricken suddenly?'

''Tis naught—'tis naught!' and the proud priest drew himself up erect, the while his eyes wandered to the face of the centurion once more,—'Thou didst say'—and he spoke with hesitation and difficulty—'that 'tis rumoured Judas is dead? Surely 'tis false,—how could he die?'

'Sir, he hath slain himself,—so runs the people's whisper.'

Caiaphas pressed one hand over his eyes to shut out the specks of red that swam before his sight like drops of blood. Then he looked round him with feigned composure—his countenance was very pale.

'See you!' he said unsteadily—'It can but move me to think that yesterday Judas was well and full of life, and that to-day he should be dead! A foolish youth,—of wild and erring impulse, but nevertheless much beloved by his father, and—his sister Judith'—Here he broke off with a fierce exclamation of mingled wrath and pain, and seizing the Arimathean by the arm, he cried boisterously—

'Come, thou subtle and righteous counsellor! On with me, and open thou thy rocky cave of death, that we may thrust within it the cause of all this mischief! Farewell, Pilate!—take health upon thee speedily and my blessing!—for thou hast done justice in this matter, albeit late, and forced from thee! And by thy legal sanction, I will set such a watch around the dead blasphemer's sepulchre as hath not been excelled in vigilance or guardianship for any treasure of the world!—his prophecy shall prove a lie! "After three days"! . . . nay!—not after a thousand and three! Let thunders crash, earth yawn, and mountains split asunder, the " Nazarene " shall never rise again ! '

And with a wild gesture of defiance he rushed from the room, dragging the Arimathean with him, and followed by Petronius in a state of wonderment and fear.

XXVII

PILATE and his wife remained standing where they were for a moment, looking at each other in silence. The mingled light of the flickering lamps around them, and the moonbeams pouring in through the open window, gave a spectral pallor to their faces, which in absorbed expression reflected the same trouble; the same perplexed unquiet thought. After a pause, Pilate turned and moved feebly back to his couch,—Justitia following him.

'Oh, to escape this terror!' he murmured, as he sank among his pillows once more and closed his eyes—''Tis everywhere,—'tis upon Caiaphas, even as it is upon us all! A terror of the unknown, the undeclared, the invisible, the deathless! What hath been done this day we cannot comprehend,—we can but feel a mystery in the air,—and we grope blindly, seeing nothing — touching nothing — and therefore doubting everything, but nevertheless afraid! Afraid of what? Of ourselves? Nay, for we have killed the Man who did so much amaze us. What more then? Why, no more, since He is dead. And being dead, what cause is there for fear?'

He sighed heavily. Justitia knelt beside him.

'Dear my lord'—she began softly, her voice trembling a little. He turned his head towards her.

'What would'st thou say, Justitia?' he asked gently —'Methinks my moods do trouble thee, thou most beloved of women,—I fain would be more cheerful for thy sake. But there is a darkness on my spirit that not even thy love can lift,—thou hast wept also, for I see the tears within thine eyes. Why art thou moved to weakness, thou strong heart?—what would they say of thee in Rome, thou who art adjudged a very queen of pride, if they beheld thee now?'

Justitia answered not, for all at once her head drooped upon her husband's breast, and clinging to him close, she gave way to a sudden paroxysm of passionate weeping. Pilate held her to him, soothing her with trembling touch and whispered words, now and again lifting his eyes to look with a kind of apprehension and expectancy round the silent room, as though he thought some one besides themselves witnessed their actions. After a while, when the violence of her sobbing ceased, he said—

'Tell me, Justitia—tell me all that troubles thee. Some secret grief thou hast kept pent up within thee through the day,—and what with storm and earth-quake, and darkness and thy fears for me, thou hast brooded on sorrow dumbly, as women often do when 'they have none to love them. But I who love thee more than life, Justitia, have the right to share thy heaviness,—I am strong enough, or should be strong, —look up!' and he raised her tearful face between his hands and gazed at her tenderly—'Unburden thy soul, Justitia! . . . tell me thy dream!'

With a cry she sprang erect, pushing back her ruffled hair from her brows, and gazing out into the moonlit garden with a strange expression of alarm and awe.

'No, no!' she whispered—'I cannot,—I dare not! 'Tis dark with the terror thou hast spoken of,—a portent and a mystery; it brings no comfort,—and thou canst not bear to hear more evil omens of disaster'——

She broke off, adding presently in the same hushed accents,

'Didst thou understand, Pontius, when Petronius spoke, that Iscariot was dead?'

'Surely I understood'—responded Pilate—'What marvel in it? 'Twas he that did betray his Master to the priests. He dared not testify of this his treachery,—and when I asked for him at this morning's trial, he could not be found. Out of remorse he slew himself, or so I judge—a fitting death for such a traitor. Thou dost not grieve for him?'

'I knew him not'—said Justitia thoughtfully—'else—perchance if I had known—I might have pitied him. But Judith loved him.'

Pilate moved impatiently among his cushions.

'Much do I marvel at thy interest in that most haughty and most forward maiden'—he said—'That she is beautiful I grant,—but vanity doth make her beauty valueless. How camest thou to choose her as a friend?'

'She is no friend of mine,' Justitia answered slowly, still looking out at the clear night—'Save that she hath been long left motherless, and is unguided and undisciplined, wherefore I have counselled her at times,—though truly my counsels are but wasted words, and she hath evil rooted in her soul. Nevertheless believe me, Pontius, now will her vanity have end,—for if she hath a heart, that heart will break to-night!'

Her husband made no reply, and a long silence fell between them. During this pause, a sound of joyous singing reached them,—a party of young men and maidens were strolling homeward from some festive meeting, thrumming on stringed instruments and carolling as they went. Over the wall of Pilate's enclosed garden their figures could be seen passing along the open street beyond, and occasional scraps of their conversation echoed distinctly through the air.

'Ephra, dost thou remember last week,' said a man's voice—'when the crowd went out to meet the "Nazarene" who died to-day? Canst recall the wild tune they sang? 'Twas passing sweet, and ended thus,—" Hosanna!"'

In a high pure tenor he sent the word pealing through the evening stillness,—his companions caught it up and chorussed all together

'Hosanna!—Hosanna!
Hosanna in the Highest!
Blessed is he that cometh,
That cometh in the name of the Lord!
Hosanna in the Highest!'

The stirring triumph and grandeur of the melody seemed to terrify Justitia, for she caught at the heavy curtain that partially draped the window, and held it clenched in her hand convulsively as though for support, her whole frame trembling with some inward excitement. Suddenly the singing stopped, broken by laughter, and another voice cried out jestingly,—

'Beware the priests! An' we raise such a chant as this, we shall all be crucified!'

They laughed again, and sauntering on, passed out of sight and hearing.

Justitia dropped the curtain from her grasp, and shivered as with deadly cold. Pilate watched her anxiously as she came slowly towards him step by step, and sat down on a low bench close to his couch, clasping her hands together in her lap and looking straight before her vaguely into empty air.

'Even so was the music in my dream'—she mur-

mured—'Methought the very dead did rise and sing
" Hosanna ! "'

Pilate said nothing,—he seemed afraid to disturb
the current of her thoughts. Presently raising her
eyes to his, she asked—

'Dost thou in very truth desire to hear? Or will
it weary thee?'

'Nay, it will comfort me '—he answered, taking
one of her listless hands and pressing it to his lips—
'If any comfort I can have 'twill be in sharing whatever sorrow troubles thee. Speak on, and tell me
all,—for from the very moment thou didst send to
me this morning at the Tribunal, my soul has been
perplexed with wondering at this act of thine,—so
unlike thee at any time.'

Justitia sighed.

'Ay, it was unlike me,—and ever since, I have
been most unlike myself. Thou knowest 'twas a
morning dream,—for night was past, and thou hadst
but lately left me to take thy place within the Hall
of Judgment. I had arisen from my bed,—but as
yet I had not called my women, and partially arrayed,
I sat before my mirror, slowly binding up my hair.
My eyes were strangely heavy and my thoughts
confused, — and suddenly the polished surface of
the metal into which I gazed, grew black, even
as a clear sky darkening with storm. Then came
a noise as of many waters thundering in my ears,
—and after that I know not what did chance to
me. Nevertheless it seemed I was awake, and
wandering solitary within some quiet region of
eternal shade.'

She paused, trembling a little, then went on—

'A solemn depth of peace it seemed to be, wherein
was neither landscape, light nor air. Methought I
stood upon a rift of rock gazing far downward,—
and there before mine eyes were laid millions on

millions of the dead,—dead men and women white
as parchment or bleached bone. Side by side in
wondrous state they lay,—and over them all brooded
a pale shadow as of outspread wings. And as I
looked upon them all and marvelled at their endless
numbers, a rush of music sounded like great harps
swung in the wind, and far away a Voice thundered
"*Hosanna!*" And lo!—the pale shadow of wings
above the dead, furled up and vanished, and
through some unseen portal came a blazing Cross
of Light, and after it, white as a summer cloud
and glorious as the sun, followed—the "Nazarene"!
"Awake, ye dead!" He cried—"Awake, for Death
is ended! Awake and pass from hence to Life!"
And they awoke!—yea, they awoke in all the plenitude of strength and wondrous beauty, those millions
upon millions of long-perished mortals,—they uprose
in radiant ranks, like flowers breaking into bloom,—
adorned with rays of light they stood, great angels
every one, and cried aloud—"Glory to thee, O
Christ, thou Messenger of God! Glory to thee,
thou holy Pardoner of our sins! Thou Giver of
Eternal Life! Glory to thee, Redeemer of the
world! we praise and worship thee for ever!" Then
was my dreaming spirit seized with shuddering and
fear,—I turned away mine eyes, unable to endure
the dazzling luminance and wonder,—and when I
looked again, the scene was changed.'

Here Justitia broke off, and leaning closer to her
husband, caught both his hands in hers, and gazed
earnestly into his face.

'Thinkest thou not,' she whispered—'that this
vision was strange? Why should it come to me?—I
who ever doubted all gods, and have in my soul
accepted death as each man's final end? 'Tis a
thought most unwelcome to me,—that the dead
should rise!'

Pilate met her eyes with a wistful woe and sympathy in his own.

'Yea, 'tis unwelcome'—he said—'I would not live again had I the choice. For we do things in this our life 'twere best not to remember,—and having sinned, one's only rescue is to die,—die utterly and so forget we ever were. Yet perchance there is no forgetfulness,— there may be an eternal part within us,'—he stopped, gazing around him nervously— 'Hast thou no more to tell?—this was not all thy dream?'

'Ah no!' cried Justitia, rising from her seat with an unconscious gesture of desperation—'Would that it were! For what remains is naught but horror,— horror and mystery and pain! 'Tis what I further saw within my vision that made me send my message in such haste to thee,—I thought I might avert misfortune and ward off evil from thy path, my husband, for if dreams have any truth, which I pray they have not, thou art surely threatened with some nameless doom!'

Pilate looked up at her troubled face, and smiled forcedly.

'Fear not for me, Justitia'—he said—'Trust me there is no other doom save death, and that doth hourly threaten every man. I marvel at thy tremors, —thou who art wontedly of so bold a spirit! Rally thy usual courage!—surely I shall not die of hearing of disaster in a dream! Speak on!—what else didst thou behold?'

'I beheld a mighty ocean'—replied Justitia, raising one hand solemnly as she spoke—'And this ocean was of human blood and covered all the earth! And methought every drop within that scarlet sea did have a voice of mingled tears and triumph, that cried aloud "Hail, Jesus of Nazareth, Son of the God Eternal!" Then on the ghastly waves there floated, even as floats a ship, a wondrous temple, gleaming with gold and precious stones, and on the summit of its loftiest pinnacle a jewelled Cross did shine. And in my dream I understood that all the kings and emperors and counsellors of the world had reared this stately fabric to the memory and the worship of the "Nazarene"!'

'To the memory and the worship of the "Nazarene"!' repeated Pilate slowly—'A temple floating on a sea of blood!—well,—what then?'

'Then,' went on Justitia, her dark eyes dilating as she grew more and more absorbed in her narration—'then I saw the heavens rent asunder, and many wondrous faces, beautiful and wise, but sorrowful, looked down. And from the waves of blood arose wild sounds of lamentation and despair, and as I listened I comprehended that the lofty floating temple I beheld was crushing underneath it the struggling souls of men. "How long, O Lord! how long!" they cried, and "Save, Lord, or we perish!" Then came a great and terrible noise as of martial music mixed with thunder, and lo! a mighty Sword fell straight from Heaven, and smote the temple in the midst so that it parted in twain, and drifted on the crimson flood a wreck,—and even as it split, I saw the secret of its wickedness,—an altar splashed with blood and strewn with dead men's bones, and overflowing in every part with bags of gold ill-gotten,—and fronting it in lewdest mockery of worship, with lies upon his lips and coin grasped in both his hands, there knelt a leering Devil in a Priest's disguise!'

She paused, breathing quickly in a kind of suppressed excitement—then continued,

'Now, as I watched the sundered halves of the smitten temple, drifting to right and left, and circling round about to sink, a wrathful voice exclaimed,

" *Many shall call upon Me, saying, Lord, Lord, have we not prophesied in thy name, and in thy name done many wonderful works?　And I will say unto them—Depart from Me, I never knew ye, ye workers of iniquity!* " And even as the Voice sounded, the temple sank ; and naught was left of it but the topmost Cross, floating alone upon the sea!'

'Always the Cross!' murmured Pilate perplexedly ; 'Doth it threaten to become a symbol?'

'I know not,' answered Justitia with a far-off dreamy expression in her face—'nevertheless 'twas ever present in my dream.　And now to hear the end,—methought I watched the lonely Cross tossed by itself upon the sea, and wondered whether, like the temple it had once adorned, 'twould also sink.　To and fro it floated, shining like a star, and presently I saw that wherever it rested for a space, it changed the waves of blood to a light like liquid fire.　Then happened a strange marvel ;—out of the far distance came a ship, sailing straightly and with speed,—'twas small and light and white as foam, and within it, steering boldly onward, sat a woman alone.　And as her vessel sped across the dreadful sea, great monsters of the deep arose and threatened her,—the pallid hands of drowned men clutched at her,—noises there were of earthquake and of thunder,—nevertheless she sailed on fearlessly, and as she journeyed, smiled and sang.　And I beheld her course with wonderment, for she was steering steadily towards the Cross that floated lost upon the waves.　Nearer she came, and soon she reached it, and leaning from her vessel's edge, she caught it in both hands and raised it up towards heaven.　"Jesus, thou Messenger of God!" she cried—"Through thy great Love we claim eternal Glory!"　And with the swiftness of lightning she was answered!—the sea of blood was changed to living flame,—her ship became a cloud of light, and she herself an angel clad in wings, and from the Cross she held streamed such a splendour as illumined all the heavens! And with thunder and with music and rejoicing, the gateways of the air, methought, were opened, and with a thousand thousand winged creatures round Him and above Him, and a new world rising like the morning sun behind Him, again, again I saw—the "Nazarene"! And with a voice of silver-sweet and overwhelming triumph He proclaimed: "*Heaven and earth shall pass away, but My words shall not pass away!*"'

She waited a moment, then went on—

'The "Nazarene"!—no other than the "Nazarene" it was whom I beheld thus gloriously surrounded!—the very "Nazarene" whom thou, Pontius, wert asked to judge and to condemn! No marvel was it that I sent to thee,—and in my scroll I would have told thee I had dreamt He was a god, but that I feared some other eye than thine might intercept and scan my words. Therefore I wrote "have naught to do with that just man,"—alas! 'twas foolish of me!—thou could'st not listen to a woman's pleading in a matter of the law, and when my slave returned I knew mine errand had been fruitless. Nevertheless I strove to warn thee '——

'Of what?' asked Pilate hoarsely,—he had covered his eyes with his hand, and spoke with difficulty—'Of naught, save that being just 'twere pity He should die. But knowest thou not 'tis ever the just who are condemned? And that thou didst suffer in a dream was better than my case;—what I saw, and what I suffered, was no dream!'

He sighed bitterly, heavily, and Justitia sitting down beside him, leaned her head upon his shoulder.

'I have not yet told thee all;'—she said in a trembling voice,—'The rest concerns thy fate!'

Pilate removed his hand from his eyes and looked round at her.

'My fate!' he echoed indifferently—'Whate'er it be, surely I shall have force enough to meet it!'

She held his hands in both her own and pressed them convulsively.

'Ay, full well I know thou hast force enough for anything'—she said—'else thou would'st not be Roman. But to perish even as Iscariot'——

He started away from her.

'As Iscariot!' he cried indignantly—'Nay, I am no traitor!'

She looked at him, her face growing very white and her lips trembling. She was evidently nerving herself to utter something which she feared would be unwelcome.

'The gods might call thee coward, Pontius!' she said at last faintly, and as though the words were wrested out of her.

He turned upon her in astonishment and wrath.

'What didst thou say, Justitia?' he demanded fiercely—'Surely I have not heard thee aright?—thou didst not dare speak such a word to me as "coward"?'

Her heart beat violently, but she kept her eyes fixed upon him tenderly, and without any visible sign of fear.

'If thou didst see supernal glory in the "Nazarene"' —she faltered slowly, and then paused, leaving her sentence unfinished.

Pilate's head drooped,—he shrank and shivered as though some invisible hand had struck him with a heavy blow.

'Go on,' he said unsteadily—'Albeit I know,—I know now what thou would'st say.'

'If thou didst see supernal glory in the "Nazarene,"' she repeated in firmer accents—'if thou didst recognise the God behind the Man, ay, even to swoon thereat, surely thou should'st have openly proclaimed this truth unto the priests and people.'

'They would not have believed me'—he answered her in a husky whisper,—'They would have deemed me mad,—unfit to rule'——

'What matter?' said Justitia dauntlessly,—'What are the beliefs of priests or people measured against the utterance of a Truth? If thou hadst spoken'——

'I tell thee they would have called me crazed'—said Pilate, rising and pacing the room agitatedly—'They would have told me that my vision was deceived,—that my brain wandered. How could'st thou ever persuade a callous crowd, of the existence of the supernatural?

'How do they persuade themselves?' demanded Justitia—'These very Jews do swear by supernatural shows that seem impossible. Do they not say that God Himself taught Moses the Commandments on Mount Sinai?—will they not even accept as truth that their most vengeful Jehovah hath oft condoned murder as a holy sacrifice, as in the story of their own judge Jephthah, who slew his innocent daughter to satisfy the horrible bloodthirstiness of Heaven! Why should the supernatural seem less to be believed in one phase of existence than another?'

'I know not—I know not!'—answered Pilate, still walking to and fro distressfully,—'Make me not answerable for the inconsistencies of man! I did my best and utmost with the people,—if I had told them what I saw, they would have dragged me from the judgment-seat as one possessed of devils and distraught; and Cæsar would have stripped me of authority.'

'Thou could'st have suffered all loss with equanimity,' said Justitia thoughtfully—'provided thine own conscience had been clear.'

He gave her no response, but still paced restlessly up and down.

Justitia moved to the window and gazed out at the dark, smooth velvet-looking foliage of the fig-trees at the end of the garden.

'It was a pale bright light, even like the beaming of this very moon'—she said—'that shone upon me in the closing of my dream. I stood, methought, in one of the strangest, loneliest, wildest corners of the world,—great mountain-peaks towered around me, white and sparkling with a seeming-bitter cold, and at my feet a solemn pool lay black and stirless. And as I looked, I saw thee, Pontius!—I saw thee flitting even as a spectre among the jagged rocks of those most solitary hills,—thou wert old and wan and weary, and hadst the livid paleness of approaching death. I called thee, but thou would'st not answer,—onward thou didst tread, and cam'st so near to me I could have touched thee! but ever thou didst elude my grasp. All suddenly'—and here she turned towards her husband, her eyes darkening with her thoughts—'I beheld thee, drifting like a cloud blown by the wind, towards a jutting peak that bent above that dreary pool of waveless waters—there thou didst pause, and with a cry that pierced my soul, thou didst exclaim "Jesus of Nazareth, thou Son of God, have mercy on me!" Then,—ere I could bid thee turn and wait for me, thou didst plunge forward,—forward and down,—down into the chill and darksome lake which closed even as a grave above thee!—thou wert gone,—gone into death and silence,—and I, shrieking upon thy name, awoke!'

'And waking thus in terror thou didst send to me?' asked Pilate gently, approaching her where she stood, and encircling her with his arm.

She bent her head in assent.

'Even then. And later, when my messenger returned from thee, I heard the people shout "*Not this man, but Barabbas.*" Who is Barabbas?'

'A thief and murderer'—said Pilate quickly—'But he hath the popular sympathy. Once he was in the honourable employ of Shadeen, the Persian jewel-merchant of this city,—and as a reward for trust reposed in him, he stole some priceless pearls from out a private coffer of his master. Moreover he was one of a band of revolutionary malcontents, and did stab to death the Pharisee Gabrias, out in the open streets. 'Tis more than eighteen months ago now—thou wert visiting thy friends in Rome, and knewest naught of it. I would have had Barabbas crucified,—nevertheless the people have given him rescue and full liberty. They celebrate their feast by the release of a murderer, and the slaughter of the Sinless. 'Tis their chosen way—and I am not to blame!'

'Iscariot also served in the house of Shadeen,' said Justitia meditatively.

'Even so I have heard.'

'And thou art not troubled, Pontius, by my dream?' she questioned earnestly—'Seest thou no omen in its end concerning thee, when I beheld thee perish in the gloom and solitude, self-slain, even as Iscariot?'

He shuddered a little and forced a faint smile.

'If I am troubled, Justitia, 'tis because thou art,—and because trouble doth vaguely press upon us all to-day. Trust me, the very Jews are not without their fears, seeing that the storm hath rent their Temple veil, and darkened the land with such mysterious suddenness. 'Tis enough to shake the spirits of the boldest,—but now perchance evil is past, and by and by the air will rid itself of all fore-bodings. Lo, how divinely clear the sky!—how fair the moon!—'tis a silver night for the slumber of the "Nazarene"!'

She looked at him with wondering, dilating eyes.

'Speakest thou in sober reason, Pontius?' she said

'Wilt thou insist upon thy fancy that He is not dead, and that He cannot die? Thinkest thou He only sleeps?'

Pilate drew her closer to him.

'Hush,—hush!' he said in a low trembling tone—'Whatever I may think, I must say nothing. Let us hold our peace,—let us live as the world would have us live, in the proud assumption that there is nothing in the universe more powerful or more wonderful than ourselves! So shall we fit ourselves for the material side of nature,—and if there be in truth, another side,—a spiritual, we can shut our eyes and swear we know naught of it! So shall we be deemed wise,—and sane!—and we shall give offence to no one —save to God,—if a God perchance there be!'

His voice grew faint—his eyes had a vacant stare, —he was looking out and upward to the brilliant sky. Suddenly he brought his gaze down from the heavens to earth, and fixed it on the open road beyond his garden where a small dark group of slowly moving figures just then appeared.

'Who goes yonder?' he said inquiringly—'Seest thou, Justitia, they take the private path towards the house of Iscariot? Surely they carry some heavy burden?'

Justitia leaned forward to look,—then drew back with a faint cry.

'Come away,—come away!' she whispered, shivering and drawing her flowing robes closer about her— 'Do not wait here—do not watch them,—they are bearing home the dead!'

'The dead!' echoed Pilate—'Then 'tis the body of Judas!'

Justitia laid her hand entreatingly against his lips.

'Hush—hush! If it be, as indeed I feel it is, do not speak of it—do not look!'—And with agitated impatience she drew the curtain across the window and shut out the solemn beauty of the night—' I am chilled with horror, Pontius,—I can bear no more ! I would not see dead Judas in my dreams ! Let us go hence and rest, and try to sleep, and,—if we can,—forget ! '

XXVIII

THAT same night, before a richly-chased mirror of purely polished silver, and gazing at her own fair face reflected in it by the brilliant lustre of the moon, Judith Iscariot sat, lost in a pleasant reverie. She was alone,—she had dismissed her attendant women,—the picture of her perfect loveliness, rendered lovelier by the softness of the lunar beams, charmed her, and she would not have so much as a small hand-lamp kindled, lest its wavering flicker should destroy the magical effect of her beauty mirrored thus and set about with glory by the argent light of heaven. Leaning back in a low carved chair, she clasped her round arms idly behind her head and contemplated herself critically with a smile. She had cast aside the bright flame-tinted mantle she had worn all day, and was now arrayed in white,—a straight plain robe of thin and silky texture that clung about her figure closely, betraying every exquisite curve and graceful line,—her fiery-golden hair unbound to its full length fell to the very floor in glistening showers, and from underneath the thick bright ripples of it clustering on her brow, her dark jewel-like eyes flashed with a mingling of joy and scorn.

'What cowards, after all, are men!' she murmured half aloud,—'Even the strongest! Yon base Barabbas

was nigh to weeping for the death of the accursëd
"Nazarene,"—methinks 'twas terror for himself, rather
than pity for the dying. And Caiaphas!—who
would have thought that he would be paralysed with
fear when they told him of the rending of the Temple
veil!'

She laughed softly,—and her lips laughing back at
her from the silver surface into which she gazed, had
so bewitching a sweetness in their smile that she
leaned forward to observe them more intently.

'Verily 'tis no marvel that they dote upon me one
and all'—she said, studying her delicate features and
dazzling complexion with complacent vanity,—'Even
smiling so, I draw the subtle Caiaphas my way,—he
passeth for a wise priest, yet if I do but set my eyes
upon him thus'—and she half closed them and peered
languorously through their sweeping lashes—'he pales
and trembles,—or thus'—and she flashed them fully
open in all their fatal brilliancy—'he loses breath for
very love, and gapes upon me, flushed and foolish like
one stricken with the burning of the sun. And
Barabbas,—I must rid me of Barabbas, though there
is something fierce about him that I love; albeit he
showed but little love for me to-day, shaken and
palsied as he was by cowardice.'

She took up a comb and began to pass it slowly
through the shining splendour of her hair. Gradually
her face became more meditative, and a slight frown
contracted her brows.

'Nevertheless there was a horror in that storm!'—
she continued in whispered accents—'And even now
my heart misgives me strangely,—I would that Judas
were at home!'

She rose up, slim and stately, and stood before her
mirror, the golden weight of half her tresses in one
hand. Round about her the moonlight fell in a
glistening halo, touching here and there a jewel on

her arm or bosom to a sudden glimmer of white fire.

'Caiaphas should have told the people what I bade him'—she murmured, 'that the tempest was awakened by the evil sorceries of the "Nazarene." He was possessed of devils; and they did cause the pitchy darkness and the tremor of the earth that rent the rocks asunder. 'Twas even so,—and Caiaphas should have spoken thus,—but he too, for the moment, lost judgment through his fears.'

Pausing, she twisted her hair mechanically round and round her fingers.

'What was the magic of the Man of Nazareth?' she queried, as though making the inquiry of her own reflection that gazed earnestly back at her from the silver oval surface she confronted—'I could see none save beauty. Beauty He had undoubtedly,—but not such beauty as a woman loves. 'Twas too austere and perfect,—too grave and passionless,—albeit He had strange light within His eyes that for a passing second moved me, even me, to terror! And then the thunder came,—and then the darkness'——

She shivered slightly, then laughed, and glanced up at the moon that shone, round and full, in at her open casement.

''Twas a malignant spell He cast,' she said—'But now 'tis ended,—and all alarms have ceased. And truly it is well for us that He is dead, for such fanatics are dangerous. And now is Judas undeceived,—he knows this prophet whom he called his Master is no god after all, but simply man,—and he will repent him of his wanderings and return to us again. When his first rage is past, he will come back ashamed and sorrowful, and seeking pardon for his fury of last night,—and we will welcome him with joy and feasting and forgiveness, and once more we shall be happy. Yea, surely Caiaphas did advise me well, and in the death of the blasphemous "Nazarene" Judas is saved from further harm.'

She threw back her hair over her shoulders and smiled. Then opening a massive brass-bound casket near her, she drew forth a handful of various jewels, and looked at them carelessly one by one, selecting at last a star-shaped ornament of magnificent rubies.

''Tis a fair gift'—she murmured, holding it up in the moonlight and watching it flash a dull red in the silver rays—' I know not that I have ever seen a fairer ! 'Twas wise of Caiaphas not to bestow this on his sickly spouse,—'twould ill become the pallid skin of the daughter of Annas.'

She studied the gems carefully,—then diving anew into the casket brought out a chain of exquisite pearls, each pearl as large as the ripe seed of Indian maize.

'How well they go together thus!' she said, setting them with the ruby star against the whiteness of her bare arm—' They should be worn in company,—the high-priest's rubies and the stolen pearls of Barabbas!'

Her lips parted in a little mocking smile, and for a moment or two she held the gems in her hand, absorbed in thought. Then, slowly fastening the pearls round her throat, she put back the ruby pendant into the jewel-coffer, and again peered at herself in the silver mirror. And as she silently absorbed the glowing radiance of her own matchless beauty, she raised her arms with a gesture of irrepressible triumph.

'For such as I am, the world is made!' she exclaimed — 'For such as I am, emperors and kings madden themselves and die! For such as I am, proud heroes abase themselves as slaves. No woman lives who can be fairer than I,—and what shall I do with my fairness when I am weary of sporting with lovers and fools?— I will wed some mighty conqueror, and be the queen and mistress of many nations!'

In her superb vanity, she lifted her head higher as
though she felt the imagined crown already on her
brows, and stepped slowly backward from the mirror,
still steadfastly regarding her own image, when all
at once the sound of a hurried footfall in the corridor
startled her. She turned in a listening attitude, her
hair falling about her, and the pearls gleaming on
her throat,—the hasty footstep came nearer,—then
paused.

'Madam! Madam!' cried a voice outside.

Moved by some swift instinct of alarm, she sprang
forward and flung the door of her chamber wide
open, thus confronting one of her father's servants,
who stared at her wildly, making dumb signs of
despair.

'What is it?' she gasped,—her lips had grown
suddenly stiff and dry and she could barely articulate,
—her heart beat violently, and the pearls about her
neck seemed strangling her.

The man opened his mouth to answer, then
stopped,—Judith clutched him by the arm.

'Speak!'—she whispered—'What evil news hast
thou?'

'Madam,' faltered the servant, trembling—'I dare
not utter it,—prithee come—thy father sends—have
patience . . . take comfort'——

He turned from her, hiding his face.

''Tis Judas!' she exclaimed—'He is wounded?—
ill? He hath returned?'

'Ay, madam, he hath returned!' replied the
messenger hoarsely, and then, as if fearing to trust
himself to the utterance of another word, he hastened
away, mutely entreating her to follow.

She paused a moment,—a ghastly pallor stole
away all the light and brilliancy of her features, and
she pressed one hand upon her bosom to control its
rising fear.

'He hath returned!' she murmured vaguely—
'Judas is at home! My father sends for me?—then
all is well,—surely 'tis well,—it cannot be otherwise
than well.'

Giving one glance backward into her moonlit
room where the silver mirror shone like a glistening shield, she began to move with hesitating step
through the corridor,—then, all at once seized by
an irresistible panic, she gathered up her trailing
white robes in her hand and ran precipitately towards
the great vestibule of the house, which her father
had had built in the fashion of an Egyptian court,
and where he was accustomed to sit in the cool of
the evening with his intimates and friends. It was
surrounded with square columns and was open to the
night, and as Judith came rushing along, her gold
hair flying about her like flame, and her dark eyes
wild with uncertain terror and expectancy, she was
confronted by the tall figure of a man who, with
extended arms, strove to intercept himself between
her and some passive object that lay, covered with
a cloth, on the ground a few steps beyond. She
gazed at him amazedly,—it was Barabbas.

'Judith!' he faltered — 'Judith, — wait! — Have
patience'——

But she pushed him aside, and ran towards her
father, whom she perceived leaning against one of
the carven columns, his face hidden upon his arm.

'Father!' she cried.

He raised his head and looked at her,—his austere
fine features were convulsed by a speechless agony
of grief, and with one trembling hand he pointed
silently to the stirless covered shape that reposed at
a little distance from him. Her eyes followed his
gesture, and, staggering forward feebly step by step,
she pushed back her hair from her brows and stared
fixedly at the outline of the thing that was so

solemnly inert. Then the full comprehension of
what she saw seemed to burst in upon her brain,
and falling upon her knees she clutched desperately
at the rough cloth which concealed that which she
craved, yet feared to see.

'Judas!' she cried—'Judas!'

Her voice broke in a sharp shriek, and she suddenly withdrew her hands and looked at them in
horror, shuddering, as though they had come in
contact with some nameless abomination. Lifting
her eyes she became dimly conscious that others
were around her,—that her father had approached,
—that Barabbas was gazing at her,—and with a
bewildered vacant smile she pointed to the hidden
dead.

'Why have ye brought him home thus wrapped
from light and air?' she demanded in quick jarring
accents—'It may be that he sleeps,—or hath swooned.
Uncover his face!'

No one moved to obey her. The veiled corpse
lying black and stirless in the full light of the moon
had something solemnly forbidding in its aspect.
And for one or two minutes a profound and awful
stillness reigned, unbroken save by the slow chime of
a bell striking the midnight hour.

Suddenly Judith's voice began again, murmuring
in rapid whispers.

'Judas,—Judas!' she said, 'waken! 'Tis folly to
lie there and fill me with such terrors,—thou art not
dead,—it is not possible,—thou could'st not die thus
suddenly. Only last night thou camest here full of
a foolish rage against me, and in thy thoughtless
frenzy thou didst curse me,—lo, now thou must
unsay that curse,—thou canst not leave me un-
forgiven and unblessed. What have I ever done of
harm to thee? I did but bid thee prove the treachery
of the "Nazarene." And thou hast proved it; where-

fore should'st thou grieve to find deception at an end?
Rise up, rise up!—if thou art ill 'tis I will tend thee,
—waken!—why should'st thou rest sullen thus, and
angry still? Surely 'tis I who should be angry at
thy churlishness, for well I know thou hear'st my
voice, though out of some sick humour, as it seems,
thou wilt not answer me!'

And once more her hands hovered hesitatingly in
the air, till apparently nerving herself to a supreme
effort, she took trembling hold of the upper part of
the pall-like drapery that hid the corpse from view.
Lifting it fearfully, she turned it back, slowly, slowly,
—then stared in horrid wonderment,—was that her
brother's face she looked upon?—that fair, strange,
pallid marble mask with those protruding desperate
eyes? Such fixed impenetrable eyes!—they gave
her wondering stare for stare,—and as she stooped
down close, and closer yet, her warm red lips went
nigh to touch those livid purple ones, which were
drawn back tightly just above the teeth in the ghastly
semblance of a smile. She stroked the damp and
ice-cold brow,—she thrust her fingers in the wild hair,
—it was most truly Judas, or some dreadful likeness
of him that lay there in waxen effigy,—a white and
frozen figure of dead youth and beauty,—and yet she
could not realise the awful truth of what she saw.
Suddenly her wandering and distrustful gaze fell on
his throat,—a rope was round it, twisted in such
a knot, that where it pressed the flesh the skin was
broken, and the bruised blood, oozing through, had
dried and made a clotted crimson mark as though
some jagged knife had hacked it. Beholding this,
she leapt erect, and tossing her arms distractedly
above her head, gave vent to a piercing scream that
drove sharp discord through the air, and brought the
servants of the household running in with torches in
the wildest confusion and alarm. Her father caught

her in his arms, endeavouring to hold and pacify her,
—in vain!—he might as well have striven to repress
a whirlwind. She was transformed into a living
breathing fury, and writhed and twisted in his grasp,
a convulsed figure of heartrending despair.

'Look you, they have murdered him!' she shrieked;
'They have murdered Judas! — he hath been
violently slain by the followers of the "Nazarene"!
O cruel deed!—There shall be vengeance for it,—
vengeance deep and bitter,—for Judas had no fault
at all save that of honesty! Caiaphas! Caiaphas!
Where is Caiaphas? Bid him come hither and
behold this work!—bid him pursue and crucify the
murderers!—let us go seek the Roman governor,—
justice, I say!—I will have justice'— Here her
shrill voice suddenly sank, and flinging herself
desperately across her brother's body, she tried with
shaking fingers to loosen the terrible death-noose of
the strangling cord.

'Undo this knot'—she cried sobbingly—'O God!
will none of ye remove this pressure that doth stop
his breath? Maybe he lives yet!—his eyes have
sense and memory in them,—untie this twisted
torture, — prithee help me, friends, — father, help
me'——

Even as she spoke, with her fingers plucking at the
cord, an awful change passed over her face, and
snatching her hands away she looked at them aghast,
—they were wet with blood. A strange light kindled
in her eyes,—a wan smile hovered on her lips. She
held up her stained fingers.

'Lo, he bleeds!' she said—'The life within him
rises to my touch,—he is not dead!'

'He bleeds as dead men oft are wont to bleed at
the touch of their murderers!'—said a harsh voice
suddenly,—'Thou, Judith, hast brought thy brother
to his death,—wherefore his very blood accuses thee!'

And the rugged figure of Peter, advancing, stood out clear in the moonbeams that fell showering on the open court.

Iscariot, tall and stately, confronted him in wrath and astonishment.

'Man, how darest thou at such a time thus rave upon my daughter'— he began, then stopped, checked in his speech by the austere dignity of the disciple's attitude and his regal, half-menacing gesture.

'Back, Jew!' he said—'Thou who art not born again of water or of spirit, but art ever of the tainted blood of Israel unregenerate, contest no words with me! Remorse hath made me strong! I am that Peter who denied his Master, and out of sin repented of, I snatch authority! Dispute me not,—I speak not unto thee, but unto her;—she who doth clamour for swift justice on the murderers of her brother there. Even so do *I* cry out for justice!—even so do *I* demand vengeance!—vengeance upon her who drove him to his doom. For Judas was my friend,—and by his own hand was he slain,—but in that desperate deed no soul took part save she who now bemoans the end that hath been wrought, through the tempting of her serpent subtilty!'

'Hast thou no mercy?' cried Barabbas in an agony, 'Not even at this hour?'

'Not at this hour nor at any hour!' responded Peter with fierce triumph lighting up his features,— 'God forbid that I should show any mercy to the wicked!'

'There spoke the first purely human Christian!' murmured a low satirical voice, and the picturesque form of Melchior shadowed itself against a marble column whitened by the moon—'Verily, Petrus, thou shalt convey to men in a new form the message of Love Divine!'

But the disciple heeded not these words. He strode

forward to where Judith lay half prone across her
brother's corpse, still busying herself with efforts to
untie the suicidal noose at the throat, which was now
darkly moist with blood.

'What doest thou there, Judith Iscariot?' he
demanded—'Thou canst never unfasten that hempen
necklet,—'tis not of pearls or sparkling gems such as
thy soul loveth,—and Judas himself hath knotted it
too closely for easy severance. Let be, let be,—weep
and lament for thine own treachery,—for behold a
curse shall fall upon thee, never to be lifted from thy
life again!'

She heard,—and raising her eyes, which were dry
and glittering with fever, smiled at him. So wildly
beautiful did she look, that Peter, though wrought up
to an exaltation of wrath, was for a moment staggered
by the bewildering loveliness of her perfect face
showered round by its wealth of red-gold hair, and
hesitated to pronounce the malediction that hovered
on his lips.

'Never again,—never again'—she murmured
vaguely; 'See!' And she showed him her blood-stained
fingers—'Life lingers in him yet!—ah, prithee, friend,'
—and she gazed up at him appealingly—'Undo the
cruel cord!—if Judas tied it, . . . didst thou not tell
me Judas tied it? . . . how could that be?'— She
paused,—a puzzled look knitting her brows,—then a
sudden terror began to shake her limbs.

'Father!' she exclaimed.

He hastened to her, and lifting her up, pressed her
against his breast, the tears raining down his face.

'What does it mean?' she faltered, gazing at him
alarmedly—'Tell me,—it is not true, . . . it cannot
be true,—Judas was ever brave and bold,—he did not
wreak this violence upon himself?'

Iscariot strove to answer her, but words failed him,
—the wonted calmness of his austerely handsome

features was completely broken up by misery and agitation. She however, gazing fully at him, understood at last,—and, wrenching herself out of his arms, stood for a moment immovable and ghastly pale, as though suddenly turned to stone. Then, lifting her incarnadined hands in the bright moon-rays, she broke into a discordant peal of delirious laughter.

'O terrible Nazarene!' she cried—'This is thy work! Thy sorceries have triumphed!—thou hast thy victory! Thou art avenged in full, thou pitiless, treacherous Nazarene!'

And with a sharp shriek that seemed to stab the stillness with a wound, she fell forward on the pavement in a swoon; as lost to sense and sight as the body of Judas, that with its fixed wide-open eyes, stared blindly outward into nothingness and smiled.

XXIX

THEY carried her to her own chamber and left
her to the ministrations of her women, who
wept for her as women will often weep when startled
by the news of some tragic event which does not
personally concern them, without feeling any real
sympathy with the actual cause of sorrow. Her
haughty and arrogant disposition had made her but
few friends among her own sex, and her peerless
beauty had ever been a source of ill-will and envy to
others less dazzlingly fair. So that the very maidens
who tended her in her fallen pride and bitter heart-
break, though they shed tears for pure nervousness,
had little love in their enforced care, and watched
her in her deep swoon with but casual interest, only
whispering vague guesses one to another as to what
would be her possible condition when she again
awoke to consciousness.

Meanwhile her brother's corpse was reverently
placed on two carved and gilded trestles set in an
arched recess of the open court, and draped with
broideries of violet and gold. In stern silence and
constrained composure, the unhappy father of the
dead man gave his formal instructions, and fulfilled
in every trifling particular the duties that devolved
upon him,—and when all had been done that was

demanded of him for the immediate moment, he
turned towards those three who had brought home
the body of his son between them, — Barabbas,
Melchior, and the disciple Peter.

'Sirs,' he said in a low voice broken by emotion—
'I have to thank ye for the sorrowful service ye have
rendered me,—albeit it hath broken my heart and
hath visited upon our house such mourning as shall
never cease. Only one of ye am I in any sort acquainted with,—and that is Barabbas, lately the
prisoner of the law. In former days he hath been
welcomed here, and deemed a worthy man and true,
and now, despite his well-proved crimes and shame
of punishment, I can but bear in mind that once he
was my son's companion in the house of El-Shadeen.'
Here his accents faltered, but he controlled himself
and went on—'Wherefore, excusing not his faults,
I yet would say that even as the people have released
him, I cannot visit him with censure, inasmuch as he
hath evident pity for my grief, and did appeal for
my beloved child against the mercilessness of this
stranger.'

Pausing, he turned his eyes upon Peter, who met
his gaze boldly.

'Stranger I truly am from henceforth to the Jews,'
said the disciple,—'Naught have I in common with
their lives, spent in the filthy worship of Mammon
and the ways of usury. Nevertheless I compassionate
thy fate, Iscariot, as I compassionate the fate of any
wretched man stricken with woes innumerable through
his own blindness and unbelief;—and as for mercilessness, whereof thou dost accuse me, thou shalt find
the Truth ever as a sword inclement, sharp to cut
away all pleasingly delusive forms. When thou dost
speak of thy beloved child, thou dost betray the
weakness of thy life, for from thy nest of over-

pampering and indulgent love hath risen a poison
snake to sting and slay! A woman left unguarded
and without authority upon her, is even as a devil
that destroys,— a virgin given liberty of will is
soon deflowered. Knowest thou not thy Judith
is a wanton?—and that thy ravening high-priest
Caiaphas hath made of her a viler thing than
ever was the city's Magdalen? Ah, strike an'
thou wilt, Iscariot!—the truth is on my lips!—tear
out my tongue, and thou shalt find the truth still
there!'

Speechless with wrath, Iscariot made one fierce
stride towards him with full intent to smite him
across the mouth as the only fitting answer to his
accusation, but as he raised his threatening hand, the
straight unquailing look of the now almost infuriate
disciple, struck him with a sudden supernatural awe,
and he paused, inert.

'The truth, the truth!' cried Peter, tossing his
arms about—'Lo, from henceforth I will clamour for
it, rage for it, live for it, die for it! Three times have
I falsely sworn, and thus have I taken the full
measure of a Lie! Its breadth, its depth, its height,
its worth, its meaning, its result,—its crushing, suffo-
cating weight upon the soul! I know its nature—
'tis all hell in a word!—'tis a "yea" or "nay" on
which is balanced all eternity! I will no more of
it,—I will have truth,—the truth of men, the truth of
women,—no usurer shall be called honest,—no wanton
shall be called chaste, to please the humour of the
passing hour! No—no—I will have none of this—
but only truth!—the truth that is even as a shining
naked scimitar in the hand of God, glittering
horribly!—I, Peter, will declare it!—I who did swear
a lie three times, will speak the truth three thousand
times in reprisal of my sin! Weep, rave, tear thy

reverend hairs, unreverent Jew, thou, who as stiff-necked righteous Pharisee didst practise cautious virtue and self-seeking sanctity, and now through unbelief art left most desolate! Would'st stake a world upon thy daughter's honour?—Fie! 'tis dross! —'tis common ware,—purchaseable for gold and gewgaws! Lo, through this dazzling woman-snare, born of thy blood, a God hath perished in Judæa! His words have been rejected,—His message is despised,—His human life hath been roughly torn from Him by torture. Therefore upon Judæa shall the curse be wrought through ages following endless ages; and as the children of the house of Israel do worship gold, even so shall gold be their damnation! Like base slaves shall they toil for kings and coun-sellors; even as brutish beasts shall they be harnessed to the wheels of work, and drag the heavier burdens of the State beneath the whip and scourge,—despised and loathed, they shall labour for others, in bondage. Scattered through many lands their tribes shall be, and nevermore shall they be called a nation! For ever and for ever shall the sinless blood of the Messenger of God rest red upon Judæa!—for ever and for ever from this day, shall Israel be cast out from the promises of life eternal,—a scorn and abomination in the sight of Heaven!'

He paused, breathless, his hands uplifted as though invoking doom. His rough cloak fell away from his shoulders in almost regal folds, displaying his coarse fisherman's dress beneath,—his figure seemed to grow taller and statelier, investing itself with a kind of mystic splendour in the shining radiance of the moon. Lifting his eyes to the stars twinkling like so many points of flame above him, he smiled, a wild and wondering smile.

'But the end is not yet!' he said—'There is a new

18

terror and trembling, that doth threaten the land.
For ye have murdered the Christ without slaying
Him!—ye have forced Him to suffer death, but He
is not dead! To-night He is buried,—shut down in
the gloom of the grave,—what will ye do if the great
stones laid above Him have no force to keep Him
down?—what if the earth will not hold Him?—what
if, after three days, as He said, He should rise to life
again? I will aver nothing,—I will not again swear
falsely,—I will shut my doubts and terrors in mine
own soul and say no more,—but think of it, O ye
unregenerate of Israel, what will ye do in the hour of
trembling, if He, whom ye think dead, doth in very
truth arise to life?'

His voice sank to a whisper,—he glanced about
him nervously,—then, as though seized by some
sudden panic, he covered himself shudderingly up in
his mantle so that his face could hardly be seen, and
began to steal away cautiously on tip-toe.

'Think of it!' he repeated, looking back once at
Iscariot with a wild stare—'Perchance He may
pardon Judas! Nay, I know nothing—I will swear
nothing,—nevertheless 'twill be a strange world,—
'twill be an altogether different, marvellous world if
He should keep His word, and after three days—no
more, no less, He should arise again!'

And still moving as one in fear, shrouded in his
cloak and stepping noiselessly, he turned abruptly
and disappeared.

Iscariot gazed after him in mingled anger and
perplexity.

'Is it some madman ye have brought hither?' he
demanded—'What manner of devil doth possess
him?'

'The devil of a late remorse!' answered Melchior
slowly—'It doth move a man ofttimes to most

singular raving, and doth frequently inspire him to singular deeds. The devil in this fisherman will move the world!'

'Fisherman?' echoed Iscariot wonderingly—'Is he no more than common?'

'No more than common,'—replied Melchior, his eyes dilating singularly—'Common as—clay! Herein will be his failure and his triumph. The scent of the sea was round him at his birth,—from very boyhood he hath contended with the raging winds and waters, —so shall he yet contend with similarly warring elements. No kings ever travelled from afar to kneel before him in his cradle,—no Eastern sages proffered gifts to honour him,—no angels sang anthems for him in the sky,—these things were for the "Nazarene" whom lately he denied, but whom he now will serve most marvellously! But for the present, as the time now goes, he is but Simon Peter, one of the fisher-folk of Galilee, and lately a companion of thy dead son Judas.'

A smothered groan escaped Iscariot's lips as his eyes wandered to the extemporised bier on which the corpse of Judas lay.

'Unhappy boy!' he murmured—'No wonder thou wert fanatic and wild, consorting with such friends as these!'

He went and stood by the covered body, and there, looking round towards his visitors with an air of sorrowful and resigned dignity, said,

'Ye will not take it ill of me, sirs, that I entreat ye now to leave me. The grief I have is almost too great to grasp,—my spirit is broken with mourning, and I am very weary. As for my daughter, thou, Barabbas, needest not that I should tell thee of the falsity of the slander brought against her by yon mad disciple of a mad reformer. Thou knowest her,—her innocence, her pride, her spotless virtue,—and to the friend thou hast with thee, thou wilt defend her honour and pure chastity. Thou hearest me?'

'I hear thee'—answered Barabbas in a choked voice—'And verily my whole heart aches for thee, Iscariot!'

The elder man looked at him keenly, and trembled.

'I thank thee, friend!' he then said quickly—'Thou hast been guilty of heinous crimes,—but nevertheless I know thou hast manliness enough, and wilt, as far as lies within thy power, defend my child from scurrilous talk, such as this coarse-tongued Galilean fisherman may set current in the town.' He paused as though he were thinking deeply,—then beckoned Barabbas to approach him more closely. As his gesture was obeyed, he laid one hand on his son's veiled corpse and the other on Barabbas's arm.

'Understand me well!' he said in a fierce hoarse whisper—'If there were a grain of truth in that vile slander, I would kill Caiaphas!—yea, by this dead body of mine only son, I swear I would slay him before all the people in the very precincts of the Temple!'

In that one moment his face was terrible,—and the sombre eyes of Barabbas glittered a swift response to his thought. For a brief space the two men looked at each other steadily, and to Barabbas's excited fancy it seemed as if at the utterance of Iscariot's oath, the body of Judas trembled slightly underneath its heavy wrappings. One second, and the sudden flash of furious comprehension that had lighted their dark features as with fire, passed, and the bereaved father bent his head in ceremonious salutation.

'Farewell, sirs,'—he said, bidding Barabbas retreat

from him by a slight commanding sign—'What poor
thanks a broken-hearted man can give are yours for
bringing home my dead. I will see ye both again,—
a few days hence,—when the bitterness of grief is
somewhat quelled,— when I am stronger,— better
fitted for reasonable speech,—but now'——

He waved his hand in dismissal, and drawing his
mantle round him, sat down by his son's corpse, to
keep an hour's melancholy vigil.

Barabbas at once retired with Melchior, only
pausing on his way out to inquire of a passing
servant if Judith had recovered from her swoon. He
received an answer in the negative, given with tears
and doleful shaking of the head, and with a heavy
heart he left the house and passed into the moonlit
street. There, after walking a little way, Melchior
suddenly stopped, fixing his jewel-like contemplative
eyes upon the brooding face of his companion.

'Dreamest thou, good ruffian, of the beauty of thy
lost Judith?' he said—'I confess to thee I never saw
a fairer woman! Even her sorrow doth enhance her
loveliness.'

Barabbas shuddered.

'Why speak to me now of her beauty?' he demanded passionately—'Hath it not wrought sufficient
havoc? Think of the dead Judas!'

'Truly I do think of him'—responded Melchior
gravely—'All the world will think of him,—he will
never be forgotten. Unhappy youth!—for history
will make him answerable for sins that are not all his
own. But the chronicles of men are not the chronicles
of God,—and even Judas shall have justice in the
end. Meantime'—and he smiled darkly—'knowest
thou, good Barabbas, I am troubled by a singular
presentiment? Poverty doth not oppress me,—nevertheless I swear unto thee, I would not in these days

stake a penny piece upon the value of the life of Caiaphas! What thinkest thou?'

Barabbas stared at him, aghast, and breathing quickly. And for a moment they remained so, gazing full at one another in the paling radiance of the sinking moon,—then walked on together, homeward, in silence.

XXX

TOWARDS three o'clock in the dawn of the Jewish Sabbath, Judith Iscariot awoke from her heavy stupor of merciful unconsciousness. Opening her eyes, she gazed about her bewilderedly, and gradually recognised her surroundings. She was in her own room,—the casement was closed and lamps were burning,—and at the foot of her couch sat two of her waiting-women sunk in a profound slumber. Lifting herself cautiously upon her pillows, she looked at them wonderingly,—then peered round on all sides to see if any others were near. No,—there was no one,—only those two maids fast asleep. Gathering together her disordered garments, and twisting up her hair in a loose knot, she noiselessly arose, and stepping down from her couch, moved across the room till she faced her mirror. There she paused and smiled wildly at herself,—how strange her eyes looked! . . . but how bright, how beautiful! The pearls Barabbas had given her long ago, gleamed on her throat,—she fingered them mechanically,—poor Barabbas!— certainly he had loved her in days gone by. But since then, many things had happened,—wonderful and confusing things,—and now there was only one thing left to remember,—that after long absence and unkind estrangement Judas was once more at home. Yes!—Judas was at home,—and she would go and see him and talk to him, and clear up whatever foolish misunderstanding there had been between them. Her head swam giddily, and she felt a feebleness in all her limbs,—shudders of icy cold ran through her, followed by waves of heat that sickened and suffocated her,—but she paid little heed to these sensations, her one desire to see Judas overpowering all physical uneasiness. She fastened her white robe more securely about her with a gold embroidered girdle, and catching sight of her ornamental dagger where it lay on a table close by, she attached it to her waist. Then she glanced anxiously round at her two women, —they still slept. Stepping heedfully on tip-toe, she passed easily out of her room, for the door had been left open for air, and there was only the curtain at the archway to quietly lift and let fall. Tottering a little as she walked, she glided along the corridor, a white figure with a spectral pale face and shining eyes,— she felt happy and light-hearted,—almost she could have sung a merry song, so singularly possessed by singular joy was she. Reaching the open-air court she stopped, gazing eagerly from side to side,—its dim quadrangle was full of flickering lights and shadows, for the moon had disappeared behind the frowning portico, leaving but a silvery trail upon the sky to faintly mark her recent passage among the stars. Everything was very still,—no living creature was visible save a little downy owl that flew with a plaint-ive cry in and out among the marble columns calling to its mate with melancholy persistence. The bereaved Iscariot, wearied out by grief, had but just retired to snatch some sorely-needed rest ; and the body of his hapless son, laid out beneath its violet pall, possessed to itself the pallid hour of the vanish-ing night and the coming morn. Judith's softly sandalled feet made a delicate sound like the pattering of falling leaves, as she moved somewhat unsteadily

over the pavement, groping in the air now and then
with her hands as though she were blind. Very soon
her perplexed and wandering gaze found what she
sought,—the suggestive dark mass of drapery under
which reposed all that was mortal of her brother, the
elder companion and confidant of her childhood, who
had loved her with a tenderness 'passing that of
women.' She hurried her steps and almost ran,—and
without any hesitation or fear, turned back all the
coverings till the face and the whole form of the dead
Judas lay before her, stark and stiff, the rope still
fastened round the neck in dreadful witness of the
deed that had been done. Terribly beautiful he
seemed in that pale semi-radiance of the sky,—
austerely grand,—with something of a solemn scorn
upon his features, and an amazing world of passionate
appeal in his upward gazing eyes. 'Call ye me a
traitor?' he mutely said to the watchful stars—'Lo,
in the days to come, there shall be among professing
saints many a worse than I!'

His sister looked at him curiously, with an expression of wild inquisitiveness,—but she neither wept nor
trembled. A fixed idea was in her distracted brain,—
undefined and fantastic,—but such as it was, she was
bent upon it. With a strange triumph lighting up
her eyes, she drew her jewelled dagger from its sheath,
and with deft care cut asunder the rope round the
throat of the corpse. As she pulled it cautiously
away, the blood again oozed slowly forth from
beneath the bruised skin,—this was mysterious and
horrible, and terrified her a little, for she shuddered from head to foot. Anon she smiled,—and
twisting the severed cord, stained and moist as it
was, in and out the embroidered girdle at her
own waist, she threw the dagger far from her into
a corner of the quadrangle, and clapped her hands
delightedly.

'Judas!' she exclaimed—'Lo! I have cut the cruel rope wherewith thou wast wounded,—now thou canst breathe!   Come!—rise up and speak to me! Tell me all—I will believe all thy marvellous histories! I will not say that thou art wrongly led,—if thou wilt only smile again and speak, I will pardon all thy foolish fancy for the teachings of the "Nazarene."   Thou knowest I would not drive thee to despair,—I would not even willingly offend thee,—I am thy little sister always who is dear to thee.   Judas—listen!—'Twas Caiaphas,—'twas the high-priest himself who bade me tell thee to betray thy Master,—and very rightly— for thy mad prophet came in arms against our creed. Why should'st thou turn rebellious and forsake the faith of all our fathers?   Come,—rise and hear reason!'—and with the unnatural force of a deepening frenzy, she bent down and partly raised the corpse, staring at its fearful countenance with mingled love and horror—'Why,—how thou lookest at me!—with what cold unpiteous eyes?   What have I done to thee?   Naught, save advise thee wisely.   As for Caiaphas,—thou knowest not Caiaphas—how much he can do for thee if thou wilt show some fitting penitence'—here she broke off with a kind of half-shriek,—the weight of the dead body was too much for her and lurched backward, dragging her with it,— she loosened her arms from about it, and it straightway fell heavily prone in its former position.   She began to sob childishly.

'Judas, Judas!   Speak to me!   Kiss me!   I know thou hearest me, and wilt not answer me for anger, because this stranger out of Nazareth is dearer unto thee than I!'

She waited in evident expectation of some response,—then, as the silence remained unbroken, she began to play with the blood-stained rope at her girdle.

'Ah well!' she sighed—'I am sorry thou art sullen. Caiaphas would do great things for thee if thou wert wise. Why should'st thou thus grow desperate because of a traitor's death? What manner of man was this much-marvelled-at "Nazarene"? Naught but a workman's son, possessed of strange fanaticism! And shall so small a thing sow rancour 'twixt us twain? Yet surely I will humour thee if still to humour Him should be thy fancy,—thou shalt have cross and crown made sacred an' thou wilt,—I can do no more in veriest kindness to appease thy wrath, — moreover thou dost maintain a useless churlishness, since thy "Nazarene" is dead, and cannot, even to please thee and amend thy sickness, rise again.'

Again she paused,—then commenced pacing to and fro in the shadowy court, looking about her vaguely. Presently spying her dagger where she had lately flung it in a corner, she picked it up and returned it to its sheath which still hung at her waist,—then she pulled down a long trail of climbing roses from the wall, and came to lay them on the breast of the irresponsive dead. As she approached, a sudden brilliant luminance affrighted her, — she started back, one hand involuntarily uplifted to shade her eyes. A Cross of light, deep red and dazzling as fire, hovered horizontally in the air immediately above the body of Judas, spreading its glowing rays outward on every side. She beheld it with amazement, — it glittered before her more brightly than the brightest sunbeams,— her fevered and wandering wits, not yet quite gone, recognised it as some miracle beyond human comprehension, and on the merest impulse she stretched forth her hands full of the just-gathered rose-clusters, in an effort to touch that lustrous, living flame. As she did so, a blood-like hue fell on her,—she seemed to be enveloped in a crimson mist that stained the whiteness of her garments and the fairness of her skin, and cast a ruddier tint than nature placed among the loosened tresses of her hair. The very roses that she held blushed into scarlet, while the waxen pallid features of the dead had for a little space a glow, as of returning life. For one or two minutes the mystic glory blazed,—then vanished,—leaving the air dull and heavy with a sense of loss. And Judith, standing paralysed with wonder, watched it disappear, and saw at the same time that a change had taken place in the aspect of her self-slain brother. The lips that had been drawn apart in the last choking agony of death were pressed together in a solemn smile,—the eyes that had stared aloft so fearfully were closed! Seeing this, she began to weep and laugh hysterically, and flinging her rose-garland across the still figure, she stooped and kissed that ice-cold smiling mouth.

'Judas, Judas!' she said in smothered sobbing accents—'Now thou art gone to sleep, without a word,—without a blessing,—thou wilt not even look at me! Ah cruel! nevertheless I do forgive thee, for surely thou art very weary, else thou would'st not lie here so quietly beneath the stars. I will let thee sleep on,—I will not wake thee till the morning dawns. At full daybreak I will come again and see that all is well with thee, thou churlish one!—good-night!' and she waved kisses to the dead man smilingly with the tears blinding her eyes—'Good-night, my brother! I will return soon, and bring thee news—yea, I will bring thee pleasing news of Caiaphas, . . . good-night! . . . sleep well!'

And still waving fond and fantastic salutations, she moved backward lightly on tip-toe step by step, her gaze fixed to the last on the now composed and

beauteous face of the corpse,—then passing under
the great portico, she noiselessly unfastened the
gate, and wandered out in all her distracted and
dishevelled beauty, into the silent streets of the
city alone.

XXXI

THE full Sabbath morning broke in unclouded loveliness, and all the people of Jerusalem flocked to the gorgeous Temple on Mount Moriah to see and to be seen, and to render their formal thanks to the Most High Jehovah for their escape from all the threatening horrors of the previous day. Some there were who added to their prayers the unconscious blasphemy of asking God to pardon them for having allowed the 'Nazarene' to live even so long as He had done, seeing that His doctrines were entirely opposed to the spirit and the faith of the nation. Yet, all the same, a singular lack of fervour marked the solemn service, notwithstanding that in the popular opinion there was everything to be thankful for. The veil of the 'Holy of Holies,' rent in the midst, hung before the congregation as a sinister reminder of the terrors of the past thunderstorm, earthquake and deep darkness ; and the voice of the high-priest Caiaphas grew wearily monotonous and indistinct long before the interminable morning ritual was ended. Something seemed missing, — there appeared to be no longer any meaning in the usually imposing 'reading of the law,' — there was a vacancy and dulness in the whole ceremonial which left a cold and cheerless impression upon the minds of all. When the crowd poured itself forth again from the different gates, many groups wended their way out of sheer curiosity to the place where the 'Prophet of Nazareth' was now ensepulchred, for the story of Joseph of Arimathea's 'boldly' going to claim the body from Pilate, and the instant vigilance of Caiaphas in demanding that a watch should be set round the tomb, had already been widely rumoured throughout the city.

'We never had a more discreet and shrewd high-priest,'—said one man, pausing in the stately King's Portico to readjust the white linen covering on his head more carefully before stepping out into the unshaded heat and glare of the open road,—'He hath conducted this matter with rare wisdom, for surely the "Nazarene's" disciples would have stolen His body, rather than have Him proved a false blasphemer for the second time.'

'Ay, thou sayest truly!' answered his companion—'And the whole crew of them are in Jerusalem at this time,—an ill-assorted dangerous rabble of the common folk of Galilee. Were I Caiaphas, I would find means of banishing these rascals from the city under pain of death.'

'One hath banished himself'—said the first speaker, 'Thou hast doubtless heard of the end of young Judas Iscariot?'

The other man nodded.

'Judas was mad,'—he said, 'Nothing in life could satisfy him,—he was ever prating of reforms and clamouring for truth. Such fellows are not fitted for the world.'

'Verily, he must himself have come to that conclusion'—remarked his friend with a grave smile, as he slowly descended the Temple steps,—'and so thinking, left the world with most determined will. He was found hanging to the branch of a tree close by the garden of Gethsemane, and last night his body was borne home to his father's house.'

'But have ye heard no later news?' chimed in another man who had listened to the little conversation,—'Iscariot hath had another grief which hath driven him well-nigh distracted. He hath lost his chiefest treasure,—his pampered and too-much beloved daughter; and hath been to every neighbour seeking news of her and finding none. She hath left him in the night suddenly, and whither she hath gone no one can tell.'

By this time the group of gossips had multiplied, and startled wondering looks were exchanged among them all.

'His daughter!' echoed a bystander—'Surely 'tis not possible! The proud Judith? Wherefore should she have fled?'

'Who can say? She swooned last night at seeing her dead brother, and was carried unconscious to her bed. There her maidens watched her,—but in their watching, slept,—and when at last they wakened, she was gone.'

The listeners shook their heads dubiously as not knowing what to make of it; and murmuring vague expressions of compassion for Iscariot, 'a worthy man and wealthy, who deserved not this affliction,' as they said, went slowly, talking as they went, homeward on their various ways.

Meanwhile, a considerable number of people had gathered together in morbid inquisitiveness round the guarded burial-place of the 'Nazarene.' It was situate in a wild and picturesque spot beween two low hills, covered with burnt brown turf and bare of any foliage, and in itself presented the appearance of a cave deeply hollowed out in the natural rock. Rough attempts at outward adornment had been made in the piling-up of a few sparkling blocks of white granite in pyramidal form on the summit,— and these glittered just now like fine crystals in the light of the noonday sun. The square cutting that served as entrance to the tomb was entirely closed by a huge stone fitting exactly into the aperture,— and between this stone and the rock itself was twisted a perfect network of cords, sealed in about a hundred places with the great seal of the Sanhedrim council. Round the sepulchre, on every side were posted the watch, consisting of about fifteen soldiers picked out from a special band of one hundred, and headed by a formidable-looking centurion of muscular build and grim visage, who, as the various groups of idle spectators approached to look at the scene, eyed them with fierce disfavour.

'By the gods!' he growled to one of his men— 'What a filthy and suspicious race are these cursëd Jews! Lo you, how they sneak hither staring and whispering! Who knows but they think we ourselves may make away with the body of the man they crucified yesterday! Worthily do they match their high-priest in cautious cowardice! Never was such a panic about a corpse before!'

And he tramped to and fro sullenly in front of the tomb, his lance and helmet gleaming like silver in the light, the while he kept his eyes obstinately fixed on the ground, determined not to honour by so much as a glance the scattered sightseers who loitered aimlessly about, staring without knowing what they stared at, but satisfied at any rate in their own minds, that here assuredly there was no pretence at keeping a watch,—these were real soldiers,—un-imaginative callous men for whom the 'Nazarene'

19

was no more than a Jew reformer who had met his
death by the ordinance of the law.

By and by, as the sun grew hotter, the little knots
of people dispersed, repeating to one another as they
sauntered along, the various wonderful stories told of
the miracles worked by the dead 'Prophet out of
Nazareth.'

'How boldly he faced Pilate!' said one.

'Ay!—and how grandly he died!'

''Tis ever the way with such fellows as he '—declared
another—'They run mad with much thinking, and
death is nothing to them, for they believe that they
will live again.'

So conversing, and alluding occasionally to the
tragic incidents that had attended the sublime
death-scene on Calvary, they strolled citywards,
and only one of all the straggling spectators was
left behind,—a man in the extreme of age, bent and
feeble and wretchedly clad, who supported himself
on a crutch, and lingered near the sepulchre, casting
timorous and appealing glances at the men on guard.
Galbus, the centurion, observed him and frowned
angrily.

'What doest thou here, thou Jew skeleton?' he
demanded roughly—'Off with thee! Bring not thy
sores and beggary into quarters with the soldiers of
Rome!'

'Sir, sir '—faltered the old man anxiously—'I ask
no alms. I do but seek thy merciful favour to let me
lay my hands upon the stone of yonder tomb, . . .
once, only once, good sir!—the little maid is sorely
ailing, and methinks to touch the stone and pray
there would surely heal her sickness '— He broke off,
trembling all over, and stretching out his wrinkled
hands wistfully.

Galbus stared contemptuously.

'What dost thou jabber of?' he asked—'The little maid?—what little maid? And what avails this touching of a stone? Thou'rt in thy dotage, man; get hence and cure thy wits,—'tis they that should be healed right speedily!'

'Sir!' cried the old man, almost weeping—'The little maid will die! Look you, good soldier, 'tis but a week agone that He who lies within that tomb, did take her in His arms and bless her; she is but three years old and passing fair! And now she hath been stricken with the fever, and methought could I but touch the stone of yonder sepulchre and say "Master, I pray thee heal the child," He, though He be dead, would hear and answer me. For He was ever pitiful for sorrow, and He was gentle with the little maid!'

Galbus flushed red,—there was a strange contraction in his throat of which he did not approve, and there was also a burning moisture in his eyes which was equally undesired. Something in this piteous old man's aspect, as well as the confiding simplicity of his faith touched the fierce soldier to an emotion of which he was ashamed. Raising his lance, he beckoned him nearer.

'Come hither, thou aged madman,' he said with affected roughness—'Keep close to me,—under my lifted lance, thou mayest lay hands upon the stone for one brief minute,—take heed thou break not the Sanhedrim seals!—And let thy prayer for thy little maid be of most short duration,—though take my word for it thou art a fool to think that a dead man hath ears to hearken thy petition. Nevertheless, come.'

Stumbling along and breathless with eagerness the old man obeyed. Close to the sacred sepulchre he came, Galbus guarding his every movement with vigilant eye,—and humbly kneeling down before the sealed stone he laid his aged hands upon it.

'Lord, if thou wilt,' he said—'Thou canst save the little maid! Say but the word and she is healed!'

One minute he knelt thus,—then he rose with a glad light in his dim old eyes.

'Most humbly do I thank thee, sir!' he said to the centurion, uncovering his white locks and bowing meekly—'May God reward thee for thy mercy unto me!'

Galbus gazed at him curiously from under his thick black eyebrows.

'Of what province art thou?'

'Sir, of Samaria.'

'And thinkest thou in very truth thou hast obtained a miracle from that tomb?'

'Sir, I know nothing of the secret ways divine. But sure I am the little maid is saved. God be with thee, soldier! . . . God guide thy lance and evermore defend thee!'

And with many expressive salutations of gratitude he tottered away.

Galbus looked after him meditatively, till his thin raggedly-clothed figure had fluttered out of sight like a fluttering withered leaf,—then the grim Roman shook his head profoundly, pulled his beard, laughed, frowned, passed his hand across his eyes, and finally, having conquered whatever momentary soft emotion had possessed him, glanced about him severely and suspiciously to see that all his men were in their several places. The noonday heat and glare had compelled them to move into their tents, which were ranged all round the sepulchre in an even snowy ring,—and Galbus, seeing this, quickly followed their example, and himself retired within the shelter of his own particular pavilion. This was pitched directly opposite the stone which closed the mystic tomb,— and as the burly centurion sat down and lifted his helmet to wipe his hot face, he muttered an involuntary curse on the sultry and barren soil of Judæa, and wished himself heartily back in Rome.

'For this is a country of fools'—he soliloquised— 'And worse still 'tis a country of cowards. These Jews were afraid of the "Nazarene" as they call Him, while He lived; and now it seems they are more afraid of Him still when He is dead. Well, well! 'tis a thing to laugh at,—a Roman will kill his enemy, true enough, but being killed he will salute the corpse and leave it to the gods without further fear or passion.'

At that moment an approaching stealthy step startled him. He sprang up, shouldered his lance and stood in the doorway of his tent expectant; a tall man muffled in a purple cloak confronted him,—it was Caiaphas who surveyed him austerely.

'Dost thou keep good watch, centurion?' he demanded.

'My vigilance hath never been questioned, sir,' responded Galbus stiffly.

Caiaphas waved his hand deprecatingly.

'I meant not to offend thee, soldier,—but there are knaves about, and I would have thee wary.'

He dropped his mantle, disclosing a face that was worn and haggard with suffering and want of sleep,— then, stepping close up to the sepulchre, he narrowly examined all the seals upon the stone. They were as he had left them on the previous evening, untouched, unbroken.

'Hast thou heard any sound?' he asked in a whisper.

Galbus stared.

'From within yonder?' he said, pointing with his lance at the tomb—'Nay!—never have I heard voice proceed from any dead man yet.'

Caiaphas forced a smile,—nevertheless he bent his ear against the stone and listened.

'What of the night?' he queried anxiously—'Were ye interrupted in your first watch?'

'By the baying of dogs at the moon, and the hooting of owls only'—replied Galbus disdainfully,— 'And such interruptions albeit distasteful, are not to be controlled.'

'I meant not these things'—said Caiaphas, turning upon him vexedly—'I thought the women might have lingered, making lamentation'——

'Women have little chance where I am,' growled Galbus,—'True, they did linger till I sent them off. Yet I treated them with kindness, for they were weeping sorely, foolish souls,—the sight of death doth ever move them strangely,—and 'twas a passing beauteous corpse o'er which they made their useless outcry. Nevertheless I am not a man to find consolements for such grief,—I bade them mourn at home;—the tears of women do provoke me more than blows.'

Caiaphas stood lost in thought,—anon he stooped again to listen at the sealed-up door of the sepulchre. Galbus, watching him, laughed.

'By the gods, sir,' he said—'One would think thou wert the chief believer in the dead man's boast that he would rise again! What hearest thou? Prithee say!—a message from the grave would be rare news!'

Caiaphas deigned no reply. Muffling himself again in his mantle, he asked—

'When does the watch change?'

'In an hour's time,' replied Galbus—'Then I,

together with my men, rest for a space,—in such heat as this, rest is deserved.'

'And when dost thou return again?'

'To-night at moonrise.'

'To-night at moonrise!' echoed Caiaphas thoughtfully. 'Mark my words, Galbus, watch thy men and guard thyself from sleeping. To-night use double vigilance!—for when to-night is past, then fears are past,—and when to-morrow's sun doth shine, and he, the "Nazarene," is proved again a false blasphemer to the people, then will all watching end. Thou wilt be well rewarded,—watch, I say, to-night!—far more to-night than any hour of to-day! Thou hearest me?'

Galbus nodded.

'I have heard much of the truth and circumspectness of the soldiery of Rome'—proceeded Caiaphas, smiling darkly—'And specially of warriors like thee, who have the mastery of a hundred men, from which this present watch is chosen. Take heed therefore to do thy calling and thy country justice,—so shall thy name be carried on the wings of praise to Cæsar, Fare-thee-well!'

He moved away—then paused, listening doubtfully, — with head turned back over his shoulder towards the tomb.

'Art thou sure thou hast heard nothing?' he asked again.

Galbus lost patience.

'By the great name of the Emperor I serve, and by the lance I carry,' he exclaimed, striking his heel on the ground, 'I swear to thee, priest, nothing—nothing!'

'Thou hast hot blood, soldier'—returned Caiaphas sedately—'Beware lest it lead thee into error!'

And he paced slowly down the dusty road and disappeared. Galbus watched his retreating form with an irrepressible disgust written on every feature of his face. One of his men approached him.

''Twas the Jewish high-priest that spoke with thee?'

'Ay, 'twas even he'—he responded briefly—'Either I choke in his presence, or the dust kicked up by his holy sandals hath filled me with a surpassing thirst. Fetch me a cup of wine.'

The man obeyed, getting the required beverage out of the provision tent.

'Ah, that washes the foul taste of the Jew out of my mouth,'—said Galbus, drinking heartily—'Methinks our Emperor hath got a beggarly province here in Judæa. Why, if history have any truth in it, 'tis the custom of this people to be conquered and sold into slavery. I believe of all my hundred, thou dost know thy lessons best, Vorsinius,—have not these Jews been always slaves?'

Vorsinius, a young soldier with a fair intelligent countenance, smiled.

'I would not say so much as that, good Galbus,' he replied modestly—'but methinks they have never been heroes.'

'No,—nor will they ever be,' said Galbus, draining his cup and shaking the dregs out on the ground—'Such names as hero and Jew, consort not well together. What other nation in the world than this one would insist on having a watch set round a tomb lest perchance a dead man should rise!'

He laughed, and the good-humoured Vorsinius laughed with him. Then they resumed their respective posts, and moved no more till in an hour's time the watch was changed. But save for the clanking of armour as one party of soldiers marched away into the city, and the other detachment took its place, the deep and solemn silence round the sealed Sepulchre remained unbroken.

XXXII

MEANWHILE Barabbas, sitting with his friend Melchior in the best room of the inn where that mysterious personage had his lodging, was endeavouring to express his thanks for the free and ungrudging hospitality that had been afforded him. He had supped well, slept well, and breakfasted well, and all at the cost and care of this new acquaintance with whom, as might be said, he was barely acquainted, — moreover the very garments he wore were Melchior's, and not his own.

'If thou seekest a man to work, I will work for thee'—he said now, fixing his large bold black eyes anxiously on the dark enigmatical face of his voluntary patron,—'But unless thou canst make use of my strength in service, I can never repay thee. I have no kinsfolk in the world,—mother and father are dead long since, and well for them that it is so, for I should have doubtless been their chief affliction. Once I could make a boast of honesty,—I worked for the merchant Shàdeen, and though I weighed out priceless gems and golden ingots, I never robbed him by so much as a diamond chip until—until the last temptation. If thou wilt ask him, he will I know say this of me—for he was sorrier for my sin than I had heart to be. I have some little knowledge

of books and old philosophies,—and formerly I had
the gift of fluent speech,—but whatsoever I might
have been, I am not now,—my hands are stained with
blood and theft,—and though the people set me free,
full well I know I am an outcast from true liberty.
Nevertheless thou hast fed me, housed me, clothed
me, and told me many wise and wondrous things,—
wherefore out of gratefulness, which I lack not, and
bounden duty, I am fain to serve thee and repay thee,
if thou wilt only teach me how.'

Melchior, leaning back on a low window-seat,
surveyed him placidly from under his half-closed
eyelids, a faint smile on his handsome mouth.

'Friend Barabbas,' he responded lazily, 'thou owest
me nothing—on the contrary, 'tis I that owe thee
much. Thou art a type of man,—even as I also am
a type of man,—and I have derived much benefit
from a study of thy complex parts,—more benefit
perchance than is discovered in the "old philosophies"
wherewith thou fanciest thou art familiar. Mark thou
the difference betwixt us!—though seemingly our
composition is the same dull mortal clay. Thou art
poor,—thou hast but yester morn left prison, naked
and ashamed,—I am rich, not by the gifts of men,
which things I spurn, or by the leavings of the dead,
but by the work of mine own brain, man's only
honest breadwinner. I have never found my way to
prison, as I despise all roads that lead one thither.
They are foul,—therefore, loving cleanness, I tread
not in them. Thou, made animal man, and ignorant
of the motive power of brain that masters matter,
didst at the bidding of mere fleshly lust resign thine
honour for a woman's sake,—I, made intelligent man,
do keep my honour for my own sake, and for the
carrying out of higher laws which I perceive exist.
Nevertheless thou art truer man than I. Thou art

the type of sheer brute manhood, against which
Divine Spirit for ever contends.'

He paused ;—and lifting his head from its recum-
bent position, smiled again.

'What wilt thou do for me, Barabbas?' he continued lightly—'Draw water, till the soil, shake my
garments free from dust, or other such slavish service?
Go to! I would not have thee spoil thy future!
Take my advice and journey thou to Rome,—I'll fill
thy pouch with coin,—settle thyself as usurer there
and lend out gold to Cæsar! Lend it freely, with
monstrous interest accumulating, for the use of the
Imperial whims, battles, buildings, and wantons! So
get thee rich and live honourably,—none will ask of
thee—"wert thou thief?"—"wert thou murderer?"
No!—for the Emperor will kiss thy sandal and put
on thee his choicest robe,—and all thou hast to do is
to keep his name upon thy books and never let it go.
"Ave Cæsar Imperator" is the keynote of the Roman
shouting—but Cæsar's whisper in thine ear will have
more meaning—"Hail, Barabbas, King of the Jews! rich
Barabbas, who doth lend me money,—noble Barabbas,
who willingly reneweth bills,—powerful Barabbas, who
doth hold the throne and dynasty by a signature!"'

He laughed, the while his companion stared at him
fascinated and half afraid.

'Or,' pursued Melchior, 'wilt thou by preference
make friends with frenzied Peter, and join the
disciples of the "Nazarene"?'

'Not with Peter—no!' exclaimed Barabbas in
haste,—'I like him not,—he is not certain of his faith!
And of the other men who came from Galilee I know
naught, save that they all forsook their Master. I
would have followed the "Nazarene" Himself into the
blackest hell!—but His followers are coward mortals
and He'——

'Was Divine, thinkest thou?' asked Melchior, fixing upon him a look of searching gravity.

Barabbas met his gaze steadily for a moment, then his own eyes fell and he sighed deeply.

'I know not what to think,' he confessed at last. 'When I first beheld Him, He did in very truth seem all Divine!—then,—the glory vanished, and only a poor patient suffering Man stood there, where I, faint from the prison famine and distraught of fancy, imagined I had seen an Angel! Then when He died —ah then, my soul was shaken!—for to the very last I hoped against all hope,—surely, I said, a God can never die! And now, if thou wilt have the truth, I judge Him as a martyred Man,—of glorious beauty, of heroic character,—one worthy to follow, to love, to serve; . . . but . . . if He had been indeed a God, He could not thus have died!'

Melchior leaned forward, resting his chin on one hand and studying him curiously.

'Knowest thou, excellent Barabbas, what is this death?' he asked—'Among the "old philosophies" thou readest, hast mastered aught concerning its true nature?'

'All men know what it is;'—replied Barabbas drearily—'A choking of the breath,—a blindness of the eyes,—darkness, silence, and an end!'

'Nay, not an end, but a beginning!' said Melchior, rising and confronting him, his eyes flashing with enthusiasm — 'That choking of the breath,—that blindness of the eyes—these are the throes of birth, not death! Even as the new-born child struggles for air, and cannot too suddenly endure the full unshaded light of day,—so does the new-born soul that struggles forth from out its fleshly womb, fight gaspingly for strength to take its first deep breathings-in of living glory! A darkness and a silence, sayest

thou? Not so!—a radiance and a music!—a wondrous clamour of the angels' voices ringing out
melodies aloft like harps in tune! And of the spirit
lately parted from the earth, they ask—"What
bringest thou? What message dost thou bear?
Hast thou made the sad world happier, wiser, fairer?"
And over all the deathless Voice of Marvel thunders;
"Soul of a man! What hast thou done?" And
that great question must be met and answered,—and
no Lie will serve!'

Barabbas gazed at him, awed, but incredulous.

'This is the faith of Egypt?' he asked.

Melchior eyed him with a touch of scorn.

'The faith of Egypt!' he echoed—''Tis not faith,
'tis knowledge!—Knowledge gained through faith!
'Tis no more of Egypt than of any land,—'tis a truth,
and as a truth is universal,—a truth the "Nazarene"
was born to make most manifest. The world is never
ripe for truth,—how should it be, so long as it is well
content to build its business and its social life on
lies!'

He paused, and recovering from his momentary
excitement, went on in his coldest and most satirical
tone—

'Worthy Barabbas, thou, like the world, art most
unfitted for the simplest learning, despite thine "old
philosophies." Such common facts as that there are
millions upon millions of eternal worlds, and millions
upon millions of eternal forms of life, would but confuse thy brain and puzzle it. Thou art a mass of
matter, unpermeated by the fires of the spirit,—and
were I to tell thee that the "Nazarene" has "died"
according to the common word, only to prove there
is no death at all, thy barbarous mind would be most
sore perplexed and troubled. Thou hast not yet
obtained the mastery of this planet's laws,—thou'rt

brute man merely,—though now, methinks thou'rt more like some fierce tiger disappointed of its mate, for thou canst not wed thy Judith '——

Barabbas interrupted him with a fierce gesture.

'I would not wed her—now!'

'No? Thou would'st rather murder Caiaphas?'

Barabbas shuddered. His black brows met in a close frown,—his lips were pressed together hard, and his eyes were almost hidden under their brooding lids.

'I have already blood upon my hands,' he muttered, 'And the man I killed—Gabrias—was innocent,— my God!—innocent as a dove compared to this wolfish priest who works his evil will by treachery and cunning. Nevertheless since I beheld the "Nazarene"'——

'Why should the "Nazarene" affect thee?' asked Melchior placidly—'A martyred Man, thou sayest— no more,—thou canst be sorry for Him, as for many another—and forget.'

Barabbas lifted his eyes.

'I cannot take a human life again,' he said solemnly, his voice trembling a little—'since I have looked upon His face!'

Melchior was silent.

A long pause ensued,—then Barabbas resumed in calmer tones—

'If thou wilt give me leave, I will go forth and ask for news of old Iscariot,—and of his daughter,—for though I may not, would not wed her, because my own great sins—and hers—have set up an everlasting barrier between us, I love her, Heaven help me, still. I have slept late and heard nothing,—wherefore to ease my mind concerning her, I will inquire how she fares. I would I could forget the face of the dead Judas!'

A tremor ran through him, and he moved restlessly.

'''Twas a face to be remembered'—said Melchior meditatively—'Set in the solemn shadows of the trees, 'twas a pale warning to the world! Nevertheless, despite its frozen tragedy, it was not all despair. Remorse was written in its staring eyes,—remorse,—repentance; and for true repentance, God hath but one reply—pity, and pardon!'

'Thinkest thou in very truth his sin will be forgiven?' exclaimed Barabbas eagerly.

'Not by the world that drove him to that sin's committal!'—answered Melchior bitterly—'The world that hunts men down to desperation, hath no pity for the desperate. But God's love never falters,—even the trembling soul of Judas may find shelter in that love!'

His voice grew very sweet and grave,—and a sudden moisture dimmed Barabbas's eyes.

'Thy words do comfort me,' he murmured huskily, ashamed of his emotion—'albeit I have been told that God is ever a God of vengeance. But Judas was so young, . . . and Judith'— He broke off—then added whisperingly—'I forgot—he bled at her touch! —'twas horrible—horrible,—that stain of blood on her white fingers!'

Melchior said nothing, and Barabbas, after a minute or two, rose up to go out.

'I must breathe the air'—he said abruptly—'The heat within the house doth choke me. I will ask where the "Nazarene" is buried and go thither.'

'Why?' inquired Melchior—'Since thou believest not in Him, what is He to thee?'

'I cannot tell'—answered Barabbas slowly—'Something there is that draws me to the thought of Him, but what it is I cannot yet discover. If I

believe not in Him as a God, 'tis because what
I hear of Him doth pass all human understanding.
Even what thou hast briefly told me doth utterly
confound all reason,—the miracle of His birth when
His mother Mary was a virgin,—how can I credit
this? 'Tis madness ; and my soul rejects that which
I cannot comprehend.'

'Did I not tell thee what a type thou wert and
art?' said Melchior—'A type of man unspiritualised,
and therefore only half instructed. If thou rejectest
what thou canst not comprehend, thou must reject
the whole wide working of the universe! " *Where
wast thou*," God said unto His servant Job, "*when
I laid the foundations of the earth? Declare if thou
hast understanding? . . . Hast thou commanded the
morning since thy days?*" Alas, most profound and
reasonable Barabbas!—if thou dost wait till thou
canst "comprehend" the mysteries of the Divine
Will, thou wilt need to grope through æons upon
æons of eternal wonder, living a thinking life
through all, and even then not reach the inner
secret. Comprehendest thou how the light finds its
sure way to the dry seed in the depths of earth and
causes it to fructify?—or how, imprisoning itself
within drops of water and grains of dust, it doth
change these things of ordinary matter into
diamonds which queens covet? Thou art not able
to "comprehend" these simplest facts of simple
nature,—and nature being but the outward reflex
of God's thought, how should'st thou understand the
workings of His interior Spirit which is Himself in
all? Whether He create a world, or breathe the
living Essence of His own Divinity into aerial atoms
to be absorbed in flesh and blood, and born as Man
of virginal Woman, He hath the power supreme to
do such things, if such be His great pleasure.

20

Talkest thou of miracles?—thou art thyself a miracle,
—thou livest in a miracle,—the whole world is
a miracle, and exists in spite of thee! Go thy ways,
man; search out truth in thine own fashion; but if
it should elude thee, blame not the truth which ever
is, but thine own witlessness which cannot grasp it!'

Barabbas stood silent,—strangely moved and
startled by the broadness of his new friend's theories.

'I would I could believe in such a God as thou
dost picture!' he said softly—'One who doth indeed
love us, and whom we could love!'

He paused and sighed;—then on a sudden
impulse, approached Melchior and taking his hand,
kissed it.

'I know not who thou art,' he said—'but thy
words are brave and bold, and to me thou hast been
more than generous. Thou must consider me thy
servant,—for as I told thee, I have no other means
of paying back the debt I owe thee. Suffer me
therefore to attend thee,—at least till I find ways of
work,—shall this be so?'

Melchior smiled.

'Thou shalt do even as thou wilt, Barabbas, albeit
I do not need attendance. Myself hath been my
bodyguard for years,—and I have never found a
more discreet and faithful confidant! Nevertheless, to
satisfy thy sudden-tender conscience, I will accept
thy service.'

A look of relief that was almost happiness, lightened
Barabbas's dark features, giving them a certain
nobleness and beauty.

'I thank thee!' he said simply—'Can I do aught
now for thee within the city?'

'Thou canst bring me news!'—returned Melchior,
fixing his eyes upon him steadily—'There may be
some of highest import. And mark me!—if thou

dost visit the tomb of the "Nazarene," take heed,—thou
wilt find it strongly guarded. Quarrel not with those
who watch, lest thou should'st be accused of some conspiracy to steal the corpse,—the Jewish priests are yet
in terror, for the "Nazarene" did swear that on the
"third day," that is, to-morrow,—remember, to-
morrow !—He would rise again.'

Barabbas stopped in the very act of leaving the
room, and turning on the threshold exclaimed,

'Impossible ! Thou dost echo the last night's
frenzy of Peter ! Rise, living, from the grave ?
Impossible ! He cannot !'

Melchior looked full at him.

'If Death be death, why truly He cannot ;'—he
responded,—'But if Death be Life, why then He can !'

XXXIII

WITH these last strange words ringing in his ears Barabbas went out, wandering almost unseeingly in the open street, and trying to concentrate his thoughts upon the things immediately around him. Somehow he found this difficult. His mind was in a dreamy whirl, and he could hardly realise the full extent of all that had occurred to him within the short space of a little more than twenty-four hours. Whole ages seemed to have passed since the early morning of the previous day when he had been released from prison and when the 'Nazarene' had been condemned to die. He had come out of his dungeon, half delirious with joy at the prospect of freedom, believing in Judith Iscariot, and loving her as a man only loves once in a lifetime. Now he knew her worthlessness,—the unrepenting vileness, treachery and corruption of her life,—and though he loved her still, he was perfectly aware that it was only because he could not yet detach his soul from the clinging memory of her bewitching bodily beauty, and this was a love, or rather a passion, of which he was vaguely ashamed. Ashamed?—he, a thief, a murderer, ashamed of anything? Since when? Why,—only —since he had looked upon the 'Nazarene.' It was strange! with all the force of his strong though un-

tutored will, he tried to understand what singularly
miraculous power this 'Man of Nazareth' possessed,
that even now,—now when He was crucified and
dead, he, Barabbas, should yet be curiously conscious
of His presence, and conscious too that this mystic
nearness of Him made all sin appear inexpressibly
hateful and humiliating. Sighing uneasily, and angry
with himself for being unable to comprehend his own
feelings, he rambled about the streets aimlessly at
first, but afterwards, recollecting part of his intention,
he visited the house of Iscariot. There for the first
time he learned from the servants of the mysterious
disappearance of Judith. Sick at heart, he listened
while the man who opened the gate told him that
search had been made everywhere throughout the
city in vain,—and that even now, Iscariot himself
was with Pilate the governor, seeking for the help of
the law to aid in the discovery of the missing girl.
The servant added in awestricken tones that they
had found the corpse of Judas uncovered, with a
branch of roses laid across it,—and that the rope
which had been round his throat was gone. ''Tis
likely she hath taken it'—he concluded—'Much
grief perchance hath driven her distraught. But
wheresoever she hath wandered we can hear no tidings
of her.'

'I will find her'—said Barabbas—'Tell her father
when he comes that I will never rest till I discover her.
I will seek for her high and low,—living or dead I
will bring her home.'

He shuddered a little as the word 'dead' escaped
his lips,—and the man who received his message was
startled at the fierce expression of his haggard face,
but nevertheless responded dismally that 'these were
sore times of trouble,' and also that the self-slain heir
of the house, Judas, would be 'buried to-morrow.'

'To-morrow!' echoed Barabbas with a wild stare, scarcely knowing what he said—'Why, to-morrow they say the "Nazarene" will rise again! Why bury Judas? If one dead man can come to life so can another!'

The servant, really alarmed this time, shut to the gate without further parley, privately considering that everybody except himself was going mad, Barabbas in particular,—while Barabbas on his part, perfectly reckless as to his appearance or manner, stumbled blindly and giddily down the sunny street, seeing nothing but the face of Judith as she had looked last night, lifting up her burning eyes from the body of her dead brother, and smiling distractedly on the stern disciple Peter, from out the golden shower of her hair.

'Gone—gone!—and whither?' he muttered as he went—'To Caiaphas? Would she have sought out Caiaphas?'

He checked his pace abruptly. The high-priest's palace was not far off,—he could see the lofty palms and thick-foliaged fig-trees of its private garden to which none had the entry save the high-priest himself, —but to obtain admittance even to the outer court of the house without the excuse of some business of high sacerdotal importance, would, he knew, be impossible. Moreover his very name, Barabbas, was sufficient to exclude him hopelessly. He sat down on a bench by the roadway and tried to think it out. There were no people passing,—the stillness of the Sabbath reigned throughout the city. Resting his head between his two hands, he pondered all ways and means of obtaining access to Caiaphas, in vain,— no fortress was more impregnable than the high-priest's abode,—no one more haughtily unapproachable in his private capacity than the high-priest in person.

'Nevertheless, he knows!' said Barabbas aloud,—
'He is her lover, curse him!—and he knows where she
hath fled. It may be she is with him even now.'

As he spoke he lifted his head, and saw that a
woman had paused near him and was looking at him
wistfully. He recognised her instantly,—by her fair
hair, her dreamy face,—her coarse grey linen gown
knotted beneath her bosom by a hempen girdle;—it
was Mary of Magdala. Instinctively he rose up,
gazing at her as steadily as she gazed at him.

'Thou art Barabbas?' she said in tremulous accents;
'Thou art he who should have died yesterday instead
of our Beloved!'

Her voice moved him deeply. It was penetratingly
sweet and pathetic,—there was a tremor in it that
unnerved him. He tried to remind himself that she
was an evil woman,—a thing polluted,—yet while he
thought of this he grew in a manner amazed at the
limpid purity and beauty of her eyes. They were of
a singularly clear blue,—but their wonderful lustre
seemed to be a brightness exhaled from inward tears.

'Thou should'st have died!' she repeated, and
faintly smiled—'Sorrowful Barabbas!'

He looked at her in vague wonderment.

'Sorrowful I am in truth,' he said—'But what
knowest thou of my sorrow? Surely I have good
reason to be glad, seeing that I am free once more,—
at liberty to live my life out to its end.'

'And dost thou love thy life and liberty?' asked
Mary softly —'Dost thou find the world so fair?
Thou wert not overburdened with rejoicing yesterday,
when in the darkness of the death of love, thou didst
kneel and weep with me!'

He did not answer her at once, but stood regarding
her with a stern intentness. Suddenly he gave a
gesture of pain and pity.

'O woman!' he exclaimed passionately—'Beautiful as thou art, why dost thou make of thy beauty degradation? I know thee!—who does not know thee!—accurst and outcast!—go thy ways—die even as Judas died, rather than live as thou dost live!'

She smiled,—a strange sad smile, that like the pureness of her eyes seemed born of weeping.

'Friend, I have died!'—she said—'At my Lord's feet I laid down all my life. Men made me what I was; God makes me what I am!'

'Thou art the Magdalen'—responded Barabbas harshly—'And neither God nor man shall alter thee!'

She crossed her small hands on her bosom, and bent her head.

'I was the Magdalen!' and she raised her eyes, full of bright tears, to the quiet sky—'Or, rather, of thy charity, say I was that poor affrighted thing, hunted by devils, whom men did torture into being Magdalen.'

'Whom men did torture!' repeated Barabbas half angrily—'Woman, for all thy sins thou hast thyself to blame!'

Her lips quivered.

'Thou'rt man'—she answered—'Therefore as man thou speakest! Lay all the burden upon woman,— the burden of sin, of misery, of shame, of tears; teach her to dream of perfect love, and then devour her by selfish lust,—slay her by slow tortures innumerable,— cast her away and trample on her even as a worm in the dust, and then when she hath perished, stand on her grave and curse her, saying—"Thou wert to blame!—thou fond, foolish, credulous trusting soul! —thou wert to blame!—not I!"'

Something in her vibrating accents struck to the heart of Barabbas with a sense of reproach. He drooped his head ashamed, and was silent.

'Hast thou a right to judge me?' she queried mildly; 'Art thou without sin? Nevertheless, let us not idly reproach one another,—I tell thee Magdalen, as Magdalen, is dead; I, Mary, live.'

'What difference dost thou make in such wise 'twixt dead and living!' murmured Barabbas with a troubled sigh.

'What difference?' echoed Mary—'What difference is there 'twixt the darkness and the light? The Magdalen was wilder than all furies,—mad with the fires of hell,—pursued of devils, bereft of hope,—and ignorant of God—poor soul, poor soul!—she died most piteously and painlessly, slain by a word of pardon from the All-Forgiving! Oh, I cannot choose but weep to think of it! And Mary lives,— Mary, who hath discovered heaven in a broken heart, —Mary, who builds up aerial hopes from tears of penitence,—Mary, whose ears have listened to the music of the Master's voice—such music!—sweeter than the sweetest song! "Go thy way," He said— "Sin no more!" O high command!—'Twas as a crown of glory set upon me! "Sin no more!" How could I sin, remembering Him! Who could look once upon Him, and return from that fair light to darkness? Lo, I am newly born, and trembling in the throes of life,—half weeping, half afraid, but full of love!—love for my Master and my King who hath forgiven me and blessed me!'

Her sweet voice had a rhythmic chime of mingled melancholy and triumph, and Barabbas listened, fascinated and wondering. Presently she came nearer to him.

'Thou dost not hate me, Barabbas? Or fear me?'

He looked at her fixedly.

'What the "Nazarene" hath blessed, that I can neither hate nor fear!'

A lovely smile irradiated her face, and her watchful
regard of him was like that of some meditative angel.

'Thou callest Him the "Nazarene" as others do,'
she said—'because He came from Nazareth. Nevertheless He was a God—He is a God! Knowest thou
they say that He will rise again?—but I believe not
this. Truly His spirit may arise; but we shall never
see Him more as we have seen Him. And that is
why last night I wept when they laid His fair body
in the tomb,—the body cannot rise, I said, and
though as godlike Spirit He will pass to Heaven,
as Man He will appear no more to us. This is the
bitterness of death;—we never see our loved ones
as we knew them,—in Heaven their faces will be
strange!'

She paused,—then went on—

'Tell me, Barabbas, of thy grief,—for grief thou hast
most visibly. I know of Judas and his death,—is it
for him thou sorrowest?'

He met her earnest gaze for a moment in silence,—
then moved by an impulse of confidence, told her of
Judith's sudden disappearance.

Mary listened attentively.

'I know her well by sight'—she said—'A fair
proud girl, beauteous and scornful; once she did
gather up her robes in haste lest I should brush
against them passing her. Thou lovest her,
Barabbas?'

He flushed and turned his head aside.

'I *have* loved her!' he answered.

'Doubtless she is all that is most perfect in a
woman?' murmured Mary, half questioningly, half
sadly,—'Chaste, holy, innocent and true?'

Her words stung him with keen agony.

'Would that she were!' he exclaimed wildly—
'But I will not lie to thee. She is—nothing! She

hath been seized by devils,—such devils as did once move . . . Magdalen!'

She started, turning very pale.

'Alas, Barabbas!' she said—'Then is she most unhappy and in far worse plight than thou! I will aid thee in thy search,—it may be she hath wandered far beyond the city precincts. Hast thou been to Gethsemane, where her brother died?'

'Not yet'—he responded wearily—'I will go thither now. Where have they buried the "Nazarene"?'

She pointed towards the west.

'Yonder, near Calvary'—she said—'In the sepulchre of Joseph of Arimathea, between two barren hills. If thou goest, thou wilt find it guarded. Caiaphas hath set a watch.'

Barabbas shuddered at the name.

'Caiaphas!'—he muttered between his set teeth —'Always Caiaphas!' And yet he could not bring himself to speak of Judith in connection with the high-priest, and forbore to give expression to his fear that the lost girl might even now be with the haughty dignitary who was in secret her lover.

'I will go to Gethsemane'—he repeated mechanically—'But the body of Judas was not found within the garden, but outside,—and his sister knoweth naught of the secret place of shadows where he perished. Nevertheless I will make search there,— and I will visit the burial-place of the "Nazarene" ere sunset. If thou hearest any news, thou wilt bring it to me?'

'Where shall I find thee?' asked Mary.

He gave her the name of the inn where he at present stayed with his acquaintance, Melchior.

'I shall remember'—she said—'And if I see the strayed girl anywhere I will follow her,—and if I hear of her I will track the rumour to its source. Meantime fare-thee-well! If thou dost truly visit my Lord's resting-place ere sunset, pray for me,— for the guard doth forbid me to approach—I may not now go thither until to-morrow.'

'Until to-morrow!' echoed Barabbas, and looked at her strangely.

'Even so,—to-morrow,'—she repeated—'When the morning breaks, I shall take flowers and sweet fragrances to strew upon the dead,—they say the guard will be removed at dawn. Farewell! God comfort thee!'

And with a gentle inclination of her head, she wrapped her mantle round her and glided softly and rapidly away.

Barabbas stood looking after her for a moment, lost in thought;—and his lips unconsciously murmured over and over again the word,

'To-morrow!'

Then, drawing his linen hood well over his brows that he might not be recognised and detained by any of his former acquaintances, he passed through the Sabbath-quieted streets of the city, and out on the road that led towards Gethsemane.

XXXIV

COOL shadows greeted him as he approached the quaint secluded garden which was now destined to be evermore renowned in the world's history. A faint wind swung the heavy foliage of the fig-trees with a solemn sound, and the clear brook that ran between two low banks of moss and turf from which some ancient olives grew, made subdued and soothing music. Down here last night, —here where the shelving ground dipped towards the water,—here where the fig-trees were dark with their darkest bunches of thick leaves, Judas had been found dead ; and it was with a dreary sense of ominous foreboding that Barabbas came to the same place now, in gloomy expectation of some new disaster. Uneasily he lifted the overhanging branches and peered among the flickering tints of dense and luminous green,—not a living creature was visible. He moved to and fro softly, looking about him everywhere in vague search for Judith,—yet doubting all the while the possibility of finding her in such a spot. Up and down he gazed wistfully,—now towards the winding path ascending to the Mount of Olives,—anon, backward to the shadowy depths of the Valley of Kedron,—and having reconnoitred all the visible landscape immediately outside Gethse-

mane, he resolved to enter the garden itself. He
lifted the latch of the small wooden gate that
separated it from the road, and went in among the
towering palm-trees and climbing roses that there
were made particular objects of cultivation and grew
in rich profusion in every available corner. As
he wandered slowly along one of the moss-grown
paths, he paused to listen. Never, surely, was there
such a silence anywhere as here! The murmur of
the brook was lost,—the wind failed to stir so much
as a small flutter among the leaves,—and the impressive stillness of the place was such, that it seemed
as if the voice of God had spoken, saying: 'Here,
where My Beloved cried to Me in His agony, let
there no more be any earthly sound!'

Barabbas hesitated. Seized with a solemn fear,
his presence in the garden appeared to himself a
strange intrusion, and after a moment or two, he
turned back, finding it impossible to proceed. He
looked dreamily at the flowers around him; roses,
red and pale, turned their faces upon him in apparent
wonderment,—a glowing cactus-tree confronted him,
all in a seeming angry blaze of bloom,—the nodding
ferns trembled as with interior agitation, and every
separate leaf and blade of grass, he fancied, questioned
him silently upon the nature of his errand in that sacred
haunt, made wonderful by a God's unselfish sorrow.
Word by word, all that the disciple Peter had related
concerning the last night spent by the 'Nazarene'
within this same Gethsemane returned to his mind.

'Will He possess all things?' he murmured half
aloud—'A Man of Nazareth, crucified and dead?—
shall we not even wander in this garden without His
memory haunting us?'

And he hastened his steps, anxious to leave the
spot, although he knew not why. A little way

beyond where he stood,—beyond the roses and the sentinel cactus-flowers, the dewy turf still reverently bore the impress of a Form Divine that there had fallen prone and wept for all the world,—wept with such tears as never yet had rained from mortal eyes, —there too had lighted for a little space, a great consoling Angel,—and there no human step had passed since the fair King of perfect Love had gone forth patiently to die.

'Judith would not be here'—Barabbas muttered, as he left the garden, closing the gate noiselessly after him,—''Twas never a resort of hers,—she would not think of coming hither.'

He paused, his heart beating with an undefinable anxiety.

'No—no,—she would not dream of it'—he repeated —'If sorrow hath distracted her, she might more likely have gone towards Calvary, the scene of yesterday. I will visit the tomb of the "Nazarene" and inquire of the guard whether she hath passed them by.'

Thus resolved he walked on his way slowly, full of the most bewildering thoughts. The question that reigned uppermost in his mind was, strange to say, not what had become of Judith Iscariot, but what and who was the 'Nazarene'? Why did His presence seem to permeate the very air? How was He different to others, that one should not be able to forget Him? He was a Teacher of new doctrine, —well, there had been other teachers of new doctrine, and would be many more. He was brave and beautiful; there were others brave and beautiful likewise. He was not a hero as the world accepts heroes,— He had fought no battles, made no conquests, and owned neither throne nor province. He was simply, or appeared to be a very poor Man, who had been

kind and sympathetic to the sorrowful; He had
healed a few sick persons, and given the comforting
hope of Heaven to those who had no consolation
upon earth. Where was the particular marvel of
these things? A life so simple, so common,—where
was its Divinity? Barabbas pondered the problem
vainly, — he was not wise enough to comprehend
that perhaps the greatest miracle of the world is
this same sort of 'simple' and 'common' life, which
is after all neither simple nor common, but most
truly complex and phenomenal. For nothing upon
earth is so singular as kindness,—nothing so rare as
sympathy,—nothing so absolutely unique, wonderful
and purely Divine, as ungrudging, unboastful, de-
voted, changeless Love that seeks nothing for itself,
but freely gives everything. What men call love is
often selfishness; what God accepts as love is the
entire and voluntary resignation of self for love's own
sake. 'In losing thyself'—He says — 'thou shalt
find Me,—and in finding Me, thou wilt find all!'

But Barabbas had not the eyes to discern the
spiritual side of nature. He could only see what
appeared on the surface of life,—of interior meanings
he knew nothing. It puzzled him to consider that
the mysterious man Melchior, whether he were
Egyptian, Greek, or any other nationality, actually
accepted this Jesus of Nazareth as a God,—without
question. Why? Because if a God, how would it
have been possible for Him to die?

'I must know everything concerning Him'—sighed
Barabbas perplexedly—'I must not accept mere
rumour. When Judith is found, and when all these
present troubles are past, I will go down to Nazareth,
and obtain a true report. It shall be my business;
for if He were Messiah, then are our people cursed
for ever with the curse of God that passeth not away.

I will not take mere hearsay,—I will prove things. As for His rising from the dead, that cannot be'——

Here, interrupting his meditations, he lifted his eyes to look at the low hills in front of him. At the distance he now was, he could plainly see the ring of white tents that circled the tomb of the 'Nazarene.'

'Truly the watch is set'—he murmured,—'And 'tis an ample guard. There can be no feigning in this fear,—the terror of the priests is real. Cowards and sceptics as they are, they surely deem this Man will rise again!'

The sight of all those soldiers' tents amazed him, —he had thought to find one or two sentinels perhaps on guard,—but that a regular military 'watch' should be encamped round the burial-place of one, who after all, according to the law's estimate, was no more than a crucified criminal, seemed to him positively astounding. The hours of the afternoon were wearing on rapidly, and he hurried his pace, anxious to reach and examine the tomb itself, but as he came within a few yards of it, a guard confronted him, and with a gruff word, forbade him to proceed further Barabbas answered the man gently, explaining the errand on which he was bound, and asking whether any one resembling the beautiful Judith had been seen wandering about in the neighbourhood. The soldier looked at him scrutinisingly,—then began to laugh.

'Why, as I live!' he said—'Thou art Barabbas! I am one of those who came to fetch thee out of prison the other morn,—thou wert drunk with the air and light as with new wine, and little didst thou deem that thou wert going to thy freedom! Thou lookest altogether a different man, thus cleansed

21

and fitly clothed ; dost find the world altered since
thy former days?'

'Nay, 'tis much the same,'—responded Barabbas
somewhat bitterly—'Evil succeeds, and good perishes;
am I not myself a living witness of this, seeing 'tis I
who should have been crucified instead of the
"Nazarene"?'

'I warrant thou dost not regret His end or thine
own escape!' returned the soldier with a grim smile ;
'Thou hast not yet been two whole days out of
prison, and already thou art searching for a woman!
'Tis ever the way with fierce rascals such as thou,
nevertheless however much I may sympathise with
thee, I cannot let thee pass me,—the orders that we
have are stringent.'

'I well believe it!' said Barabbas, looking wistfully
at the sealed-up door of the rocky Sepulchre,—'And
I do not urge thee unto disobedience. And concerning the woman I have spoken of, I seek her not
for mine own sake,—'tis the daughter of Iscariot that
hath strayed from home,—the same Iscariot whose
son Judas hung himself for shame that he betrayed
the Man of Nazareth. 'Tis thought she is distracted
at her brother's death, and that she roams wildly,
unknowing whither.'

'By my faith 'tis a sad history!' said the Roman,
not without a touch of sympathy,—'This old Iscariot
is truly in a piteous case. But no woman, fair or
foul, hath been near these precincts all the day so
far as I can tell thee. Nevertheless when the watch
doth change at moonrise, and Galbus the centurion
takes chief command, I will inform him what thou
sayest,—he hath two children of his own, young
maidens both,—and should he chance on this strayed
lamb he may be trusted to persuade her home. But
for thyself, I do advise thee not to linger,—for here,

all idlers are suspected thieves,—and if I do mistake
not thou hast some past reputation for skilled
robbery! Perchance thou would'st not steal a corpse,
—for truly 'tis not valuable,—yet all things counted,
thou'rt safer at a distance from this place. Frown
not! I mean thee well.'

'I thank thee!' said Barabbas briefly, and then
stood for a moment, lost in thought and uncertain
what to do. It was growing late,—the sun was
verging towards its setting. Flecks of crimson, like
floating rose-leaves, drifted in the sky immediately
above the hill of Calvary, and below these delicate
flushes, spread a watery band of green, a translucent
sky-lagoon, into which, ere long, the glorious orb of
day would plunge and sink like a ship on fire. The
landscape, though nearly barren of verdure, had a
wild beauty of its own seen thus in the afternoon
glow of the warm Eastern light,—and so Barabbas
thought, as his tired eyes roved from point to point
unrestfully and with a strained expression of regret
and sorrow. The centre of all visible things seemed
to be that sealed and guarded Sepulchre; and
presently, bringing back his gaze to the bold and
martial form of the Roman soldier who still watched
him half suspiciously, half curiously, he waved his
hand with an expressive gesture towards the tents
that were clustered round the mystic tomb.

'Surely all this is needless waste of trouble and
of time?' he said with forced lightness—'Who that
is sane would fear that a dead man can rise?'

'Thou mistakest the nature of the fear;'—returned
the soldier,—'No one, not even Caiaphas, is such
a fool as to believe in a resurrection of the dead.
No, no!—we guard against the living;—this
"Nazarene's" disciples are all within the neighbourhood, and they would steal the body of their former

Master willingly, if by this deed, they could assume
His prophecies were true. But now are they baffled;
they cannot break our ring or pass our ground; and
if the dead Man comes to life again He must Himself
find force to rend the rocks asunder, for no human
hand will aid the miracle!'

''Twould be a miracle indeed!' murmured
Barabbas dreamily.

'Ay!—and 'twill not happen,'—laughed the
Roman—'We all know that. And to-morrow, praise
be to the gods, the test will have been made and the
watch ended, for 'tis the third day,—and if He rise
not in keeping with His own saying, 'tis a finished
matter, and we shall no more be teased with follies.
To-morrow thou canst wander here at will unmolested—to-day I bid thee get hence and home.'

'And I obey thee'—rejoined Barabbas, turning
away—'Thou wilt speak to thy centurion of Iscariot's
daughter?'

'Most faithfully.'

'Again I thank thee. Farewell!'

'Farewell!'

The soldier resumed his slow pacing to and fro,
and Barabbas with a last lingering look at the
Sepulchre, went on his reluctant way back towards
the city. He noticed as he passed the further one
of the little hills between which the tomb was
situated, that there was a deep hollow in the ground
such as might have been burrowed out by some wild
animal for its sleeping-place. It was large enough
to hold a man unseen in its sandy depths,—and as
he measured it with a glance, the bold idea struck
him that he would come there that very night and
hide, as it were, in ambush to watch the Sepulchre
also.

'For if aught should chance that is in any wise

miraculous, then I shall witness it,'—he soliloquised ;
'Or if the disciples of the "Nazarene" should strive
to steal His corpse, why then I shall behold the fight
'twixt them and the Roman guard. Most surely I
will return hither,—for whatsoever happens it will
not be a night for sleep, but vigilance. I can watch,
—I too, as well as any other man,—moreover, if
marvellous things are to be seen, 'twere well that I
should see them. If the dead Man rise again then
shall I know He is not man but God ; but unless I
see Him living with my own eyes I never will believe.
Wherefore to prove this thing I will return hither
this night, and nothing shall prevent me. The
judgment and the heart may be deceived,—the
reason and the sight, never ! 'Twill please me well
to play the secret sentinel !—and, as I live, no force
shall move me from my post till dawn !'

XXXV

AS he resolved on this plan, he stopped to take a careful survey of the exact situation of the sheltering hollow in which he meant to pass the night. The dust of the road was grey and thick about his feet,—above him the heavens were reddening into sunset-glory. The landscape had no touch of human life about it, save his own solitary figure,—Jerusalem lay before him, a dream of white roofs rather than a reality, and not a sound stirred the heated air. Therefore, in the great hush that prevailed, he was unaccountably startled to see the form of a woman, walking, or rather gliding slowly towards him ; she was coming up from the city carrying a sheaf of large white lilies. She was herself, like the blossoms she bore, clad in white, and as she approached with perfectly noiseless footsteps, Barabbas, moved by a sudden instinct, placed himself directly in her path, fully confronting her, and staring at her with burning, eager, wistful eyes. Her face, pale and marvellously beautiful, was the same he had seen so strangely illumined on Calvary when the bells had begun to ring, and the darkness had slowly dispersed,—a face expressing neither youth nor age, nor any mark of earthly time, but reflecting on its pure and perfect features both maidenhood and motherhood in one, combined with such angelic sweetness, wisdom, sorrow, purity and love as never had before adorned the fairness of any woman born. Barabbas held his breath for very wonderment at sight of her,—something supreme and queenly in her aspect disposed him to fall upon his knees before her in reverence,—yet he refrained from this and stood erect, trembling greatly, but resolved to keep the position he had taken up in the centre of the narrow road, so that she might not pass him without at least a look, a word or a gesture.

''Tis the Mother of the Crucified !'—he murmured ; 'I will speak to her, and ask of her the truth concerning all the marvellous history of her Son,—surely she will answer !—surely she must answer, seeing it may become a matter of life and death, not only with me, but with the world.'

He waited,—and she came on, holding her lilies with both hands against her breast. Within two or three yards of him, however, she paused, and stood still. So still indeed was she that she might have been a figure of ivory or marble ; not a fold of her garments stirred,—not a petal of the lilies she carried quivered,—her calm eyes, clear as heaven, regarded him steadily,—one tress of her fair hair escaping from the white linen head-covering she wore, glittered against her throat,—and on her lips rested the tender shadow of a smile. Behind her flamed the sunset,—round her the very air grew dense and brilliant, as though powdered through with the fine dust of finest amber,—and at her feet one fallen lily-bud opened its satin petals to the light, disclosing its interior heart of gold. Vaguely awed by her very quiescence, Barabbas gazed upon her enthralled, and for the moment stricken speechless,—a wondering, doubting and bewildered sinner, face to face with the Angel-

Virgin of the world! The red light of the sinking sun playing on the whiteness of her garments dazzled him,—she seemed to grow in stature and in majesty even while he looked; and with a sigh of mingled pain, dread and desire, he extended his hands appealingly.

'Mary of Nazareth!'

The shadow of the smile upon her lips deepened and softened with an infinite compassion. But she neither answered nor moved.

'Mary, Mother of the "Nazarene"!' he faltered, trembling more and more, for there was something supernatural in her beauty, something almost terrifying in the mingled meekness and majesty of her regard—'Hear me, I beseech thee! Thou knowest who I am,—Barabbas,—an evil man of many sins,— and, had the people's voice been just, 'tis I who should have perished yesterday instead of thy beloved Son. I swear I would have died most willingly,—not at the first—no!—for I did long for liberty and all the joys of free existence; but after I had seen His face, my life seemed to mine own self worthless, and I would have given it gladly to save His!'

Still not a word from her!—only that same mild tenderness of look and smile.

'They say thy Son blasphemed;'— pursued Barabbas with increasing agitation, 'Because He spoke familiarly of God and called Him "Father"! 'Twas a wild utterance,—for now a foolish rumour floats upon the people's lips,—a rumour most incredible,—alleging that He was in very truth the only Son of God. Why didst not thou, Mary, disprove this idle tale?—for thou, of all the world, dost know the manner of His birth! Thou should'st have warned Him of the danger of His words,—and so might He have saved Himself from the penalty of the law. For were He the holiest man that ever breathed, still in this way of speech He was guilty of a vast presumption,—the great God, the terrible Almighty hath never vested His Divinity in human guise! Knowest thou not, Mary, that this false impression of Him still abides?—and that the whisper of it, passing from mouth to mouth, doth waken the strangest fears and doubts within the souls of men? —and even I, Barabbas, ignorant, guilty, and all unbelieving as I am, grow troubled and perplexed, seeking the truth and finding none! With thee this matter rests,—thou art the Mother of this "Nazarene," —'tis not too late to speak—thou canst unravel all the mystery, wherefore I do beseech thee answer me!'

His entreating eyes studied her tranquil face eagerly, but not a sound escaped her lips, not even a faint responsive sigh.

'Why wilt thou thus keep silence?' he exclaimed passionately—'Hast thou thought, Mary, what the result will be, if thou dost suffer this mad and strange report to travel on uncontradicted? For if thy dead Son be declared a God, of birth miraculous and Divine, then must a curse rest on the people of Judæa for having slain Him, and all the world will make a scorn of Israel for endless time! On us will fall the blame and punishment for our rejection of the God-Messiah,—and the nations of the earth will loathe us for our cruelty, our wickedness, perversity and unbelief. Mary, thou knowest! Speak!—wilt thou let the whole world worship a Legend and a Lie?'

As he uttered the last word, a sudden cold shudder ran through him,—he grew dizzy and faint, but with an effort held his ground, gazing full at her to whom he made his bold and desperate appeal. She had not moved,—but there was an indefinable change in her that startled him. Some mystic light that was not of the sunset seemed cast upon her face, and in her steadfast eyes there shone a radiance more softly brilliant than the glittering of moonbeams on the sea. Half swooning with the force of his own emotions, Barabbas suddenly fell on his knees, grasping the edge of her white robe in one hand.

'Mary of Nazareth!' he whispered hoarsely— 'In pity to me a sinner,—in mercy to the world— declare the truth! Who was the Father of thy Son?'

Deep silence followed his daring question. Above the fragrant lilies, her radiant face grew warm with speechless eloquence,—and lifting her eyes she gazed upward—upward,—far into the vistas of ethereal blue;—transfigured by some inward glorious thought, she seemed about to float away upon the air in answer to a voice calling her heavenward! The sun dropped below the horizon and disappeared,—the skies began to pale into that rapid Eastern twilight which paves the passage of the stars.

'Not a word!—not a word!' cried Barabbas then, springing to his feet, and carried out of himself by mingled fervour and ferocity—'O Woman!—wilt thou deceive Man unto the bitter end? Shall our very God be of thy making? Shall our very creeds be of thy teaching? Must thou command our souls even to the very hope of Heaven? If thou art human, if thou art holy, if thou desirest truth made manifest, speak, Mary, thou who didst bring into the world this "King" to whom hath now been given a Cross for throne and thorns for Crown! Dost thou meditate eternal vengeance on us all? Hast thou sworn within thy soul that men shall worship what

they once despised and pray to Him they slew? If
so, such monstrous compensation ne'er was dreamed
of — 'tis a revenge more subtle than the fiercest
tortures! Is it for wrath or love, Mary, that thou
dost hold thy peace?'

Her sweet mouth trembled a little, but she did not
speak,—her eyes were still uplifted as in prayer.

'How can silence in aught avail thee?' pursued
Barabbas impetuously—'Lo, if the great God Invisible
hath filled thee with His mystic Spirit, art thou not
thereby made a creature marvellous?—a very queen
of wonders?—and by thy very life dost thou not
glorify thy sex and make it sacred and revered for
evermore? Wherefore then hesitate to take full
majesty and power upon thee? But if thou hast no
miracle to tell, surely thou art a cruelty incarnate,
for by thy dumb refusal to be true, thou mayest
weave around the hapless world a web of error such
as the ages never yet have seen! Think for a
moment,—picture it!—shall wise men of the earth
and conquerors and kings bow their proud heads
before mere Woman and Child? The symbol of all
Nature, in which there is no touch Divine but everything of common!—wilt thou make fools of tribes
and nations, thou Mother of the so-called Christ, who
art accredited with being Virgin still? No man hath
touched thee, say the people,—yet thou hast a
husband, and thou hadst a Son!—art thou thyself a
Miracle?—or dost thou out of pleasure in an unde-
served fame, suffer these wild things to be said of
thee?'

Still she answered nothing. But bringing her
eyes down from their rapturous survey of heaven,
she fixed them on him with a grave regard in which
there was something of mild rebuke as well as compassion.

'I would not wilfully offend, or seem to offer thee reproach,'—he went on, vaguely troubled by her look—'I know thou art a sorrowing Mother at this present time ; though to me thou hast an air of gladness rather than of grief. But I am only one of many who will clamour, ay, with tears and prayers, for an answer from thee,—I am a lonely, wretched sinner with a broken heart,—life is nothing to me, forms are nothing, the opinions of the world less than nothing, —I seek the truth, that I may rest thereon and find some comfort,—there are and will be thousands such as I. Could I believe, I would believe ; but an' thou wilt not speak, thou leavest me in ignorance. If thy Son be born of the Spirit of God, then will I worship Him and thee,—but if He be no more than Man, then will I think of Him with pity as one noble and heroic who was foully slain, and of thee as patient woman sore afflicted, and there an end. On thy word do I rely,—oh, thou must have a heart of steel or adamant, if still thou wilt not answer me !'

This time she stirred slightly, but she did not speak. Bending her head a little forward over the lilies she held, she gazed at him with an earnest and tender thoughtfulness,—and then — Barabbas started back amazed and terror-stricken. For behind her and around her a sudden great light shone,—a fiery halo, radiating to right and left like two glittering wings between which her tranquil and majestic figure held its place in queenly and serene unconsciousness. The unearthly glory palpitated with a thousand hues of delicate and changeful colour,—and Barabbas with a faint cry of wonderment, dropped again upon his knees.

'God have mercy on me !' he muttered, staring with dazzled eyes at the pulsating splendour, and the gentle figure that in the midst of those unearthly fires stood half framed in flowering lilies—'God have mercy on me! Methought 'twas to a woman that I spoke,—this is an Angel!'

A soft surprise flitted over her face,—it was evident that she herself was unaware of the mystic light that circled her as with a ring. It vanished even while Barabbas spoke, and he, kneeling in the dust and gazing upward, fancied his sight had surely been deceived. But now she moved,—and coming quite close up to him, looked him full and steadfastly in the eyes. A whisper light as the flutter of a leaf fell on his ears,

'To-morrow!'

And with noiseless footsteps she passed him by, seeming to float aerially, like a spirit, upward on her way towards the Sepulchre between the hills. Barabbas, springing erect, ran recklessly a few steps after her, crying aloud—

'Mary! Mary of Nazareth! Woman or angel, whatever thou art, judge me not wrongfully! I have but sought the truth, even as the world will seek it! —the truth of Him who was thy Son!'

She turned her head gently back towards him with an air of queenly patience.

'To-morrow!' she repeated, and her voice sounding like a soft chime, seemed carried through the air, over the quiet landscape into every nook and corner of rock and field, bearing as a message to all creation the one word 'To-morrow!'

Then, gliding on, she disappeared.

Breathless and overcome with excitement, Barabbas flung himself down on the arid turf that edged the road, his senses all aswoon and trembling.

'To-morrow!' he said—'Why—what shall to-morrow bring? Will her dead Son live again? Doth she

also cherish this mad delusion ? If He in truth doth
rend the rocks asunder and arise, 'twill be sufficient
proof of God for all ; but such a miracle can never be,
—'tis out of very Nature, yet I cannot but believe that
some strange mystery doth invest the world,—some
thought of God is working in its depths. For long
long ages God hath well-nigh forgotten us,—doth He
now remember at the very time when *we* forget?
Hath He visited us in very truth, to be rejected?
And if this should be so, what will be the purport of
our doom? Ah me, we men are ever fools and blind,
—and I the wretchedest fool of all, for methought
I saw a heavenly radiance round yon woman of
Nazareth, even as I deemed I saw the same in Pilate's
Hall around the figure of her Son—'twas but a dazzlement of sight and sense,—a weariness and faintness
which quickly passed, and then the light had fled.
How soon our fancies are deceived!—a sick man
seeth visions, and thinks that they are real,—and I,
weak with long imprisonment and fasting, fretted
with griefs, and poisoned with despairs, am made the
dupe of mine own feebleness. How full was I of
strength once!—and now,—why the very look of this
Mary of Nazareth doth easily unman me! To-morrow!
I would that it were here! 'Tis growing late and
dark—I will return to Melchior and tell him whither
I am bound to-night,—then will I come back hither
and take up my secret vigil till the marvellously-
expected day shall dawn.'

He started running down the road towards Jerusalem, and as he entered the city gates, he met a
detachment of soldiers, headed by Galbus, marching
out. They were going to relieve the watch at the
Sepulchre, and encamp themselves there for the night.
He drew aside to let them pass, and as their
burnished helmets and pikes went in a narrow

glittering line up the road, the moon, large as a golden shield, suddenly lifted herself above the city, gazing, as it were, over the hills in open wonderment, at the Divine Mystery hidden in the earth below.

XXXVI

'THY command must be obeyed,—nevertheless, Caiaphas, 'tis strange and unusual.'

The speaker was an elderly scribe,—a man with a pale lean intellectual face, and a high forehead, which just now was puckered in a puzzled frown. He was seated in the private audience-room of the high-priest, and the high-priest himself was majestically throned in a gilded chair opposite to him. Lamps were kindled,—the table was strewn with slips of parchment, — through the open casement the gardens of the palace could be seen richly illumined by the moon,—it was the evening of the Sabbath-day.

'Strange and unusual as it may be,' returned Caiaphas coldly, 'it is my order. Thy business is not to question or dispute, but to perform the will of those that are set over thee. Wherefore should'st thou and thy fellows chronicle the brief career and ignominious death of a mad blasphemer?'

'There is no answer to thy "wherefore," save the one,' replied the scribe, with a little smile,—'It is the custom, and hath been so for many ages, to faithfully set down all things within our records,— even to small items, whether concerning our evil men or good. The story of this fanatic of Nazareth

is worthy to be written, if only to disprove all supernatural legends that are in rumour and connection
with Him. Some things He taught were wise, and
some were foolish, because impracticable,—and possibly His best suggestions may be traced to Egypt,
and He be proved the merest echo of some ancient
perished creed. I do confess unto thee, Caiaphas,
I see no reason for the absolute omission of His
name in circumstantial history.'

Caiaphas flushed a dark red, then grew pale, and
grasped the projecting edges of his chair with both
hands convulsively.

'Thou art a narrow pedant!'—he said angrily—
'Thou canst not see what I see. Knowest thou not
there is a change of feeling even now among the
people?—that they bemoan their "Prophet's" death,
and weep, saying He wrought much good among
them? Moreover that the end of Judas Iscariot
hath moved them most profoundly, knowing that
the unhappy youth did slay himself for pure remorse at having given the "Nazarene" over to the
law? All this will grow upon report,—we, the
Sanhedrim, shall be branded perchance, as murderers,
and this crucified criminal be made a martyr.
Wherefore I will not have Him mentioned in our
records, Shebna,—let His name perish and His teachings be forgotten!—lest in the future, men should
ask—"Who was this Man of Nazareth and wherefore
was He slain?"'

'They will ask that the more, maybe, if thou leave
it unto rumour'—said Shebna drily, collecting his
parchments together—'If thou would'st make a man
immortally renowned, let him be spoken of from
mouth to mouth, and nothing of any written fact
be found concerning him! Gossip hath whispered
a man into a god ere now, when whole volumes of

22

history would have failed to make him one. I tell
thee I would rather be talked of than written of,—
'tis the more lasting fame. If, in impassive language,
I should coldly pen the story of this Jesus of
Nazareth, and classify Him as a poor crazed creature
who gave Himself out to be the Son of God, and
was crucified for His blasphemy, no one, either in
the present or the future, would trouble their heads
further concerning Him.'

'If thou write one thing thou must write all,'
declared Caiaphas with irritation — 'Thou must
relate the terrors of the darkness and the earthquake ;
and what could'st thou make of the rending of the
Temple veil ?'

Shebna looked meditative.

'True,—these things were strange and terrifying,'
—he murmured — 'But after all—the heat of these
late days has been intense,—an earthquake and a
storm are natural disturbances which might occur
at any time,—and the Temple veil was probably rent
by an oblique flash of lightning. Thou art moved
from thy wonted calmness, Caiaphas, else thou
would'st see naught so particular in such events
that they should not be written.'

The high-priest rose, trembling with the interior
force of an inexplicable fury.

'Thou obstinate slave, thou shalt not write them !'
he cried vehemently—''Tis I who scan thy leaves,—
'tis I who set my sign upon thy chronicle to warrant
and approve its truth. Now if thou darest so much
as write the name of Jesus of Nazareth in these
present annals, I will cut thy parchment into
shreds before thy face and depose thee from thine
office !'

Shebna rose also, and stood staring at his irate
superior in blank astonishment.

'Anger not thyself thus needlessly, Caiaphas'—
he said quietly—'I argue not against thy order,
which shall be fulfilled,—I simply seek to show thee
'tis in a manner unnecessary, as no fear can now be
had of this troublous "Nazarene," seeing He is dead.
Nevertheless thou shalt have complete obedience;
no word shall be inscribed upon our documents
pertaining to this so-called "King of the Jews;" we
will consign Him to oblivion.'

'Ay!—so best!' returned Caiaphas, recovering
composure, and re-seating himself—'For what the
pen does not write, the eye cannot read. Ye scribes
are after all, the only powers of a land,—ye are more
than kings,—for if ye chronicle not a victory, the
world will never know 'twas gained,—and if ye speak
not of a Man, who shall ever know that he existed?
I believe not in the force of rumour as thou dost,—
who doth credit mere garrulity?'

'Why—every one!' responded Shebna satirically—
'A man will doubt and seek to disprove the written
facts of history,—but he will oft believe the first thing
told him by his neighbour! And touching this
matter, Caiaphas, thou must not forget that there
are others who have known the "Nazarene" who may
write some memorial of Him; His followers were
many'——

'Ignorant fools all and common folk'—retorted the
high-priest—'none of whom know the use of letters.
A goodly company forsooth!—idle Galilean fisher-
men, hill-thieves, publicans, lepers and street-outcasts;
such as these shall never write a line that can be read
hereafter. Moveover, even if they did, what would
their report be worth, if we, who make the Jewish
annals, are silent?'

Shebna found no answer to this trenchant question,
which indeed seemed to settle the matter. He had

his own ideas upon the point,—every man has his own ideas upon every point,—but he was afraid to give them any further utterance. So he merely made a little deprecatory gesture of submission and assent, and, after a few more general remarks on ordinary subjects, he gathered up his parchments and humbly bowed himself out of his sacerdotal ruler's presence.

Left alone, Caiaphas sat for some moments in his chair absorbed in thought. His face was careworn,—his eyelids heavy with want of sleep.

'How is it I am thus unmanned?' he murmured wearily—'Moved for the merest fancies!—troubled by the wandering humours of a tired brain! I cannot rid me of the memory of the Man of Nazareth,—there was a triumph in His dying eyes mingled with lightning-wrath that did appal my soul! But I have baffled Him!—there shall be no new creeds to conquer time; the one Jehovah shall suffice,—the one revengeful, blood-demanding, jealous God whose very name doth terrify the world! If God were Love then would man grow too proud;—shall a worm assume that the Divine hath care for it? An' such folly were believed in, we could not hold our mastery upon the people,—each wretched unit would appeal from us to God, and deem himself our independent equals. Ah, what a Sabbath this hath been!—how desolate in every moment, from the anguish and amazement of the morning when old Iscariot did seek me out with furious upbraidings, and frenzied clamour for his lost daughter, as if I knew whither she hath strayed! Would that I did know! Who is it that hath mouthed a scandal round her name and mine, and turned Iscariot's heart against me? The released Barabbas? Nay, he could guess nothing. I have been ever cautious,—and yet,—a whisper and a slander fly on swifter wings than light or wind, and who shall stay them? I must be on my guard,—and though I love Judith, I will not look upon her face for many days even when she is found, lest harm come of it.'

He rose, and moved to the open casement, from which a light wooden stairway led down into the shaded precincts of his luxurious private garden. Leaning against the intertwisted trellis-work, he looked out at the placid, star-strewn heavens with troubled and indifferent eyes.

''Tis the last night of the watch'—he said—'And to-morrow all suspense will cease. The counsellor of Arimathea hath kept his word,—he hath not visited the tomb since the burial,—likewise the followers of the "Nazarene" are scared, and reft of settled plan or purpose, wherefore, so far all is well. To-morrow we shall attest unto the people the falseness of the Prophet they believed in,—then, there will be no more cause for fear. So will the matter be forgotten; these fanatics for truth are more troublous than seditious rebels; open truth is most impolitic,—one cannot rule the world except by lies!'

He smiled a little at his own cynicism,—then started nervously, hearing a slight rustling in the thick foliage below his balcony. Moving from his indolent posture he bent forward to listen, and as he did so, two brilliant wild eyes peered up at him from the dusky shadows.

'Caiaphas!' and the whisper thrilled like the hiss of a snake through the silence,—'Caiaphas!'

Seized with a chill terror, he stepped swiftly and noiselessly down the stairway, and bending back the bushes, gazed eagerly into what seemed a nest of leaves,—and there perceived the form of a woman crouched down on the ground as though seeking to

hide herself,—a woman in draggled white garments,
with a fair, strangely agonised face that smiled at
him in a sort of forlorn joy as he discerned it among
the sheltering shrubs and flowers. He uttered a
smothered cry—

'Judith!'

And half in rage, half in love, he dragged her from
her hiding-place, and caught her up in his arms,
looking about him in dread lest any one should see
them, and trying to cover her with his own flowing
mantle.

'Judith!—Judith!' he muttered, his heart beating
heavily, the while he sought to put back from her
brows all the tangled gold of her dishevelled hair—
'What doest thou here? Where hast thou been?
Knowest thou not that thy father hath sought thee
all throughout the day with tears and heart-break?
And why hast thou ventured hither thus alone?
Rememberest thou not the scandal of tongues—the
gossip of the city? Consider the folly of it!—if my
wife saw thee,—if my servants spied thee!—oh, thou
must not linger here one moment, Judith,—thou must
go home ;—come,—I myself will take thee through
the private way, and naught will be suspected,—
come!—there is no time to be lost if thou would'st
silence slander.'

With unnatural violence she wrenched herself from
his grasp and retreated step by step looking full at
him. Leaves and brambles clung about her,—a
spray of the scarlet cactus-blossom was twisted in
her girdle, and against her breast she held some dark
object which she appeared to cherish with a jealous
care.

'Thou art Caiaphas!' she said, dreamily surveying
him—'Thou art God's great high-priest who hath
become a slave for love of me! I have watched for

thee all day and have not found thee, though, up at a
casement yonder I saw thy wedded spouse, the pale
daughter of Annas, weeping. Did she weep for thee,
thinkest thou?—if so 'twas strange. Who that is
wise would shed tears for any man! Listen, Caiaphas,
—thou who dost exact obedience from all the people
of Jerusalem,—the hour is come when thou must
obey me!'

Alarmed at her wild look and manner, Caiaphas
went towards her, trying again to take her in his
arms,—but she still retreated, her eyes flashing with a
fierceness that startled him.

'What can I do for thee, Judith?' he murmured,
speaking as gently as he could, and hoping to soothe
her by soft words—'Thou knowest how willing I
always am to give thee pleasure. Only I beseech
thee, come with me out of this place, lest we be seen
and spoken of'——

'All the world may see,'—responded Judith with
an air of triumph—'All the world may hear! I care
naught. What is the world to me, so long as Judas
still is angry? Judas will not speak to me for wrath,
—he deems 'tis I did bring the "Nazarene" to death,—
whereas 'tis thou!—thou only. And thou must
tell him so,—thou must declare thy full part in
the matter, for neither he nor I will bear the un-
deserved blame. He is at home sleeping; I told him
thou hadst sworn to make him great and famous in
the land,—but he answered nothing. I promised I
would bring him news,—come thou now and wake
him—thou knowest not how fast he sleeps!—and tell
him all, — tell him how thou didst teach me to
persuade him to betray his friend the "Nazarene."
For though the "Nazarene" is dead, it seems He was
not altogether evil,—and methinks 'tis pity He is
dead, since Judas loved Him. I knew not that his

love was such, or of so great a tenderness,—and now
I suffer for my ignorance, for Judas will not pardon
me, or look at me, or say as he was wont to say—
" Fair sister, morning is fairer for thy presence ! "—yea,
he would oft speak so, smilingly, for I was beautiful,
—the fairest woman in Judæa was I, till I grew old !'
Here she paused with a puzzled expression,—her own
words seemed to frighten her,—but presently she
went on, muttering to herself—

' Till I grew old,—ay !—cruel age creeps on apace
with us all,—we should not stint love, lest those we
love be taken from us,—we must not wait too long,
Judas and I, or we shall be buried in our graves ere
we be friends. And once shut in that darkness we
shall never rise, not even on the waves of many
tears !'

Her voice sank tremulously, — then suddenly it
rang out clear and shrill.

' See !' she exclaimed wildly, —'Thus died the
King !'

And unclasping her hands from the object she
had hugged so closely to her bosom, she held up
a Cross, made of two small olive branches tied
together with a strand of silk drawn out of her own
girdle.

Caiaphas staggered back, struck speechless by her
words and the swiftness of her action, and involuntarily
he made a gesture of repugnance and offence. She
saw it and sprang up to him, still brandishing the
Cross before his eyes.

' Thus died the King !' she repeated with a kind
of exultation—'Slain by His own high-priest on the
altar of the world !'

And with all the madness of her tortured brain
lighting her looks as with fire, she stood transfigured
into an unearthly loveliness that appalled while it

fascinated her quondam lover, — and for one absorbing moment the twain confronted each other
as though they were restless ghosts met by
moonlight, — the Cross between them uplifted like
a sign of parting, — a mystic barrier dividing them
for ever!

XXXVII

IT was but an instant that they remained thus
inert,—then, shaking off the amazement and
fear that had held him motionless and dumb, Caiaphas
seized the crazed girl in his arms and strove to snatch
the Cross from her grasp.   But she clung to it fiercely
in an access of fever and frenzy; and with a swift
lithe spring like that of a young leopardess, she again
escaped from him and stood apart, eyeing him venge-
fully yet with a wan smile.   Never had the proud
priest been brought to such a verge of despair as
now,—for what was he to do with this distracted
creature, whose very presence in his private garden,
if discovered, would bring scandal on his name, ruin
his character, and degrade him from his lofty post!
Even the words she uttered in her madness would
betray the secret of their illicit loves,—the position
was wholly intolerable,—yet how was he to extricate
himself from it!   And why did she threaten him with
the Cross?—she who had openly declared the intensity
of her hate for the 'Nazarene'?   It might be merely
the working of a delirious brain toying with chaotic
contradictions, yet it troubled Caiaphas strangely.
He advanced a step or two extending his hands in
appeal.

'Judith, come to me'—he said in a low tone of

mingled coaxing and command,—'Thou art ill,—
distraught,—and perchance weary with wandering,—
thou knowest not what thou sayest. Thy father waits
for thee at home,—let me take thee to him now,—
surely thou would'st not break his heart and mine?
Come!'—and he ventured still nearer to her—'Do I
not love thee, Judith?—and wilt thou not trust thyself unto my tenderness?'

She looked at him strangely, her large eyes dilating
with vague wonder.

'Thy tenderness?' she echoed. 'What tenderness
canst thou boast of, Caiaphas, unless it be that of
the wolf for its prey? Speakest thou of love? Thou
hast not loved me,—nor I thee,—moreover there is
no love left in all the world,—'tis dead, and thou,
methinks, hast slain it.' Here she paused, passing
one hand over her brow with a puzzled expression,—
'I know not how the message came to me'—she
continued murmuringly—'for Judas said nothing!'

'What message?' asked Caiaphas softly, drawing
nearer to her, and resolving in his own mind that he
would coax her away from the garden by degrees—
'Tell me what it is that troubles thee.'

A faint smile crossed her lips.

'Nay, naught troubles me!' she said—'I have
lived too long to grieve for bygone things. Look
you, since my time the world is changed,—old days
are passed for ever,—and Judæa is no more what it
hath been. And of the message,—why, that was
strange,—it told me that God lived and that Death
was dead! Listen!' and with a swift capriciousness
that startled him she flung herself into his arms and
leaned her head against his breast, looking upwards
into his face—'I have heard that now there is some
curse upon us and that we shall never die! 'Tis
bitter,—for I am tired of life, and so, surely, art thou.

We have lived long enough; 'tis centuries since I
was young and since thou didst slay the " Nazarene."
Rememberest thou His shining face in death?—methought He wore the lightning as a crown! But
darkness came; and then I lost my brother Judas;
Barabbas found him afterwards, and brought him
home.'

'Barabbas!' muttered Caiaphas, the while he held
Judith half roughly, half caressingly, in his embrace
and sought to guide her steps imperceptibly towards
the private gate leading out from the garden—
'Barabbas is a murderer!'

'Then should'st thou be his friend'—said Judith—
'for thou art murderer likewise! Hast thou not
subtly slain the "Nazarene"? 'Twas aptly planned,
Caiaphas,—men are as blind fools without reason,
and none will think of blaming thee. And as for
Judas,—Judas is not dead; he sleeps; if he indeed
were dead the world should know that thou hadst
killed him!'

Caiaphas frowned, and a sudden rage began to
kindle itself in his blood against this woman he had
once recklessly adored.

'Hold thy peace, Judith!' he said fiercely—'Thou
ravest!—thou art unlike thyself, else should I be
wroth with thee. Talk not so wildly of the accursëd
"Nazarene," or it may be I shall hate thee even as
ardently as I have loved. Thou thyself didst loathe
this Prophet and desire His death; thou thyself
didst mock Him ere He died; now, out of mere
woman's wantonness thou pratest of Him almost as
if His memory were dear to thee! Such folly passeth
patience,—but thou'rt ill, and canst not comprehend
thine own distraction,—why now!—what new fancy
doth torment thee?'

For she suddenly withdrew herself from his arms,

and, sighing piteously, began to play idly with
a piece of coarse rope that dangled loosely from her
girdle. Presently untying it, she held it out to him.

'Prithee take this, Caiaphas,'—she murmured
plaintively—'Place it among the holy treasures of
the Temple,—'twill serve! 'Twas round the throat
of Judas,—see! his blood doth stain it here!'

He started back with a cry of horror. She came
nearer still, with mute gestures praying him to
accept the hideous gift she proffered.

'Wilt thou not receive it?' she asked, fixing her
wild eyes on his alarmed and pallid countenance—
'Then art thou no true priest, for on the altar thou
dost serve, there are the things of blood and sacrifice,
and this should be amongst them. Lo!—it doth
express the penitence of Judas,—he hath done wrong
and his remorse is great; he prays for pardon! And
I have told him for his comfort, that he hath not
been in all to blame, for that it was thou,—thou and
the creatures of thy craft, of whom I was one, that
did destroy the "Nazarene." And he is glad, I think,
—for when I told him this, a light fell on him and
he smiled,—for, ever did he hate the priests, and that
they should outrage innocence, and crucify a god is
no great wonder!'

Speechless with inward fury and despair, Caiaphas
stood helplessly staring at her, while she in a kind
of sad resignation, re-fastened the blood-stained cord
at her own waist. Then she drew the roughly-made
Cross from her bosom and smiled.

'This is a strange charm!' she said softly—'It
makes the old world new! In rays of light this same
sign fell on Judas as he slept and seemed to give him
peace. I found these olive-branches in Gethsemane,
and tied them thus together,—if it could comfort
Judas, so shall it comfort me!'

And raising it to her lips she kissed it.

'Judith—Judith!' cried the high-priest desperately; 'Wilt thou kiss the symbol of ignoble death?'

'Why not?' said she—'If Death thereby is dead? I told thee of the message,—'twas that God lived and Death was dead. We wept for Judas, believing he was gone from us into the grave for ever,—but now we know he lives, we shall be comforted. 'Tis a new wisdom we have learned, albeit there was something sweet in the old ignorance. For when we were sure that we should die,—it mattered little whether we lived well or ill,—a few years and all was at an end,—sins were not counted then,—but now, we dare not sin lest we be burdened with the memory of wrong through everlasting time. Methinks there is a misery in this joy of endless life!— what will become of thee, Caiaphas?—of me?—shall we forget our sins, thinkest thou?—or must we evermore remember?'

He met her large appealing eyes,—then gently advancing, encircled her with one arm.

'Judith,—beloved Judith'—he whispered—'As thou art dear to me, do not torment thyself and me with these wild fancies. Come,—I will not force thee homeward against thy will,—come within the palace, and I will hide thee where thou knowest of,— the secret nook where we have passed so many hours of love'——

'Flatter not thyself I ever loved thee!' she said with a returning flash of her former pride and scorn; 'Men were my slaves, and thou the most abased of all!' She paused, shuddering violently,—then went on in feeble tones,—'But that was long ago,— when I was young; rememberest thou how fair I was?—with eyes like jewels and hair like gold?'

'Thou art not changed, Judith'—murmured

Caiaphas, pressing her to his heart with involuntary force and passion—'Thou art as thou wert ever, the most beautiful of women!'

'Thou dost mock me,' she sighed, leaning against him languidly—'But I heed not what thou sayest, as I never loved thee. No man did ever move me to a sorrow for his sake—not even poor Barabbas who in very truth did worship me. Out of his love he slew Gabrias who had grown too boastful of my favour,—and for his crime he suffered long imprisonment,—yet I cared naught! If men are fools they needs must pay the price for folly.'

She roused herself, and shook back her long hair over her shoulders.

'Come!' she said—'Come and wake Judas. He has slept a long long while, and it will soon be morning.'

She moved swiftly and with an air of resolve over the grass, and Caiaphas, relieved that she seemed bent on departure, made an elaborate pretence of accompanying her. Her exquisite form, light, supple and stately, glided along before his eyes like some fair spectre, and the fascination of her beauty was such that he had much ado to keep himself from snatching her in his arms, all distraught as she was, and covering her with the last kisses of despairing love and farewell. But the fear of discovery held his passions in check,—and he was careful to walk beside her with an assumption of protecting dignity and compassion, so that if any chance beholder should spy him, he would be able to explain that he had found her wandering through his gardens in a state of fever and distraction, and that he was merely fulfilling his duty as a priest in taking her back to her father's house.

Suddenly she stopped, and surveyed him with frowning suspicion.

'Thou wilt make full confession to Judas?' she demanded—'Thou wilt declare how it was *thy* scheme and thine alone that brought to death the "Nazarene"? Thou wilt absolve him from the sin that troubles him?—the sin whereunto we both persuaded him?'

He looked away from her.

'Be at peace, I pray thee, Judith'—he murmured evasively—'I will say what I can '——

'Nay, it is not what thou canst say but what thou must say!' cried Judith excitedly—'Thou *canst* say any lie,—thou *must* say the truth! Thou cruel priest! Thou shalt not darken my brother's name and fame by thy treachery,—thou shalt not screen thyself behind him in this history! *Thou*, the priest, didst hate the god, if any god there was within thy Victim,—and thou didst slay Him. The very people would have set Him free hadst thou not bidden me cry out "Crucify Him" to keep them in their vengeful humour. I tell thee thou shalt confess this thing,— I will not go from hence till thou dost promise me,— Judas waits for us at home,—swear to me thou wilt tell him all!'

Driven to desperation, and bethinking himself that after all, Judas was dead, though his distraught sister would not realise it, Caiaphas answered hurriedly,

'Be it as thou wilt, Judith. I swear!'

She peered at him distrustfully, her eyes glittering with a sparkle of malevolence.

'I do not believe thee!' she said deliberately— 'Thou canst so aptly play the spy and traitor that thou art not to be trusted! If thou wilt be true to thy word for once, swear to me by this!'

And she again held up the Cross before him. At the suddenly renewed sight of it such a fury seized him that for the moment he lost all control over himself.

'Darest thou thus taunt me!' he cried—'Thou art not Judith Iscariot, but some devil in her aspect! Crazed fool or fiend, thou shalt no longer provoke me!'

And closing with her, he endeavoured to violently wrench the offending Symbol from her hands, the while she fought for its retention with the breathless rage and tenacity of some savage creature, till in the struggle, the Cross bent and snapped in twain. At this, she gave a cry of despair, and snatching her dagger from her girdle, sprang upon her priestly lover and stabbed him with a furious thrust that sent him reeling. Staggering backward, he fell senseless on the ground, the blood gushing freely from his wound, and she, stooping over him, stared at her own work in a dazed, wild wonder. Then, dropping both the dagger and the fragments of the Cross upon his bleeding body, she rushed away in frantic fear, and fled, like a phantom of the moon and shadow, out into the brooding silence of the night.

XXXVIII

MEANTIME, around the holy Sepulchre the guard kept vigilant watch. Behind it and on either side, armed men paced evenly to and fro,— in front of it the fierce and martial Galbus stood at the doorway of his tent, leaning upon his tall lance and surveying the scenery around him. There was a singular soft freshness in the air,—a bland and soothing perfume, as though the breathings of a thousand flowers were floating over the land on the drifting wings of a lazy southern wind. The moon, airily rolling through the clear ether like a golden bubble, cast long mellow beams upon the piled-up glistening rocks of the sacred tomb and the burnt brown turf that sparsely covered the little hills,—the stars, dimmed in lustre by this greater radiance, seemed wandering through a labyrinth of light mist and rainbow-tinted haloes. A great calm prevailed; the small pennon on the top of Galbus's tent, hung limp without the faintest flutter; a bush of myrtle close by had such a stillness in its leaves that it looked like an artificial semblance of itself, deftly carved and coloured by some ingenious human craftsman. Not a sound could be heard, save the muffled tread of the soldiers' sandalled feet, and Galbus, somewhat oppressed by the silence as well as by the heat of the atmosphere, began to grumble to himself *sotto-voce* for want of anything better to do.

'How they will laugh in Rome at this folly!' he said—'Did any one ever dream the like! I, Galbus, a man who hath seen war,—one who hath counted his ten corpses to a round of fighting, set here to watch that a corpse escape not! By the gods! The suspicious imagining of these Jew priests doth pass all patience; they deem that the poor, wild, half-starved-looking followers of the crucified "Nazarene" will steal His body, forgetting that it would need at least half-a-dozen men of stout sinew to move so much as yonder stone that closeth up the grave; and even then 'twould be displaced with difficulty. Well, well! The night will soon be gone and this crazy business finished; 'twill be as I say, matter for laughter in Rome when I tell them how I and fourteen picked men out of my hundred, were forced to guard a poor dead body lest it should rise again!'

Lifting his helmet to cool his brows, he rubbed his eyes and yawned.

'Were I to sleep now,' he soliloquised—'yon crafty Caiaphas, discovering it, would manage so as to lose me my post. Was ever such a petulant priest! and subtle therewithal, even as Volpian, he who doth serve Diana's altar in Rome, and out of purest zeal, doth ravish many a fair virgin! They're all alike, these so-called "holy" men,—no son of mine shall ever be a priest I warrant! This was the crime of the dead "Nazarene" from all that I can gather,—He sought to do away with priestcraft,—a mighty task, Jove knoweth! And now I call to mind yon aged soul who prayed here in the morning for his "little maid"—the feeble fool!—he met me in the town yonder, a-shaking like a wind-blown reed for joy—

"Good sir!" cried he, "the little maid is saved!"
And then he swore, with tears, that the fever left her
at the very hour he made petition to yon sealed-up
tomb! Heaven help him for a crazed frail creature!
—the superstitions of these country folk are strange
and sometimes devilish,—nevertheless I hear on all
sides that this young Prophet out of Nazareth was a
good man, and pitiful. By my soul!' and he yawned
again—''Tis a night for peaceful slumber, yet I may
not drowse, lest while I close my eyes, unheard-of
powers disturb the air '——

'Galbus! Galbus! Hist! Galbus!'

'What now?' he answered sharply, as the soldier
who had thus called him hurriedly approached—
'Why leavest thou thy post?'

'Fidius is there,'—said the young man apologetically, as he paused to salute his superior officer—' I
called thee so that thou should'st listen.'

'Listen? To what?' demanded Galbus impatiently;
'There is no sound but thy gruff voice and mine.
Thou art a dreamer, Maximus,—thy mother told
me so.'

Maximus, a tall stalwart Roman of handsome face
and figure, smiled deprecatingly, but at the same
time held up his hand to enjoin attention.

'Nay, I dream not, Galbus; I pray thee hearken!—
'tis some unknown bird that sings!'

The grim centurion stared at him, half in indignation, half in surprise.

'Bird!' he echoed—'There are few birds in
Palestine I warrant thee!—and what there are must
be as dry-throated as the locusts in the corn.'

'Hush!' whispered Maximus—'It begins again!'

And before Galbus could utter another word, a
silvery ripple of music floated towards him,—a flow
of gurgling notes, full and pure and honey-sweet,—

notes such as no nightingale in moonlit woods ever sang, even in the most ardent time of nesting tenderness. The amazement on the centurion's face deepened into rapture,—grasping his lance firmly with both hands he leaned against it, silently listening, and lost in wonder. The hidden bird sang on; and it seemed as if some wondrous meaning was enclosed within its song, for the fascination of striving to follow the thread of its rich rhythm intensified with every sweet tone that sounded on the still air. All at once it ceased,—but its broken melody was taken up by a companion singer who had evidently found a resting-place within the bush of myrtle that grew close by the sacred tomb. This second bird warbled even more rapturously than the first,—and while the clear torrent of tune poured forth passion to the silence, another soldier hastily advanced, eagerly exclaiming,

'Galbus! Hearest thou this music?'

Galbus started, . . . there was a strange moisture in his eyes,—he had been lost in thought, and the face of his little daughter who had died when barely three years of age had flitted, or appeared to flit, for a moment between him and the glittering moon. The sight of a second man wandering away from his post served as a timely check to his emotions, and he struck the butt-end of his lance into the ground with a well-affected air of anger.

'By the gods! Canst thou not hear a bird sing, without running hither like a prattling babe to tell me of it? Back to thy place, and quickly! Knowest thou not that we are bound to keep guard to-night with more than usual circumspection?—and shall we all be scattered like sheep at the twittering of birds? Maximus, be ashamed! Thou hast set a bad example; get hence, thou too,—and pay closer heed to thy duty,—who knows whether there may not be sorcery in this singing!'

A flush of vexation mounted to the brows of the young Maximus at the implied reproach, but he said nothing, and immediately retired. His post was not more than three or four yards from where Galbus stood; and feeling somewhat weary, he sat down inside one of the tents to rest. There, leaning his head on his hand, he still listened to the sweet chirping voices that now sounded louder and clearer than ever. The other soldier also went back to his place, crestfallen, but obedient, and Galbus was left to himself, to gaze at the sailing moon, and drink in the magical tenderness of the chorus that floated round and round the quiet sepulchre of the Crucified in ever-widening circles of delicious harmony. And presently,—all the men on guard, rather than disturb such music by the clank of their armour or the tread of their sandals, sat within their tents, all silent,—all enthralled into languid peace by a mystic and imperceptibly deepening spell.

''Tis wondrous,—I will not deny it,'—murmured Galbus after a while, seating himself also just within the door of his own small pavilion, and composing himself to fresh attention—'First it was one bird, and now it seems as if there were twenty. Never did I hear such singing in Palestine! They may be birds of passage,—yet from whence would they come, and whither would they speed? And wherefore should they choose such a resting-place as these arid hills?—or such an hour for tuning up their songs as now?'

He sat absorbed, his mind soothed and satisfied by the delicate pipings of the invisible little throats that seemed as if they must burst with the fulness and delight of song.

And, farther off, there was another listener to the
marvellous music,—one whose presence there that
night was totally unsuspected by the guard. This
was Barabbas. He lay unseen in the hollow of the
hill behind the sepulchre, and heard the melting
melody in rapt wonder. He knew the country round
Jerusalem well,—he had known it from boyhood;
but he had never heard sweet singing-birds till now.
He could not understand it; it was to him much
more than what was called a miracle. The air was
so very still,—the little trees were so motionless,—
the very blades of stunted grass so stiffly upright,
that the rippling notes seemed produced by some
power unearthly. It might have been the liquid
sounding of fairy flutes in the air, or dainty *arpeggi*
struck from golden strings, only that the voices were
most truly bird-like, full of nightingale-warbles and
luscious trills. And by and by the same sense of
peace and happiness stole on the tired soul of
Barabbas as had come to the war-worn centurion on
guard; gradually he grew lost in a sort of blissful
dream, scarcely knowing what he thought or what
he felt. When he had told Melchior of his intent
to keep secret vigil near the tomb of the 'Nazarene,'
that incomprehensible personage had looked grave,
but had not forbidden him, only saying gently—

'*Take heed, lest when the Master cometh, He find
you sleeping!*'

This was a strange saying!—nevertheless here he
was; determined not to sleep, but to remain broadly,
fully awake, so that he might be able to testify in
plain language as to what happened,—if indeed anything should happen. Yet he was conscious of a
drowsiness in the air,—of a lulling rhythm in the
dulcet singing of the unseen feathered choir, that was
inexpressibly soothing,—and he found difficulty in

resisting the tempting languor that by slow and insensible degrees began to take possession of him. He tried to think of various practical things,—of the terror which had evidently seized the disciples of the dead 'Nazarene,' causing them to hide themselves in the lowest quarters of the city, and entirely give up any attempt to visit the guarded tomb of their perished Master,—of the extreme precautions of Caiaphas,—of the continued indisposition of Pilate,— of the suicide of Judas Iscariot,—then,—of the strayed Judith, . . . and here his mind recoiled upon itself as it were, with inward trembling. The thought of her was singularly depressing and unwelcome to him just at this moment,—he could not have told why, but so it was. It would be well for her if she were dead, he told himself sorrowfully,—better for her, a thousand times,—better even for him. He would be glad to die, he thought,—that curious sense of detachment from earth and utter indifference to existence had come to him, as it comes at certain epochs to us all,—when death with its darkness and deep silence, seems a sweeter, kinder, and more valuable boon than life.

He flung himself back full length in the turfy hollow and lay staring up at the stars and the moon. How those birds sang! How sweetly the fragrant wind breathed through the dried and faintly rustling grass! He stretched his arms out on either side of him with a sigh of lazy comfort,—and presently took a singular pleasure in observing that he had unconsciously assumed the attitude of one preparing to be crucified. He began to wonder idly how it would feel if huge nails were driven forcibly through his open palms, as had been done to his former comrade Hanan, and to Him they called the 'Nazarene.' Involuntarily closing his fingers on a tuft of grass, he suddenly felt that he had grasped something foreign to the soil, and looking to see what he held, he found he had pulled up a small bell-shaped blossom, pure white and delicately scented. He examined it attentively ; he had never beheld its like before. But there was such a listless heaviness upon him that he had no desire to lift himself up and search for more such flowers,—had he done so he would have witnessed a fairy-like and strange spectacle. For, from base to summit of the hills around, the brown turf was rapidly being covered up out of sight by masses of snowy bloom, breaking upwards like white foam !— thousands and thousands of blossoms started from the trembling earth,—that earth which panted with the knowledge of a Divine Redemption, and yearned to pay its glorious Master homage. And the hidden birds sang on,—sweetly, passionately, triumphantly ; and round the holy sepulchre the soldiers nodded on the benches within their tents, half sleeping, wholly dreaming,—of love, of home, of kindred, of dear and precious memories such as never were expressed or written. Only the young Maximus forced himself to keep wide awake ; the reproach of Galbus had stung his military pride, and he resolved to be more than doubly vigilant in his watch. So, though he longed to fling himself down upon the turf and rest a while, he resisted the oppression that lay heavy upon him, and rising, walked slowly to and fro, glancing now and then dubiously and half compassionately at his drowsing comrades. He was not inclined to rouse them,—he meant to win some special praise for keener vigilance than they. His tall figure cast a gigantic shadow in the moonlight, as he paced leisurely up and down, and he watched this spectral exaggeration of himself in a curiously philosophic mood. What kind of a world would it have been, he thought, if the shadow of man had never fallen upon it? Dreamily pondering this wholly unanswerable question, he was all at once startled out of his reverie by a great light that fell in one, keen, dazzling flash straight from the heavens, sweeping the shadow of himself into naught, and playing about him in running, intertwisting rings of flame. Amazed, he looked up, and saw in the east a vivid rose-red radiance that widened out swiftly even as he gazed upon it,—while across the ruddy tint there appeared bright perpendicular bars of gold, like a vision of the gates of Eden. Shaking off the strange stupor that numbed his senses and held him for a moment inert, he sprang quickly to the side of Galbus, who, seated in his tent and leaning against his spear was all but fast asleep.

'Galbus! Galbus!'

Galbus at once leaped fiercely erect with a defiant look, as though threatening with death any one who should presume to say that he had slumbered.

Maximus, trembling, seized him by the arm, and half in terror, half in expectancy, pointed eastward.

'Galbus, the watch is ended! Lo,—the Dawn!'

XXXIX

GALBUS stared wildly with dazzled eyes.
'The dawn? . . . the dawn, sayest thou?'
he muttered thickly—'Nay, nay! . . . never did dawn
break thus strangely!' And his bronzed features
grew pale. ''Tis fire! . . . or lightning! . . . Maximus,
—Maximus,—my sight fails me, . . . yonder glory
hath a marvel in it! . . . 'tis blinding to the sight!
Ye gods,—look! . . . look there!'

Dropping his lance, he stretched out both arms
towards the sky, losing breath and utterance in the
excess of his amazement and fear; Maximus, speechless too, clung to him, gazing with equal dread and
wonder at the terrific splendour that cast its glory
round them and illumined all the visible earth. For
now, out of the burning centre of that eastward blaze
of crimson, there rose up a double fan-shaped, diamond-
shining whiteness, as of huge unfolding misty wings,
—towering aloft, these aerial pinions extended towards
the south; while from the north, another exactly
similar and equally dazzling Appearance made itself
visible against a gleaming background of smooth gold.
Then,—all at once, with a sudden sharp tremor the
earth shook; and there came the impetuous rush and
whirl of a mighty wind that bent the trees like
blades of grass and seemed to scatter the very stars

in heaven like a swarm of frightened fireflies; and with the surging sound that mysterious Winged Whiteness began to sweep forward at the swift and flashing pace of lightning!

'Galbus, Galbus!' gasped Maximus, falling down and covering his face in a paroxysm of fear—'Kneel —kneel!—for we must die! The gods descend! Behold them where they come!'

With straining eyeballs and panting breath, Galbus gave one upward frenzied stare, . . . his swooning senses could but just dimly realise that surely the powers of Heaven were upon him, and that death, sudden and relentless, must be his inevitable fate. How could mortal strength uphold mortal man at such a sight! . . . How could human vision bear the fearful dazzlement and marvel of what he, for one dizzy second, gazed upon! . . . Two majestic Shapes, —the transfigured and ethereal semblances of a glorified humanity, flashing with a brightness celestial, a splendour invincible, grew up, as it were, in stately stature out of the molten-golden east; and seemingly impelled by wind and fire, floated meteor-like through space, and together silently descended at the closed tomb of the 'Nazarene'! One of these supernal Beings appeared robed in white fire,—his lustrous countenance, gleaming as with lightning, shone from between pale glistening locks of gold, on which a halo rested, like a crown. As this glorious Messenger touched earth, the ground rocked, and the divided air recoiled upon itself with a roll and roar of thunder. Prone on the turf Galbus fell senseless and dead for the time being, . . . and in that one thrilling moment no living man beheld the splendid declaration of the Divine, save one,—Barabbas. He, when the great light flashed around him, when the whirlwind and the thunder swept surgingly across the hills, had crawled forth from his hiding-place; and now, crouching on the grass in a dumb agony of trembling, stared at the supernatural sight, unforbidden for a brief space, too dazzled to realise all its meaning and majesty, and believing that he must be wrapt in some wild and glittering dream, . . . when, even as he looked, a sharp brilliance, like the cutting sting of a lash, struck him across the eyes,—and he, too, swayed blindly back and plunged into the darkness of a swoon that was like death.

Quivering to its deepest underground fibres, the earth supported the glowing forms of God's ethereal Envoys;—together they stood, the fire of their white transparent wings quenching the silver reflex of the sinking moon,—their radiant faces turned towards the closed sepulchre wherein their Master slept. Again the great wind rushed in resonant harp-like chords through heaven,—again the ground rocked and trembled, and again the thunder sounded its deep trump of wakening eloquence! And all the mystic voices of the air seemed whispering the great Truths about to be made manifest;—'Death is dead; Life is Eternal! God is Love!'

Like kindled flames upon the sombre soil, the Angels of the Message waited side by side, their heavenly eyes luminous with Divine rapture, and the light upon their brows flinging glorious reflections far up in twinkling points of radiance to the vanishing stars. The dawn was near,—the strong suspense of Nature was at its keenest pitch,—it seemed as if what we know of Creation could endure the strain no more, —as if the world, the sun, the moon, the visible planets, must melt away like drops of dew in the burning fervour of so vast an ecstasy of expectation! The dawn was near!—that Dawn which would be like no other dawn that ever heralded a day,—the dawn

of all the hope, the joy, the faith, the love that waits
upon the promised certainty of life immortal ; that
priceless promise given to those who are willing to
accept it without question or mistrust; and who,
loving their fellow-men better than themselves, in
God and for God, touch heavenly ecstasy while yet
on earth.

And now a deep silence reigned. All the soldiers
of the watch lay stretched on the ground unconscious,
as though struck dead by lightning,—the previous
mysterious singing of the birds had ceased ; and only
the lambent quivering of the wing-like glory surrounding the angelic Messengers, seemed to make
an expressed though unheard sound as of music.
Then, . . . in the midst of the solemn hush, . . . the
great stone that closed the tomb of the Crucified
trembled, . . . and was suddenly thrust back like a
door flung open in haste for the exit of a King, . . .
and lo ! . . . a Third great Angel joined the other
two ! Sublimely beautiful He stood,—the Risen
from the Dead ! . . . gazing with loving eyes on all
the swooning, sleeping world of men ; the same grand
Countenance that had made a glory of the Cross of
Death, now, with a smile of victory, gave poor
Humanity the gift of everlasting Life ! The grateful
skies brightened above Him, — earth exhaled its
choicest odours through every little pulsing leaf and
scented herb and tree ; Nature exulted in the touch
of things eternal,—and the dim pearly light of the
gradually breaking morn fell on all things with a
greater purity, a brighter blessedness than ever had
invested it before. The Man Crucified and Risen,
now manifested in Himself the mystic mingling of
God in Humanity ; and taught that for the powers of
the Soul set free from sin, there is no limit, no
vanquishment, no end ! No more eternal partings for

those who on the earth should learn to love each other, — no more the withering hopelessness of despair,—the only 'death' now possible to redeemed mortality being 'the bondage of sin' voluntarily entered into and preferred by the unbelieving. And from this self-wrought, self-chosen doom not even a God can save.

Reverently bent were the radiant heads of the angelic Beings that had descended in full flight from Heaven; but He who stood erect between them, tall and majestically fair, looked upward once; then straight across the silent landscape; and, stretching forth His hands, semeed by the tenderness of the gesture to place His benediction on the world. A light grey mist was rising incense-like from the eastern edge of the horizon, — the crimson glory lately flaming there had paled into the faint pink of a blush rose-petal, and a soothing shadow stole imperceptibly over the scene, toning down into silver lines the departing rays of that supernatural splendour which had been like the beginning of a new creation. Slowly, very slowly, the transcendent brightness round the form of the Risen Redeemer faded into air,—His Human Shape became more and more clearly defined, till almost He looked with the same aspect He had worn in the Hall of Pilate, when man's law had condemned Him to suffer man's death. Only there rested a sublimer glory on His countenance: the expression of a power omnipotent; a beauty terrific; a knowledge supernal that made Him wonderful even in the sight of His serving-angels of Heaven. To them presently His high command was silently expressed, for one bright Being vanished like a melting cloud within the opened sepulchre,—and the other, moving to the great stone of burial that had been rolled away, rested upon it, a shining Wonder, clothed in white wings.

Meanwhile He who had proved Death to be but another name for Life, began to pace pensively to and fro among the tangled shrubs and vines that in their careless and untrained luxuriance gave to the otherwise dreary burial-spot, something of a wild beauty. He moved as though He loved the world; even to the very blades of grass His feet passed gently over; the leaves upon their branches bent towards Him as taking health and joy from His fair Presence, and fearlessly seeking His blessing. And ever as He moved, His aspect grew more human; out of the secret depths of space He seemed to clothe Himself anew with the fleeting semblance of mortality. Now and again He paused, and gazed at the senseless forms around Him of all those who had been set to guard His resting-place, and then the mystic watchfulness and deep compassion of His eyes reflected the vast, impersonal and changeless love which emanates from the Divine alone. Passing slowly among them with noiseless tread, the while they lay inert, unconscious of His nearness (even as we, at this time, in our blind and selfish torpor are unconscious or indifferent when He comes), He presently approached the spot where the sinner who should, in justice, have suffered instead of Him had fallen as one dead,—Barabbas. Stretched flat upon the turf, with arms extended on either side of him as though the earth were a cross and he the criminal nailed to it, his dark countenance and closed eyes fronting the sky, the erring, passion-haunted man was ready for some punishment, some instant withering doom. Stained with the crime of murder, branded as a thief, and full of a thousand follies and germinating sins, what had he done that he should

merit all the pity and the pardon that flashed upon
him like a glory from the tender glance of the risen
Christ! What had he done?—why, nothing in truth,
—he could, he would do nothing worthy. Only a
thought of love had been in his dark soul for the
sorrows of the Man Crucified,—and he had shed tears
for the sufferings of the holiest Innocence that ever was
maligned by human malice; he had longed to understand, to know, to serve this splendid Ideal of the Ages,
—and—this was all. Yet this sufficed to bring the
glorious Master to his side; though as that Master
looked upon him, a shade of sorrow darkened the
beautiful Divine brows,—the shadow and presentiment of what was yet to be. There, made visible in
Barabbas, was the symbol of the animal man, blindly
conscious of the creative Soul of the Universe, yet
doubting all manifestations of that Soul, and thrusting his own narrow fears and scepticisms forward
to obstruct and bar out the very presence of the
Eternal. And beside him, in strange contrast, stood
the pure and stately embodiment of the Spirit of
God made human, — the example of a perfect
manhood, the emblem of life, and the symbol of
Genius, which slandered and tortured and slain
and buried, rises eternally triumphant over evil and
death.

A faint sigh stirred the air,—the sigh of One who
knew that by the pitiless will of Man, He should be
wronged and spiritually re-crucified for ages; and
then the risen Light of the World turned away and
glided among the little trembling trees, His figure
gradually becoming a mere misty outline, vague
and undefinable as though it were the floating
shadow of a dream. Two hours had yet to pass
ere the sun would rise, — meanwhile a fragrant
freshness sweetened the breaking dawn, and all

24

Nature remained absorbed in a sacred silence of enraptured worship, conscious that the Master and Lord of Life was now, as once before in oldest time, 'walking in His garden in the cool of the day'!

XL

SHUDDERING in every limb with pain and chilly fear, Barabbas presently awoke from his long swoon. Something had happened,—but what? He rubbed his aching eyes and lifted himself into a half-sitting posture, looking uneasily about him. Dully he considered his position; he was in his old place on the hill behind the sepulchre; the place where he had watched, until—until, as it seemed, a strange thing had chanced to him which now he could not quite remember. A dream had dazzled him, he thought, and scared his senses from him. He imagined he had seen two supernatural Shapes, formed as it were, out of floating pyramidal fire, descending near the tomb of the 'Nazarene,' —but ere he had had time to look upon them straightly, a dizziness had seized him, and he saw no more.

'*Take heed, lest when the Master cometh, He find you sleeping.*' These words, spoken to him by the man Melchior, ere he had started to take up his self-imposed vigil, recurred to him unpleasantly now and troubled him; had he slept after all? And had the 'Master' come?

Rising slowly to his feet, he gazed from left to right of him; all things seemed the same. The tents of the soldiers on guard gleamed whitely in the pallid grey of dawn; the men had evidently not yet left their posts, though the night was fully past and the sense of sunrise was in the air. There was something peculiarly beautiful in the clear freshness of that wondrous morning. The world appeared new; as though it were conscious of the victory of the Soul over Death; and Barabbas, pained and puzzled though he was, felt the comfort of the deep tranquillity and restfulness around him. Dismissing his forebodings, he began to think he would boldly go to the sepulchre, and seek out Galbus to ask him how he had fared during the night,—then, on further reflection he hesitated, for if, after all, anything unusual should have occurred, he, Barabbas, might be suspected of having had some share in it. While he stood thus irresolute, soft approaching steps startled him, and he quickly crouched down again behind a bend of the hill where he could see without being seen. Three women were coming up the road from the city,—the foremost one of the group was Mary Magdalene. Her head was bent sorrowfully; she moved listlessly and with an air of deep melancholy,—in her hands she carried flowers and sweet herbs, and delicate odours seemed to be exhaled from her garments as she moved. She and her companions exchanged no words; they all seemed stricken by the silence of an absolute despair. As they passed by the spot where Barabbas lay concealed, he lifted himself cautiously up to look after them, and wondered whether it would be safe or prudent to follow in their track. They appeared like misty phantoms floating along in the pearly hues of dawn; but he could see the golden glint of the Magdalen's hair flash like a sunbeam as she turned round by the shelving rocks of the sepulchre and disappeared. Poor, wistful, woebegone

women, he thought!—they went to visit the dead,—
the dead 'Man of Nazareth' whose wondrous smile
of love and pardon would never lighten their lonely
lives again! Alas, for them, that in their clinging
faithfulness, they should of sad and morbid choice
renew their useless anguish by gazing once more
upon the cruelly unflinching stillness and rigidity
of the frozen monster Death, who never yields
his once-gained prey for all the clamour of tender
women's tears! So Barabbas mused compassionately, though his mind was swayed between doubt
and fear whenever the recollection of his last
night's 'dream' occurred to him,—that dream of
angels which had blinded him with its excess of
light.

Suddenly a piercing cry echoed through the
silence, and two of the women came rushing back
along the road in a panic of haste and fear. Throwing personal precaution to the winds, Barabbas
sprang out from his hiding-place and confronted
them.

'What now?' he demanded excitedly—'Speak—
speak! What news?'

'He is risen! He is risen!' they cried, their eager
voices struggling together for quickest utterance—
'The seals of the tomb are broken,—the stone is
rolled away,—and an Angel of the Lord is there!
He is risen!'

Trembling with agitation, Barabbas thrust
himself in their path as they strove to run past
him.

'Ye are mad!—surely ye are mad!' he exclaimed;
'Whither go ye?'

Impatiently they pointed towards the city.

'Yonder!—to summon His disciples. Go! see the
place where the Lord lay! None shall hinder thee;

the keepers are as dead men! He is risen!—He is risen!'

And they pursued their swift course down the road as though impelled along by invisible wings.

Barabbas waited no longer, but ran impetuously at a headlong pace towards the sepulchre, every pulse in his body beating with feverish excitement. As he approached it, however, he involuntarily slackened his speed, stricken with wonder and affright at the strange scene. It was true!—the 'keepers' were 'as dead men;'—Galbus and his band of soldiers were all prone upon the ground like corpses flung there after a battle,—and what had seemed the impossible had been effected, in that the tomb was open, and the huge stone rolled away. And the Angel of whom the women spoke? Barabbas could see no Angel,—though he fancied that on the displaced stone, there glittered a singular bright light that made it shine like a block of polished gold. He rubbed his eyes dubiously: such marvels made him distrust the evidence of his own senses,—yet, there at the entrance of the opened tomb, lay something human,—something in distress,—the fallen form of the Magdalen, who seemed to have swooned. Barabbas would have approached her,—but an invisible force held him to the spot where he stood, smitten with strong awe and fear, and he dared not advance a step. And while he yet looked, he saw her move; and presently she rose up feebly, and with tottering steps stooped towards the sepulchre as though to enter in. Then all suddenly a calm Voice sounded on the deep silence,—a Voice of pure unearthly music sweeter than all we know of sweetest sound:

'*Woman, why weepest thou?*'

Thrilled with amazement and dread, Barabbas saw her sink upon her knees and raise her hands in passionate supplication.

'*Because*,' . . . and her trembling accents were broken by low weeping—'*they have taken away my Lord, and I know not where they have laid Him!*'

A deep silence followed. The golden glory vanished from the stone that had been rolled away,—and another light began to shine—the first heraldic blazon of the rising sun. Unanswered and uncomforted, the Magdalen hid her face in her clasped hands,—she had seen a vision of angels; one at the head and one at the foot of the sepulchred niche where her Master had reposed in temporary death,—but what are all the angels in paradise worth to Love, if the Beloved be missing? And stricken to the heart by despair and loneliness, she wept on, crouched at the entrance of the vacant tomb, her slight frame shaken by the tempest of her grief for the loss of the dead outward Semblance of Him whose pardon had reclaimed her life. But while she thus gave way to the abandonment of sorrow, the enchained spectator of the scene, Barabbas, suddenly became conscious of a majesty and a terror filling the air; some great Splendour suggested itself vaguely like the thunderous thrill of the atmosphere preceding a storm. Faint and trembling he felt rather than saw, that a Figure was advancing from the sheltering shadow of the few trees that surrounded the sepulchre, . . . and slowly, slowly, in a mortal anguish of dread and expectation he turned,—and beheld in very truth, in very life, . . . the 'Nazarene'! He, the Crucified, the Slain and Buried, stood there living; looking even as He looked before He had been nailed upon the Cross to die,—the same, the same in every feature, as

human-seeming as Humanity itself, save that His
vesture appeared woven out of glittering mist and
fire! Breathless, giddy, and unable to articulate the
feeblest cry, Barabbas stared upon Him, fully recog-
nising the fair beauty of His countenance, the
lustrous love and wisdom of His eyes, yet afraid to
believe this Miracle a Truth. In aerial stateliness
He passed by without sound, and glided, a Kingly
Spirit in mortal aspect, to where the Magdalen wept
alone. There, pausing, He spoke, His dulcet accents
charming the stillness to responsive pulsations of
harmony.

'*Woman, why weepest thou ! Whom seekest
thou ?*'

Moving restlessly, she half turned round and gazed
vaguely up through the obscuring cloud of her
tears and falling hair, only seeing that some one, she
knew not who, stood beside her, questioning her as
to her cause of grief. And with a shuddering
sigh she drooped her head again and answered
wearily—

'*Sir, if thou hast borne Him hence, tell me
where thou hast laid Him, and I will take Him
away.*'

'*Mary !*'

The sweet name, set among holy things for ever,
fell softly on the silence like a song.

She started,—sprang up to her full height,—gazed
wildly, . . . wonderingly, . . . incredulously, . . .
then,—with a shriek of joy that seemed to echo to
the very skies, she fell on her knees.

'Master! Master!' she cried, and stretched
forth her hands towards that Risen Saviour whose
living Presence was the sign of rescue for the
world.

But now a light celestial environed Him,—the

earth trembled where He stood,—and with a warning yet gentle gesture He motioned her away.

'*Touch Me not; for I am but newly risen!*'

And as He said these words a splendour flashed about His form like fire,—He lifted His eyes to the brightening heavens, and all the radiant hues of morning seemed to float around Him and melt above Him in rings upon rings of ever-widening lustre, while the arrowy beams of the sun, shooting upwards through the clear ether, formed as it were upon the edge of the horizon a great Crown of the Universe for the glory of Him alone. Divinity invested Him with an unspeakable grandeur and majesty; and when His voice again sounded through space, it rang with the clarion note of supreme command and resistless power.

'*Go!*'—and extending His arms, He appeared to indicate by one royal, all-comprehensive gesture His sovereignty over things visible and invisible; '*Go, tell My brethren that I ascend! Unto My Father and your Father,—unto My God and your God!*'

One thrilling instant more His creatures looked upon Him,—the Magdalen in rapt and speechless ecstasy,—Barabbas in stupefied, fascinated amazement mingled with a strange qualm of unbelief and misgiving,—then, all at once there came a great blankness over the land,—an emptiness and sense of desolation,—the Kingly Conqueror of Death no longer lent the lustre of His beauty to the breaking day. He was gone!—He had vanished like a summer cloud absorbed in space; and only a fragrant cluster of snow-white flowers marked the spot where He had stood! And presently, across the deep stillness that followed His departure, there came the far-off ringing of bells from the city,—then the faint stir and hum of wakening life ;—the mystic marvels of the night were ended,—the first Easter morn spread fully forth its glorious golden blazon; and all aflame with wonder at the scene, the sun rose.

XLI

LIKE the breaking of a charm woven by some wizard incantation, the spell which had held Barabbas dumb with awe and fear was suddenly dispersed. Recklessly springing forward without stopping to consider what he did, he confronted the Magdalen, who still knelt where her Lord had left her, her enravished eyes upturned to heaven as though she saw some mystic vision of eternal joys. With hasty ruthlessness, born of a dark suspicion that rankled in his mind, Barabbas seized her by the hands.

'Wherefore dost thou pray to emptiness?' he cried loudly—'The "Nazarene" was here a moment since! Whither hath He fled?'

Mary started from her trance of worship, trembled, and looked at her fierce questioner in vague yet sweet bewilderment, with the half-sad, half-happy smile of one who has been brusquely wakened out of an ecstatic dream.

'Yea, truly He was here!' she answered in soft accents that thrilled with rapture—'Yea truly, though my faltering soul could not at first believe it, He hath risen from the dead! From henceforth who shall fear the terrors of the grave! He hath risen! Verily God hath manifested Himself unto us, and given comfort for the sorrow of the world!'

She seemed yet entranced,—her eyes were luminous, her face glowingly beautiful as that of some inspired angel. Barabbas grew more and more impatient.

'Woman, thou art dazed or in a vision!' he exclaimed — 'Thy Master was ever a worker of miracles, and surely He hath worked them in the night that now is past! Prate not thus of His rising from the dead,—for of a truth methinks thou knowest that He hath never died!'

Slowly Mary rose from her knees, and putting back the falling tresses of her long bright hair gazed at him amazedly.

'Never died!' she echoed—'What meanest thou? Art thou not Barabbas, and didst thou not behold Him die? Didst thou not weep with me for His long agony? And hast thou not looked upon Him here alive again? Art thou distraught that thou believest not in God? How camest thou hither?'

Barabbas made no answer. His dark brows were knitted frowningly; his limbs yet trembled from the agitation through which he had passed; but there was a lowering doubt within him to which he was ashamed to give utterance. He moved to the opening of the vacant tomb and peered in mistrust-fully,—then after a second's hesitation, stooped down and entered. There was nothing to be seen save the empty stone niche where the 'Nazarene' had slept, and the linen grave-clothes which had enswathed Him. These were rolled together and flung aside in one corner. Coming out of the dark recess, he stood silent and dissatisfied; he longed to give voice to the suspicion that like a mocking devil assailed him and worked mischief in his mind; yet he remained abashed before the tender ecstasy, deep humility and adoring faith of the woman who in the sublimity of perfect love, seemed stronger than himself, made weak and wavering by doubt. Meanwhile, as he waited hesitatingly, watching the Magdalen, the broad beams of the sun pouring over the landscape appeared to cause a sudden movement among the hitherto inert forms of the soldiers of the watch,— and presently one of the men sprang up erect with an amazed look as though he had fallen out of the clouds.

'Ye gods!' he cried loudly—'What! All asleep? Galbus! Maximus! Dion! Antinus! What! Broad day and not a man waking!'

The clamour he made, and his fashion of prodding his still only half-conscious comrades with the end of his lance, began to take effect, but before he could thoroughly rouse them all, Barabbas caught the Magdalen by the arm, and dragging her with him round the bend of the rocks in which the sepulchre was hewn, escaped from sight ere he could be discovered.

'Lo there!' he muttered breathlessly, when he stood safely on the high-road beside Mary, who in her dreamy bewilderment had scarcely comprehended the hurry and alarm of his action—'If yonder Romans had seen me by the open tomb they would have sworn I had stolen the body of the " Nazarene,"—for I am branded already as a robber. And thou, even thou would'st not have gone without suspicion,—frail woman as thou art, thou mightest have been deemed capable of treachery!'

His sombre black eyes rested darkly upon her,— but she was quite unconscious of any latent significance hidden in his words. Her countenance looked singularly fair and youthful, while it was irradiated by a holy joy that made its natural loveliness almost unearthly.

'Wilt thou now go upon thine errand?' he

continued, regarding her steadfastly—'Thy Master gave thee some command,—wilt thou fulfil it? Two of thy friends have sped before thee crying "*He is risen!*"—now, do but add thy voice in all its sweet persuasiveness to theirs,—and lo! perchance the world will take thy word for truth Divine!'

She looked at him, first in amazement, then in sorrow and compassion.

'Thou poor Barabbas!' she said—'Hast thou then looked upon the Master's face, and yet canst not believe in Him? What aileth thee, thou blind and suffering soul? In such a time of joy, why chainest thou thyself to misery? Speak all thy thought!— what hast thou in thy mind against me?'

'Naught against thee in very truth'—answered Barabbas slowly and reluctantly, 'save that I deem thee overwrought by such a frenzy of strange faith that thou would'st almost force a miracle! Truly I saw thy Master; and that He lived and walked and spoke I am prepared to swear,—but I repeat to thee my words—He is not dead,—He never died! And thou, Mary of Magdala, knowest this!'

Nothing but wonder now filled her clear childlike eyes.

'What meanest thou?' she asked anxiously—'I cannot follow thee,—surely thou wanderest in thy speech and reason'——

'Nay, not so!' he interrupted her harshly—'I am no woman, that I should be duped by feverous visions and the crazed distemper of a vain imagining! Last night, here on these hills, I too kept secret vigil,— and nothing of any import chanced, save a sudden rising of the wind with lightning and thunder. And towards the middle of the watch, a swooning came upon me,—my senses reeled, and in the dazzlement of brain and sight, methought the lightning took

strange shape and walked upon the land arrayed
in wings. This blinded me, and I recall no more,
for I lost hold on life till morning. Then, waking,
I saw thee and thy companions coming from the city
stealthily,—and afterwards while I yet waited, the
twain who were thy friends came running back
possessed by some distraction, and, meeting me, they
swore the Crucified had risen from the dead! I
believed it not,—and even now I still believe it not,
though with mine own eyes I have looked upon Him
living! I say that He hath never died,—upon the
Cross He did but swoon! Ay!—'twas a seeming
death!—and thou, Mary, didst so melt the hearts of
those who crucified Him, that when they took His
body from the tree, they gave it into thy charge, and
to His Mother, and for pure clemency, did forbear to
break His limbs. Doubtless thou also didst confer
with the Arimathean counsellor, to the end that He
should be laid within yon unused quiet cave, where
in the darkness and cool silence He hath recovered,—
for was He not a master of the secrets of all healing?
Nay, I am sure of nothing,—as man I can but
reason!—one must be even as a bat or mole not to
see through this scheme wrought by the unwise love
of women! Go thy ways, Mary!—perjure thyself no
more,—'tis no miracle to me that thus thy Master
liveth!'

While he thus spoke in mingled resentment and
scorn, she never moved. Listening patiently, her
steadfast gaze fixed upon him, she looked the very
incarnation of heavenly pity. Her lips trembled
apart; she was about to speak, when another voice,
clear and imperative, unexpectedly joined in the
conversation—

'Go thy ways, Mary! Fulfil thine errand and
delay not; for 'tis the errand of all true women

henceforth unto the end of this world's time! An errand of love and mercy!—be thou the first one to perform it,—tell the "brethren" even as thy Master bade thee, that He hath risen!—that death is conquered by immortality, and that He ascends!— unto His Father, whom now through Him we know as Father of us all.'

And Melchior stood before them, his eyes flashing a mingled sorrow and satire. Barabbas stared at him afraid and ashamed; how had he managed to arrive on the scene so silently that his approach had not even been observed? Meeting his cold ironic regard, Barabbas felt suddenly humiliated, though he could not have told why; Melchior meanwhile continued,—

'Well hast thou kept thy vigil, friend Barabbas!— as faithfully and observantly in very truth as those admirable followers of the "Nazarene," who when He besought them to watch beside Him for one hour, could not deprive themselves of sleep for all their boasted love and faithfulness! Thou, erring and wilful sinner as thou art, hast been privileged to see the Divine and live,—and yet thou dost deem a very God imposture, measured by the ruling of thy finite reason! Did I not tell thee thou wert man's true type?—and a perfect representative of thy unbelieving race? Mary,' and he turned to the Magdalen with a gentle reverence—'I pray thee linger here no longer, —but haste to bear thy news to those who are bidden to receive it; though verily 'tis certain that not one, not even the repentant Petrus, will at first believe thy tidings. Men will work bravely to support their own lies; but scarce a soul shall be found on earth, willing to bear pure witness to God's Truth. But keep thou thy faith, Mary!—on woman's love and patience rests the world's future.'

She gave one fleeting startled glance at him of

questioning surprise and fear,—then instinctively obeying his authoritative gesture she hastened away, her grey garments and gold hair floating together like mingled sun and cloud as she sped city-wards.

'Thou dark distrustful soul!' then said Melchior to his moody companion,—'How deservest thou any kindness of fate, seeing thou hast looked upon a God and known Him not? Heavy would be thy punishment wert thou alone in thy perversity and sin,—but take good comfort!—all thy race are with thee!—thou art, despite thyself, the true "King of the Jews!" Behold the watch where they come, all agape with wonder and dismay!—well may they look thus wildly, for their news is of that strangeness that some among them will scarce have skill to utter it. Stand we aside a space while they pass by.'

He drew Barabbas apart, and they both observed with differently mixed feelings, the disorderly and scrambling approach of the soldiers who were coming away from the sepulchre and hurrying towards the town. They all looked only half awake and dazed with bewilderment ; the centurion Galbus no longer headed the band, but walked, or rather stumbled along in the midst, supported by two of his men who held him up apparently despite himself. He was ghastly pale,—his eyes had a fixed unseeing stare, —he seemed like one stricken by paralysis and rendered suddenly old. Melchior glanced at him, and stepped forward—

'Greeting to Rome!' he said, confronting the party—'What ails your leader?'

The soldiers halted, and Maximus who was in command replied curtly—

'We answer no questions from strangers. Stand back and let us pass!'

25

Quietly Melchior lifted his right hand, displaying a broad jewelled ring on the centre finger.

'Be civil, good Roman!' he said—'Respect the Emperor's signet.'

The astonished Maximus hastily saluted,—there was no mistake about the matter,—the mysterious stranger did indeed possess the Imperial talisman; and its authority was immediately recognised.

'I crave pardon, sir' — murmured Maximus apologetically—'But in this tributary province of Judæa each man of Rome must be upon his guard'——

'Ay! and keep good vigil too, as no doubt ye all have done throughout the night;'—interrupted Melchior—'Nothing, of course, hath chanced of any import? Ye have left the dead safely entombed?'

Silence followed. The soldiers looked down confusedly,—Maximus shivered as though the warm morning sun chilled him,—but the pallid-featured Galbus made no sign, and only stared on vaguely, straight ahead, like a blind man dreaming of light.

'Sir'—replied Maximus after a pause—'Of the past night there is much to tell,—but methinks it must be told first to those who have the ruling of the law among the Jews. Rome did not slay the "Nazarene," and for that death our governor hath publicly refused to be accountable. Neither can Rome be blamed for what hath now so strangely chanced—for lo, the seals of the Sanhedrim council are broken; the stone that closed the tomb is rolled away; and the body of the crucified Prophet hath been taken from thence,—but how these things were done I know not. I do confess we slept when we should have watched,—but truly there were strange sorceries all about us! A singing of birds was in the air; so sweet that we were fain to listen—and

towards morning we beheld the heavens on fire,—
that is, Galbus and myself beheld it, for these others
slept:'— Here he lowered his voice and spoke
almost in a whisper—'The burden of the telling of
this tale devolves on me, for Galbus is deprived of
speech,—he can express nothing of what he saw,—
the lightning that flashed across the land hath
stricken him wholly dumb!'

'So shall he bear no garrulous witness to the
wonders of the night'—said Melchior with a grave
and kindly glance at the bent and drooping figure of
the lately stalwart centurion, —'Yet be consoled,
good soldier. 'Tis but a temporary silence and will
pass. Whither go ye now? To Pilate?'

'Yea, to Pilate first and then to Caiaphas'—
answered Maximus—'There shall I plainly speak of
what I know. And if thou be the Emperor's friend,
good sir, I do beseech thee to mistake us not,—we
have been ever honoured in the legion for prowess
and vigilance till now, and truly I cannot tell how
we were all entranced away from watchfulness.
Nevertheless I will assert before the Tribunal, yea,
and before the whole Sanhedrim, that no man's force,
be he Jew or Roman, can stand against the powers
of Heaven!' And he looked round at the dazed
and helpless Galbus, marking him out by an impressive gesture as the living proof of the terrors
of the past vigil.

Melchior drew back.

'Fear not, soldier! Thou shalt not lose place in
the legion, nor shalt thou lack protection from Cæsar.
On to the city!—present this dumb centurion to
Caiaphas,—and speak thou the truth as it is apparent
unto thee, but doubt not that a lie will be quickly
substituted for it! The lie will best suit the Jews,—
'twill cost little trouble to keep up, being prone to

propagate itself in endless forms,—but the Truth
will need fighting for and dying for through ages
yet to come! Farewell! In whatsoever way I can,
I will commend thee to the Emperor.'

Again Maximus saluted profoundly, and the men
resumed their dusty hurried march. As they went,
one said to his fellow,

'Yonder stranger who doth wear our Emperor's
signet is not particular in choice of comrades, for
with him was Barabbas.'

'Barabbas!' echoed the other, — 'He that was
released from punishment of death in place of the
" Nazarene "?'

'Even he! 'Tis said he was a robber.'

They trudged on through the thick white dust,
and presently the whole company arrived at the
gates of the city, where they were met by a rabble
of the Jewish populace who hailed them with shouts
of derision. The rumour had already gone abroad
that the crucified Prophet of Nazareth had risen from
the dead, and though none believed in the miracle,
there were a few superstitious souls in the crowd
who imparted to others their notion that He had
not really died, and moreover could not die. But
the general impression was that the Body had been
stolen from the tomb in spite of all precaution,—
that the soldiers had been plied with wine, and in
all probability drugged into a lethargy, and that
while they slept off the effects of over-much liquor,
the disciples of the 'Nazarene' had moved away
the stone from the sepulchre and carried off their
dead Master. In any case Roman vigilance had
been baffled, and to the Jewish mob there was something peculiarly pleasing in this defeat. They yelled
and hooted round the discomfited 'watch,'—pointing
out the tottering Galbus with jeers as 'one that hath

not yet recovered from his winebibbing!' and formed a disorderly cortège up to the house of Pilate. There, when the great portal was unbarred to admit the soldiers, and these passed in, the malcontents remained for a little time outside, shouting ironical applause for the valour of Rome,— then, tired of their own clamour, gradually dispersed.

Meanwhile, Barabbas once more in the shelter of the inn where Melchior lodged, turned to that strange personage and asked abruptly,

'How camest thou to wear the Emperor's signet?'

'That is my business, not thine, Barabbas!' responded Melchior tranquilly—'Learn thou the first rule of civility, which is, to ask no questions on matters which do not concern thee. The Emperor is my friend,—and for a service I have done him I hold Rome itself in fee.'

Barabbas opened his eyes wide in astonishment, and would certainly have pressed for further information had he not been interrupted at that moment by a soft knocking at the door, and the sound of a voice calling eagerly—

'Open! Open quickly! I have news for Barabbas. It is I,—Mary of Magdala.'

XLII

IN answer to this summons they unlatched the door, and confronted the Magdalen on the threshold. She was breathless with running, and her eyes expressed a great and compassionate anxiety.

'I promised thee, Barabbas,'—she began hurriedly, —'I promised thee that if I heard aught of Judith Iscariot I would tell thee,—lo now, I have found her! She is in the wooded grove of Gethsemane,—alone, strangely distraught and ill,—dying perchance! I pray thee tarry not, but come with me straightway, —thou may'st persuade her from thence. I cannot. She weeps and sings,—anon she clasps her hands and prays,—then she flies from me as one in fear,—'twill need much tenderness to move her,—but thou as one familiar to her sight may haply entice her homeward —prithee come!'

'Yea, go quickly now, Barabbas,'—said Melchior gently—'In the sorrow of a broken heart, love must needs pardon sin, and make an end of bitterness.'

He turned away, and Barabbas, needing no second bidding, hastened out of the house with the Magdalen, in a tremor of excitement and apprehension. The way to Gethsemane seemed interminably long, and yet they lost no time, not even in converse, for both were full of thoughts that baffled words. At last they reached the gate of the garden, and as she lifted the latch, Mary held up one hand warningly.

'Listen!' she said.

Faint fragments of song came floating towards them,—broken scraps of melody, sweet and solemn and wild,—and presently Barabbas recognised the sonorous rhythm of the stanzas of Solomon the Poet-King:

> 'Whither is thy beloved gone, O thou fairest among
>   women?
> Whither is thy beloved turned aside?
> Tell us, that we may seek him with thee.
>
> My beloved is gone down into his garden,
> To the beds of spices and to gather lilies;
> My beloved is mine and I am his!
>
> Awake, O north wind, and come thou south!
> Blow upon my garden and on the spices thereof;
> Let my beloved come into his garden '——

Here the voice broke with a sharp discordant cry—

'Judas! Judas! Judas!'

This name three times repeated, sent shuddering echoes of shrill despair through the solemn tranquillity of Gethsemane, and Barabbas trembled as he heard.

'Where is she?' he demanded, in a hoarse whisper.

Mary Magdalene made no reply, but took him by the hand and led him onward.

They followed a winding path, so overgrown with

moss that their footsteps made no sound upon it, and presently came in view of a grassy knoll tufted with palms, and furthermore adorned by the broken shell of a disused fountain. Here a white figure sat droopingly, all alone; surrounded by a fantastic tangle of creepers and flowers that lay in straggling lengths upon the turf, apparently just gathered and thrown idly down to perish. Mary and Barabbas moved cautiously on, till they were within a few steps of that solitary woman-shape, upon whose fiery-gold hair the sunlight shed a deeper flame.

'Pause here a while'—whispered Mary then—'She hath a singular suddenness of violence in her,—and if we come upon her unpreparedly, she will take instant flight. Best let me go before, and speak with her.'

But some instinctive sense of being watched, already moved the distraught girl. Springing to her feet, she shaded her eyes with one hand and looked straight down upon them. Then lifting up her voice once more in that wailing cry, 'Judas!' she came rushing forward. With flying hair and feverishly glittering eyes she confronted them, and as her wild gaze fell on Barabbas, she uttered an exclamation of joy:

'Judas!' and she ran to him, flinging her arms about him in delirious ecstasy—'Judas, thou art here at last! Why didst thou not come sooner? I have wandered all about the city seeking thee,—yea! I have even killed Caiaphas for thy sake! Didst thou not know of this, and art thou not glad? Of a truth he was a traitor; but alas! I learned his treachery too late to serve thee in the saving of thy friend the "Nazarene." And willingly do I confess my share of blame,—not thou, poor Judas, wert in fault; 'twas all my doing, and Caiaphas persuaded me,—therefore grieve thou no more for others' crimes. And now I have done all I could to make amends, thou wilt forgive me? Is it not so? Thou wilt forgive thy little sister? Thou wilt love her still?'

While thus she moaned and murmured, with mingled sobs and smiles, pressing her soft face against his breast and lifting up her beautiful dark anguished eyes entreatingly, Barabbas felt as if his heart must break,—tears rose in his throat and choked his power of speech,—he pressed her convulsively in his arms but could say nothing,—and she whose madness was capable of endless fluctuations, from tenderness to ferocity, grew irritated at his silence. Tearing herself away from him she stood apart, eyeing him at first with wonder,—then with complete repugnance and scorn.

'Thou art not Judas after all!' she said—'How darest thou break in upon my solitude? Knowest thou not that this is my garden of dreams? I dwell here always,—and I will have none but Judas with me. I saw him last night,—he came to me and said that all was well with him,—that he would meet me here,—and for a moment I did fancy thou wert he. But no, thou art some insolent intruder!—get thee hence and trouble me not,—I have many flowers to gather yet, wherewith to strew my grave. For I am dead, and this is the borderland of vision,—Judas is dead also,—and we both wander yet apart,—but we shall meet,—I know not when or how,—but sure I am 'twill not be long!'

She paused in her incoherent speech, and Mary Magdalene ventured to approach her.

'Judith!—poor Judith!' she murmured gently and took her hand. Judith looked at her dubiously and somewhat resentfully,—then smiled, a piteous wan smile.

'Thou art very kind!' she sighed,—'I do re-member,—thou wert here before, not long since, and didst whisper words of comfort passing sweetly. Albeit I know thee not,—still, thou art woman,—thou canst understand my grief. I cannot go from hence,—for I have promised to abide here until Judas comes, therefore I pray thee do not vex me by entreaty. Moreover I must hide me for a while, for I have slain the high-priest Caiaphas,—do they know it yet in the city?—and will they search for me? I have sworn they shall not find me,—Judas will come at sunset and bear me hence with him,—'tis very lonely waiting, and if thou dost desire it thou canst stay with me a while,—but send away yon stranger.'

And she pointed to Barabbas, who drew back sorrowfully, stricken to the heart by an anguish he could scarcely conceal. But Judith did not compre-hend his torture,—apparently she had no memory or recognition of him,—her errant fancy was already drifting elsewhere.

'Take me away to the trees yonder'—she said to Mary supplicatingly—'And let us sit down and sing. Or thou shalt sing and I will sleep. I am tired,—the way is endless; one meets too many dreams. They rise one after the other,—some beautiful, some dreadful, and Judas is in them all. And there is a red streak round his throat just where the cord pressed it,—this cord'—and she touched a frayed rope hanging at her waist—'I cut the noose,—never-theless he still seems to suffer, though he should not, and methinks at times he looks upon me wrathfully. 'Tis cruel of him,—he should remember the old days when we were children,—one should never forget the love of home. And though age has crept upon me now, I once was young,—and such beauty was mine as is seldom seen! *"The fairest woman in Judæa"* I was called, and this was true, — Judas should think of it, and not despise me now, because, through suffering, that fairness hath departed. Moreover of this "Nazarene" he served, he hath not told me aught; save that He was wise and good, and poor and all unrecognised, — but this is the history of all wise good men, and is not strange. Some say He was a god, — but there be many gods in Rome! Justitia, Pilate's wife, thinks naught of gods. And I have even heard the daughter of Annas say that she did doubt and hate the great Jehovah, — and this, when she was wife of Caiaphas, Jehovah's priest. Perchance she was unhappy, — and had good cause to doubt her husband's faithfulness! — who knows! — but of a very truth she loved not God! Methinks 'tis difficult to love a Power Unseen. Such thoughts weary me; but this doth comfort me' — and she drew from her bosom the same kind of roughly-made cross she had before possessed, formed of two twigs of olive, — 'Caiaphas did break one in his fury, — and for that, as well as other things, I slew him, — this is another I have made, and 'tis a magic symbol! for when I raise it — so!' and she lifted it above her head in a sort of rapture — 'methinks I hear most wondrous music, and a sweet voice saying "Peace!"'

She nestled close to the Magdalen, who with pitying tears, placed one arm round her and strove to lead her away. But she quickly perceived that the direction taken was towards the exit from the garden, and she obstinately refused to move a step further on that path.

'No, no!' she said — 'We will go deeper in among the trees. There is a place of palms yonder, and many flowers, and shade and fragrance. Come! —

sing me to sleep—be thou my friend, and stay with me till sunset, when Judas will be here.'

She began to gather up all her fallen garlands, and while she was thus occupied, the Magdalen whispered to Barabbas—

'Comfort thyself, friend,—I will stay with her a little. Thou canst follow and see the place where she will choose to rest—then go thou quickly to her father and tell him she is here. Prepare him well to use with her both force and gentleness,—be not thus sorrowful and amazed at her dislike of thee—she knows thee not at all,—a cloud is on her brain;— have patience!'

'Hath she slain Caiaphas?' muttered Barabbas unsteadily—'Or is the fancy born of her distraction?'

'I know not!' answered Mary—'Thou must inquire and learn. I have heard nothing—for to me the Master's rising from the dead hath sufficed as news for all the world! Of men's doings I know naught.'

As she spoke thus in hurried accents, Judith caught her impatiently by the arm and drew her away.

'Bid yon stranger depart'—she said—'I like him not! He doth resemble one Barabbas! He was my lover and I did betray him,—he would slay me if he knew!'

And she quickened her pace. The Magdalen accompanied her, and Barabbas followed slowly at a little distance, striving to conceal himself as much in the background as possible. At last, after various erratic ups and downs, Judith arrived at what she called 'a place of palms.' The feathery foliage towered high up against the deep blue sky, and smaller trees of thicker branch and leaf cast their green gloom on

the smooth turf, while numberless climbing roses
and passion-flowers had grown up arch-wise so as to
form a complete bower of shade. Here the frenzied
girl seemed to grow suddenly calm,—she sighed
profoundly, and her troubled countenance cleared.
She sat down under the natural canopy of flowers
with Mary beside her. A smile parted her lips,—
the old sweet witching smile that on that perfect
mouth had been a resistless snare for the souls of
men.

'Sing!' she said—'Some simple song of tenderness
that will banish all the spectres flitting round me!
I will not ask thee who thou art,—thou hast a look
of love within thine eyes and thou art beautiful.
Yea!—thou hast long fair tresses full of sunshine,—
but see!' and she held up a mass of her own luxuriant
hair which was like gold and fire commingled—'This
is a brighter colour methinks!—and 'tis even as silk
unto the touch. Lo, when I die thou shalt sever it
and make a rope thereof,—twine it around the throat
of Judas,—and maybe it will heal his wound. Now
sing!'

She leaned her head against Mary's breast and
half closed her eyes. Barabbas ventured nearer and
stood in the shadow of the trees, listening while the
voice of the Magdalen, honey-sweet yet shaken by
tears sounded plaintively on the silence. And the
song that she sang ran thus;

> The earth hath many flowers; in all the fields and
>   bowers
> Their radiant blossoms open 'neath the glory of
>   the sun,—
> But their leaves are scarce unfurl'd to the summer
>   of the world,
> When they perish in their beauty, every one.

Brief is their fair delight; 'tis ended ere the night:
Sad emblems are they all of the sadder lives of
    men!
Better be a rose, the wildest one that blows,
And safe in the shelter of the King's gardèn!

The lofty laurels stand, at a conqueror's right hand,
To deck the feasts of triumph and the revellings of
    mirth,
Lilies and bays are bound for the brows of heroes
    crowned,
As symbols of the evanescent earth,—
But beauty, pride, and power, are the blossoms of
    an hour,
Bringing sorrow more than safety to the weary
    souls of men;
Better be a rose, the wildest one that blows,
And safe in the shelter of the King's gardèn!

The soft, quaint, almost solemn melody ceased, and
Judith began to rock herself to and fro restlessly,
wringing her hands as though she were in pain.
'The King's garden!' she wailed—'Ay!—but
where is the King? He was crowned with thorns
and He is dead,—dead! they have crucified Him!
I, Judith Iscariot, *by subtilty*, betrayed Him!—on me,
on me, let the curse fall—not on Judas, not on Judas,
merciful God!—but on me! On me let the thunders
crash vengeance,—let the fires of earth consume me,
—mine was the sin—mine, I say!—Judas was
innocent! In the King's garden one should meet
the King,—but He is dead; I would that He were
living, for since He died I have been lost in
darkness!'
And she broke into a passion of wild weeping.

Mary drew her compassionately into her arms and glancing backward made a slight sign to Barabbas. He understood, and turning away, hastened out of Gethsemane, his heart aching and his eyes full of scalding blinding tears, while the strange refrain of the Magdalen's song echoed itself over and over again in his ears—

Better be a rose, the wildest one that blows,
And safe in the shelter of the King's gardèn !

Better, ay, far better! Best of all things in life, death and eternity it is, to be the humblest creature ever born, and 'safe,'—safe in the shelter of that mystic 'garden' where Christ is King!

XLIII

MAKING his way with all possible speed towards the house of Iscariot to bear the ill news of Judith's distraught condition to her already broken-hearted father, Barabbas found the whole city in strange confusion. The streets were blocked by disorderly crowds of people wandering to and fro, many of whom were weeping and wailing hysterically, while others were wildly crying out that '*the graves were opened*' and that the world was coming to an end. Elbowing a difficult passage through the throng, Barabbas inquired the cause of the seeming tumult, and learned that the rumour of the 'Nazarene's' miraculous resurrection had excited what some practical persons called 'a fever of imagination' among the populace, and that numbers of men and women had been suddenly seized by frenzy and had run out of their houses in frantic terror, shrieking aloud that they had 'seen the dead!' Long-perished friends, and loved ones who had slept entombed for years, now appeared again among the living, so these living swore; spirit-hands touched them, spirit-voices called them,—all the air was full of mystic sound. Possessed by superstitious fear, they could not be persuaded to return to their usual daily occupations, and were only pacified by crowding together in the open thoroughfares, and leaguing themselves as it were, in a band of mutual support and protection against the overwhelming Supernatural that on that wondrous morning seemed to invest the land. Iscariot was not in the city, so Barabbas learned,—his unhappy son Judas had been buried in haste and privacy early in the morning, and he himself, after the dreary obsequies were over, had taken horse and ridden out towards Bethany in renewed search for his lost daughter. Nevertheless, in spite of this information, Barabbas pressed on in the vague hope of meeting him, till finally he could go no further, being completely hemmed in by an excited mob that was pouring itself towards the house of Caiaphas. In the midst of the howling, hooting, unreasoning rabble, were the Roman soldiers who had been set to guard the sacred sepulchre; they had just undergone examination by Pontius Pilate, and by him were now sent on to tell the story of their night's adventure to the high-priest. They could scarcely keep the order of their march, so roughly were they hustled by the irritated and impatient crowd, and they had much ado to refrain from responding wrathfully to the repeated jeers of impudent half-grown lads, and beggars of both sexes who helped to swell the riotous cortège, shouting insults all the way.

'Lo, what drunken varlets are these men of Rome! They could not guard even a dead Jew!'

'Where is the Prophet of Nazareth?'

'Who broke the seals of Sanhedrim?'

'What have ye done with the King of the Jews? Give Him back to us and we will crucify Him a second time more surely!'

Meanwhile as the noisy concourse came roaring and jostling onward, within the high-priest's palace

26

itself there was a great hush and shadow. All the
servants and officers of the household knew that
Caiaphas had been dangerously wounded on the
previous night by some secret assassin who had
stabbed him and left him for dead. He had been
found lying senseless and bleeding on the piece of
grass immediately below his private balcony; and
the attempted murder was, without any hesitation,
judged to be the act of one of the disciples of the
'Nazarene,' who had, in all likelihood, considered it
a rightful means of avenging his dead Master. A
surgeon had been hastily summoned, who gave it
as his opinion that the injury inflicted would not
necessarily prove fatal, but that to ensure recovery
the patient must have the greatest care and the
utmost quiet. Accordingly, the gates of the palace
were closed against all comers ; the servants went
about on tip-toe,—Rachel, 'the pale daughter of
Annas' as Judith had been wont to call her, sat
somewhat apart from the couch of her priestly spouse,
occasionally ministering to his wants with that
dutiful yet frigid exactitude which might distinguish
a paid nurse rather than a wife,—the curtains at the
casement of the sick man's chamber were closely
drawn to exclude the dazzling sunlight, and every
possible precaution had been taken to ensure absolute
tranquillity. But all this care was of little avail, since
Caiaphas himself was the despair of his physician.
He groaned and swore,—tossing and tumbling among
his pillows in a restless fury at his own enforced
inactivity,—and he could scarcely respond to the
soothing and bland inquiries of Annas, his colleague
and father-in-law, with any show of patience or
civility.

'Truly thou dost chafe thy spirit needlessly,
Caiaphas'—observed that sleek personage sedately—

'Seeing that I am here to act for thee and carry out thy duties of the Temple ministration. Moreover thou art singularly unwise and obstinate in with-holding from us all description of thy would-be murderer. He must be tracked and punished as thou knowest,—this weapon that was found beside thee, and with which thou wert well-nigh slain, will aid us in discovery.'

Caiaphas flung aside his coverings and made an attempt to sit up. The attendant physician remon-strated, but he paid no heed.

'What weapon dost thou speak of?' he mut-tered hoarsely—'Give it to me! Let me look upon it!'

Annas, alarmed at the fierce expression of his face, at once gave it to him. He clutched it,—then glared angrily round the room.

'Leave me, all of ye!' he said—'All, save my wife. I would speak with her alone.'

His irritability was such that they dared not provoke him further by contradiction,—his command was therefore obeyed. He waited in silence till the door closed behind the retiring figures of Annas, the physician, and two servants who had been in waiting, —then he sank back on his pillows exhausted, still holding fast the jewelled dagger with which Judith Iscariot had in her frenzy so nearly made an end of his life.

'Rachel, come to me!' he called faintly yet imperatively.

His wife approached him. She was a slight dark pensive-looking woman with pale composed features and cold calm eyes.

'Thou hast seen this toy before,'—he said, showing her the dagger, 'Thou knowest it?'

She glanced at it indifferently.

'Full well!' she answered—''Tis Judith's jewelled plaything—a gift to her from the dead Gabrias!'

Caiaphas turned himself restlessly.

'Ay! 'tis Judith's. The girl is frenzied for her brother's death,—she came to me last night,—she knew not what she said or did. 'Twas she who stabbed me,—but none must know of it. Take thou the weapon therefore, and cast it in the well below the garden,—thou wilt do this and say nothing,— passionless as thou art, I feel that I can trust thee!'

She took the dagger, and a curious smile flitted across her features.

'Alas, poor Judith!' she said.

Caiaphas gave her a quick surprised look.

'Thou dost pity her?'

'With all my soul!'

A feverish rush of blood crimsoned the high-priest's features.

'I loved her!' he cried hoarsely, in a sudden reckless access of pain and passion—'Hearest thou, Rachel! I loved her!'

Rachel's cold eyes rested scornfully upon him.

'I hear, Caiaphas! And I know!'

'Learn then yet another thing!' he continued wildly—'For her sake I have been faithless unto thee!'

'That also do I know!' responded Rachel with chill equanimity.

'And sayest thou nothing?—carest thou nothing?' he demanded, amazed and exasperated.

Over the face of the pale daughter of Annas came the warm flush of a righteous disdain.

'I say nothing because I feel nothing, Caiaphas!' she replied—'To know thee as I have known thee, ever since the day when my father Annas gave my life into thy cruel keeping, would make the softest woman's heart as hard as steel or adamant! I care nothing,—for who could care for the loss or the retaining of a love so valueless as thine! Speak we no more of this, for I have schooled myself to silence; —I am thy wife,—only thy wife, who according to thy measure is little more than dog or slave! And I will do thy bidding as dog and slave till death releases me, for out of mine own self-respect and pride I will not let thee boast that I have failed in aught. And of thy sensual passions I heed nothing, —thou art free to follow them, seeing thou dost walk in the holy ways of Abraham, to whom most surely all women born were of less account than the cattle of the field!—yet he was the favourite of the self-same God thou servest,—and so perchance art thou! But for me, henceforth, there shall be other gods than one who doth reward with favour the lies and infidelities of man!'

Such passion vibrated in her voice, such wrath flashed within her eyes, that for the moment her husband was stupefied with astonishment;—but as she turned to leave the room, he called her back angrily—

'Rachel!'

'What now?'

'How darest thou' . . . he panted huskily—'How darest thou assault me with thy shrewish tongue thus furiously'——

She smiled coldly.

'I dare all things, being wronged!' she answered; 'And for Judith Iscariot I have naught but love!— love and gratitude that she did seek to rid the world of thee! 'Twas bravely done! I would she had succeeded!'

And with haughty step and slow, she passed out of the apartment, just as Annas, white and trembling with alarm entered it again, accompanied by the physician.

'Caiaphas! . . . Caiaphas!' . . . he stammered.

'Sir, be calm!' interposed the physician anxiously, hastening to the bedside of his patient,—'I sought to keep intruders from thee,—but now this business seemeth strange and urgent'——

He broke off, and Caiaphas, still agitated by the unexpected conduct of his wife towards him, stared wonderingly from one to the other.

'What ails ye both?' he asked feebly—'How! dost thou tremble, Annas?—thou who art moved by nothing save a lack of delicate food? Speak, man! What news is on thy lips?'

'Pilate hath sent his men to thee'—faltered Annas; 'The watch hath been broken,—the sepulchre is empty'——

With a frightful cry Caiaphas almost leaped from his bed.

'Cowards! Thieves! Let them not dare to say the Man of Nazareth hath risen from the dead, for if His body be no longer in the tomb, it hath been stolen! Where are these laggards?—these worthless Romans? Pilate hath sent them?—then bid them enter!'

Annas glanced at the physician, who shrugged his shoulders and threw up his hands, implying by these gestures his resignation of all responsibility in a matter so entirely beyond his control.

'Bid them enter!' shouted Caiaphas again, his face convulsed with impatience and fury. And in another moment, Maximus, with the speechless Galbus and the rest of his men keeping behind him, appeared.

'Sir,' said he, looking full at the high-priest, who glared at him in return with an expression of implacable and vengeful ferocity — 'Methinks I am come at an ill time, seeing thou art wounded and suffering; nevertheless I am bound to fulfil the received command of the governor. Pilate hath sent me hither to tell thee that our watch hath been in vain,—the Heavens have interposed, and a miracle hath been enacted; the "Nazarene" hath risen!'

'Liar!' and Caiaphas well-nigh foaming at the mouth, clutched at the purple coverings of his couch and leaned forward as though he were about to hurl some deadly weapon at the speaker; 'Liar! Who art thou, dastard Roman, that darest presume upon my patience by the bringing of a false report? *Thou* wert not placed in charge! Galbus did head thy band of scoundrels,—let *him* speak!'

Maximus, pale with rage at the insult thus offered to himself and his comrades, had much ado to control his rising temper.

'Sir priest,' he said, breathless with suppressed anger—'Thou goest too far in the manner of thy speech, seeing Judæa is the slave of Rome, and thou thyself a payer of tribute unto Cæsar. I have not brought thee any false report,—I scorn to lie,—and I am here to tell the truth of what I saw. That these men about me slept I deny not,—but I was wakeful, —and with mine own eyes I did behold, at the first quarter after midnight, the heavens opened, and two god-like Shapes descending towards the tomb. Galbus looked on the marvellous sight with me,—and with the lightning of the glory we were smitten to the ground even as dead men. At morning when we woke, we found the great stone rolled away from the sepulchre, and the tomb itself empty of all save the linen cerements wherein the body of the "Nazarene"

was swathed. And as for Galbus, I would that any
bidding of thine or mine could make him speak,—for
since the fearful fires did fall upon us both at midnight, he hath been smitten feeble as thou seest him
now, and dumb.'

While Maximus thus spoke the countenance of
Caiaphas had grown livid and hideous with the restrained passion and bitter malice of his soul.

'Would I had had my way!' he muttered thickly
between the slow gasps of his labouring breath—'I
would have hewn the body of the crucified blasphemer
asunder limb from limb, and flung each portion to
the dogs that roam the city!' He paused, choking
back the terrible oath that rose to his lips, and then
went on slowly, addressing himself again to Maximus:
'So!—this is the story of the thieves' trick played
upon ye by the Galilean rogues who, like their
Master, practised evils' magic! Think not I am
deceived; no dead man rises from the grave, and I
will sift this matter! Galbus hath lost the power
of speech thou sayest,—nevertheless he is not deaf
methinks,—he is capable of signs. Let him stand
forth and face me! I will question him, and by the
God of Israel he shall answer me, if only in dumb
show!'

His irate order was obeyed,—the two soldiers who
supported the tottering, half-paralysed Galbus, led
him forward. Caiaphas, leaning out of bed, grasped
him by the arm roughly.

'Galbus!'

Slowly the wandering lack-lustre eyes of the
centurion lifted themselves and rested vaguely on
the high-priest's pale and resentful visage. At first
there was no expression whatever in their fixed
regard,—but gradually the light of returning intelligence and memory brightened and dilated them

and a sudden change began to manifest itself in the whole demeanour of the stricken man. Drawing a deep breath, he straightened his drooping figure, and shook himself free of his two supporters, who stared upon him in amazement,—with one hand he felt for his sword, and as he touched the familiar hilt, he smiled, and raised his head with his former proud and martial bearing. Caiaphas watched him in astonishment and suspicion — the man's former crushed and helpless demeanour seemed now an elaborate pretence, — his very dumbness might be assumed!—and believing this to be the case, a black frown wrinkled the high-priest's brows as he fiercely demanded—

'How now, Galbus! What report hast thou to offer of thy duty?—what knowest thou of last night's vigil? If thou art dumb, make signs; if thou hast any utterance, speak! Who made thy watch of no avail, and turned thy Roman valour into trembling?'

With sudden and startling vehemence the unexpected answer came:

'Jesus of Nazareth, Son of the living God!'

It was Galbus who spoke,—the spell of silence was all at once lifted from him, — and his voice, resonant, clear and convincing, rang like a trumpet-note through the room. Wonder and dismay fell upon all who heard him,—but he, expanding and glorying as it were in the utterance of a truth, exclaimed again loudly and fearlessly—

'Jesus of Nazareth, Son of the living God!'

Maddened with rage, Caiaphas made a frantic attempt to strike him on the mouth, but was prevented by the politic Annas.

'Away with him, away with him!' he cried furiously, impotently beating the air with his clenched fists—'Bind him,—gag him!—slay him! I will be answerable for his death to Cæsar! Gag him, I say!—silence him in earnest!—he is a liar, a liar!—he shall be branded as such to his nation!—bear him hence quickly,—let him not shout his blasphemies through the town! Gag him!—ye villains, ye will not obey me!—ye will let the people think the crucified malefactor a god divine,—curse him, I say! —curse ye all for a band of liars!—ye foul brutes, ye cowards of Rome,—ye base panderers to the scum of Galilee'——

His voice broke in a sharp cry,—his wound began to bleed afresh and the crimson stain welled rapidly through the linen wrappings; the physician, seriously alarmed, declared to Annas that he could not be answerable for his patient's life if this scene were allowed to continue. Annas therefore took it upon himself to put an end to the inquiry.

'Get ye all hence!' he said, addressing himself to Maximus angrily—'And take this raving Galbus out of hearing! His dumbness was better than his speech. But think not we shall let this matter rest thus,—what reasoning man would of sane will accept a fool's report such as thou bringest! We are not to be duped either by Galileans or Romans!'

Maximus gave him no reply save a look of supreme scorn,—Galbus meanwhile had been coldly watching the pallid and convulsed face of Caiaphas.

'Lo, how the devils in this Jewish priest do torture him!' he said meditatively—'Hell itself cries out upon Christ's murderer!'

'Silence, thou knave!' cried Annas.

'Silence thyself, thou Jew!' retorted Galbus— 'Thou canst not so command a soldier of Tiberius!'

Annas grew livid with rage. The physician who

was engaged in stanching the blood that flowed from Caiaphas's wound, again interposed, entreating that the room might be cleared and his patient left tranquil. Annas therefore, with difficulty restraining the torrent of invective that rose to his lips, assumed an air of dignified rebuke.

'Centurion, 'tis beneath me and my sacred calling to argue with the base and the unworthy. Hence !—with thy men,—through Pilate we shall yet communicate with thee, and report thy conduct to the Emperor. Doubt not that justice will be done !—both unto thee and unto us,—and whosoever broke the seals of the Sanhedrim affixed upon the tomb ye all were set to guard, shall be tracked and punished with the extremest penalty of the law.'

Galbus smiled grimly.

'Track ye the angels then, and find the path to Heaven !' he said—'To false priests the task will not be easy !'

And turning abruptly on his heel he placed himself at the head of his company as if he had never left command of it. In the momentary pause before the little troop departed, one soldier hung back and made a secret sign to Annas.

'What would'st thou ?' said Annas impatiently—'Seest thou not the high-priest almost swoons ?—he can stand no more of this rude clamour.'

'I would but say one thing to him '—said the man, who was a dark-browed, evil-looking fellow from Sicily—'Haply it might give him a clue.'

Annas looked at him scrutinisingly, then quickly approached Caiaphas, who had sunk back on his pillows in a sort of lethargy.

'This soldier hath a private word for thee, my son, he said.

Caiaphas opened his languid bloodshot eyes.

'Vex me no more!' he muttered feebly—'I suffer!
—let me rest!'

'Sir'—said the soldier quickly—''tis but a hint to
thee, which may serve to some good purpose. 'Tis
true we slept upon our watch last night, lulled into
slumber by a wondrous singing as of nightingales,—
and of ourselves we saw no marvels, despite what
Maximus hath told thee. But on this morning as
we came away from the sepulchre, a stranger met us
on the road who did inquire most particularly as to
the nature of our vigil. He had a foreign aspect,
and to our wonder, wore the Emperor's signet. And
with him was Barabbas.'

Caiaphas started, and heedless of his wound, sat
up.

'Barabbas?'

'Yea, sir. Barabbas. He that was a robber.'

A sudden gleam of malicious joy sparkled in the
high-priest's eyes.

'Soldier, I thank thee! Thou hast done well in
telling me of this. Come back hither later on, and
thou shalt have gold from the treasury as thy reward.
And mark me, friend!—to all thy comrades who did
sleep, seeing *no* miracle, but only seeing Barabbas
on the road next morning, gold shall be meted out
full lavishly, provided they will tell this thing
throughout the town. Barabbas did defend the
"Nazarene," and therefore may be ranked among
His followers and disciples. Thou sayest truly,—
Barabbas was a robber!'

And when the soldier had rejoined his companions,
and the sound of the retreating footsteps of all the
men had died away in the outer corridor, Caiaphas
lay back again upon his couch with a sigh of deep
relief and contentment. Smiling an evil smile, he
murmured to himself softly—

' Barabbas ?—*Barabbas was a robber.*'

And in an hour's time, despite his recent rage and excitement, he slept tranquilly,—while on his thin closely-compressed lips, even in deep slumber, still lingered the shadow of that wicked smile.

XLIV

EMERGING at last with difficulty from the
turbulent throng that had accompanied the
Roman soldiers to the high-priest's palace and that
now waited in a dense mass outside the gates for
their return, Barabbas managed finally to reach
Iscariot's dwelling. The house was shut up and in
mourning; and none of the servants could truly tell
where their master had gone after his son's melancholy
funeral. Uncertain what to do, and shrinking from
the idea of confiding to paid menials the news that
their mistress was wandering about distraught, with
no other companion or friend than the evilly-reputed
Magdalen, Barabbas could see no other course open
to him than to return at once to Gethsemane and
consult with Mary as to what next could be done
to restore the unhappy girl to her no less unhappy
father. He therefore made the best of his way back
to the garden through certain by-streets where the
crowd had not penetrated, and as he came out upon
the open road leading to the Mount of Olives, within
sight of the trees of Gethsemane, he perceived a
group of persons standing together in earnest conversation. Drawing nearer he recognised one of them
as Simon Peter; the others he did not know, but
judged from their appearance and dress that they

were Galileans, and followers of Him that was called
the 'Nazarene.' He would have passed them by, in
his haste to reach his destination, but that Peter saw
him and called to him. He approached reluctantly.

'This is Barabbas!' said Peter slowly—'He who
was released unto the Jews instead of the Lord. He
hath repented of his crimes; shall we not persuade
him to go with us?'

The others looked upon him curiously,—one, a fair
tall man with a noble head and brilliant yet dreamy
eyes, addressed him gently—

'Friend, thou art welcome! Knowest thou that
He whom the wicked crucified, hath risen gloriously
from the dead? Wherefore, we, His disciples, grieve
no more, seeing that now we have such hope as
faileth not! We are journeying from hence to
Bethany and on towards Galilee, even as He, our
Master bids us,—He hath promised to meet us on
the way.'

Barabbas gazed steadily at the speaker.

'Believest thou, with all thy soul, that He hath
risen from the dead?'

'Yea, truly!'

'Prithee, who art thou?'

'My name is John.'

A pause ensued. Barabbas stood silent, his brows
knitted, his eyes burning sombrely like clouded fire
beneath their thick black lashes.

'Wilt thou go with us?' demanded Peter,—'Perchance thou also, on the way, wilt meet and see the
risen Lord!'

'Nay, I have seen Him!' answered Barabbas, and
as he said the words, the listening disciples started
and exchanged amazed glances one with the other—
'And from your words I gather that ye have not!
Truly He lives!—that I will swear! Ye have received

this news from Mary Magdalene,—and ye are ready
to accept the woman's version as a miracle,—but I,—
I was near her when He did converse with her,—
I watched His face,—I heard His voice,—I saw Him
glide, or melt away! Whither He went I know
not; for though I searched the tomb He was not
there,'—

'We also searched the tomb'—began Peter.

'What! Then ye doubted of His rising from the
dead?—even ye?' And Barabbas smiled darkly.
'Will ye know Him, think ye, if ye meet Him by
the way?'

'Know Him?' cried Peter —'Ay!—among a
thousand thousand!'

Barabbas looked straight at him, with a melancholy
scorn in his black eyes.

'Take heed, Peter! Swear nothing. Thou didst
deny Him thrice!'

He waited a moment; then went on in slow
deliberate accents.

'Righteous sirs, I am beholden to ye all for the
offer of your comradeship; nevertheless I may not
join your company. Methinks my destiny is ordered
elsewhere. I am a man of many sins, and cankered
o'er with doubts and fears that would not well consort with your fidelity. Nevertheless I deem the
Truth can never hurt a man, being most surely part
of God, if God there be,—therefore the truth of my
refusal ye shall have from me. Lo then, when your
Master was betrayed, ye did most pitilessly all forsake Him; and for that one abhorrent deed, my soul
rebels against ye! Sooner would I companion Judas
in his self-sought grave than follow in your track!—
I could not break my bread in peace with one
deserter of the sinless "Nazarene"!'

He paused, agitated by strange passion, and they

were all silent, amazed and inwardly stung at the pitiless veracity and daring of his speech.

'I am Barabbas,'—he continued, 'And my name may serve, an' ye choose it, for all that is worst in man. I have been both thief and murderer,—I am a vagabond of no value in the world, and I speak without learning, — but I strive not to hide my crimes,—I make no pretence of being what I am not. Ye perchance are righteous, and think ye may exalt mankind,—I am a sinner, and know that men can seldom be exalted. I make no secret of my disbelief; and I say unto you all plainly, that to my thought the Man of Nazareth hath never died, inasmuch as since that so-called death I have myself this very morn, beheld Him living. Wonderful in truth was His aspect,—I do confess it!—marvellous beauty and great light attended Him,—but even thus He always looked, ay, even in the Hall of Pilate when first I saw His face. That He swooned upon the Cross is possible,—that He recovered in the tomb is also possible; yea, I would even credit that with the force pent up in His most noble and heroic frame, He could Himself roll back the sealed stone from the sepulchre; but of "miracles" and things *impos*-sible I needs must doubt till they are proved. And if ye would confess it, ye have your doubts also, even as mine. Nevertheless had I served the " Nazarene " and dwelt with Him as ye have done, as Man and Friend and Teacher merely; I never would have left Him to His enemies, or denied Him, as this Peter whom despite his late repentance, I despise!'

He spoke with force and eloquence, and Peter, shuddered and paled at his rebuke.

'Thou strange ruffian!' he said tremulously — 'Canst thou not understand the terrors and the hesitations of a man'——

27

'I can understand all things,' interrupted Barabbas fiercely, 'save cowardice! Lo, if this Master whom ye boast of is a god, and hath risen truly from the dead,—let Him but come and speak to me—to me, the wretched, sinful, doubting, fearing Barabbas,— let me know Him as He is, and what matter even if I die of the terror and the splendour of His presence! Doubt would shake my soul no more,— I would endure eternities of pain to prove His godhead! Ye have known Him, so ye say, and yet ye doubted and deserted Him!—lo, ye yourselves have made it seem that ye mistrusted Him,—for if ye did believe that He were God, why did ye all forsake Him?'

Great tears gathered in the eyes of the disciple called John.

'Prithee, say no more, Barabbas!' he murmured— 'We know our faults; we are but men.'

'True!' said Barabbas mournfully—'We are but men! We should be gods to serve a God; and some there be who swear we can become as gods, knowing both good and evil if so we will it. But methinks we only choose to master half the lesson—Evil;— of Good there is little knowledge and less liking. I pray ye all to pardon me the roughness of my speech, —I am a sad, embittered, broken-hearted man, and all life looks upon me frowningly. And though I may not go with ye—I say "god-speed!" and—if ye meet your Lord, may your eyes have love enough to know Him when ye see Him! So—farewell!'

'Stay!' cried Peter—'All thy reproaches shall not go unanswered! *Thou* knowest on whom should fall the rightful blame, though these my companions here are yet in ignorance. I told thee all,—thou and the stranger whom thou hadst with thee,—wherefore carry thy rebuke where most it is deserved, to that arch-traitress whom thy soul doth cherish with a secret passion, uncontrolled, despite her infamy! Ah, who will ever truly tell the story of the Lord's betrayal! None!—for a woman-wanton is the dearest joy of man, and the very laws he makes protect her foulness, and defend his lust!'

'Coward art thou still, Peter!' retorted Barabbas hotly—'Would'st thou shelter thine own weakness behind that of woman?—'tis an unmanly deed! Does it make thy sin or the sin of Judas less that ye were so easily tempted by woman's voice and per-suaded by woman's eyes? Nay! it doth prove your fickleness the more,—go to! bear thy part in crime without mean subterfuge; 'tis nobler to con-fess a sin than cover it'— Here he broke off abruptly, startled by a sudden movement among the disciples, who were all with one accord looking amazedly down the road in the direction of Geth-semane. He followed their wondering glances, and saw to his utter consternation the white-robed form of a woman flying forth like a phantom from under the sheltering shadows of the olive-trees. The fiery gold of her streaming hair flashing in the sun identi-fied her at once to his grieved sight,—it was the frenzied Judith,—and behind her ran the Magdalen, making signals of anxiety and distress. Swaying to and fro, sometimes stumbling, anon rushing impetu-ously as though borne by a swift wind, the distracted girl fled along like some furiously hunted animal, till her course was interrupted by the presence of the disciples, and Barabbas, with whom she came suddenly face to face. He, going close up to her, tried to take her gently by the hands, but she flung him off with a violent gesture and stood still, panting for breath and trembling. The very fury of mania possessed her, her face was livid and convulsed, her lips were blue

and drawn in against her teeth in a thin unnatural
line, and in startling contrast to the pallor of her
features, her great dark eyes blazed with a feverish
thirsty glare as of some inward longing unappeased.

'Where is the King?' she cried shrilly, fixing a
wild look on Peter—'I have been in His garden—all
among the flowers and the palms,—but He is not
there! He has come out of the grave, they say,—
devils and angels alike whisper it, — nevertheless
though I seek Him I cannot find Him! But surely
He must be found,—I have need of Him speedily, for
I must ask Him to pardon Judas,—Judas frowns at
me and will not be consoled!'

Here, interrupting herself, she flung her long hair
backward over her shoulders, and smiling faintly,
looked from one to the other of the disciples in a sort
of vague anticipation and inquiry. Peter's stern
eyes rested upon her austerely and without compassion,—she shrank a little away from him,—and
again her glances wandered wildly, till a sudden
magnetism appeared to attract them fixedly to the
calm fair face of John. With a sharp cry she threw
herself on her knees before him, lifting her clasped
hands and still smiling piteously.

'Good sir, be gentle with me! I am full of sin,
and I have never been merciful to any man,—yet for
my brother's sake I must find the King! I know He
cannot have gone so very far away, for last night I
beheld Him in a vision. He slept, all white and cold,
upon a bed of stone; the blood-stained thorns were
in His golden hair,—the grave-clothes were His robes
of state,—but even as He lay thus, a great world
came to pay Him homage. A strange world—a vast
world, — the world of the Dead!— they gathered
round His couch and smiled upon Him, — their
shadowy forms grew warm and colourful with life,—

and as they came they chanted all together—" Thus is Death slain that we may live!" And hearken, sir, hearken!—Judas was there,—Judas, with gentle eyes and smiling lips, but ah!—he never looked on me! —he never smiled at me!—but I was glad, because the cruel mark had gone from round his throat, and he seemed happy, though I, his sister, stood apart, alone! And presently the white King rose!—'twas marvellous!—His thorny crown was changed to stars! —His grave-clothes glittered into light and fire!— and like the morning Sun itself He shone upon the world! And all the buried men and women lived again,—yea, all the earth was full of life and joy,— but there was one strange terror in the glory, for I heard a voice proclaim with thunder—" From hence-forth every soul created is immortal ; Life rules the universe for ever, and only thou, Judith Iscariot, art dead!" '

She gave vent to a shuddering moan, and writhing herself to and fro, clung to the mantle of John as though for protection. He did not repulse or try to raise her, but stood silently, gazing down upon her crouching figure in solemn compassion. Mary Magdalene had also approached, and now bent above the unfortunate girl with whispered words of more than a sister's tenderness, but Judith seemed uncon-scious of her presence, and still lifted her appealing face to John.

'Think of it, gentle sir!' she murmured sobbingly; 'Is it not hard, very hard, that I, only I, out of all Creation, should thus be dead? In all the joy and moving of the world, that my heart should be frozen thus and still?—that I should feel no love, no hope, no memory? Yet it is true!—I know the curse has fallen upon me, for I am stricken dull and foolish,—I am even as a stone upon the road for every foot to

spurn at! Beauty I had,—but 'twas of no avail to
me ; love I had, but love was powerless to defend
me ; and lo, while all the universe rejoices in its life
eternal, I, Judith, must remain the one dead soul
accursed,—unless—unless, so the whisperers in the air
tell me, I may haply find the King. For though He
looked in anger on me once, 'tis said He hath great
tenderness, and patience more than all men,—He will
perchance forgive. He is not in His garden,—I have
sought Him everywhere, and Judas has not come.
Help me, friend, I do beseech thee!—take me to the
presence of the King,—for Judas is angered with me,
—Judas must be consoled!'

XLV

SHE knelt,—her wide-open wild eyes upturned;
—and as she finished her incoherent appeal,
she lifted the roughly twisted Cross she had made,
and held it close up before the wondering gaze of
the 'beloved' disciple.

'Will this not move thee?' she asked plaintively.

John started as from a dream.

'Is not this the sister of dead Judas?' he said
softly and in amazement—'What doeth she with
such a symbol?'

'Alas, who knows! and who can follow the
wanderings of her distempered fancy!' answered
Barabbas, struggling with the tears that rose in his
throat—'Her brother's death hath maddened her
thus. Prithee have patience!—I would we could
persuade her to her father's house!' And he looked
distressfully at the Magdalen, who shook her head
sorrowfully.

'I fear me 'twill be difficult,'—she said—'She
hath the strangest fits of passion. She was quite
happy in the garden till a little while agone, then
suddenly convulsed, she rose and shrieked aloud,
and wringing her hands fled swiftly from me. I
followed fast,—and she ran forth into the high-road
thus demented, nor would she let me touch her.'

They spoke in low tones, and Judith heeded nothing that was said. She remained on her knees, looking at John.

'Where is the King?' she reiterated.

Before John could reply, Peter suddenly advanced.

'If thou dost speak of Him whom thou didst aid the priests to crucify,'—he said sternly—'thou dost ask news of Him in vain. He doth not answer to the call of the wicked, and for the treacherous He hath no sympathy. Shall a murderer ask for his victim?—shall he that hath wilfully wrested life from the innocent expect that life to live again? Cry, Judith, to the heavens, for the King of Heaven is there,—but such as thou art, wilt find Him on this earth no more!'

'How canst thou tell, Peter?' interposed John quickly—'Thou art too harsh,—thou should'st not too presumptuously declare the ways of the Divine! Hast thou no pity?—Our Master had, when we were with Him, and of a truth methinks He would have comforted this broken and afflicted soul!'

'Thy Master had strange servants!' said Barabbas hotly—'And this Peter doth commiserate his own sins only!'

'Hush, oh hush!' prayed the Magdalen fervently; 'Dispute not now among yourselves!—see ye not a change in her? Judith! Judith!'

Judith had risen slowly to her feet, and was now standing upright, though feebly,—the hot sunshine fell full on the uncovered splendour of her hair and made it appear to burn like flame, but her face was wan and sad as the face of the dying. She had turned her eyes upon Peter, though with an almost unseeing look.

'Thou hast a harsh note in thy voice'—she said faintly—'Methinks thou didst never love a woman,

not even the mother that bore thee. Who art thou?
—I know thee not, but sure am I thou wilt do cruel
things in the world. With love, one is cruel,—but
without it,—ah!—what is it to be without love?—
I cannot tell, for I have lost what love I had, and
I am dead. Alas, alas! It seems that none of ye
know where the King hath now His dwelling,—
I must go seek Him further. 'Tis useless to waste
time in cursing me,—'twere kinder to bestow on me
some hope.'

Here she staggered slightly, and seemed about to
fall,—Mary Magdalene caught her round the waist.
'I am not well'—she went on—'There is such
a strange weight at my heart,—and an aching heat
upon my brows. Thou'—and turning, she put her
arms about Mary's neck and looked her full in the
eyes—'thou art my friend,—we were in the King's
garden together, were we not?—two sinful, sorrowful
weak women,—but we did not find Him there. Had
He seen us He would have pitied us. And Judas
did not come. He promised,—but he did not
come.'

'Didst thou not say that he would come at
sunset?' murmured Mary soothingly—''Tis not yet
sunset.'

'Not yet sunset!' and Judith sighed, opening her
beautiful pained eyes in mournful languor and
bewilderment—'Surely it should be near, for the skies
are growing very dark,—it will soon be difficult to
see one's way'——

She broke off, gasping for breath; the disciples
exchanged grave and alarmed glances, while Barabbas,
seized by a spasm of fear, sprang forward.

'Judith, speak to me!' he cried.

She looked at him, smiling a little, but still clinging
to Mary.

'Who is this?' she asked—'He calls me by my name,—then surely he should know me.'

'Judith, Judith! I am Barabbas!' And he stretched out his arms towards her in a passion of despair and yearning agony.

Feebly she extended one hand to him.

'Art thou indeed Barabbas?' she said, with an echo of the old sweetness in her failing voice—'Alas, Barabbas!—Believe me, I am sorry for thee. Thou didst love me!'

He grasped the little hand convulsively, and turned away to hide the scalding tears that fell. A great compassion for him was expressed in the earnest faces of the disciples,—even Peter's rugged features softened, and a troubled shame and remorse for his recent harshness appeared to vex his shifting and uneasy spirit.

Just then a terrible paroxysm of trembling seized Judith's limbs,—Mary Magdalene could scarcely support her, and appealed to the others, with a frightened glance, for aid. Barabbas and three of the disciples went to her assistance, but the insane Judith was possessed of unnatural strength, and twisted and writhed about with so much fury that it seemed as though her whole frame were being torn and tortured by devils, and they were afraid to seize her by force lest this action should increase her frenzy.

'Lay her down under the trees by the roadside'— said Peter, in gentler tones than he had yet used— ''Tis a feverish convulsion, and in the shade and cool, it will pass quickly.'

But it was impossible to move her a step. She stood, clutching Mary, obstinately forcing herself to remain upright, and fighting against the physical anguish that was gradually overcoming her,—her

eyes were fixed, and stared straight upward to the
cloudless sky. All at once the horrible tremors
ceased,—her face flushed suddenly into the radiance
of its former dazzling beauty, and with a violent
movement, she thrust the Magdalen aside. Like
some great queen she lifted her head with an imperial
gesture, and her eyes flashed fire.

'What news bring ye from the city?' she demanded—'Do they mourn there or rejoice for the
death of Caiaphas?'

'Alas, Judith, dream not so wildly!'—murmured
Barabbas quickly—'Caiaphas is not dead,—some
enemy hath wounded him in the night,—but he doth
live, and will live on,—trouble not thyself!'

As he spoke she looked at him strangely,—and
over her features came a swift dusky pallor as of
death.

'What! Caiaphas doth live and will live on?' she
cried—'He is not dead? Then upon him, O God of
Israel, send down thine everlasting curse!—let loose
on him the fiends of darkest hell! Betrayer, seducer,
liar and self-seeking hypocrite, remember, O just God,
remember the sins of this thy so-called righteous
servant in the Holy Place, and let thy judgments
meet the measure of his vileness! Not upon Judas'
—and she raised her arms aloft in passionate appeal—
'not upon Judas, nor on any blind and ignorant
sinner, visit thy vengeance, O dread Lord, but on thy
priest, who in pretence of serving the Divine hath
murdered it! A curse on Caiaphas!—the curse of
dead Judas,—the curse of dying Judith!—the never-
lifting curse of the wretched, who are led by a priest's
Lie out of Heaven, into Hell!'

Dilating with her inward passion, she looked like
a pale fierce prophetess denouncing the evils of the
time,—reason for the moment seemed to have re-

turned to her,—her voice was clear, her sentences connected,—and Peter and the others stared upon her amazed, awed and fascinated. But the rush of her wild eloquence exhausted her,—she lost breath, and looked vaguely about her, groping with her hands in a blind way, as though she had become suddenly enveloped in darkness. All at once she sprang forward eagerly with an impetuous grace and swiftness that caused those around her to fall hastily back, except Barabbas, who still tried to hold and support her, though she with a gesture of her old pride and scorn motioned him away. Alone on the white dusty road she stood in a listening attitude, —her eyes glittering, her lips apart; evidently she heard, or thought she heard something that to the others who watched her was but silence. The sun poured straightly down upon her,—she looked like a fair startled sylph in the amber glow of the burning Eastern noonday,—gradually an expression of surprise and then of rapture lighted her pallid face,—she lifted her gaze slowly, and with seeming wonder and incredulity, fixed her eyes on the near grassy slope of the Mount of Olives, where two ancient fig-trees twining their gnarled boughs together made an arch of dark and soothing shade. Pointing thither with one hand, she smiled,—and once more her matchless beauty flashed up through form and face like a flame.

'Lo there!' she exclaimed joyously—'How is it that ye could not find Him? There is the King!'

Throwing up her arms, she ran eagerly along a few steps, . . . tottered, . . . then fell face forward in the dust, and there lay; . . . motionless for ever! She had prayed for the pardon of Judas,—she had sought—and found—the 'King'!

Barabbas, Mary Magdalene and the disciples

quickly surrounded the prone figure shrouded in its
gold hair, but ere they could raise it, the sound of
a horse's hoofs galloping fast down the road came
closer and closer, and finally stopped. A man's
voice called out anxiously—

'What have ye there? Need ye any service?'

They looked up,—and a solemn silence fell upon
them. For it was Iscariot. He had just returned
from a vain search for his daughter in the villages
of Bethphage and Bethany. In one keen glance he
read in their awestricken faces his own new misery,
and dismounting from his horse he dispersed the
little group with a single tragic gesture of supreme
despair. The white figure fallen in the dust, the
lustrous wonder of the hair that covered it as with a
mantle, swam before his eyes,—flinging himself down
he clutched wildly at the corpse of that fair child of
his, who had been to his heart above all earthly
things beloved.

' Judith!' he cried.

Then, slowly and shudderingly he lifted the body
and turned the face upward to the light, . . . alas,
the piteous beauty of that face!—what sadness, and
what wonder in its fixed grave smile! So strongly
too did it resemble the face of the dead Judas, that
had it not been for the wealth of woman's hair falling
about it, it might have been taken for the fine fair
remorseful countenance of that self-slain disciple.
Yet a certain vague joy rested on the quiet features ;
—one little hand pressed against the bosom, held a
cross ; this Iscariot saw, and wrenching it from the
stiffening fingers, flung it in the dust.

'Get hence!' he cried fiercely—'Ye madmen of
Galilee, get hence! Out of my sight, and linger
not to triumph in my misery! Behold, my house
is desolate!—I have no more place or honour in the

world! Rejoice at that, ye enemies of Israel!
What care I for your promised heaven!—ye have
reft from me the joy of earth! What are your
boasted miracles! your resurrections from the grave!
—will ye give me back my children? Will ye raise
up my son, self-slaughtered for your Prophet's sake?
Will ye restore to me this maid, the daughter of
my blood, the treasure of my care? Nay! ye are
liars all!—ye have no power to comfort the afflicted,
ye cruel preachers of a loveless creed,—ye cowards
and accurst! Leave me, I say!—leave me . . . alone
with my dead!'

And clasping the body of his daughter in his arms,
he laid his grey head upon her still breast and wept,—
wept as only strong men weep when they are broken-
hearted.

Awed and troubled, and vaguely perplexed too,
by the mystery of a grief and pain too great as it
seemed for human or divine consolement, the disciples slowly moved away, the Magdalen accompanying them sorrowfully, her face veiled to hide
her tears,—and only Barabbas remained beside the
stricken father to share with him his bitter agony.
Once Peter looked back and seemed to consider
whether he should speak. But he hesitated,—for
what, after all, could he say? He had not the
secret of his Divine Master, who by a mere look
could calm a tempest. True, he might have said
'Be patient, Iscariot! God will comfort thee!'
What! This, to a Pharisee and usurer? Never!
Let him, instead of children, hug his bags of ill-
gotten gold,—what Jew with wealth hath need of
other comfort? So Peter thought; yet there was an
uneasiness in his mind; his Master, he well knew,
would not have acted thus, and he was by his lack
of broad sympathy, already falsifying and distorting

the Divine example. Tormented by, yet wilfully deaf to the teasing whisper of conscience, he walked on 'to meet the Lord' by the road to Galilee, half hoping, half fearing, half doubting, half believing, an image of the future on which he was destined to set his lasting mark. Meanwhile John lingered a moment,—his earnest gaze rested compassionately on the tragic group beneath the olive-boughs,—the aged Jew clasping his dead daughter, his grey locks mingling with her gold,—and the rugged dark figure of Barabbas standing near ;—then, stooping, he raised reverently from the dust the cross Iscariot had thrown there, kissed it, laid it against his breast, and with fair head bent musingly, and eyes full of dreams, went slowly on his way.

XLVI

NEARLY a week had elapsed since the miracle of the Resurrection of the Crucified had been reported in Jerusalem. The high-priest Caiaphas was recovering rapidly from his well-nigh deadly wound, and had so far carried out certain secret plans of his as to have had the centurion Galbus, together with his companion Maximus, sent hastily out of Judæa and back to Rome. Petronius too, the other centurion, suspected of sympathy with the followers of the 'Nazarene,' was likewise dismissed,—but all three officers had no sooner reached their native country than they were at once promoted in the Roman legions, by whose good office and influence no one knew, unless the stranger Melchior who wore the Emperor's signet had something to do with the matter. Meanwhile, it was generally understood among the Jews that the body of the 'Prophet out of Galilee' had been stolen,—moreover, that the authorities of the Sanhedrim council were already on the track of the criminal concerned in the robbery. Public attention, however, had been somewhat diverted from the matter by the grand and picturesque obsequies of Judith Iscariot. Never had the city seen such a sight as the long procession of white-robed, lily-wreathed maidens who attended the corpse of 'the fairest woman in Judæa' to its last resting-place beside that of her ill-fated brother. White flowers and white draperies symbolised to the people's gaze the dead girl's pure virginity,—and though some shook their heads and shrugged their shoulders and whispered rumours of scandal, none dared speak boldly of the truths they knew. For Iscariot was a power in Jerusalem,—his usurer's grip held fast the fortunes of many a struggling household,—the secret fear of him kept would-be rancorous tongues mute. But the proud priest Caiaphas hid his burning eyes in the pillows of his sick-bed, and smarted in his guilty conscience as he heard the sound of the dreary funeral chant passing by his palace walls,—yet he maintained a rigid silence,—and his pale wife Rachel, coldly watching him, also held her peace. Between them lay the full and true knowledge of Judith's deep dishonour,—nevertheless, like the murderous dagger she had used, which now was rusting at the bottom of a well, that knowledge remained buried in their hearts by unspoken yet mutual agreement.

All the disciples and followers of the 'Nazarene,' men and women alike, had left Jerusalem, some for fear of the priests, some to return to their own homes in the country districts,—and the city inhabitants were beginning to fall back into their usual methods of living,—methods which had been so strangely disorganised by late events. Joseph of Arimathea had had his tomb, now rendered so sacred, hewn open from the top, that it might be more readily examined within and without, and, disgusted with the callousness and suspicions of the priests, himself entirely believing in the Divine Resurrection from the Dead, sold his fine house in Jerusalem, gave all the proceeds to the poor, and departed to his native humble town of Arimathea, there to dwell in retirement for good.

28

Among other gossip of the town it was rumoured that Pilate, the governor, had written letters to the Emperor Tiberius, asking to be recalled to Rome on the plea of ill-health, but of this, nothing was known for certain.

It was about the eighth day after the first Easter, —and over the little village of Nazareth the sun was sinking. A blaze of royal gold and purple falling aslant from the west reddened the outlying fertile valley and surrounding cornfields, and poured warm splendour through the open doorway of a small dark dwelling where sat an aged man alone at a carpenter's bench, working busily; though sunset was the usual sign for rest from labour. He was finishing a wooden cradle, of which every portion was panelled into squares of curious and elaborate carving. His wrinkled hands manipulated the carving tools with singular swiftness and dexterity; and as he fashioned a flower or a leaf in the design, he worked with the minute and fastidious care of an artist who loves the labour he has chosen. Beside him on the bench lay a fresh-gathered branch of field-lilies,—he was copying these on a square of wood with extraordinary fidelity. The red glow of the skies illumined his bent, roughly-clad figure, and set a rose-halo round his snow-white hair,—he was completely absorbed in his toil,—so much so that he did not hear an approaching slow footstep at his door, or see the shadow which darkened it and partially robbed him of the sun.

'Art thou Joseph, the carpenter of Nazareth?' said a harsh sad voice, suddenly addressing him— 'And dost thou work thus peacefully without mourning, thy son being dead yonder in Jerusalem?'

The old man started. Laying down the panel he was carving, he shaded his eyes with one hand from the light, and looked up dimly and wonderingly at his questioner. He saw before him a tall broad-shouldered man, dark and fierce-featured, travel-worn and dusty, with terrible black eyes that burned beneath his shaggy brows with the danger-fires born of long pent-up unshed tears.

'What stranger art thou?' he demanded—'Why comest thou hither?'

'I am an outcast of the world, by name Barabbas,'—and as the intruder gave this answer, he moved a step or two within the shed—'Thus have I answered thee straightway, but to me thou offerest no quick reply. I have come hither from Jerusalem, impelled by a desire to find thee and to speak with thee, if peradventure thou art he of whom the people tell me. Wherefore I ask again, art thou or art thou not Joseph, son of Jacob, a descendant of the House of David, and father of him who was called "the King of the Jews"?'

Rising from his bench, the venerable man confronted his importunate visitor.

'Yea, I am Joseph;'—he answered mildly.

Barabbas, gaunt and worn with sorrow, sleeplessness and fatigue, fixed upon him a piercing look as though he sought to read the inmost secrets of his soul.

'Surely thou art a poor and aged man'—he muttered faintly—'On the brink of the grave thy feet are treading;—with that darkness waiting for thee, that darkness in which we know not what may chance to us,—thou wilt not lie! I shall find truth in thee doubtless,—truth—truth at last'——

His voice failed him,—his eyes closed,—he dropped wearily on a low bench near the door. He had travelled for two days with scarcely any rest or food, and in his exhausted condition it was some minutes before he perceived that Joseph was proffering him a wooden bowl full of pure cool water. He drank gratefully, and recovering himself a little he again turned his eyes on the imposing, reverend figure beside him.

'I am Barabbas'—he repeated presently after a pause,—'But perchance that name doth tell thee nothing. Hear then its meaning. I have been thief, rebel and murderer,—no good thing is there in my mind towards any man; by right and justice I should have been crucified instead of Him who was thy Son, for He was innocent, and I am guilty. But if thou knowest the world's ways, this will not seem unto thee strange, for man's laws are made to excuse man's guilt,—and innocence is ever slain, being a virtue unrequired, an aggravation and reproach to wickedness. So hath it been in Jerusalem these past wild days,—and so methinks will it ever be, in all the labyrinths of this life. Freedom hath done me little service,—I have lived centuries of grief since the doors of my prison were unbarred,—I thirsted for my liberty,—it came, but brought me naught but sorrow, —rather would I have died than suffered as I have suffered,—death did never seem to me so sweet and welcome as now,—God knoweth it! Thou lookest at me with most unmoved and placid face,—carest thou not that they have slain thy son?'

Joseph said no word, but stood immovably erect,— the sunset-glow shining warmly about him and widening its ring of glory round his silvery hair.

'Howbeit now it seems they have not slain Him after all, and thou perchance dost know it'—went on Barabbas, watching for some change of expression in the old man's peaceful countenance—'And all the world is growing mad with talk of "miracles." He hath arisen living from the dead; and hath appeared

to His followers—part of this tale is true, but has no
" miracle " in it, inasmuch as I am sure He never
died! He swooned upon the Cross and recovered in
the tomb, and doubtless will appear to men for many
years to come, and thus will be confirmed the story
of His resurrection. Markest thou this? No
Divinity was in this Man, nor any sort of " miracle ; "
thou, Joseph, dost not assume Divinity for the child
begotten of thy will and born of thy blood in mortal
fashion, as all creatures of mortality are born?'

He had spoken in tones that were purposely cold
and matter-of-fact, yet under his assumed composure
there was concealed a keen and painful anxiety.
Still silent, Joseph stood, a regal figure, bathed in the
purple and gold reflections of the evening skies. At
last Barabbas could bear the suspense no longer,—
his suppressed impatience broke forth in a kind of
fury.

'Speak, man, speak!' he cried passionately—'Oh,
if thou knewest my tortures! Lo, I have seen this
Man,—this " King of the Jews," in all His fair, heroic,
appalling beauty! His face, His voice, His aspect
haunt me!— His patient eyes consume my soul!
Man or God, whiche'er He be, in very truth His
looks were more of God than Man,—His tenderness
was more than human! Men are cruel to each
other,—He was pitiful ;—men complain,—He never
murmured! I watched Him die,—He made a glory
out of pain!—and on the morn when it was said He
had arisen from His grave, I, even I myself, saw
Him walking softly 'mid the shadows of the dawn
and speaking—ay! to whom, thinkest thou, did He
speak? To a broken - hearted woman whose sins
He had forgiven! 'Twas marvellous, — no man
newly escaped from the grave would have stopped
for this methinks, — yet God, we are taught, is

vengeful, — wherefore it seems this "Nazarene" is neither man nor god! Oh that I knew Him as He truly is!—I would dare all things for this one instruction! Lo, I have pleaded even with His mother, thy wife, praying her to tell me of His birth, which now is also said to be a "miracle"—but she was dumb, even as thou art, and while I looked upon her a great light shone about her face, — a light mystic and wonderful, that filled my soul with fear. Even such a splendour did invest the "Nazarene" when I beheld Him in the Hall of Judgment,— beauty and light seemed portion of His nature. Nevertheless the terror of this mystery doth madden me; hence I have come to thee;—speak thou the truth, Joseph, as simple man and honest, and tell me all thou canst of this same Jesus, the wonder of Judæa,—thou, as His father, must know everything concerning Him, even from the very hour that He was born into the world! Wherefore, if only out of mercy to my pain and ignorance, I do beseech thee, speak!'

'What can I tell thee, tortured soul,' said Joseph at last, in solemn compassionate accents—'Save that the Man Divine was not my Son?'

Barabbas sprang up and caught him convulsively by the arm.

'Not thy Son!' he echoed—'Was not Mary thy wife? Hast thou no children?'

'None who call Her their mother,'—replied Joseph; 'Children indeed I have, but these were born to me in early manhood by my first wedded wife long dead. Mary I knew not save as one removed from earth,—a heavenly Virgin, whose white purity and singular destiny I was commanded to defend.'

'But didst thou not espouse her?'

'Even as I was bidden;'—answered Joseph
simply—'And worshipped her as Angel and as
Queen!'

'Ah, now thou also dost confuse me with
vain words'—exclaimed Barabbas half angrily—
'Why dost thou name her thus royally? Many
of the people say she was a stray maiden out of
Egypt.'

A dreamy rapt look came into Joseph's deep-set
eyes.

'If she was of any earthly land she was of Egypt,'
he said musingly—'And to Egypt I was bidden to
take her for protection when Herod the tyrant
threatened the life of her young Child. When first
I met her, 'twas in spring,—a quiet evening in the
month of May;—she walked alone across the fields,
like a phantom of the moon with a strange light
in her hair, and a stranger glory in her eyes!—
methought that I had met an angel out of heaven,
and down among the flowerets at her feet I knelt
adoringly!' He paused in a sort of ecstasy—then
resumed calmly—''Twas at her will and wish that
I espoused her in the sight of man; once, to speak
truth, I hesitated, fearing evil,—but then again the
bidding came, and I obeyed it.'

'Why speakest thou of bidding or forbidding?'
cried Barabbas, perplexed and baffled—'What
meanest thou? Was not this Jesus born of Mary?
—and didst thou not espouse her, woman or angel
or queen;—no matter whence she came or at what
hour, was she not thine?'

'No!' answered Joseph with sudden and passionate
vehemence—'Dare not to utter such a blasphemy!
She was never mine,—never, by look or word or
touch or breath! The angels were her friends,—
they sang to her from the farthest stars on the night

of her Child's birth ;—I was her faithful servant
only!'

'Thou ravest!' and Barabbas, strung up to a
nervous pitch of excitement, could scarcely restrain
his deepening sense of incredulity and anger—'Thou
art as mad as all the rest of those concerned in this
strange business! But I have come to thee for
truth; and truth I will wrest from thee despite
evasion! Thou poor, frail man!—dost thou not
fear death?—and wilt thou on the very edge of thy
near tomb, play with delusion, and pronounce a lie?
Thou knewest of the birth of Mary's Child ;—if He
was not thy Son, whose Son was He?'

A sudden shadow swept the floor,—the sun had
sunk; there was a momentary dread silence that
made itself almost felt. The chill grey of the
evening crept stealthily over the outside landscape, and in the semi-gloom of the hut, the two
men stood facing each other, speechless and
trembling.

'Whose Son'—repeated Barabbas in a faint awed
whisper—'was He?'

A vague terror and bewilderment clouded Joseph's
features. Raising his hands with an eloquent gesture
of solemn earnestness, he looked full at the daring
questioner.

'In the name of the great God that made us,' he
said tremulously—'I swear I never knew! I never
knew!—I only . . . dreamed!'

As he spoke, a flashing light poured itself swiftly
aslant in a golden blaze athwart the deepening dusk;
—affrighted at the sudden brilliancy, he turned
quickly round towards the open doorway, . . . then
with a wild cry ;—

'Lo there!—there!' he gasped—'Behold Him
where He stands! Ask Him,—not me! Question

Him concerning that to which no mortal man hath answer!'

And falling to the ground he covered his face,—while Barabbas staggered back, amazed, blinded, breathless, and smitten with terror;—before him, in silent, royal, radiant beauty stood—the 'Nazarene'!

XLVII

THE same lustrous Face that had shone in pale splendour on the Cross,—the same deep Eyes that had looked their dying pardon on the world,— the same, the very same!—the one recognisable Beloved through all ages, —'the same yesterday, to-day and for ever.'   And yet how transfigured was that Human Semblance! how permeated through and through with the glory of the Divine! Light streamed above and below the Kingly Form that seemed clad in cloud and fire,—rays of celestial gold flashed round the god-like brows; all the majesty of morning, noon and night, and all the mystic secrets of creation, were centred in the lightning glances that with power shed forth love,—love unutterable and vast,—love beyond any mortal comprehension,—love flung out illimitably as sunshine, as widely as the sweet ungrudging air!   Fearing greatly, but still doubting the testimony of his own sight and sense, Barabbas knelt and gazed appealingly at the supernal Vision, asking himself the while whether it were a phantom of his mind, or the reflex of a marvellous Reality!   Seeking to be convinced, he forced himself to note the trivial things of every day around him,—the carpenter's bench, the branch of lilies lying across it, the implements of wood-carving,

—all these evidences of practical toil and daily life he realised in every detail. There too, a little apart from him, knelt the aged Joseph, his face covered in his mantle,—a figure real and tangible and earthly; and out through the open doorway, beyond the Angel-stature of the Shining One, stretched the cool length of the meadow opposite, and the further cornfields dimly seen in the darkening eve. It was no dream then!—the world was the world still, and not a chaos of spectral fancies; this great 'King' standing patiently upon the humble threshold of His childhood's habitation was no phantom, but a glorious living Truth,—and as Barabbas gradually became conscious of this, he prayed inwardly that he might die at so supreme a moment of transcendent ecstasy! And presently he felt a yearning impulse to draw nearer to the Divine Presence;—and at the first thrill of this desire in his soul, the Vision seemed to smile a welcome. Nearer and nearer still he crept, with beating heart and struggling breath,— he a poor mortal sinner dared to approach Immortal Purity,—till at last he could almost feel the quivering of the lambent light that glittered in a golden aureole round the risen Form of the world's Redeemer.

'Master, is it Thou!' he whispered—'Thou, in very truth! why hast Thou come to me when I have doubted Thee? Punish me, I beseech Thee, with the judgment due unto my sin and disbelief;—I am unfit for life or death;—here at Thy feet I fain would perish utterly!'

Deep silence answered him,—such tender silence as soothes the weary into rest. Trembling, he ventured to lift his eyes,—the wondrous love and glory of the Countenance he looked upon filled him with rapture, —his long-imprisoned suffering soul awoke at last to the full consciousness of an immortal destiny.

'I believe! I believe in Thee, O Thou Divine!' he
cried—'Let me follow Thee wheresoe'er Thou goest!
Let me not lose Thee, the one Truth in a false
world!—Take me with Thee, the servant of Thy will,
beyond the things of earth and time,—no matter
where—all must be well if Thou dost guide!'

As he thus made his passionate supplication, the
luminous Figure moved slowly backward,—turned,—
and passed floatingly in a path of light across the
meadows,—Barabbas hastily rose to his feet and
followed fast. Seeing nothing, knowing nothing,
remembering nothing, save that crowned Wonder of
the Ages that glided on before him, he brushed his
way through fragrant flowers, and seemed to walk
on air. A great joy possessed him,—such joy as
once he would have deemed impossible to win,—the
soft breeze blowing against his face felt like a caress
from heaven,—he was dimly aware that a few stars
were hanging like drops of dew in the dusky ether,
—but the exaltation of his spirit was such that earth
and all its manifold beauty weighed but as one drop
in the wave of ecstasy that absorbed his every sense.
All at once, on the shadowy bend of a little hill, the
radiant Vision paused, . . . then like a cloud dissolv-
ing into air, suddenly vanished!

Barabbas halted abruptly and looked about him.
He was already some miles away from Nazareth ; and
there was darkness before him where there had been
light. But happiness stayed within his soul and he
was not in any way anxious or disheartened. The
great 'King' had disappeared, but what then!—His
departure was but temporary,— He lived and He
would come again. Exulting in the joy of faith,
Barabbas raised his eyes to the quiet heaven, and
wondered whether there were truly such a thing as
misery ?—Could man be wretched with a God for his

friend, and the certainty of life immortal? Who would sit down and grieve for loss of love, for death or ill fortune in the world, when all evil was destined to be changed to good in the end? And the once sorrowful and embittered Barabbas was content,—his doubts were set at rest for ever.

''Twas a God they slew!' he said — ''Tis a God that is arisen from the grave! And to that God, the Christ and Saviour of mankind, I render up my soul!'

He uttered the words aloud, in the full belief that they were heard. And though no answer came in mortal speech, there was bestowed upon him the sweetest sense of rest and peace and gladness his life had ever known. Cheerily and in perfect confidence he moved onward in the path where he had found himself set, according to the following of the ' Master ;' it led straight over the hills and back to Jerusalem. As he went, he resolved his plans. He would return to his strange acquaintance Melchior, who had always bidden him to believe in the Divinity of the ' Nazarene,' and who had placed no obstacles whatever in the way of his endeavouring to find out truth for himself, and to him first he would narrate his adventure at Nazareth. Then he would declare his faith, not only to Melchior but to every one who asked him concerning it,—he would show no hesitation or shame in the full confession of his happy change. What the result would be he did not consider,—the inward spiritual strength he felt made him totally indifferent to earthly consequences. The cruelty, the rancour and malice of men were powerless to touch him henceforth ; for the bitterest suffering, the most agonising martyrdom, would seem easy of endurance to one who had truly seen the Christ, knowing that it was Christ indeed !

Of Joseph, to whom he had paid so abrupt a visit,

he thought no more. Could he have known what had chanced, the shadow of a vague regret might in part have clouded his own personal joy. Some people of Nazareth going early to their labour in the cornfields noticed that the familiar and reverend figure of the old man was not seen at work as usual, and they straightway went to enquire the cause. They found him resting easily on the ground ; his white head leaning against the carpenter's bench, on which a branch of lilies lay slowly withering,—his eyes were closed in apparent deep and placid slumber. Two of his sons came in and strove to rouse him ; and not till they had lifted him up and carried him out to the open air, where they laid him down on the grass among the nodding field-flowers, with face upturned to the sun, did they discover that he had quietly passed away into the living splendour of eternal things, where age is turned to youth, and the darkest 'dreams' make their meanings clear.

XLVIII

THE broad lustre of a full moon spread itself like powdered silver over the walls and turrets of Jerusalem on the night Barabbas returned thither from his journey to Nazareth. He arrived late, and the gates of the city were locked, but he succeeded in rousing a sleepy watchman who came out of the guard-room in answer to his summons, and who was about to unbar a side-portal and let him through, when suddenly pausing in his intent, he rubbed his drowsy eyes and stared, astonished.

'Why, art thou not Barabbas?' he exclaimed.

'Yea, truly am I! What then? Hast business with me?'

But the watchman gave him no direct reply. Dropping the bolt he had just withdrawn back into its place, he shouted aloud—

'Ho there! Waken, ye lazy rascals, and come forth! Here is the man ye seek,—Barabbas!'

There followed a hoarse shout, a hasty trampling of feet and the clash of armour, and almost before the bewildered Barabbas could realise what had happened, he was surrounded by soldiers, seized and taken prisoner. Perplexed but not dismayed, he made no effort to escape. He glanced from one to the other of his captors,—they were Romans and all strangers to him.

'What jest is this?' he demanded—'Why do ye suddenly maltreat me thus? Surely ye know the people's vote hath set me free,—for what cause am I again a captive?'

'Hold thy peace, ruffian!' said one of the men angrily—''Tis not for criminals to question law!'

'Full well I know I am a criminal'—responded Barabbas patiently—'Nevertheless by law my crimes were lately pardoned. Of what new fault am I accused?'

'Of a base attempt to murder the high-priest Caiaphas!'—answered an officer who seemed to be the leader of the band—'He hath nearly died of a deadly wound inflicted by a secret assassin, and he doth swear thou art the man! Moreover thou art also judged guilty of connivance with the followers of the "Nazarene," in plot to steal His body from the tomb officially sealed. Thou wert seen in converse with a woman of ill fame named Magdalen,—thou wert also in the company of Simon Peter,—and again, certain comrades-at-arms of ours met thee on the morning when the corpse of the "Nazarene" was missing, on the high-road to the sepulchre. These be proofs enough against thee, remembering thy former reputation!—and for these things thou shalt surely die.'

Barabbas heard all this with a curious passiveness.

'Caiaphas doth accuse me thus?' he asked.

'Caiaphas hath denounced thee unto Pilate, and most furiously demands thy punishment'—was the reply —'Question thy fate no more; but come thou with us quietly, and fight not uselessly against thy destiny.'

Barabbas smiled. The plans of Caiaphas were singularly transparent reading! To shield the dead Judith Iscariot and himself from suspicion and slander, he had cunningly devised this false accusation against

an already known criminal,—moreover he was hereby
able to indulge his own private spite and vengeance
against Barabbas for ever having been one of Judith's
many lovers. The additional charge made,—that of
stealing the body of the Crucified from the tomb,—
was to throw dust in the people's eyes, and silence, if
possible, all rumours respecting the miracle of the
Resurrection. The whole situation was perfectly
clear,—but the victim of the high-priest's crafty
scheme was in no wise disconcerted by evil circumstance. Addressing the officer who had condescended
to give him an explanation of the cause of his sudden
arrest, he said gently—

'Friend, be assured that whatsoe'er my destiny I
am prepared to meet it!'—and he held out his wrists
that they might be more easily manacled—'I am
innocent this time of the deeds whereof I am
accused,—howbeit, innocence doth count as nothing
in the working of the world's laws,—wherefore I say,
in the name of Jesus of Nazareth I am willing and
ready to die!'

'Rash fool!' cried a soldier, striking him—'Dare
not to speak thus if thou dost value life! That
utterance of thine alone is blasphemy!—rank blasphemy enough to slay thee!'

'And as I shall be slain, the manner of my speech
doth little matter'—responded Barabbas tranquilly—
'Methinks a man should speak the truth that is
within him, no matter whether death or life be
imminent. Come, come! lead on! Quarrel not; this
is no time for quarrelling. Ye are but the hirelings
of the law, and cannot help but do the deeds that are
commanded; let us be friends, good Romans!—I
bear ye no ill-will. See!—I struggle not at all; ye
are well within your right—ye must obey authority,
albeit that authority be of earth and brief withal. I

also must obey authority,—but the commands that I
receive are changeless, and whosoever disobeys them
is accurst!'

His eyes flashed a sombre glory as he spoke,—as
the fetters were fastened on his wrists, he smiled
again.

'He is mad!' said the soldiers, vaguely awed and
exchanging wondering glances—'They say he loved
Judith Iscariot; perchance her death hath turned
his brain.'

Barabbas heard them whispering thus among
themselves, but gave no outward sign of attention.
Judith Iscariot!   Yes, he had loved her and he loved
her still,—being dead, she was far dearer to him than
if she had lived on.   For she was now no longer
Judith Iscariot,—she was a new creature, removed,
indefinable and mystic,—a spirit released,—to good
or evil, who could say?—but at any rate safe from
the clamour of the world and the deeper taint of sin.
Full of his own meditations, he maintained an
absolute silence while the soldiers marched him
quickly through the streets of the slumbering city
to the gloomy prison, where the formidable gates
that had so lately opened to release him, once more
enclosed him, and shut out, as he felt for ever, all
hope of earthly freedom.

'What!   Art thou back again, Barabbas?' growled
the gaoler, flashing his lantern in the prisoner's eyes
as he spoke—'Well, well!—what folly will do for a
man! 'Tis but a fortnight surely since thou wert
set at liberty, with all the people cheering thee,—yet
thou hast such an ingrained bad nature thou canst
not keep thee out of mischief.   They crucified thy
yelping dog of a comrade, Hanan,—now it is likely
they will crucify thee.   What sayest thou to that for
a finish to a rogue's career?'

Barabbas was mute. Sudden tears swam in his eyes,—he was thinking of a Supreme Figure, and a Divine Face, that on the Cross had made death glorious.

'Mum as a post,—sullen as a bear!' continued the gaoler gruffly—'Such as thou art are the worst characters. There is no hope for the surly and impenitent! Come hither and take possession of thy former cell—not a soul hath been in it, save perchance a starving rat, since thou wert there. Get thee in and make thy peace with Heaven!'

He opened the door of the very same wretched den in which Barabbas had already passed eighteen months of rebellious pain and misery,—and made as though he would thrust his captive in. Barabbas paused on the threshold, and looked him frankly in the face.

'Nay, be not rough with me!' he said gently— 'There is no need for anger. This time I am innocent of all the faults whereof I am wrongfully accused. Nevertheless I was most wrongfully released,—'twas the people's caprice and no true justice; wherefore I am ready now to atone. And surely as thou sayest, I will strive to make my peace with Heaven!'

A great beauty illumined his dark features,—his eyes were soft and earnest,—on his lips there rested a faint grave smile.

The gaoler stared at him, perplexed and dimly touched.

'An' thou art civil-tongued I will not vex thy last hours'—he said, in friendlier accents—'Thou'lt have a full day's penitence,—the Council will not sit to-morrow. Thou shalt not starve or thirst meanwhile,—for though I know thou art a rank villain, I'll see to that,—more I cannot do for thee,—so make the best of thy old lodging.'

He closed the iron door, bolting and barring it with heavy noise, — Barabbas listened, with an instinctive sense that for him it barred out the world eternally. Standing upright, he looked about him. The same dungeon !—the same narrow line of light piercing the thick obscurity ! It fell from the moon, a pure stream of silver,—and he sat down presently on a stone projection of the wall to watch it. In this attitude, with face lifted to the mild radiance, he was happy and at rest,—his wretched prison seemed beautiful to him,—and the prospect of a speedy death contained no terror but rather joy.

He passed the night tranquilly, in wakeful meditation, till the arrowy moonbeam in his cell changed to a golden shaft shot aslant from the rising sun. With the morning the gaoler brought him food and drink, and asked him whether he had slept.

'Not I !' he answered cheerfully—''Twas nigh on the approach of dawn when I came hither,—and the pleasure of my thoughts did banish slumber. Is it a fair day ?'

'Yea, 'tis a fair day,'—replied the gaoler, secretly marvelling at the composure of the captive—'Though methinks thou should'st be little interested in the weather fair or foul. Thou hast another day and night to pass alive, in the pleasure of thy thoughts as thou sayest,—and after that thou wilt think no more ! Knowest thou of what thou art suspect ?'

'Something have I heard,'—responded Barabbas— 'But truly I suspect myself of more sins than Councils wot of !'

The gaoler stared and shrugged his shoulders.

'Thou speakest in riddles,' he said—'And thou art altogether a strange rascal. Nevertheless I have made enquiry concerning thee. Thy case is hopeless —for 'tis Caiaphas who doth accuse thee.'

'This doth not astonish me ;'—said Barabbas.

'He hath reason then ?'

'Nay, he hath no reason. But I find nothing marvellous in that a priest should lie!'

The gaoler chuckled hoarsely.

'I like thee for that saying!—rogue as thou art I like thee!' and he rubbed his hands complacently— 'Thou hast wit and sense withal!—Why, man, if God is anything of the likeness His priests would make Him out to be, He is the worst and most boastful tyrant that ever wreaked havoc on mankind! But take heed to thyself!—speak not thus rashly,—think on the "Nazarene" who set Himself against this priestcraft, and would have had it all abolished or made new had He obtained His will. He had a daring spirit, that young Man of Nazareth!—I myself once heard Him say that it was not well to pray in public places to be seen of men. This was a blow direct at the keeping-up of temples, and fat priests to serve in them,—but look you He suffered for His boldness—and though 'twas said He was the Son of God, that did not save Him '——

'Prithee be reverent in thy speech,'—interposed Barabbas gently — 'Take heed thyself that thou blaspheme not! He was,—He is the Son of God!— the Risen from the Dead, the Saviour of the world,— as such I know and do acknowledge Him!'

'By Israel, now do I see that thou art mad!' cried the gaoler, backing away from him—'Mad, raving mad!—touched by the fever of miracles that hath lately plagued Jerusalem ; this "Nazarene" hath bewitched the very air! Prate to thyself of such follies, not to me ;—I have no patience with distempered brains. Prepare thee for thy cross tomorrow!—this will be more wholesome meditation for thy mind. Thou wilt see me no more ;—I was

sorry for thy ups and downs of fortune; thy brief
glimpse of freedom finishing in new imprisonment;
but now,—verily as I live I think thee dangerous, and
only fit to die!'

With these words he turned to leave the dungeon;
Barabbas extended his fettered hands.

'Farewell, friend!' he said.

The gaoler looked round grudgingly and in ill-
humour,—he was vexed with himself at the singular
interest this man Barabbas had awakened in him,
and he was ashamed to show it. He eyed the tall,
muscular figure up and down severely, and met the
full calm gaze of the dark earnest eyes,—then, as it
were against his own will, he hastily grasped the
hands and as hastily let them go.

'Farewell!' he responded curtly — 'When thou
diest, die bravely!'

And he disappeared, making more clanging noise
than usual in his impatient bolting and barring of
the door.

Left alone, Barabbas fell back into his former train
of happy musing. Of the narrow discomfort, heat
and darkness of his miserable dungeon he was
scarcely conscious,—he was more triumphant than
any conquering king in the fulness and joy of the
knowledge of things eternal. He had been lifted to
that sublimity and supremacy of pure faith which
alone enables a man to bear sorrow nobly, to dare all
things, and hope all things; the warm sweet certainty
of something higher, grander, and lovelier than this
life and all that it contains, nestled in his heart like a
brooding bird and kept him glad and tranquil. At
times he felt a strong desire to pray to that Divine
Friend who after guiding him a little way had
suddenly departed from him on the hills above
Nazareth;—to ask Him to bestow the beauty of His

glorious Presence on His worshipping servant once
again. But he checked this longing,—it seemed like
a renewal of doubt,—as if he sought to be convinced
and re-convinced of Truth immutably declared. To
pray for further benefit after so much had been
bestowed, would surely be both selfish and ungrateful.
Therefore he made no appeal, but sat in solitary
communing with his own soul, which now, completely
aroused to the long-withheld consciousness of immortality, already aspired to its native sovereignty in
glorious worlds unseen.

The day wore slowly onward,—and again the
night dropped down its dusky purple curtain pat-
terned with the stars and moon. A pleasant sense
of weariness overcame Barabbas at last,—he took
no thought for the morrow on which it seemed
likely he would be tried before Caiaphas, found
guilty and put to death,—except in so far that he
had resolved to make no defence, as he could not
do so without implicating the dead Judith. Also,
he had determined that when questioned concerning
the supposed theft of the body of the Christ from
the sepulchre, he would openly declare his faith, and
would pronounce before all the scribes and Pharisees
the adjuration ; '*Jesus of Nazareth, Son of the living
God!*' And with this very phrase upon his lips, he
threw himself down upon the straw that was heaped
in one corner of his dungeon, closed his eyes and
fell fast asleep.

In his sleep he dreamed a pleasing dream. He
fancied he was lying on a couch of emerald moss,
softer than softest velvet,—that flowers of every hue
and every fragrance were blossoming round him,—
and that beside him sat a shining figure in white,
weaving a crown of thornless roses. 'Where have
I wandered?' he murmured—'Into what wondrous

country of fair sights and sounds?' And the
angelic shape beside him made musical response,—
'Thou hast reached a place of shelter out of storm,—
and after many days of watching and of trouble
we have persuaded thee hither. Rest now and take
thy joy freely ;—thou art safe in the King's Garden!'

With these words ringing yet in his ears he
suddenly awoke, and waking, wondered what ailed
him. He felt faint and giddy ; the walls of his
prison appeared to rock to and fro as in an earthquake, and the nightly moonbeam falling aslant,
struck his eyes sharply like a whip of fire. Something cold and heavy pressed with numbing force
upon his heart,—an icy sense of suffocation rose in
his throat,—and in the acute suffering of the moment,
he struggled to his feet, though he could scarcely
stand and only breathed with difficulty. The blood
galloped feverishly in his veins, — then abruptly
stilled itself and seemed to freeze, — the chill pang
at his heart ceased, leaving his limbs numb and
quivering. Exhausted by this spasm of physical
agony, his head dropped feebly on his breast; and
he leaned against the wall for support, panting for
breath, . . . when, . . . all at once a great light,
like the pouring-out of liquid gold, flashed dazzlingly
into his cell! He looked up, . . . and uttered a cry
of rapture!—Again, again!—face to face with him in
his lonely dungeon, — he beheld the 'Nazarene'!
The Vision Beautiful! — the shining Figure, the
radiant Face of the Divine 'Man of Sorrows'!—this
was the marvellous Glory revealed within the gloom!

Awed, but not afraid, Barabbas raised his eyes to
his supernal Visitant.

'Lord—Lord!' he gasped, faintly stretching his
manacled hands blindly forth—'I am not worthy!
Why hast Thou come to me?—I, Barabbas, am unfit

to look upon Thee! I should have died upon the cross, not Thou! Command me therefore to some place of punishment,—some desert in the darkest ways of death!—there let me rid myself of sin, if this be possible, by faith in Thee—by love!'——

He broke off, trembling,—and the great Christ seemed to smile. Filled with excess of joy, he now beheld that Divine Figure bending tenderly towards him,—gentle Hands were laid upon his bruised and fettered wrists; Hands that drew him close and closer yet, slowly and surely upwards,—upwards into such light and air as never gladdened earth;—and a thrilling Voice whispered—

'Whosoever believeth in Me shall not abide in Darkness! Enter thou into the joy of thy Lord!'

The light widened into a rippling sea of gold and azure,—the dungeon walls appeared to totter and crumble to nothingness,—bright forms of beauty grew up like flowers out of the clear pure space; and such symphonic music sounded as made the rolling of planets in their orbits seem but the distant lesser notes of the vast eternal melody; and thus,—clinging close to the strong Hands that held his, and looking with wondering grateful ecstasy into the Divine Eyes that smiled their pardon and eternal love upon him, Barabbas left his prison and went forth,—into the 'glorious liberty of the free'!

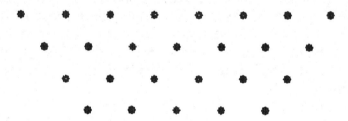

With the early dawn of the next day two men

descended together in haste to visit the dungeon.
One was the gaoler—the other was the stranger
Melchior.

'They shall not crucify Barabbas'—said the latter
resolvedly—'I will be answerable for him, and
myself defend him at his trial.'

'Thou speakest boldly!' returned the gaoler,
eyeing him dubiously—'But though thou hast the
Emperor's signet, and Caiaphas hath given thee
permit to see the prisoner, these favours will not
stay the progress of the law.'

'Maybe not!'—said Melchior impatiently—
'Nevertheless the makers of the law in Jerusalem
are corrupt; and their corruption shall be blazoned
to the world if this lately pardoned man be again
made to suffer. What influence can be obtained for
him shall most assuredly be used. There is much
good in this Barabbas.'

Here they reached the dungeon. Quickly un-
locking the door, the gaoler peered in.

'Barabbas!'

No answer was returned.

'Barabbas, come forth!'

Still silence.

'He sleeps soundly,'—said the gaoler, taking down
a lantern which hung on the outside wall for use and
lighting it,—'We must needs go in and rouse him.'

Lamp in hand he entered the dismal cell, Melchior
following. Barabbas lay on the ground, apparently
sunk in a deep and peaceful slumber; his manacled
hands were folded cross-wise on his breast.
Melchior stepped hurriedly forward and bent down
over him.

'Barabbas!'

But Barabbas rested gravely mute. A flash from
the prison-lantern showed that a smile was on his

face; and that his dark and rugged features were smoothed and tranquillised into an expression of exceeding beauty. There was something grand and impressive in the aspect of his powerful figure lying thus passive in an attitude of such complete repose, —his crossed hands and closed eyes suggested that eternal calm wherein, as in a deep sea, is found the pearl of Infinite Knowledge.

Melchior rose from his brief examination of the quiet form; a vague melancholy shadowed his face.

'We need argue no more concerning the fate of Barabbas!' he said in hushed accents—'Neither signets of emperors nor authority of priests can avail him now! We come too late! Whatever were his passions or crimes they are pardoned;—and a Higher Power than ours hath given him his liberty. Carry him forth gently;—he is dead!'

EPILOGUE

ONE afternoon at sunset two travellers stood together, looking their last on the white walls and enclosed gardens of Jerusalem. Silently absorbing the scene, they watched from a little hill above the city, the red sky-glow like a furnace over the roofs and turrets, and flash fire upon the architectural splendour of that 'jewel of the earth' known as Solomon's Temple. They could see the summit of Calvary, bare and brown and deserted,— and in the lower distance the thick green foliage of Gethsemane. One of them, a man of singular height and massive build, knelt on the turf, and fixed his eyes with a passionate intensity on Calvary alone,— there his looks lingered with deep and wondering tenderness as though he saw some beatific vision on that lonely point which shone with a blood-red hue in the ardent flame of the descending sun. His companion, no other than Melchior, turned and saw him thus entranced.

'Sorrowest thou, Simon,' he said gently—'to leave this land which God hath visited? Vex not thy soul,—for God is ever with thee; and Calvary is not the wonder of Judæa, but of the wider world from henceforth. Judæa hath rejected the Divine, where-fore she herself shall be rejected.'

Simon of Cyrene, for it was he, looked up.

'Yea, thou dost speak truly,' he answered, 'in this as in other things. Nevertheless I can but remember how I bore the Cross up yonder hill! Words can never tell the sweetness of the toil,—the joy and glory that surrounded me! And greater still the marvel of the raising of that Cross!—methought I held Salvation! Let me not speak of it,—my soul doth reel too near the verge of Heaven!—and once again I see His face—the face of God that smiled on me!'

Melchior did not speak for some minutes,—his own eyes were turned thoughtfully towards some scattered rocks on a plain to the left of the city, which was sometimes called the 'Place of Tombs' on account of its numerous hewn-out sepulchres and burial-caves.

'Over there,'—he said presently, pointing thither; 'sleeps Barabbas whom I told thee of, — there where that solitary palm nods its half-withered leaves. 'Twas I who gave him burial,—no other living friend he seemed to have in all Jerusalem, despite the rapture of the foolish crowd the day he was set free. He was an untaught erring soul, yet not without some nobleness—a type of human Doubt aspiring unto Truth; methinks out of this aspiration only, he hath found both peace and pardon.'

He was silent a little,—then continued,

'Cyrenian, to thee was given the strength to bear the Cross; and in thy task thou didst obtain both faith and knowledge. All men may not win such sweet and sudden happiness,—for humanity is weak, not strong. Humanity can rarely sacrifice itself for God, and doth not willingly accept a burden not its own. Thou, who dost now resign thy home and kindred, thy fertile valleys of Cyrene, thy free and

thoughtless serving of thyself, for sake of serving the
Divine, art wise before the days of wisdom, and wilt
perchance know swiftly and at once, what it will take
this wild unspiritual world long centuries to learn.
The Messenger has come, and the Message has been
given;—the Christ hath been slain and hath arisen
from the dead, as symbol of the truth that Good shall
triumph over Evil everlastingly,—nevertheless it will
be long ere the lesson of Divine Perfection is understood by man.'

Simon, rising from his kneeling attitude, looked
wistfully and with some curiosity at the speaker.

'Why should it be long?' he asked—'Since thou
so speedily hast learned to recognise the Christ?
Art thou more skilled in mysteries than other
men?'

'If I should say so, 'twould be a boast unworthy;
Melchior answered slowly—'And of the things
occult I may not tell thee. But this much thou
shalt hear. In early youth I was a king, . . . nay,
man, wonder not!—kings are no marvel! The
puppets of the nations merely,—prisoned round with
vain trappings and idle shows,—the very scorn of all
who have obtained a true and glorious independence!
I learned in my brief kingship the worthlessness of
sovereignty, the fickleness of crowds, the instability
of friends, the foolishness of earthly power. When
Christ was born in Bethlehem, a vision came upon
me in the midwatches of the night, and an Angel
stood before me, saying—"Arise, Melchior! be thou
the first monarch in the world to resign monarchy;
for the time hath come when crowns and kingdoms
shall be utterly destroyed, as obstacles to the Brotherhood of Man. Get thee to Bethlehem of Judæa,—
there shalt thou find the new-born God, the Prince
of Peace, who will unite in one all nations,—and link

Humanity to Heaven by the splendour of His Everlasting Name"!'

He paused enrapt,—Simon of Cyrene watched him awed and fascinated.

'The Angel vanished;'—he continued—'And I arose straightway and went, and stayed not on my journey till I came to Bethlehem; there . did I lay my crown before the Child of Mary, and swear to Him my faith. I have followed Him from the cradle to the Cross; I follow Him now from the rent sepulchre of Earth, to the unbarred gate of Heaven!'

'And I with thee!' exclaimed Simon with eager fervour,—'Lo, I am humble as a child—and I will learn of thee all that I should do!'

'Nay, I can teach thee nothing;'—said Melchior gently—'Thou hast borne the Cross—thou hast lifted the Christ,—the rest will be granted thee!'

He looked once more over the city which now seemed to float like a glittering mirage in the circling glory of the after-glow: the sun had sunk.

'"*If thou hadst known, even in this thy day*"'—he quoted dreamily—'Alas, alas! What of those who wilfully prefer ignorance to knowledge!'

'Speakest thou of the misguided who have scorned and rejected the Divine?' asked Simon—'Surely ere long they all will be convinced,—yea, even Caiaphas'——

'Thou simple soul!—thinkest thou that a liar can ever be convinced of truth? Nay—'tis a miracle past all working! Through Caiaphas the stain of treachery will rest on the dead Judas; through Caiaphas will be denied the Resurrection,—through Caiaphas the very name of Christ will be banished from the Jewish annals. Bear thou this in mind,— that a so-called priest of God did crucify God's

Messenger. 'Twill help thee to more clearly read the future!'

'Knowest thou,' said Simon suddenly—'that Peter hath returned from Bethany and boldly preacheth Christ crucified and risen?'

'Ay, doth he preach?' queried Melchior, with satiric melancholy—'And hath he grown so sudden bold? Even so doth he make late atonement! He hath a wondrous destiny—for half the world will grasp the creed devised by him who did deny his Master!'

Sighing, he turned away from the city view.

''Tis God's symbolic teaching,' he said, 'which few of us may understand. A language unlettered and vast as eternity itself! Upon that hill of Calvary to which thou, Simon, turnest thy parting looks of tenderness, hath been mystically enacted the world's one Tragedy—the tragedy of Love and Genius slain to satisfy the malice of mankind. But Love and Genius are immortal; and immortality must evermore arise, wherefore in the dark days that are coming let us not lose our courage or our hope. There will be many forms of faith,—and many human creeds in which there is no touch of the Divine,—keep we to the faithful following of Christ, and in the midst of many bewilderments we shall not wander far astray. The hour grows late,—come, thou first hermit of the Christian world!—let us go on together!'

They descended the hill. Across the plains they passed slowly; taking the way that led towards the mystic land of Egypt, where the Pyramids lift their summits to the stars, and the Nile murmurs of the false gods forgotten. They walked in a path of roseate radiance left by a reflection of the vanished sun; and went onward steadily, never once looking back till their figures gradually diminished and disappeared. Swiftly the night gathered, and spread itself darkly over Jerusalem like a threatening shadow of storm and swift destruction; thunder was in the air, and only one pale star peered dimly forth in the dusk, shining placidly over the Place of Tombs, where, in his quiet burial-cave, Barabbas slept beside the withering palm.

THE END.

MORRISON AND GIBB, PRINTERS, EDINBURGH.

PRESS OPINIONS

ON

'BARABBAS'

————◆————

THE GUARDIAN.

'By the dignity of its conceptions, the reserve around the Central Figure, and the fine imagery of the scene and circumstance, it has a likeness to the Ammergau Play, with the introduction of more modern problems and suggestions. . . . Not a single word beyond the Scripture utterances is placed in the mouth of the Redeemer, while the Blessed Virgin is treated in a wholly ideal way. . . . The studies of character are very striking. . . . There is much that is elevating and devout in this remarkable literary work.'—*November* 8, 1893.

ILLUSTRATED CHURCH NEWS.

'Marie Corelli has too much reverent and artistic feeling to degrade the ideal of mankind. . . . A glorious mystery surrounds the Son of Man in her pages, as in those of the first Church historians. . . . Her characters move, not as puppets, but as men and women, instinct with life, warm with passion. . . . The best proof of the success of "Barabbas" is that, in spite of its free handling of generally received facts, it is interesting to the end. . . . It is human, broad-based on the rock of our common nature, appealing to what is best in it, and fashioned by an artist hand.'—*December* 12, 1893.

MR. ZANGWILL in the PALL MALL MAGAZINE for January 1894.

'I am not the proper person to review *an attack upon Christianity.*'

MR. ZANGWILL in the PALL MALL MAGAZINE for March.

'*I in no way intended to convey the idea that Miss Corelli had directly assailed the Christian faith.* . . . I have no doubt that Miss Corelli wrote her book with the best intentions and the highest motives, and I regret that I should have employed a phrase which might lend itself to a misconception of her work by persons who had not perused it.'

ILLUSTRATED LONDON NEWS.

'It may be said at once, and without hesitation, that Marie Corelli has written many pages of real power and great beauty. . . . The scene around the sepulchre on the last night of the watch, with the mysterious music, the blossoming of the hills, the sudden radiance of the skies, and the great Vision which Barabbas alone beholds from a cleft in the rock, has a sincerely spiritual character.'—*November* 4, 1893.

ACADEMY.

'There is no reason why we should not do full justice to the picturesque fancy and fertile imagination of this author. Marie Corelli is a word-painter of more than ordinary exuberance, and she is certainly remarkable in her choice of themes. . . . With regard to the management of her story, it is enough to say that she has contrived to steer clear of any such violation of good taste as might conceivably have been created by the introduction of lighter themes in a narrative so solemn. She has consistently adhered to the scriptural account. . . . But a work so ambitious must necessarily provoke criticism at every turn.'—*December* 30, 1893.

COURT JOURNAL.

'Miss Marie Corelli has come to the relief of the dull season with a daring book, which she has flung down like a gauntlet, challenging the verdict of the public and the critics. . . . She is realistic, dramatic, even sensational, but so have been some of the greatest painters of the same subjects. . . . If Rembrandt or Doré may represent in pigment " The World's Tragedy," and win homage by their work, it is not quite easy to understand why a writer should be held to have violated the canons of good taste by making what is plainly a reverent and earnest effort to treat the same subject. . . . For freshness and originality of idea many passages in Marie Corelli's work are entirely admirable. . . . No one with a spark of imagination will fail to appreciate them.'—*December* 9, 1893.

COURT JOURNAL (Second Notice).

'We are glad to see that the leading journals representative of the Church and religion view "Barabbas" with favour. Our own opinion of the book is already known; but in view of attacks which we consider to be without foundation or excuse, we would like to add that we cannot conceive it possible that the faith of a believer could be shaken by a perusal of Marie Corelli's work, while, on the contrary, we can readily imagine a sceptic being won to a belief in the biblical story of the Life and Passion of Christ by the realism and reasonableness with which the author has invested the narrative.'—*December* 23, 1893.

BIRMINGHAM DAILY POST.

'The subject is treated with great reverence, and the expansion of the Scripture narrative is marked with vivid imaginative force. . . . The author has not put into the lips of Christ any words other than those to be found in our Bibles. . . . The story is told with much intensity and with opulence of imaginative power.'—*November* 25, 1893.

NEWCASTLE DAILY JOURNAL.

'"Barabbas" is appallingly well written. I use the adverb advisedly. In the boldness of its conception, in the fearlessness of its characterisation, in the lurid brilliancy of its execution, "Barabbas" is appalling. As a religious novel, "Barabbas" stands alone. The religious novel, as we now know it, belongs either to the goody-goody class or the "up-to-date up-to-doubt" class. Anybody can write such novels, but no one, save Marie Corelli, could write "Barabbas."'—*November* 30, 1893.

SHAFTS.

'"Barabbas" is a masterpiece, and will hold its own more and more as time passes, clearing thought and destroying prejudice. That it contains much which will not obtain the universal vote, is of no account ; the best and noblest literature always does. It is not only one of the books of the year, but with the author's other works may be said to be among the most powerful literary productions of the nineteenth century. The last fifty years, which have witnessed such radical changes in our literature, have produced nothing greater of their kind than the works of this gifted writer. . . .

'This book, "Barabbas," is a work of genius ; containing lofty flights of imagination. Justice has not been done to it by the criticisms flashed over it ; it glows with power ; it fills the heart and understanding with the truthfulness and beauty of its pictured scenes and characters. We rise to heights ;—we gladden in quick sympathy ;—we shrink from vice rampant and cruelty triumphant in quick changes of mood, spell-bound by this pen of power that bears us along. "Barabbas" is the gospel story glorified, quickened, transfigured, stamped with an awful reality, instinct with life not before known, never to be forgotten.   What then? is it inconceivable that the powerful pen of a cultured woman of genius should write a more potent picture of the World's Tragedy than was written by the fisher-men of Judæa?   Surely the world is the better of this wondrous concept of a dream,—whatever be the creed it may hold; or whether it be free of creeds, holding only to the indestructible inner truths.   For by nothing is our nature so exalted, as by the contemplation of the Ideal; whether that Ideal be purity, truth, nobility, heroism, in the abstract, or these virtues carried to their concrete perfection in great actions, and earnest, de-termined human effort.'—*January* 1894.

AMERICAN OPINION

PHILADELPHIA BULLETIN.

'A notable book is "Barabbas," not only by reason of the universality of interest which the very name arouses, but in virtue of a dignity of treatment which can hardly be too highly commended, in a work dealing with so perilous a subject. That the book is of a nature to do good through a deepening of feeling, and an increased vividness of realisation, there can be little doubt. . . . We have suggestions of a new set of motives for the betrayal, . . . we see motive and action working out to logical ends, and the Scripture narrative begins to glow with new meanings. . . . If there is value in its historical suggestiveness, there is yet more in the union of dignity with intense dramatic fire in its composition. The tremendous theme is handled with perfect reverence, yet with an eye to the total effect which, as a narrative of an epochal tragedy, it is bound to maintain. An author who undertakes so difficult a task may rightly claim recognition of the fact.'—*October* 28, 1893.

BOSTON INTERIOR.

'A strong story, strong in description, strong in feeling. The single conception of "Barabbas" raises it to a high level; and the tone of the whole, exalted and passionate, makes it impressive, and impressive tor good.'—*December* 1893.

BOSTON LITERARY WORLD.

'Marie Corelli in her work of " Barabbas" may be said to have achieved a somewhat remarkable success. . . . A deep and reverent enthusiasm fills the writer, and makes her narrative very real as well as impressive.'—*November* 18, 1893.

BOSTON CONGREGATIONALIST.

'A remarkable work in many ways, bold yet reverent in its handling of the great and solemn facts of the trial, crucifixion, and resurrection of Jesus ; striking in its fresh and sympathetic representations of Judas, Barabbas, and others ; uplifting in its tender and beautiful conception of Christ, and brilliant in its descriptions. It will promote true devotion to Christ in every one.'—*December* 1893.

CHICAGO TIMES.

'The portrayal of Jesus is a singularly noble and striking one, gathered indeed from the Gospels, but given a warm, breathing, human setting which is wholly absent from the gospel narratives.'—*December* 20, 1893.

BURLINGTON HAWK-EYE (Iowa).

'A wonderfully interesting and fascinating story of the greatest of earth's tragedies . . . full of intensely dramatic power.'—*November* 24, 1893.

A LIST OF NEW BOOKS AND ANNOUNCEMENTS OF METHUEN AND COMPANY PUBLISHERS : LONDON 18 BURY STREET W.C.

CONTENTS

	PAGE
FORTHCOMING BOOKS,	2
POETRY,	10
HISTORY AND BIOGRAPHY,	11
GENERAL LITERATURE,	13
WORKS BY S. BARING GOULD,	15
FICTION,	17
NOVEL SERIES,	18
BOOKS FOR BOYS AND GIRLS,	20
LEADERS OF RELIGION,	22
UNIVERSITY EXTENSION SERIES,	22
SOCIAL QUESTIONS OF TO-DAY,	23

OCTOBER 1893

MESSRS. METHUEN'S
ANNOUNCEMENTS

———◆———

Gladstone. THE SPEECHES AND PUBLIC ADDRESSES OF THE RT. HON. W. E. GLADSTONE, M.P. With Notes. Edited by A. W. HUTTON, M.A. (Librarian of the Gladstone Library), and H. J. COHEN, M.A. With Portraits. *8vo. Vol. IX.* 12s. 6d.

Messrs. METHUEN beg to announce that they are about to issue, in ten volumes 8vo, an authorised collection of Mr. Gladstone's Speeches, the work being undertaken with his sanction and under his superintendence. Notes and Introductions will be added.

In view of the interest in the Home Rule Question, it is proposed to issue Vols. IX. and X., which will include the speeches of the last seven or eight years, immediately, and then to proceed with the earlier volumes. Volume X. is already published.

Henley & Whibley. A BOOK OF ENGLISH PROSE. Collected by W. E. HENLEY and CHARLES WHIBLEY. *Crown 8vo.*

Also small limited editions on Dutch and Japanese paper. 21s. and 42s. *net.*

A companion book to Mr. Henley's well-known *Lyra Heroica.* It is believed that no such collection of splendid prose has ever been brought within the compass of one volume. Each piece, whether containing a character-sketch or incident, is complete in itself. The book will be finely printed and bound.

Henley. ENGLISH LYRICS. Selected and Edited by W. E. HENLEY. In Two Editions :

A limited issue on hand-made paper. *Large crown 8vo.*

A small issue on finest large Japanese paper. *Demy 8vo.*

The announcement of this important collection of English Lyrics will excite wide interest. It will be finely printed by Messrs. Constable & Co., and issued at first in limited editions.

Dixon. ENGLISH POETRY FROM BLAKE TO BROWNING. By W. M. DIXON, M.A. *Crown 8vo.* 5s.

A Popular Account of the Poetry of the Century.

Prior. CAMBRIDGE SERMONS. Edited by C. H. PRIOR, M.A., Fellow and Tutor of Pembroke College. *Crown 8vo.* 6s.

A volume of sermons preached before the University of Cambridge by various preachers, including the Archbishop of Canterbury and Bishop Westcott.

Oscar Browning. GUELPHS AND GHIBELLINES: A Short History of Mediæval Italy, A.D. 1250-1409. By OSCAR BROWNING, Fellow and Tutor of King's College, Cambridge. *Crown 8vo.* 5s.

O'Grady. THE STORY OF IRELAND. By STANDISH O'GRADY, Author of 'Finn and His Companions.' *Small crown 8vo.*

A short sketch of Irish History, simply and picturesquely told, for young people.

Scott. THE MAGIC HOUSE AND OTHER VERSES. By DUNCAN C. SCOTT. *Extra Post 8vo, bound in buckram.* 5s.

Lock. THE LIFE OF JOHN KEBLE. By WALTER LOCK, M.A. With Portrait from a painting by GEORGE RICHMOND, R.A. *Crown 8vo., buckram, 5s. Fifth Edition just ready.*

'A fine portrait of one of the most saintly characters of our age, and a valuable contribution to the history of that Oxford Movement.'—*Times.*

Classical Translations

Irwin. LUCIAN—Six Dialogues (Nigrinus, Icaro-Menippus, Cock, Ship, Parasite, Law of Falsehood). Translated into English by S. T. IRWIN, M.A., Assistant Master at Clifton; late Scholar of Lincoln College, Oxford. *Crown 8vo.*

Morshead. SOPHOCLES—Electra and Ajax. Translated into English by E. D. A. MORSHEAD, M.A., late Scholar of New College, Oxford; Assistant Master at Winchester. *Crown 8vo.*

Two new volumes of the 'Classical Translations' series.

Fiction

Corelli. BARABBAS: A DREAM OF THE WORLD'S TRAGEDY. By MARIE CORELLI, Author of 'A Romance of Two Worlds,' 'Vendetta,' etc. 3 vols. *Crown 8vo.* 31s. 6d.

Baring Gould. CHEAP JACK ZITA. By S. BARING GOULD, Author of 'Mehalah,' 'In the Roar of the Sea,' etc. 3 vols., *Crown 8vo.* 31s. 6d.

A Romance of the Ely Fen District in 1815.

Fenn. THE STAR GAZERS. By G. MANVILLE FENN, Author of 'Eli's Children,' etc. 3 vols. *Crown 8vo.* 31s. 6d.

Esmé Stuart. A WOMAN OF FORTY. By ESMÉ STUART, Author of 'Muriel's Marriage,' 'Virginie's Husband,' etc. 2 vols. *Crown 8vo.* 21s.

Parker. THE TRANSLATION OF A SAVAGE. By GILBERT PARKER, Author of 'Pierre and His People,' 'Mrs. Falchion,' etc. *Crown 8vo.* 5s.

A picturesque story with a pathetic and original motive, by an author whose rise in the estimation of the critics and the public has been rapid.

Gilchrist. THE STONE DRAGON. By MURRAY GILCHRIST. *Crown 8vo. Buckram,* 6s.

A volume of stories of power so weird and original as to ensure them a ready welcome.

Benson. DODO: A DETAIL OF THE DAY. By E. F. BENSON. *Crown 8vo. Seventh Edition.* 2 *vols.* 21s.

A story of society by a new writer, full of interest and power, which has already passed through six editions, and has attracted by its brilliance universal attention. The best critics were cordial in their praise. The 'Guardian' spoke of *Dodo* as *unusually clever and interesting*; the 'Spectator' called it *a delightfully witty sketch of society*; the 'Speaker' said the dialogue was *a perpetual feast of epigram and paradox*; the 'Athenæum' spoke of the author as *a writer of quite exceptional ability*; the 'Academy' praised his *amazing cleverness*; the 'World' said the book was *brilliantly written*; and half-a-dozen papers declared there was *not a dull page in the two volumes*.

FOR BOYS AND GIRLS

Baring Gould. THE ICELANDER'S SWORD. By S. BARING GOULD, Author of 'Mehalah,' etc. With twenty-nine Illustrations by J. MOYR SMITH. *Crown 8vo.* 6s.

A stirring story of Iceland, written for boys by the author of 'In the Roar of the Sea.'

Cuthell. TWO LITTLE CHILDREN AND CHING. By EDITH E. CUTHELL. Profusely Illustrated. *Crown 8vo. Cloth, gilt edges,* 6s.

Another story, with a dog hero, by the author of the very popular 'Only a Guard-Room Dog.'

Blake. TODDLEBEN'S HERO. By M. M. BLAKE, Author of 'The Siege of Norwich Castle.' With 36 Illustrations. *Crown 8vo.* 5s.

A story of military life for children.

NEW AND CHEAPER EDITIONS

Baring Gould. MRS. CURGENVEN OF CURGENVEN. By S. BARING GOULD, Author of 'Mehalah,' 'Old Country Life,' etc. *Crown 8vo. Third Edition.* 6s.

A powerful and characteristic story of Devon life by the author of 'Mehalah,' which in its 3 vol. form passed through two editions. The 'Graphic' speaks of it as *a novel of vigorous humour and sustained power*; the 'Sussex Daily News' says that *the swing of the narrative is splendid*; and the 'Speaker' mentions its *bright imaginative power*.

Parker. MRS. FALCHION. By GILBERT PARKER, Author of 'Pierre and His People.' *New Edition in one volume.* 6s.

Mr. Parker's second book has received a warm welcome. The 'Athenæum' called it *a splendid study of character*; the 'Pall Mall Gazette' spoke of the writing as *but little behind anything that has been done by any writer of our time*; the 'St. James'' called it *a very striking and admirable novel*; and the 'Westminster Gazette' applied to it the epithet of *distinguished.*

Norris. HIS GRACE. By W. E. NORRIS, Author of 'Mademoiselle de Mersac,' 'The Rogue,' etc. *Third and Cheaper Edition. Crown 8vo.* 6s.

An edition in one volume of a novel which in its two volume form quickly ran through two editions.

Pearce. JACO TRELOAR. By J. H. PEARCE, Author of 'Esther Pentreath.' *New Edition. Crown 8vo.* 3s. 6d.

A tragic story of Cornish life by a writer of remarkable power, whose first novel has been highly praised by Mr. Gladstone.

The 'Spectator' speaks of Mr. Pearce as *a writer of exceptional power*; the 'Daily Telegraph' calls it *powerful and picturesque*; the 'Birmingham Post' asserts that it is *a novel of high quality.*

Pryce. TIME AND THE WOMAN. By RICHARD PRYCE, Author of 'Miss Maxwell's Affections,' 'The Quiet Mrs. Fleming,' etc. *New and Cheaper Edition. Crown 8vo.* 6s.

'Mr. Pryce's work recalls the style of Octave Feuillet, by its clearness, conciseness, its literary reserve.'—*Athenæum.*

'It is impossible to read the book without interest and admiration.'—*Scotsman.*

'He has, in fact, written a book of some distinction, and the more his readers have thought and observed for themselves the more are they likely to appreciate it.'—*Pall Mall Gazette.*

'Quite peculiar fascination is exercised by this novel. The story is told with unusual cleverness. 'Time and the Woman' has genuine literary distinction, and the rarity of this quality in the ordinary novel needs no expression.'—*Vanity Fair.*

Dickenson. A VICAR'S WIFE. By EVELYN DICKENSON. *Cheap Edition. Crown 8vo.* 3s. 6d.

Prowse. THE POISON OF ASPS. By R. ORTON PROWSE. *Cheap Edition. Crown 8vo.* 3s. 6d.

UNIVERSITY EXTENSION SERIES

NEW VOLUMES. Crown 8vo.

A MANUAL OF ELECTRICAL SCIENCE. By GEORGE J. BURCH, M.A. With numerous Illustrations. 3s.

A practical, popular, and full handbook.

THE CHEMISTRY OF FIRE. By M. M. PATTISON MUIR, M.A. Illustrated. 2s. 6d.

An exposition of the Elementary Principles of Chemistry.

A TEXT-BOOK OF AGRICULTURAL BOTANY. By M. C. POTTER, M.A., F.L.S. Illustrated. 3s. 6d.

THE VAULT OF HEAVEN. A Popular Introduction to Astronomy. By R. A. GREGORY. With numerous Illustrations. Crown 8vo. 2s. 6d.

METEOROLOGY. The Elements of Weather and Climate. By H. N. DICKSON, F.R.S.E., F.R. Met. Soc. Illustrated. 2s. 6d.

SOCIAL QUESTIONS OF TO-DAY

NEW VOLUMES.

Crown 8vo, 2s. 6d.

WOMEN'S WORK. By LADY DILKE, MISS BULLEY, and MISS ABRAHAM.

TRUSTS, POOLS AND CORNERS. As affecting Commerce and Industry. By J. STEPHEN JEANS, M.R.I., F.S.S.

Educational Books

Davis. TACITI GERMANIA. Edited with Notes and Introduction. By R. F. DAVIS, M.A., Editor of the 'Agricola.' *Small crown 8vo.*

Stedman. GREEK TESTAMENT SELECTIONS. Edited by A. M. M. STEDMAN, M.A. *Third and Revised Edition.* *Fcap. 8vo.* 2s. 6d.

Stedman. A SHORTER GREEK PRIMER OF ACCIDENCE AND SYNTAX. By A. M. M. STEDMAN, M.A. *Crown 8vo.*

Stedman. STEPS TO FRENCH. By A. M. M. STEDMAN, M.A. 18mo.

An attempt to supply a very easy and very short book of French Lessons.

Stedman. THE HELVETIAN WAR. Edited with Notes and Vocabulary by A. M. M. STEDMAN, M.A. 18mo. 1s.

Methuen's Commercial Series

Crown 8vo. Cloth.

Gibbins. BRITISH COMMERCE AND COLONIES FROM ELIZABETH TO VICTORIA. By H. DE B. GIBBINS, M.A., Author of 'The Industrial History of England,' etc., etc. 2s.

Bally. A MANUAL OF FRENCH COMMERCIAL CORRESPONDENCE. By S. E. BALLY, Modern Language Master at the Manchester Grammar School.

Lyde. COMMERCIAL GEOGRAPHY, with special reference to Trade Routes, New Markets, and Manufacturing Districts. By L. D. LYDE, M.A., of The Academy, Glasgow. 2s.

Simplified Classics

A series of Classical Readers, Edited for Lower Forms with Introductions, Notes, Maps, and Illustrations.

Herodotus. THE PERSIAN WARS. Edited by A. G. LIDDELL, M.A., Assistant Master at Nottingham High School.

Plautus. THE CAPTIVI. Edited by J. H. FREESE, M.A., late Fellow of St. John's College, Cambridge.

Livy. THE KINGS OF ROME. Edited by A. M. M. STEDMAN, M.A.

Methuen's Novel Series

A Series of copyright Novels, by well-known Authors, bound in red buckram, at the price of three shillings and sixpence. The first volumes will be :— **3/6**

1. JACQUETTA. By S. BARING GOULD, Author of ' Mehalah,' etc.

2. ARMINELL : A Social Romance. By S. BARING GOULD, Author of ' Mehalah,' etc.

3. MARGERY OF QUETHER. By S. BARING GOULD.

4. URITH. By S. BARING GOULD.

5. IN THE ROAR OF THE SEA. By S. BARING GOULD.

6. DERRICK VAUGHAN, NOVELIST. With Portrait of Author. By EDNA LYALL, Author of 'Donovan,' etc.
7. JACK'S FATHER. By W. E. NORRIS.
8. MY DANISH SWEETHEART. By W. CLARK RUSSELL.

HALF-CROWN NOVELS.

A Series of Novels by popular Authors, tastefully bound in cloth.

2/6

1. THE PLAN OF CAMPAIGN. By F. MABEL ROBINSON.
2. DISENCHANTMENT. By F. MABEL ROBINSON.
3. MR. BUTLER'S WARD. By MABEL ROBINSON.
4. HOVENDEN, V.C. By F. MABEL ROBINSON.
5. ELI'S CHILDREN. By G. MANVILLE FENN.
6. A DOUBLE KNOT. By G. MANVILLE FENN.
7. DISARMED. By M. BETHAM EDWARDS.
8. A LOST ILLUSION. By LESLIE KEITH.
9. A MARRIAGE AT SEA. By W. CLARK RUSSELL.
10. IN TENT AND BUNGALOW. By the Author of 'Indian Idylls.'
11. MY STEWARDSHIP. By E. M'QUEEN GRAY.
12. A REVEREND GENTLEMAN. By J. M. COBBAN.
13. THE STORY OF CHRIS. By ROWLAND GREY.

Other Volumes will be announced in due course.

Books for Girls

A Series of Books by well-known Authors, bound uniformly.

Walford. A PINCH OF EXPERIENCE. By L. B. WALFORD, Author of 'Mr. Smith.' With Illustrations by GORDON BROWNE. *Crown 8vo. 3s. 6d.*

'The clever authoress steers clear of namby-pamby, and invests her moral with a fresh and striking dress. There is terseness and vivacity of style, and the illustrations are admirable.'—*Anti-Jacobin.*

Molesworth. THE RED GRANGE. By Mrs. MOLESWORTH, Author of 'Carrots.' With Illustrations by GORDON BROWNE. *Crown 8vo. 3s. 6d.*

'A volume in which girls will delight, and beautifully illustrated.'—*Pall Mall Gazette.*

Author of 'Mdle. Mori.' THE SECRET OF MADAME DE Monluc. By the Author of 'The Atelier du Lys,' 'Mdle. Mori.' *Crown 8vo. 3s. 6d.*

'An exquisite literary cameo.'—*World.*

Parr. DUMPS. By Mrs. PARR, Author of 'Adam and Eve,' 'Dorothy Fox,' etc. Illustrated by W. PARKINSON. *Crown 8vo. 3s. 6d.*

'One of the prettiest stories which even this clever writer has given the world for a long time.'—*World.*

Meade. OUT OF THE FASHION. By L. T. MEADE, Author of 'A Girl of the People,' etc. With 6 Illustrations by W. PAGET. *Crown 8vo. 3s. 6d.*

'One of those charmingly-written social tales, which this writer knows so well how to write. It is delightful reading, and is well illustrated by W. Paget.'—*Glasgow Herald.*

Meade. A GIRL OF THE PEOPLE. By L. T. MEADE, Author of 'Scamp and I,' etc. Illustrated by R. BARNES. *Crown 8vo. 3s. 6d.*

'An excellent story. Vivid portraiture of character, and broad and wholesome lessons about life.'—*Spectator.*

'One of Mrs. Meade's most fascinating books.'—*Daily News.*

Meade. HEPSY GIPSY. By L. T. MEADE. Illustrated by EVERARD HOPKINS. *Crown 8vo. 2s. 6d.*

'Mrs. Meade has not often done better work than this.'—*Spectator.*

Meade. THE HONOURABLE MISS: A Tale of a Country Town. By L. T. MEADE, Author of 'Scamp and I,' 'A Girl of the People,' etc. With Illustrations by EVERARD HOPKINS. *Crown 8vo. 3s. 6d.*

Adams. MY LAND OF BEULAH. By MRS. LEITH ADAMS. With a Frontispiece by GORDON BROWNE. *Crown 8vo. 3s. 6d.*

New and Recent Books

Poetry

Rudyard Kipling. BARRACK-ROOM BALLADS; And Other Verses. By RUDYARD KIPLING. *Sixth Edition. Crown 8vo. 6s.*

A Special Presentation Edition, bound in white buckram, with extra gilt ornament. *7s. 6d.*

'Mr. Kipling's verse is strong, vivid, full of character. . . . Unmistakable genius rings in every line.'—*Times.*

'The disreputable lingo of Cockayne is henceforth justified before the world; for a man of genius has taken it in hand, and has shown, beyond all cavilling, that in its way it also is a medium for literature. You are grateful, and you say to yourself, half in envy and half in admiration: "Here is a *book*; here, or one is a Dutchman, is one of the books of the year." '—*National Observer.*

'"Barrack-Room Ballads" contains some of the best work that Mr. Kipling has ever done, which is saying a good deal. "Fuzzy-Wuzzy," "Gunga Din," and "Tommy," are, in our opinion, altogether superior to anything of the kind that English literature has hitherto produced.'—*Athenæum.*

'These ballads are as wonderful in their descriptive power as they are vigorous in their dramatic force. There are few ballads in the English language more stirring than "The Ballad of East and West," worthy to stand by the Border ballads of Scott.'—*Spectator.*

'The ballads teem with imagination, they palpitate with emotion. We read them with laughter and tears; the metres throb in our pulses, the cunningly ordered words tingle with life; and if this be not poetry, what is?'—*Pall Mall Gazette.*

Henley. LYRA HEROICA: An Anthology selected from the best English Verse of the 16th, 17th, 18th, and 19th Centuries. By WILLIAM ERNEST HENLEY, Author of 'A Book of Verse,' 'Views and Reviews,' etc. *Crown 8vo. Stamped gilt buckram, gilt top, edges uncut. 6s.*

Mr. Henley has brought to the task of selection an instinct alike for poetry and for chivalry which seems to us quite wonderfully, and even unerringly, right.'—*Guardian.*

Tomson. A SUMMER NIGHT, AND OTHER POEMS. By GRAHAM R. TOMSON. With Frontispiece by A. TOMSON. *Fcap. 8vo. 3s. 6d.*

Also an edition on hand-made paper, limited to 50 copies. *Large crown 8vo. 10s. 6d. net.*

'Mrs. Tomson holds perhaps the very highest rank among poetesses of English birth. This selection will help her reputation.'—*Black and White.*

Ibsen. BRAND. A Drama by HENRIK IBSEN. Translated by WILLIAM WILSON. *Crown 8vo.* 5s.

'The greatest world-poem of the nineteenth century next to "Faust." "Brand" will have an astonishing interest for Englishmen. It is in the same set with "Agamemnon," with "Lear," with the literature that we now instinctively regard as high and holy.'—*Daily Chronicle.*

'Q.' GREEN BAYS: Verses and Parodies. By "Q.," Author of 'Dead Man's Rock' etc. *Second Edition. Fcap. 8vo.* 3s. 6d.

'The verses display a rare and versatile gift of parody, great command of metre, and a very pretty turn of humour.'—*Times.*

"A. G." VERSES TO ORDER. By "A. G." *Crown 8vo, cloth extra, gilt top.* 2s. 6d. *net.*

A small volume of verse by a writer whose initials are well known to Oxford men.
'A capital specimen of light academic poetry. These verses are very bright and engaging, easy and sufficiently witty.'—*St. James's Gazette.*

Hosken. VERSES BY THE WAY. BY J. D. HOSKEN.
Printed on laid paper, and bound in buckram, gilt top. 5s.
Also a small edition on large Dutch hand-made paper. *Price* 12s. 6d. *net.*

A Volume of Lyrics and Sonnets by J. D. Hosken, the Postman Poet, of Helston, Cornwall, whose interesting career is now more or less well known to the literary public. Q, the Author of 'The Splendid Spur,' etc., writes a critical and biographical introduction.

Langbridge. A CRACKED FIDDLE. Being Selections from the Poems of FREDERIC LANGBRIDGE. With Portrait. *Crown 8vo.* 5s.

Langbridge. BALLADS OF THE BRAVE: Poems of Chivalry Enterprise, Courage, and Constancy, from the Earliest Times to the Present Day. Edited, with Notes, by Rev. F. LANGBRIDGE. *Crown 8vo. Buckram* 3s. 6d. School Edition, 2s. 6d.

'A very happy conception happily carried out. These "Ballads of the Brave" are intended to suit the real tastes of boys, and will suit the taste of the great majority.'—*Spectator.* 'The book is full of splendid things.'—*World.*

History and Biography

Collingwood. JOHN RUSKIN: His Life and Work. By W. G. COLLINGWOOD, M.A., late Scholar of University College, Oxford, Author of the 'Art Teaching of John Ruskin,' Editor of Mr. Ruskin's Poems. *2 vols. 8vo.* 32s. *Second Edition.*

This important work is written by Mr. Collingwood, who has been for some years Mr. Ruskin's private secretary, and who has had unique advantages in obtaining materials for this book from Mr. Ruskin himself and from his friends. It contains a large amount of new matter, and of letters which have never been published, and is, in fact, a full and authoritative biography of Mr. Ruskin. The book contains numerous portraits of Mr. Ruskin, including a coloured one from a water-colour portrait by himself, and also 13 sketches, never before published, by Mr. Ruskin and Mr. Arthur Severn. A bibliography is added.

'No more magnificent volumes have been published for a long time than "The Life and Work of John Ruskin." . . .'—*Times.*

'This most lovingly written and most profoundly interesting book.'—*Daily News.*

'It is long since we have had a biography with such varied delights of substance and of form. Such a book is a pleasure for the day, and a joy for ever.'—*Daily Chronicle.*

'Mr. Ruskin could not well have been more fortunate in his biographer.'—*Globe.*

'A noble monument of a noble subject. One of the most beautiful books about one of the noblest lives of our century.'—*Glasgow Herald.*

Gladstone. THE SPEECHES AND PUBLIC ADDRESSES OF THE RT. HON. W. E. GLADSTONE, M.P. With Notes and Introductions. Edited by A. W. HUTTON, M.A. (Librarian of the Gladstone Library), and H. J. COHEN, M.A. With Portraits. *8vo. Vol. X. 12s. 6d.*

Russell. THE LIFE OF ADMIRAL LORD COLLING-WOOD. By W. CLARK RUSSELL, Author of 'The Wreck of the Grosvenor.' With Illustrations by F. BRANGWYN. *8vo. 15s.*

'A really good book.'—*Saturday Review.*

'A most excellent and wholesome book, which we should like to see in the hands of every boy in the country.'—*St. James's Gazette.*

Clark. THE COLLEGES OF OXFORD: Their History and their Traditions. By Members of the University. Edited by A. CLARK, M.A., Fellow and Tutor of Lincoln College. *8vo. 12s. 6d.*

'Whether the reader approaches the book as a patriotic member of a college, as an antiquary, or as a student of the organic growth of college foundation, it will amply reward his attention.'—*Times.*

'A delightful book, learned and lively. —*Academy.*

'A work which will certainly be appealed to for many years as the standard book on the Colleges of Oxford.'—*Athenæum.*

Hulton. RIXAE OXONIENSES: An Account of the Battles of the Nations, The Struggle between Town and Gown, etc. By S. F. HULTON, M.A. *Crown 8vo. 5s.*

James. CURIOSITIES OF CHRISTIAN HISTORY PRIOR TO THE REFORMATION. By CROAKE JAMES, Author of 'Curiosities of Law and Lawyers.' *Crown 8vo. 7s. 6d.*

Perrens. THE HISTORY OF FLORENCE FROM THE TIME OF THE MEDICIS TO THE FALL OF THE REPUBLIC. By F. T. PERRENS. Translated by HANNAH LYNCH. In three volumes. *Vol. I. 8vo. 12s. 6d.*

This is a translation from the French of the best history of Florence in existence. This volume covers a period of profound interest—political and literary—and is written with great vivacity.

'This is a standard book by an honest and intelligent historian, who has deserved well of his countrymen, and of all who are interested in Italian history.'—*Manchester Guardian.*

Kaufmann. CHARLES KINGSLEY. By M. KAUFMANN, M.A. *Crown 8vo. 5s.*

A biography of Kingsley, especially dealing with his achievements in social reform.

'The author has certainly gone about his work with conscientiousness and industry.'—*Sheffield Daily Telegraph.*

Oliphant. THOMAS CHALMERS: A Biography. By Mrs. OLIPHANT. With Portrait. *Crown 8vo. Buckram, 5s.*

'A well-executed biography, worthy of its author and of the remarkable man who is its subject. Mrs. Oliphant relates lucidly and dramatically the important part which Chalmers played in the memorable secession.'—*Times.*

'Written with all the facile literary grace that marks this indefatigable authoress' work, it presents a very complete picture of Chalmers as he lived and worked. . . . The salient points in his many-sided life are seized with unerring judgment.'—*North British Daily Mail.*

Wells. THE TEACHING OF HISTORY IN SCHOOLS. A Lecture delivered at the University Extension Meeting in Oxford, Aug. 6th, 1892. By J. WELLS, M.A., Fellow and Tutor of Wadham College, and Editor of ' Oxford and Oxford Life.' *Crown 8vo. 6d.*

Pollard. THE JESUITS IN POLAND. By A. F. POLLARD, B.A. Oxford Prize Essays—The Lothian Prize Essay 1892. *Crown 8vo. 2s. 6d. net.*

Clifford. THE DESCENT OF CHARLOTTE COMPTON (BARONESS FERRERS DE CHARTLEY). By her Great-Granddaughter, ISABELLA G. C. CLIFFORD. *Small 4to. 10s. 6d. net.*

General Literature

Bowden. THE IMITATION OF BUDDHA: Being Quotations from Buddhist Literature for each Day in the Year. Compiled by E. M. BOWDEN. With Preface by Sir EDWIN ARNOLD. *Third Edition. 16mo. 2s. 6d.*

Ditchfield. OUR ENGLISH VILLAGES : Their Story and their Antiquities. By P. H. DITCHFIELD, M.A., F.R.H.S., Rector of Barkham, Berks. *Post 8vo.* **2s. 6d.** Illustrated.

'An extremely amusing and interesting little book, which should find a place in every parochial library.'—*Guardian.*

Ditchfield. OLD ENGLISH SPORTS. By P. H. DITCH-FIELD, M.A. *Crown 8vo.* **2s. 6d.** Illustrated.

'A charming account of old English Sports.'—*Morning Post.*

Burne. PARSON AND PEASANT : Chapters of their Natural History. By J. B. BURNE, M.A., Rector of Wasing. *Crown 8vo.* **5s.**

'"Parson and Peasant" is a book not only to be interested in, but to learn something from—a book which may prove a help to many a clergyman, and broaden the hearts and ripen the charity of laymen.'—*Derby Mercury.*

Massee. A MONOGRAPH OF THE MYXOGASTRES. By GEORGE MASSEE. With 12 Coloured Plates. *Royal 8vo.* **18s. net.**

This is the only work in English on this important group. It contains 12 Coloured Plates, produced in the finest style of chromo-lithography.

'Supplies a want acutely felt. Its merits are of a high order, and it is one of the most important contributions to systematic natural science which have lately appeared.'—*Westminster Review.*

'A work much in advance of any book in the language treating of this group of organisms. It is indispensable to every student of the Mxyogastres. The coloured plates deserve high praise for their accuracy and execution.'—*Nature.*

Cunningham. THE PATH TOWARDS KNOWLEDGE : Essays on Questions of the Day. By W. CUNNINGHAM, D.D., Fellow of Trinity College, Cambridge, Professor of Economics at King's College, London. *Crown 8vo.* **4s. 6d.**

Essays on Marriage and Population, Socialism, Money, Education, Positivism, etc.

Bushill. PROFIT SHARING AND THE LABOUR QUES-TION. By T. W. BUSHILL, a Profit Sharing Employer. With an Introduction by SEDLEY TAYLOR, Author of 'Profit Sharing between Capital and Labour.' *Crown 8vo.* **2s. 6d.**

John Beever. PRACTICAL FLY-FISHING, Founded on Nature, by JOHN BEEVER, late of the Thwaite House, Coniston. A New Edition, with a Memoir of the Author by W. G. COLLINGWOOD, M.A., Author of 'The Life and Work of John Ruskin,' etc. Also additional Notes and a chapter on Char-Fishing, by A. and A. R. SEVERN. With a specially designed title-page. *Crown 8vo.* **3s. 6d.**

A little book on Fly-Fishing by an old friend of Mr. Ruskin. It has been out of print for some time, and being still much in request, is now issued with a Memoir of the Author by W. G. Collingwood.

Anderson Graham. NATURE IN BOOKS : Studies in Literary Biography. By P. ANDERSON GRAHAM. *Crown 8vo.* 6s.

The chapters are entitled : I. 'The Magic of the Fields' (Jefferies). II. 'Art and Nature' (Tennyson). III. 'The Doctrine of Idleness' (Thoreau). IV. 'The Romance of Life' (Scott). V. 'The Poetry of Toil' (Burns). VI. 'The Divinity of Nature' (Wordsworth).

Wells. OXFORD AND OXFORD LIFE. By Members of the University. Edited by J. WELLS, M.A., Fellow and Tutor of Wadham College. *Crown 8vo.* 3s. 6d.

This work contains an account of life at Oxford—intellectual, social, and religious— a careful estimate of necessary expenses, a review of recent changes, a statement of the present position of the University, and chapters on Women's Education, aids to study, and University Extension.

'We congratulate Mr. Wells on the production of a readable and intelligent account of Oxford as it is at the present time, written by persons who are, with hardly an exception, possessed of a close acquaintance with the system and life of the University.'—*Athenæum.*

Driver. SERMONS ON SUBJECTS CONNECTED WITH THE OLD TESTAMENT. By S. R. DRIVER, D.D., Canon of Christ Church, Regius Professor of Hebrew in the University of Oxford. *Crown 8vo.* 6s.

A welcome volume to the author's famous 'Introduction.' No man can read these discourses without feeling that Dr. Driver is fully alive to the deeper teaching of the Old Testament.'—*Guardian.*

Cheyne. FOUNDERS OF OLD TESTAMENT CRITICISM: Biographical, Descriptive, and Critical Studies. By T. K. CHEYNE, D.D., Oriel Professor of the Interpretation of Holy Scripture at Oxford. *Large crown 8vo.* 7s. 6d.   [*Ready.*

This important book is a historical sketch of O.T. Criticism in the form of biographical studies from the days of Eichhorn to those of Driver and Robertson Smith. It is the only book of its kind in English.

'The volume is one of great interest and value. It displays all the author's well-known ability and learning, and its opportune publication has laid all students of theology, and specially of Bible criticism, under weighty obligation.'—*Scotsman.*

'A very learned and instructive work.'—*Times.*

WORKS BY

S. Baring Gould, Author of 'Mehalah,' etc.

OLD COUNTRY LIFE. With Sixty-seven Illustrations by W. PARKINSON, F. D. BEDFORD, and F. MASEY. *Large Crown 8vo, cloth super extra, top edge gilt,* 10s. 6d. *Fourth and Cheaper Edition.* 6s.

'"Old Country Life," as healthy wholesome reading, full of breezy life and movement, full of quaint stories vigorously told, will not be excelled by any book to be published throughout the year. Sound, hearty, and English to the core.'— *World.*

HISTORIC ODDITIES AND STRANGE EVENTS. *Third Edition, Crown 8vo. 6s.*

'A collection of exciting and entertaining chapters. The whole volume is delightful reading.'—*Times.*

FREAKS OF FANATICISM. *Third Edition. Crown 8vo. 6s.*

'Mr. Baring Gould has a keen eye for colour and effect, and the subjects he has chosen give ample scope to his descriptive and analytic faculties. A perfectly fascinating book.'—*Scottish Leader.*

SONGS OF THE WEST: Traditional Ballads and Songs of the West of England, with their Traditional Melodies. Collected by S. BARING GOULD, M.A., and H. FLEETWOOD SHEPPARD, M.A. Arranged for Voice and Piano. In 4 Parts (containing 25 Songs each), *Parts I., II., III., 3s. each. Part IV., 5s. In one Vol., roan, 15s.*

'A rich and varied collection of humour, pathos, grace, and poetic fancy.'—*Saturday Review.*

YORKSHIRE ODDITIES AND STRANGE EVENTS. *Fourth Edition. Crown 8vo. 6s.*

STRANGE SURVIVALS AND SUPERSTITIONS. With Illustrations. By S. BARING GOULD. *Crown 8vo. 7s. 6d.*

A book on such subjects as Foundations, Gables, Holes, Gallows, Raising the Hat, Old Ballads, etc. etc. It traces in a most interesting manner their origin and history.

'We have read Mr. Baring Gould's book from beginning to end. It is full of quaint and various information, and there is not a dull page in it.'—*Notes and Queries.*

THE TRAGEDY OF THE CAESARS: The Emperors of the Julian and Claudian Lines. With numerous Illustrations from Busts, Gems, Cameos, etc. By S. BARING GOULD, Author of 'Mehalah,' etc. *Second Edition. 2 vols. Royal 8vo. 30s.*

This book is the only one in English which deals with the personal history of the Caesars, and Mr. Baring Gould has found a subject which, for picturesque detail and sombre interest, is not rivalled by any work of fiction. The volumes are copiously illustrated.

'A most splendid and fascinating book on a subject of undying interest. The great feature of the book is the use the author has made of the existing portraits of the Caesars, and the admirable critical subtlety he has exhibited in dealing with this line of research. It is brilliantly written, and the illustrations are supplied on a scale of profuse magnificence.'—*Daily Chronicle.*

'The volumes will in no sense disappoint the general reader. Indeed, in their way, there is nothing in any sense so good in English. . . . Mr. Baring Gould has presented his narrative in such a way as not to make one dull page.'—*Athenæum.*

JACQUETTA, and other Stories. *Crown 8vo. 3s. 6d.*

ARMINELL: A Social Romance. *New Edition. Crown 8vo. 3s. 6d.*

'To say that a book is by the author of "Mehalah" is to imply that it contains a story cast on strong lines, containing dramatic possibilities, vivid and sympathetic descriptions of Nature, and a wealth of ingenious imagery. All these expectations are justified by "Arminell."'—*Speaker.*

URITH: A Story of Dartmoor. *Third Edition. Crown 8vo. 3s. 6d.*

'The author is at his best.'—*Times.*

'He has nearly reached the high water-mark of "Mehalah."'—*National Observer.*

MARGERY OF QUETHER, and other Stories. *Crown 8vo. 3s. 6d.*

IN THE ROAR OF THE SEA: A Tale of the Cornish Coast. *New Edition. 3s. 6d.*

MRS. CURGENVEN OF CURGENVEN. *Third Edition. 6s.*

Fiction

Pryce. TIME AND THE WOMAN. By RICHARD PRYCE, Author of 'Miss Maxwell's Affections,' 'The Quiet Mrs. Fleming,' etc. New and Cheaper Edition. *Crown 8vo. 6s.*

'Mr. Pryce's work recalls the style of Octave Feuillet, by its clearness, conciseness, its literary reserve.'—*Athenæum.*

Gray. ELSA. A Novel. By E. M'QUEEN GRAY. *Crown 8vo. 6s.*

'A charming novel. The characters are not only powerful sketches, but minutely and carefully finished portraits.'—*Guardian.*

Anthony Hope. A CHANGE OF AIR: A Novel. By ANTHONY HOPE, Author of 'Mr. Witt's Widow,' etc. 1 *vol. Crown 8vo. 6s.*

A bright story by Mr. Hope, who has, the *Athenæum* says, 'a decided outlook and individuality of his own.'

'A graceful, vivacious comedy, true to human nature. The characters are traced with a masterly hand.'—*Times.*

Edna Lyall. DERRICK VAUGHAN, NOVELIST. By EDNA LYALL, Author of 'Donovan.' *Crown 8vo. 31st Thousand.* 3s. 6d. ; *paper,* 1s.

Lynn Linton. THE TRUE HISTORY OF JOSHUA DAVIDSON, Christian and Communist. By E. LYNN LINTON. Eleventh Edition. *Post 8vo.* 1s.

Dicker. A CAVALIER'S LADYE. By CONSTANCE DICKER. With Illustrations. *Crown 8vo. 3s. 6d.*

Author of 'Vera.' THE DANCE OF THE HOURS. By the Author of ' Vera,' ' Blue Roses,' etc. *Crown 8vo.* 6s.

'A musician's dream, pathetically broken off at the hour of its realisation, is vividly represented in this book. . . . Well written and possessing many elements of interest. The success of "The Dance of the Hours" may be safely predicted.'— *Morning Post.*

Norris. A Deplorable Affair. By W. E. NORRIS, Author of ' His Grace.' *Crown 8vo.* 3s. 6d.

'What with its interesting story, its graceful manner, and its perpetual good humour, the book is as enjoyable as any that has come from its author's pen.'— *Scotsman.*

Dickinson. A VICAR'S WIFE. By EVELYN DICKINSON. *Crown 8vo.* 3s. 6d.

Prowse. THE POISON OF ASPS. By R. ORTON PROWSE. *Crown 8vo.* 3s. 6d.

Parker. PIERRE AND HIS PEOPLE. By GILBERT PARKER. *Crown 8vo. Buckram.* 6s.

'Stories happily conceived and finely executed. There is strength and genius in Mr. Parker's style.'— *Daily Telegraph.*

Marriott Watson. DIOGENES OF LONDON and other Sketches. By H. B. MARRIOTT WATSON, Author of ' The Web of the Spider.' *Crown 8vo. Buckram.* 6s.

' By all those who delight in the uses of words, who rate the exercise of prose above the exercise of verse, who rejoice in all proofs of its delicacy and its strength, who believe that English prose is chief among the moulds of thought, by these Mr. Marriott Watson's book will be welcomed.'— *National Observer.*

Methuen's Novel Series

A series of copyright Novels, by well-known Authors, bound in red buckram, at the price of three shillings and sixpence. The first volumes (ready) are :— **3/6**

1. JACQUETTA. By S. BARING GOULD, Author of ' Mehalah,' etc.

2. ARMINELL : A Social Romance. By S. BARING GOULD, Author of ' Mehalah,' etc.

3. MARGERY OF QUETHER. By S. BARING GOULD.

4. URITH. By S. BARING GOULD.

5. IN THE ROAR OF THE SEA. By S. BARING GOULD.

6. DERRICK VAUGHAN, NOVELIST.. With Portrait of Author. By EDNA LYALL, Author of 'Donovan,' etc. Also paper, 1s.

7. JACK'S FATHER. By W. E. NORRIS.

8. MY DANISH SWEETHEART. By W. CLARK RUSSELL.

Other Volumes will be announced in due course.

HALF-CROWN NOVELS

A Series of Novels by popular Authors, tastefully bound in cloth.

2/6

1. THE PLAN OF CAMPAIGN. By F. MABEL ROBINSON.

2. DISENCHANTMENT. By F. MABEL ROBINSON.

3. MR. BUTLER'S WARD. By MABEL ROBINSON.

4. HOVENDEN, V.C. By F. MABEL ROBINSON.

5. ELI'S CHILDREN. By G. MANVILLE FENN.

6. A DOUBLE KNOT. By G. MANVILLE FENN.

7. DISARMED. By M. BETHAM EDWARDS.

8. A LOST ILLUSION. By LESLIE KEITH.

9. A MARRIAGE AT SEA. By W. CLARK RUSSELL.

10. IN TENT AND BUNGALOW. By the Author of 'Indian Idylls.'

11. MY STEWARDSHIP. By E. M'QUEEN GRAY.

12. A REVEREND GENTLEMAN. By J. M. COBBAN.

13. THE STORY OF CHRIS. By ROLAND GREY.

Other volumes will be announced in due course.

NEW TWO-SHILLING EDITIONS

Crown 8vo, Ornamental Boards.

2/-

ELI'S CHILDREN. By G. MANVILLE FENN.

DISENCHANTMENT. By F. MABEL ROBINSON.

THE PLAN OF CAMPAIGN. By F. MABEL ROBINSON.

Crown 8vo. Picture Boards.

A REVEREND GENTLEMAN. By J. MacLaren Cobban.

MR. BUTLER'S WARD. By Mabel Robinson.

JACK'S FATHER. By W. E. Norris.

THE QUIET MRS. FLEMING. By Richard Pryce.

Books for Boys and Girls

Cuthell. ONLY A GUARD-ROOM DOG. By Mrs. Cuthell. With 16 Illustrations by W. Parkinson. *Square Crown 8vo.* 6s.

'This is a charming story. Tangle was but a little mongrel Skye terrier, but he had a big heart in his little body, and played a hero's part more than once. The book can be warmly recommended.'—*Standard.*

Collingwood. THE DOCTOR OF THE JULIET. By Harry Collingwood, Author of 'The Pirate Island,' etc. Illustrated by Gordon Browne. *Crown 8vo.* 6s.

'"The Doctor of the Juliet," well illustrated by Gordon Browne, is one of Harry Collingwood's best efforts.'—*Morning Post.*

Clark Russell. MASTER ROCKAFELLAR'S VOYAGE. By W. Clark Russell, Author of 'The Wreck of the Grosvenor,' etc. Illustrated by Gordon Browne. *Crown 8vo.* 3s. 6d.

'Mr. Clark Russell's story of "Master Rockafellar's Voyage" will be among the favourites of the Christmas books. There is a rattle and "go" all through it, and its illustrations are charming in themselves, and very much above the average in the way in which they are produced.'—*Guardian.*

Manville Fenn. SYD BELTON : Or, The Boy who would not go to Sea. By G. Manville Fenn, Author of 'In the King's Name,' etc. Illustrated by Gordon Browne. *Crown 8vo.* 3s. 6d.

'Who among the young story-reading public will not rejoice at the sight of the old combination, so often proved admirable—a story by Manville Fenn, illustrated by Gordon Browne? The story, too, is one of the good old sort, full of life and vigour, breeziness and fun.'—*Journal of Education.*

Walford. A PINCH OF EXPERIENCE. By. L. B. Walford, Author of 'Mr. Smith.' With Illustrations by Gordon Browne. *Crown 8vo.* 3s. 6d.

'The clever authoress steers clear of namby-pamby, and invests her moral with a fresh and striking dress. There is terseness and vivacity of style and the illustrations are admirable.'—*Anti-Jacobin.*

Molesworth. THE RED GRANGE. By Mrs. MOLESWORTH, Author of 'Carrots.' With Illustrations by GORDON BROWNE. *Crown 8vo. 3s. 6d.*

'A volume in which girls will delight, and beautifully illustrated.'—*Pall Mall Gazette.*

Author of 'Mdle. Mori.' THE SECRET OF MADAME DE Monluc. By the Author of 'The Atelier du Lys,' 'Mdle. Mori.' *Crown 8vo. 3s. 6d.*

'An exquisite literary cameo.'—*World.*

Parr. DUMPS. By Mrs. PARR, Author of 'Adam and Eve,' 'Dorothy Fox,' etc. Illustrated by W. PARKINSON. *Crown 8vo. 3s. 6d.*

'One of the prettiest stories which even this clever writer has given the world for a long time.'—*World.*

Meade. OUT OF THE FASHION. By L. T. MEADE, Author of 'A Girl of the People,' etc. With 6 illustrations by W. PAGET. *Crown 8vo, 3s. 6d.*

'One of those charmingly-written social tales, which this writer knows so well how to write. It is delightful reading, and is well illustrated by W. Paget.'—*Glasgow Herald.*

Meade. A GIRL OF THE PEOPLE. By L. T. MEADE, Author of 'Scamp and I,' etc. Illustrated by R. BARNES. *Crown 8vo. 3s. 6d.*

'An excellent story. Vivid portraiture of character, and broad and wholesome lessons about life.'—*Spectator.*
'One of Mrs. Meade's most fascinating books.'—*Daily News.*

Meade. HEPSY GIPSY. By L. T. MEADE. Illustrated by EVERARD HOPKINS. *Crown 8vo. 2s. 6d.*

'Mrs. Meade has not often done better work than this.'—*Spectator.*

Meade. THE HONOURABLE MISS: A Tale of a Country Town. By L. T. MEADE, Author of 'Scamp and I,' 'A Girl of the People,' etc. With Illustrations by EVERARD HOPKINS. *Crown 8vo. 3s. 6d.*

Adams. MY LAND OF BEULAH. By Mrs. LEITH ADAMS. With a Frontispiece by GORDON BROWNE. *Crown 8vo. 3s. 6d.*

Leaders of Religion

Edited by H. C. BEECHING, M.A. *With Portrait, crown 8vo.* 2s. 6d.

A series of short biographies of the most prominent leaders of religious life and thought.

The following are ready—

2/6

CARDINAL NEWMAN. By R. H. HUTTON.

> 'Few who read this book will fail to be struck by the wonderful insight it displays into the nature of the Cardinal's genius and the spirit of his life.'—WILFRID WARD, in the *Tablet.*

> 'Full of knowledge, excellent in method, and intelligent in criticism. We regard it as wholly admirable.'—*Academy.*

JOHN WESLEY. By J. H. OVERTON, M.A.

> 'It is well done: the story is clearly told, proportion is duly observed, and there is no lack either of discrimination or of sympathy.'—*Manchester Guardian.*

BISHOP WILBERFORCE. By G. W. DANIEL, M.A.

CHARLES SIMEON. By H. C. G. MOULE, M.A.

Other volumes will be announced in due course.

University Extension Series

A series of books on historical, literary, and scientific subjects, suitable for extension students and home reading circles. Each volume is complete in itself, and the subjects are treated by competent writers in a broad and philosophic spirit.

Edited by J. E. SYMES, M.A.,

Principal of University College, Nottingham.

Crown 8vo. Price (with some exceptions) 2s. 6d.

The following volumes are ready :—

THE INDUSTRIAL HISTORY OF ENGLAND. By H. DE
B. GIBBINS, M.A., late Scholar of Wadham College, Oxon., Cobden Prizeman. *Third Edition.* With Maps and Plans. 3s.

> A compact and clear story of our industrial development. A study of this concise but luminous book cannot fail to give the reader a clear insight into the principal phenomena of our industrial history. The editor and publishers are to be congratulated on this first volume of their venture, and we shall look with expectant interest for the succeeding volumes of the series.'—*University Extension Journal.*

A HISTORY OF ENGLISH POLITICAL ECONOMY. By
L. L. Price, M.A., Fellow of Oriel College, Oxon.

PROBLEMS OF POVERTY: An Inquiry into the Industrial
Conditions of the Poor. By J. A. Hobson, M.A.

VICTORIAN POETS. By A. Sharp.

THE FRENCH REVOLUTION. By J. E. Symes, M.A.

PSYCHOLOGY. By F. S. Granger, M.A., Lecturer in Philosophy at University College, Nottingham.

THE EVOLUTION OF PLANT LIFE: Lower Forms. By
G. Massee, Kew Gardens. With Illustrations.

AIR AND WATER. Professor V. B. Lewes, M.A. Illustrated.

THE CHEMISTRY OF LIFE AND HEALTH. By C. W.
Kimmins, M.A. Camb. Illustrated.

THE MECHANICS OF DAILY LIFE. By V. P. Sells, M.A.
Illustrated.

ENGLISH SOCIAL REFORMERS. H. de B. Gibbins, M.A.

ENGLISH TRADE AND FINANCE IN THE SEVEN-
TEENTH CENTURY. By W. A. S. Hewins, B.A.

Social Questions of To-day

Edited by H. de B. GIBBINS, M.A.

Crown 8vo. 2s. 6d. **2/6**

A series of volumes upon those topics of social, economic,
and industrial interest that are at the present moment foremost in the public mind. Each volume of the series is written by an
author who is an acknowledged authority upon the subject with which
he deals.

The following Volumes of the Series are ready :—

TRADE UNIONISM—NEW AND OLD. By G. Howell,
M.P., Author of 'The Conflicts of Capital and Labour.'

THE CO-OPERATIVE MOVEMENT TO-DAY. By G. J.
Holyoake, Author of 'The History of Co-operation.'

MUTUAL THRIFT. By Rev. J. FROME WILKINSON, M.A., Author of ' The Friendly Society Movement.'

PROBLEMS OF POVERTY : An Inquiry into the Industrial Conditions of the Poor. By J. A. HOBSON, M.A.

THE COMMERCE OF NATIONS. By C. F. BASTABLE, M.A., Professor of Economics at Trinity College, Dublin.

THE ALIEN INVASION. By W. H. WILKINS, B.A., Secretary to the Society for Preventing the Immigration of Destitute Aliens.

THE RURAL EXODUS. By P. ANDERSON GRAHAM.

LAND NATIONALIZATION. By HAROLD COX, B.A.

A SHORTER WORKING DAY. By H. DE B. GIBBINS and R. A. HADFIELD, of the Hecla Works, Sheffield.

BACK TO THE LAND : An Inquiry into the Cure for Rural Depopulation. By H. E. MOORE.

Edinburgh: T. & A. Constable, *Printers to Her Majesty.*

CPSIA information can be obtained
at www.ICGtesting.com
Printed in the USA
LVOW04s2308260317
528559LV00021B/419/P